Bastard Feudalism, English Society and the Law

Bastard Feudalism, English Society and the Law

The Statutes of Livery, 1390–1520

Gordon McKelvie

THE BOYDELL PRESS

First published 2020
The Boydell Press, Woodbridge

ISBN 978-1-78327-477-2

The Boydell Press is an imprint of Boydell & Brewer Ltd
PO Box 9, Woodbridge, Suffolk IP12 3DF, UK
and of Boydell & Brewer Inc.
668 Mt Hope Avenue, Rochester, NY 14620–2731, USA
website: www.boydellandbrewer.com

A catalogue record of this publication is available
from the British Library

This publication is printed on acid-free paper

Printed and bound in Great Britain by TJ International Ltd, Padstow, Cornwall

Contents

Acknowledgements

This book has taken a long time to write and I therefore have many friends and family to thank for their help and support in both a personal and professional capacity. My former supervisor, Michael Hicks, has always been immensely generous with his time, expertise and advice and has read various parts of this book. Michael's help over the years in various capacities has been immense and he has been nothing short of the ideal supervisor and mentor. Neil Murphy has always been helpful with advice and criticism and his constant probing to draw out wider points has improved this book immeasurably. Philip Morgan has asked many perceptive questions about my research, giving me a lot to ponder and has been kind enough to read over the initial proposal and draft chapters. The University of Winchester is a good place for any historian to work in a teaching and research capacity and I have many friends who have made working here much easier. James Ross deserves thanks for numerous conversations on a range of late medieval topics and his willingness to share references which have helped to refine many of the arguments in this book. Katherine Weikert has listened to my various musings over many years in at least three shared offices. History in many ways is a collaborative discipline that relies on people being able to share ideas with each other. For historians of the fifteenth century, the Late Medieval Seminar at the Institute of Historical Research is the ideal place to learn and share ideas, and I have benefited from presenting at, and attending, the seminar for many years. I should also like to thank Alexander Brondarbit, Paul Cavill, Adam Chapman, Sean Cunningham, Daniel Gosling, John Hare, Samantha Harper, Nicholas Kingwell, Hannes Kleineke, Ryan Lavelle, Mark Whelan, Simon Payling and Deborah Youngs for numerous discussions and observations that have helped to improve this book. Boydell & Brewer have been immensely helpful to this first-time author, in particular Caroline Palmer with her invaluable advice and support to this first time author. I should also thank Robert Kinsey, whose prompting to get a proposal in and to finish the book has become something of an annual tradition at the International Medieval Congress at Leeds. I would also like to thank the anonymous reader for their valuable suggestions that have improved this book. Unless stated otherwise, all archival references in this book are to The National Archives, London. In terms of finance, I would like to thank the University of Winchester for awarding me a studentship between 2009 and 2012 to undertake the initial thesis and for helping to fund subsequent archival visits and conferences. As a PhD student I was fortunate to obtain a bursary from the IHR to undertake archival research in London. I would also like to thank the Richard III & Yorkist History Trust, who provided funds towards the cost of publication. Finally, I would like to thank my parents, Jim and Isabel, for all of their help, support and encouragement over the years.

Abbreviations

BIHR	*Bulletin of the Institute of Historical Research.*
BL	British Library, London.
CCR	*Calendar of Close Rolls Preserved in the Public Record Office,* 42 vols. (London, 1900–47).
CIPM	*Calendar of Inquisitions Post-Mortem and other Analogous Documents Preserved in the Public Record Office,* 26 vols. (London, 1905–54; Woodbridge, 2002–10).
CPR	*Calendar of Patent Rolls Preserved in the Public Record Office,* 49 vols. (London, 1893–1916).
CRO	Cumbria Record Office, Carlisle.
EHD	*English Historical Documents.*
EHR	*English Historical Review.*
HMC	Historic Manuscripts Commission.
HRO	Hampshire Record Office, Winchester.
L&P	*Letters and Papers, Foreign and Domestic, of the Reign of Henry VIII, 1509–1547,* ed. J.S. Brewer et al., 21 vols. (London, 1862–1932).
ODNB	*Oxford Dictionary of National Biography,* eds. Brian Howard Harrison and H.C.C. Mathews, 60 vols. (Oxford, 2000).
P&P	*Past and Present.*
PL	*Paston Letters and Papers of the Fifteenth Century,* vols. 1 and 2, ed. Norman Davis (Oxford, 1971–6), vol. 3, ed. Richard Beadle and Colin Richmond (Early English Text Society, special series xxii, 2005).
PROME	*Parliamentary Rolls of Medieval England,* eds. Christopher Given-Wilson et al., 16 vols. (Woodbridge, 2005).
Stat. Realm	*Statutes of the Realm,* 11 vols. (London, 1810–28).
TRHS	*Transactions of the Royal Historical Society.*

Timeline of Parliamentary Activity[1]

1377 – Act preventing the distribution of liveries for the maintenance of lawsuits.[2]

1384 – Report in the *Westminster Chronicle* about a dispute between the Commons and the Lords over the issue of badges during which John of Gaunt claimed that he was able to discipline his own men and that there was no need for a statute on the issue.[3]

September 1388 – No surviving parliament roll but the *Westminster Chronicle* notes a Commons petition about the distribution of liveries.[4]

1390 – First statute restricting the distribution of liveries to certain categories of servants.[5]

1393 – Complaint from the Commons that the statutes were not being upheld. Law to be upheld with powers given to justices of the peace and assize to enquire into those breaking the law.[6]

1397 – Problem of liveries included in Haxey's petition along with complaints about the size of the royal household, the state of the Scottish marches and that sheriffs and escheators of insufficient standing were being appointed.[7]

1399 – First act to place restrictions on the distribution and wearing of the royal livery, with the king's knights and esquires only allowed to wear the king's livery in his presence.[8]

---

[1] The specific details of all of the relevant acts are discussed in Chapters 3 and 4. Therefore, this timeline is intended to be brief, highlighting only the key points to give a sense of the chronological development of the laws. For more detailed timelines see: Gordon McKelvie, 'The Legality of Bastard Feudalism: The Statutes of Livery, 1390 to c.1520' (unpublished PhD thesis, University of Winchester, 2013), 143–57; Jonathan Rose, *Maintenance in Medieval England* (Cambridge, 2017), 371–9.

[2] *PROME*, vi, 50.

[3] *The Westminster Chronicle, 1381–1394*, eds. and trans. L.C. Hector and Barbara F. Harvey (Oxford, 1982), 80–3.

[4] *PROME*, vii, 124.

[5] Ibid., 147–50. Also printed in *EDH*, iv, 1116.

[6] Ibid., 239–40.

[7] Ibid., 313–14.

[8] Ibid., viii, 38.

1401 – Commons petition about the problem of liveries. Statutes were to be upheld but the king's knights and esquires were allowed to wear the king's livery in their own counties and the Prince of Wales was exempt from the statutes.[9]

1406 – Commons petition about the problem of liveries. Statutes to be upheld with larger fines included.[10]

1411 – Commons petition reiterating most of the 1406 petition.[11]

1427 – Failed Commons petition about liveries requesting that the law be extended to the palatinate counties and more efficient methods of enforcement.[12]

1429 – Commons petition largely reiterating the 1427 petition successful. First act to state explicitly that women and the palatinate counties were bound by the law. More stringent methods of enforcement included. This was the last act about the distribution of liveries to originate in the Commons petition.[13]

1449 – A surviving copy of a parliamentary debate from the Winchester sessions of this parliament states that 'The Lord Sturton thinketh that ther wold be certain comyssioners of *oyer et terminer* to enquiere of murders and ryottes don ageinst the peace and *also of lyveries* and that every shireve certify therof.' Not included in parliament rolls.[14]

1461 – New act further regulating the distribution of livery badges.[15]

1468 – New act during the third session of the parliament that opened in June 1467. Law extended to cover other forms of retaining beyond the distribution of liveries.[16]

1474–5 – Prince of Wales exempt from the statutes relating to retaining and the distribution of liveries.[17]

1483 – Commons request that the statutes of livery, along with the first statute of Westminster, the statutes of Winchester, the statutes of weights and measurements and the statutes of servants and labourers, mendicants and vagabonds are upheld and enforced.[18]

---

[9]   Ibid., 148–9.
[10] Ibid., 400–1.
[11] Ibid., 547–8.
[12] Ibid., ix, 354–5.
[13] Ibid., 394, 402–3.
[14] *EHD*, iv, 468–9.
[15] *PROME*, xiii, 65.
[16] Ibid., 384–6.
[17] Ibid., xiv, 324–5.
[18] Ibid., 413.

1485 – The attending ecclesiastical and secular lords swore an article, in parliament, that they would not harbour any known felons nor give livery or retain anyone contrary to the statutes.[19]

1487 – Act about retaining the king's tenants.[20]

1504 – Act passed at Henry VII's final parliament, only to last for the life of the king. Stricter penalties and more efficient methods for enforcement. Those in receipt of a royal licence permitted to retain beyond the restricted categories of servant.[21]

---

[19]   Ibid., xv, 131–2.
[20]   Ibid., 371–2, 375–6.
[21]   Ibid., xvi, 365–8.

Introduction

All history is social history and almost all history is political history. History is concerned with past societies and the politics of those societies are formed by various social, cultural, technological, religious and economic pressures. In one sense all are intertwined. Therefore, an understanding of the politics of a society is essential for understanding the nature of that society, its structure, its people and their concerns. Fundamental to this understanding are the political alignments and social bonds within that society. For the later middle ages, the affinity was 'the most important political grouping'.[1] It was composed of a lord and his various servants and followers, who were retained by a variety of methods. Historians have dubbed this system 'bastard feudalism'. The phrase itself was not a contemporary one but it is a useful term to describe a set of socio-political relations that were most prominent during the late medieval period. At its heart was retaining, the most formal method of which was the indenture of retainer which bound a retainer to his lord, stating the expected service and rewards, notably fees, annuities and the benefits of 'good lordship'. Other methods were more informal in character, such as the distribution of annuities and liveries to estate officials, or even more intangible, such as 'hospitality, entertainment and favours incapable of precise definition and description'[2] which by their very nature rarely leave a trace in the surviving records. These relationships and groupings enabled late medieval governments and nobles to obtain the service they required, whether administrative, military or legal. In short, it was how late medieval politics, society and government functioned.

These relationships possessed the potential for social cohesion but they could also be used as a method of recruitment for serious breaches of public order. Retaining and distributing livery became associated with public order problems such as maintenance, riots, assaults, intimidation and, in extreme cases, rebellion. To prevent such abuses parliament passed a series of acts between 1390 and 1504 that restricted the distribution of livery, and later of fees, to members of a lord's family, his permanent household servants and his legal counsel. There have been numerous articles which have examined specific acts or retaining over a short

---

[1] Christopher Given-Wilson, *The Royal Household and the King's Affinity: Service, Politics and Finance in England, 1360–1413* (London and New Haven, 1986), 203.

[2] J.R. Maddicott, 'Law and Lordship: Royal Justices as Retainers in Thirteenth and Fourteenth Century England', *P&P*, supplement iv (1978), 56.

period of time,[3] while others have briefly considered the development of the laws.[4] But this book is the first long-term study of illegal livery, examining the development of the law and all of the resultant cases found in the records of the King's Bench between 1390 and the 1520s. It examines the relationship between law-making in parliament and law enforcement in the localities. Retaining and the distribution of liveries were key political issues from the late fourteenth to early sixteenth centuries and helped to facilitate many of the political upheavals of the period. This study therefore provides new insights into the politics of the long fifteenth century, but its significance extends beyond the political history of the period. The lord–servant relationship was a product of social structures and therefore an examination of the acts regarding retaining elucidates important aspects of medieval society, culture and values.

Bastard Feudalism and Political Society

The phrase bastard feudalism was coined by Reverend Charles Plummer, who regarded it as 'a sort of ignoble caricature of the feudal system' that was corrupt from the apex to the base.[5] It was characterised by men being retained by lords 'who wore his livery and fought his battles ... while he in turn maintained their quarrels and shielded their crimes from punishment'.[6] Plummer's contemporary, Bishop William Stubbs, saw livery and maintenance, the two manifestations of bastard feudalism deemed to be the most socially disruptive, as 'signs of faction and oppression, and were two great sources of mischief'.[7] The views

---

[3]   Alan Cameron, 'The Giving of Livery and Retaining in Henry VII's Reign', *Renaissance & Modern Studies*, xviii (1974), 17–35; M.A. Hicks, 'The 1468 Statute of Livery', *Historical Research*, lxiv (1991), 15–28; Dominic Luckett, 'Crown Office and Licensed Retinues in the Reign of Henry VII' in *Rulers and Ruled in Late Medieval England*, eds. Rowena E. Archer and Simon Walker (London, 1995), 223–38; Gordon McKelvie, 'The Livery Act of 1429' in *The Fifteenth Century XIV: Essays in Honour of Michael Hicks*, ed. Linda Clark (Woodbridge, 2015), 55–65; Gordon McKelvie, 'Henry VII's Letter to Carlisle in 1498: His Concerns about Retaining in a Border Fortress', *Northern History*, liv (2017), 149–66; Nigel Saul, 'The Commons and the Abolition of Badges', *Parliamentary History*, ix (1990), 302–15; R.L. Storey, 'Liveries and Commissions of the Peace, 1388–90' in *The Reign of Richard II*, eds. F.R.H. Du Boulay and C.M. Barron (London, 1971), 131–52.

[4]   William H. Dunham, *Lord Hastings' Indentured Retainers, 1461–83: The Lawfulness of Livery and Retaining under the Yorkists and Tudors*, Transactions of the Connecticut Academy of Arts & Sciences, xxxix (New Haven, 1955), 67–89; J.M.W. Bean, *From Lord to Patron: Lordship in Late Medieval England* (Manchester, 1989); Given-Wilson, *King's Affinity*, 234–45.

[5]   J. Fortescue, *Governance of England*, ed. C. Plummer (Oxford, 1885), 25.

[6]   Ibid., 15–16.

[7]   William Stubbs, *Constitutional History of England in the Middle Ages*, 3 vols. (Oxford,

of Plummer and Stubbs were grounded in a nineteenth-century worldview that adopted a Whig interpretation of history. Victorian historians sought to explain medieval history as a prelude to what they regarded as the ideal democracy of Victorian Britain. For them the study of parliament, its evolution and the rule of law was central. Anything that brought England closer to the settlements after the Glorious Revolution or the Great Reform Act received approval; anything that caused England to stray from its supposed inevitable course towards an ideal democracy headed by a constitutional monarch was castigated. Whig history was 'genealogical' because 'it searched for the antecedents of the present condition'.[8] This approach championed the development of the state and implicitly castigated the private power of the nobility as inevitably a disruptive force in society. In this view, the disorders of late medieval England were caused by nobles being 'over-mighty' and kings needed to curb their power.

During the twentieth century this view of history, and therefore the interpretations of historians, changed. A less moralistic tone was adopted and abstract concepts of constitutional progression and regression gave way to detailed understanding of the contemporary records. Although his attention was on the thirteenth and fourteenth centuries, the work of T.F. Tout was important because his focus on administrative history turned attention from abstract concepts to the daily workings of royal administration and how that affected the relationship between the king and his subjects. A focus on the administrative structures led to the development of a better understanding of their functions and those who worked them.[9] However, the significant change in the understanding of bastard feudalism and late medieval political society came in the work of K.B. McFarlane, who stripped bastard feudalism of its negative connotations. For McFarlane, bastard feudalism was a system that had 'the appearance of [feudalism]', with its key characteristic being retaining and payment for service in the form of fees and annuities as opposed to grants of land.[10] The late medieval nobility were not 'over-mighty' or constantly looking for means of perverting the legal system and causing disturbances to public order. As McFarlane noted, 'only an undermighty ruler had anything to fear from overmighty subjects; and if he were undermighty his personal lack of fitness was the cause, not the weakness of his office and its resources'.[11]

1880), iii, 579.

[8] P.R. Cavill, *The English Parliaments of Henry VII, 1485–1504* (Oxford, 2009), 2.

[9] T.F. Tout, *Chapters in Administrative History of Medieval England*, 6 vols. (Manchester, 1920–33). For the significance of Tout see in particular: Ralph Griffiths, 'Public and Private Bureaucracies in England and Wales in the Fifteenth Century', *TRHS*, 5th series, xxx (1980), 109–12.

[10] K.B. McFarlane, 'Bastard Feudalism', *BIHR*, 20 (1947 for 1945), 161–80, quotation on 161. See also: K.B. McFarlane, 'Parliament and Bastard Feudalism', *TRHS*, 4th series, xxvi (1944), 53–79.

[11] K.B. McFarlane, 'The Wars of the Roses', *Proceedings of the British Academy*, i

McFarlane's approach became the foundation on which later studies of late medieval English political society were built. The earliest studies can be divided into two interconnected categories: those focused on noble families, their estates and affinities,[12] and those focused on particular geographical areas such as counties or regions, centred on the local gentry which were also influenced by studies of the early modern gentry.[13] These prosopographical studies tackled the large quantity of central government records, supplemented by those available in local and private archives, to illuminate the importance of the nobility and gentry for the operation of royal government. They found that 'bastard feudalism was a perfectly respectable tie, binding lesser to greater landowners' and that it could be a force for social cohesion in later medieval England.[14] The main dissension from the idea that bastard feudalism was inherently a force for stability comes from historians of the high middle ages seeking to explain the emergence of bastard feudalism who highlight the more disruptive aspects of bastard feudalism. Peter Coss saw bastard feudalism as the reaction of nobles to Angevin legal reforms by corrupting the new legal system to ensure the continuation of their power, particularly in response to the waning influence of the honorial system between 1180 and 1230. It was 'a response to the resurrection of public authority within

---

(1964), 94–5.

[12] For book-length studies see: J.M.W. Bean, *The Estates of the Percy Family, 1416–1537* (Oxford, 1958); Michael Hicks, *False, Fleeting, Perjur'd Clarence: George, Duke of Clarence 1449–78*, revised edition (Bangor, 1992); G.A. Holmes, *The Estates of the Higher Nobility in Fourteenth-Century England* (Cambridge, 1957); P.A. Johnson, *Duke Richard of York, 1411–1460* (Oxford, 1988); Carole Rawcliffe, *The Staffords: Earls of Stafford and Dukes of Buckingham* (Cambridge, 1978). For single articles see: Christine Carpenter, 'The Beauchamp Affinity: A Study of Bastard Feudalism at Work', *EHR*, xcv (1980), 205–37; M. Cherry, 'The Courtenay Earls of Devon: The Formation and Disintegration of a Late Medieval Aristocratic Affinity', *Southern History*, i (1979), 71–97. For a more recent study see: James Ross, *John de Vere, Thirteenth Earl of Oxford (1442–1513): 'The Foremost Man of the Kingdom'* (Woodbridge, 2011).

[13] Michael J. Bennett, *Community, Class and Careerism: Cheshire and Lancashire Society in the Age of Sir Gawain and the Green Knight* (Cambridge, 1983); Christine Carpenter, *Locality and Polity: A Study of Warwickshire Landed Society* (Cambridge, 1992); Simon Payling, *Political Society in Lancastrian England: The Greater Gentry of Nottingham* (Oxford, 1991); A.J. Pollard, *North-Eastern England during the Wars of the Roses: Lay Society, War and Politics, 1450–1500* (Oxford, 1990); Nigel Saul, *Knights and Esquires: The Gloucestershire Gentry in the Fourteenth Century* (Oxford, 1981); Nigel Saul, *Scenes from Provincial Life: Knightly Families in Sussex, 1280–1400* (Oxford, 1986); Susan M. Wright, *The Derbyshire Gentry in the Fifteenth Century*, Derbyshire Record Society, viii (Chesterfield, 1983). See also: Malcolm Mercer, *The Medieval Gentry: Power, Leadership and Choice during the Wars of the Roses* (London, 2010).

[14] Christine Carpenter, 'Bastard Feudalism in Fourteenth-Century England' in *Kings, Lords and Men in Scotland and Britain, 1300–1625*, eds. Steve Boardman and Julian Goodacre (Edinburgh, 2014), 59–92.

feudal society and within the feudal state'.[15] David Carpenter noted that bastard feudalism was caused by 'a multiplicity of factors' including Angevin reforms and the appointment of gentry to local offices giving 'the magnates the opportunity to pervert the whole system'.[16] This historiographical divide between high and late medievalists can in part be attributed to differing definitions of bastard feudalism. Andrew Spencer has noted that historians have used two definitions of the concept: a narrow definition in which bastard feudalism was the method by which nobles altered the way they obtained service from using the 'feudal' method of granting land to a newer method of using cash payments as rewards for service; and a broader definition in which the nobility dominated localities in a corrupt and intimidating manner.[17] The statutes of livery were concerned about bastard feudalism in the broader sense of corruption and abuse but sought to prevent such abuses by restricting bastard feudalism in the narrower sense of the creation of social bonds.

Since McFarlane, the two historians of late medieval England who have examined bastard feudalism in the greatest depth, albeit with differing interpretations, are Michael Hicks and Christine Carpenter, both of whom have offered powerful critiques of older approaches. Two essays by Michael Hicks in 1991 noted problems with earlier studies and have shaped how the problem of liveries and retaining should be viewed. The first, on bastard feudalism, highlighted the implicit assumptions in earlier studies and the problems associated with privileging particular sets of sources at the expense of others.[18] The second argued the need to reintroduce principles into our understanding of late medieval politics, noting that historians have mentioned ideas and idealism but then 'ignore them when explaining what actually happened, which stemmed from self-interest, self-preservation and self-advancement'.[19] These two essays were precursors to a later book on bastard feudalism in which Hicks adopted a broad definition that equated bastard feudalism with the need for service. Like feudalism, bastard feudalism was a system that enabled nobles to obtain the service they required, whether it was domestic, legal, military or administrative. The key point in this approach was that bastard feudalism was 'morally neutral'. It was not the cause of disorder, nor part of an attempt to subvert governmental systems, but a necessary

---

[15] P.R. Coss, 'Bastard Feudalism revised', *P&P*, cxxv (1989), 54.

[16] David A. Carpenter, 'Debate: Bastard Feudalism Revised', *P&P*, cxxxi (1991), 177–89, quotation on 180.

[17] Andrew Spencer, *Nobility and Kingship in Medieval England: The Earls and Edward I* (Cambridge, 2014), 100–9, quotation on 100.

[18] Michael Hicks, 'Bastard Feudalism: Society and Politics in Fifteenth-Century England' in *Richard III and His Rivals: Magnates and their Motives in the Wars of the Roses* (London, 1991), 1–40.

[19] Michael Hicks, 'Idealism in Late Medieval English Politics' in *Richard III and His Rivals: Magnates and their Motives in the Wars of the Roses* (London, 1991), 41.

means of obtaining service. The lack of readily available land to grant meant non-tenurial ties between lords and men were necessary.[20] Bastard feudalism as a whole was never banned or abolished. The key thing was that it was a mechanism for both stability and disorder. By examining what were viewed as unacceptable forms of retaining, the acceptable forms also emerge.

The workings of bastard feudalism and the legal system are also key to the work of Christine Carpenter, who together with Edward Powell was one of the first advocates of the new constitutional history, which developed as a reaction against what they regarded as the simplistic reduction of politics to patronage. Christine Carpenter in particular criticised the static nature of developments in late medieval historiography from the 1970s to 1990s, stating that 'McFarlane's legacy has been a barrage of detailed studies of nobles and gentry', which have enhanced present knowledge and understanding, but have failed to produce a new synthesis. This lack of a new synthesis led Carpenter to argue for a new form of constitutional history that is 'conceived in terms of the world that our late medieval protagonists knew and grappled with'.[21] For Mark Ormrod the new constitutional history has shown historians that political history cannot be understood 'without appreciating the ideas, values, principles and traditions that underpinned it'.[22] Political principles and ideology could clearly influence someone's actions as much as personal interest, and provided the intellectual framework for much contemporary political rhetoric. Indeed, it is shown later that the statutes themselves cannot properly be understood without some explanation of the broader social and cultural milieu in which they were passed.

Yet the new constitutional history is problematic for two reasons. Though relatively minor, the first problem is the term 'constitutional', which has too many Whiggish connotations. Granted, the focus is not deterministic in nature. Indeed much of what is discussed pertains to ideas about the nature of government, and a more apt term would be 'ideological history'. Second, as Christian Liddy

---

[20]   Michael Hicks, *Bastard Feudalism* (London, 1995).
[21]   Christine Carpenter, 'Political and Constitutional History: Before and After McFarlane' in *The McFarlane Legacy: Studies in Late Medieval Politics and Society*, eds. R.H. Britnell and A.J. Pollard (Stroud, 1995), 190, 198. See also: Christine Carpenter, *Locality and Polity: A Study of Warwickshire Landed Society, 1401–1499* (Cambridge, 1992), 628–47, especially 642. See also: Edward Powell, 'After "After McFarlane": The Poverty of Patronage and the Case for Constitutional History' in *Trade, Devotion and Governance: Papers in Later Medieval History*, eds. Dorothy J. Clayton, Richard G. Davies and Peter McNiven (Stroud, 1994), 13; Edward Powell, *Kingship, Law and Society: Criminal Justice in the Reign of Henry V* (Oxford, 1989), 1–22; John Watts, *Henry VI and the Politics of Kingship* (Cambridge, 1996), 1–81.
[22]   W. Mark Ormrod, 'The Rebellion of Archbishop Scrope and the Tradition of Opposition to Royal Taxation' in *The Reign of Henry IV: Rebellion and Survival, 1403–13*, eds. Gwilym Dodd and Douglas Biggs (York, 2008), 174.

observed, 'parliament … does not appear to have much of a place'.[23] One reason for this, as Mark Ormrod has noted, is that most 'new constitutional' historians tend to focus their attention on the fifteenth century, when parliaments were more infrequent than in the fourteenth century.[24] Another reason is the prominence given to the peerage by the new constitutional school who regard the nobility, not parliament, as being the primary link between central government and the localities. The older constitutional traditional of the nineteenth century, best characterised by Stubbs, placed too much importance on parliament, particularly the Commons, mistaking their theoretical power to refuse royal requests of taxation for genuine political authority. Parliaments were only in session for around ten per cent of the time during the later middle ages and were therefore as much of an event as an institution at this time.[25]

The crown's most important relation was with the landed aristocracy, which is why crown–magnate relations are at the heart of the historiography of late medieval politics. This, however, does not means that parliament was irrelevant. Older constitutional historians placed too much emphasis on parliament but the new constitutional school has reversed this trend and placed too little emphasis on it. There were fewer parliaments during the fifteenth century than the fourteenth century, but Paul Cavill has shown that during Henry VII's reign parliament could have a real impact on people's lives which helped to 'expand and refine social policy'.[26] Parliament was not a detached entity but reflected the social, economic and political expectations in its acts and is therefore crucial for understanding the social and political history of late medieval England. Parliament is particularly relevant for this study as it was the vehicle through which those who wanted to restrict certain forms of retaining ensured that laws to address such problems were passed. These acts were enrolled in the parliament rolls, which provide a window into what were deemed to be acceptable and unacceptable forms of retaining. Political ideas had a role in the shaping of late medieval politics and these ideas were embedded in a broader social and cultural milieu which influenced the terms of the laws and their subsequent enforcement.

Another approach to bastard feudalism has been to reject the utility of the term. In 1992 Colin Richmond confidently declared: 'Bastard Feudalism is

---

[23] Christian Liddy, *War, Politics and Finance in Late Medieval English Towns: Bristol, York and the Crown, 1350–1400* (Woodbridge, 2005), 17.

[24] W.M. Ormrod, 'The New Political History: Recent Trends in the Historiography of Later Medieval England' in *New Approaches to the History of Late Medieval and Early Modern Europe*, eds. Troels Dahlreup and Per Ingesman (Copenhagen, 2009), 51.

[25] As noted in: Chris Given-Wilson, *Henry IV* (London, 2016), 539.

[26] P.R. Cavill, 'The Problem of Labour and the Parliament of 1495' in *The Fifteenth Century V: 'Of Mice and Men': Image, Belief and Regulation in Late Medieval England*, ed. Linda Clark (Woodbridge, 2005), 143–55, quotation on 155.

dead: I do not think I ever believed it was alive.'[27] Richmond made this bold statement while reviewing several monographs written during the late 1980s and early 1990s, in particular Simon Walker's study of John of Gaunt's affinity and Simon Payling's study of Lancastrian Nottinghamshire. Both Walker and Payling demonstrated that magnates could not simply dominate the politics and local government of a particular county.[28] Richmond's argument rests on the assumption that bastard feudalism was about members of the peerage creating affinities comprising members of the local gentry to dominate particular counties. Yet one of the recurring themes of this book is that bastard feudalism extended beyond the retaining practices of the peerage. The acts of parliament and resultant cases examined here show that retaining was not the sole preserve of the peerage and that similar relations occurred further down the social scale, some of which were perfectly acceptable to contemporaries. Bastard feudalism can be regarded as 'shorthand for complex structures of social and political relationships'.[29]

In accepting the validity of the term bastard feudalism, this book shares one of the professed aims of Andrew Spencer's recent study of earls during Edward I's reign, which was to 'perform a little historical necromancy' by reviving the use of the term.[30] The second half of this book in particular will highlight how pervasive retaining was across late medieval society.

The Records of the King's Bench

The main contemporary sources examined in this study are the records of the King's Bench, which was the highest court in the kingdom; its rulings could only be overturned by parliament.[31] Three specific classes were examined in detail: the controlment rolls (KB29), the ancient indictments (KB9) and the *coram rege* rolls (KB27). The controlment rolls are arranged by regnal year and were originally compiled by the clerk of the court of the King's Bench in order to keep a record of all the crown cases dealt with by the court of the King's Bench. These were the working indexes for the clerk of the court and provide references in the form of

[27] Colin Richmond, 'An English Mafia?', *Nottingham Medieval Studies*, 36 (1992), 240.
[28] Simon Payling, *Political Society in Lancastrian England: The Greater Gentry of Nottingham* (Oxford, 1991), 87–108; Simon Walker, *The Lancastrian Affinity, 1361–1399* (Oxford, 1990), 231–5.
[29] Carpenter, 'Bastard Feudalism in England in the Fourteenth Century', 61.
[30] Spencer, *Nobility and Kingship*, 100.
[31] For a discussion of the role of the King's Bench see: Marjorie Blatcher, *The Court of King's Bench, 1450–1550: A Study in Self-Help* (London, 1978), 1–9. A more in-depth discussion of this source material is given in: Gordon McKelvie, 'The Legality of Bastard Feudalism: The Statutes of Livery, 1390 to c.1520' (unpublished PhD thesis, University of Winchester, 2013), 36–50.

regnal year and legal term to the case in other classes of documents. They contain enrolled writs of *venire facias*, ordering local justices to make those accused appear in court, which was the first stage of the legal process. The controlment rolls are a valuable source because clerks diligently updated them, as shown in the case of Sir Ralph Greystock in Yorkshire. When Greystock finally appeared at King's Bench to produce a pardon on 11 July 1445[32] after being indicted at Michaelmas 1423 for illegally distributing livery to seven yeomen and one gentleman, the clerk of the court updated the controlment roll from twenty-two years earlier.[33] The controlment rolls are a useful guide to the various stages of the same case but the information contained in them is brief and omits important detail such as the date of the offence and where it was committed, meaning other records are necessary. This information is available in the ancient indictments because they were the 'formal written accusation[s] of a crime recorded by a presenting jury before a court'.[34] They also include returned commissions of *oyer et terminer* in which powerful commissions were imported into a locality and to hear and determine cases quickly, the details of which do not always appear in the controlment rolls.[35] The final class examined is the *coram rege rolls,* which include the original indictment; record of the payment of fines paid to the King's Bench; the entire legal process; and the outcome of the case. All three classes are examined in conjunction with each other because certain cases were only recorded in one of these classes.

The cases discussed in this study are from the crown side of the King's Bench, which were those cases prosecuted by local JPs or commissions of *oyer et terminer* acting as agents of the crown. However, there are some cases that survive in the plea, or civil, side of these documents from private prosecutions for illegal livery brought about by individuals, such as in Nottinghamshire in 1451 when Sir John Talbot (later earl of Shrewsbury) brought a suit against Sir John Stanhope in connection to an election dispute[36] and in Essex in 1490 when Peter Pekham, esquire, brought a suit against Sir Ralph Hastings.[37] Such instances are rare, making it difficult to identify any clear patterns. Private suits are only discussed in this book where they help to illuminate wider points. However, the records from counties in which King's Bench was not the main law court are included in this study. Lancashire, Cheshire and County Durham were all palatinates, which meant that they had their own legal and administrative

---

[32] KB27/737 rex rot. 1.
[33] KB29/57 rot. 5.
[34] Powell, *Kingship, Law and Society,* 303.
[35] For instance, a series of cases from Derbyshire in 1468 do not appear in the controlment rolls: KB9/13 mm. 11, 19–23.
[36] CP40/763 rot. 483; CP40/769 rot. 138; Payling, *Political Society,* 162–4.
[37] KB27/916 plea rot. 74.

system and did not return cases to King's Bench. Such cases are comparable to those found on the crown side of the King's Bench and therefore have been included in this study.

Although they are voluminous and contain a rich variety of information, it has long been recognised that legal records must be treated with caution. Charles Ross noted that indictments were formulaic and 'by their very nature ... deserve to be treated with scepticism, since they were often produced by interested parties, private enemies, informers or spies working for the government'.[38] Indictments were not a collection of neutral facts but narratives that had to be fitted into a pre-determined formula. Moreover, allegations could be false or malicious. They were not a comprehensive catalogue of every instance of a particular crime such as illegal livery. Ralph Griffiths argued that it is impossible to chart statistically criminal activity from the fifteenth century and therefore conclusions are, at best, impressionistic. The records produced by the law courts 'varied in degree of accuracy' and 'were couched in formalised language that included supposititious rather than actual details'.[39] More recently, Hannes Kleineke has stated that the regional variations in the readiness of the population to take cases to the law courts results in an analysis of levels of litigiousness rather than levels of crime, noting that such records should be used qualitatively, not quantitatively.[40] Despite these valid criticisms, the records of the King's Bench are fundamental to understanding retaining and bastard feudalism. The records provide an indication of how the statutes were enforced. It is probable that many instances of illegal livery or retaining were not prosecuted and therefore nothing can be said about them. Yet levels of enforcement raise important questions about why the statutes were enforced at certain times, and not necessarily during other periods. This is a key issue addressed throughout this book.

This study is based on 336 cases of illegal livery and retaining identifiable in the relevant records between the passing of the first act in 1390 and 1522, after which no other cases can be identified before 1530. The book is divided into two broad parts that examine the nature of bastard feudalism in England during the long fifteenth century, and the way in which society and government

---

[38] Charles Ross, 'Rumour, Propaganda and Popular Opinion during the Wars of the Roses' in *Patronage, the Crown and the Provinces in Later Medieval England*, ed. Ralph Griffiths (Gloucester, 1981), 16.

[39] Ralph Griffiths, *The Reign of Henry VI: The Exercise of Royal Authority, 1422–1461* (London, 1981), 128.

[40] Hannes Kleineke, 'Poachers and Gamekeepers: Four Fifteenth Century West Country Criminals' in *Outlaws in Medieval and Early Modern England: Crime, Government and Society, 1000–1650*, eds. John C. Appleby and Paul Dalton (Farnham, 2009), 129; Hannes Kleineke, 'Why the West was Wild: Law and Disorder in Fifteenth-Century Cornwall and Devon' in *The Fifteenth Century III: Authority and Subversion*, ed. Linda Clark (Woodbridge, 2003), 78–9.

sought to restrict the creation of bastard feudal relationships. The first part of this book examines the political events and legal processes surrounding illegal livery, by exploring the nature of the legislation and its enforcement, particularly the relationship between law-making in parliament and law enforcement in the localities. Thereafter, it examines the legal processes and outcomes of the cases and explains the various options that royal government had to deal with offenders. The second part of this book uses these cases to address wider points about the nature of retaining in late medieval England, and the ways in which retainers were used. This begins by considering the social status of those indicted for illegal livery and retaining, before considering the various networks through which such relationships were formed. It then considers the extent to which illegal livery and retaining was used to raise men for the purpose of lawlessness and feuding, before looking at the urban context of illegal livery and retaining. In doing so, it demonstrates the importance of bastard feudalism in understanding the nature of law, politics and society in late medieval England.

1

The System – Liveries and Retaining

In order to understand the enforcement of the statutes, it is important to clarify what the problems were that the statutes were addressing. The key point about the statutes is that they were never designed to end bastard feudalism or prevent retaining or the granting of liveries, but instead sought to restrict such practices to acceptable categories of servants. The simple reason for this is that parliament did not enact legislation in a vacuum. Various social and political pressures led to the issue being discussed in parliament and the acts being passed. The wider social, political, ideological and cultural contexts need consideration because they influenced what could and could not be legislated against. In one sense this draws on the insights of the 'new constitutional' school of late medieval historiography which emphasises the need to take account of the language and norms of medieval political life.[1] The term 'constitutional' is inherently problematic because of its Whiggish connotations and the lack of any written constitution at any point or in any place in British history. There was no formal constitution; instead there was a set of norms and implicit values that were shared by many and influenced political life, including the drafting and enforcement of laws. A more fruitful way of conceptualising the need to look beyond materialistic interests for understanding political and legal history is to think, as Michael Hicks has done, in terms of idealism.[2]

The law and acts passed in parliament similarly illuminated the society in which a law was passed, what that society valued and its principles and preoccupations. A key source for understanding the social values that underpinned the legislation are provisos which permit the distribution of liveries beyond those defined by the statutes. These exemptions explain wider social practices and expectations and highlight the precise problems that the statutes were addressing. Stanley Chrimes argued that amendments to laws which, among other things, exempt certain persons or groups 'cannot be dismissed as insignificant'.[3] This chapter explains the social and cultural contexts in which the statutes were passed and operated because this enables a better understanding of the nature of the enforcement of the statutes as a whole. As such the chapter considers the nature

---

[1] See above, pp. 6–7.
[2] Hicks, 'Idealism in Late Medieval English Politics', 41–60.
[3] Stanley Chrimes, *English Constitutional Ideas in the Fifteenth Century* (Cambridge, 1936), 163.

and function of the late medieval affinity before considering the broader cultural context of livery giving in late medieval England.

The Noble Affinity

At the heart of bastard feudalism was the noble affinity, which comprised all of the followers of a particular lord, though the precise connections could differ between individuals in the affinity. T.B. Pugh noted that the recruitment of members of the gentry was essential for 'the political and military power of a late medieval magnate'.[4] The relationship was also beneficial for the retainer – hence the affinity was key to how late medieval England functioned. K.B. McFarlane characterised late medieval England as being 'full of patrons seeking clients and clients in need of patronage', noting that 'the substantial men of every shire were much courted by those above and below them'.[5] The service a lord obtained from his servants in his household, his tenants and his wider affinity of estate officials and retainers was vital for providing him with the necessary resources to advance his interests. The system cannot be viewed as exploitative, as relationships were reciprocal and lay at the heart of all avenues for social advancement.[6] Members of the affinity benefited from their lord's 'good lordship', a rather vague but meaningful concept that, at a basic level, meant that a lord would advance the interests of his servants whenever possible. It was this very vagueness that gave the concept of 'good lordship' its strength. Although never rigorously defined or theorised in the manner that chivalry was, Maurice Keen's argument that definitions of chivalry were tonal as opposed to precise is also applicable to the notion of good lordship.[7]

Bastard feudalism developed as a means for the nobility to obtain the services they required without creating permanent tenurial bonds, giving them more flexibility in those with whom they forged a personal connection.[8] In many ways permanent tenurial bonds, characteristic of the high middle ages in England after the Norman Conquest, could only be created sporadically when new lands became available to grant. Scott Waugh identified evidence for over 100 examples of contractual relations between lords and clients prior to 1300 in various types of surviving records.[9] Nobles from earlier generations

4   T.B. Pugh, 'The Magnates, Knights and Gentry' in *Fifteenth Century England*, eds. S.B. Chrimes, C.D. Ross and R.A. Griffiths (Manchester, 1972), 101.
5   McFarlane, *The Nobility of Late Medieval England*, 113.
6   Bennett, *Class, Community and Careerism*, 192.
7   Maurice Keen, *Chivalry* (London, 1984), 2.
8   See above, p. 00.
9   Scott L. Waugh, 'Tenure to Contract: Lordship and Clientage in Thirteenth-Century England', *EHR*, ci (1986), 819–20.

including Thomas of Lancaster, Simon de Montfort, William de Valence and William Marshall all led affinities of men who wore a lord's livery and/or were in receipt of his fees.[10] Explanations for bastard feudalism's origins tend to highlight the disruptive element of bastard feudalism as nobles created affinities of non-tenurial servants as a means of subverting royal authority.[11] Although the interpretations of high and late medievalists may differ, the key point is that from at least the thirteenth century, and possibly earlier, nobles looked beyond their own lands for servants with him they did not share ties of tenure. Yet this does not mean that tenurial-based feudalism lost its relevance. Tenants on various estates remained a vital component for many aristocratic followings. David Carpenter has shown that feudal ties remained key during the thirteenth and early fourteenth centuries.[12] Andrew Spencer has warned against over-emphasising the importance of retaining in late thirteenth-century armies since land, as opposed to fees, was the main method of rewarding permanent associates and comments that 'although lords had begun to act in a "bastard-feudal" way, they were still thinking in a "feudal" way'.[13] Even in the fifteenth and sixteenth centuries which were the high point of bastard feudalism, more traditional feudal relations and structures remained an important element in the development of a noble's power. James Ross has highlighted the importance of mesne feudalism as a key source of income for the English aristocracy in the fifteenth century, noting that it is too easy to dismiss feudalism as meaningless by this point. The continued importance of tenurial relation also meant that the socio-political relationships between landlords and tenants remained.[14] Throughout the fifteenth century tenants on a noble's land continued to form the bulk of most noble affinities.[15] Bastard feudalism did not replace feudalism, which was not formally abolished until the Restoration of the Stuarts in 1660, as both were key methods by which power and politics functioned.[16]

---

[10] David Crouch, *William Marshall: Court, Career and Chivalry in the Angevin Empire* (London, 1990), 157–68; J.R. Maddicott, *Thomas of Lancaster, 1307–1322: A Study in the Reign of Edward II* (Oxford, 1970), 40–66; J.R. Maddicott, *Simon de Montfort* (Cambridge, 1994), 59–76; Huw Ridgeway, 'William de Valence and his *Familiares*, 1247–72', *Historical Research*, lxv (1992), 239–57.

[11] David Crouch has suggested this can be backdated to the civil war during the reign of King Stephen: David B. Crouch, 'Debate: Bastard Feudalism Revised', *P&P*, cxxxi (1991), 165–77.

[12] David Carpenter, 'The Second Century of English Feudalism', *P&P*, clxviii (2000), 30–71.

[13] Andrew Spencer, 'The Comital Military Retinue in the Reign of Edward I', *Historical Research*, lxxxiii (2010), 54.

[14] James Ross, 'The English Aristocracy and Mesne Feudalism in the Late Middle Ages', *EHR*, cxxxiii (2018), 1027–59.

[15] Hicks, *Bastard Feudalism*, 48–52.

[16] *Stat. Realm*, v, 259–66.

By the late fourteenth century, when the first statutes were enacted, the ties that bound men to their lords were multifaceted and connections were forged in several ways. The two most obvious connections were the indenture of retainer whereby a servant (normally a member of the gentry) bound themselves to a particular lord (normally a member of the parliamentary peerage) and the granting of liveries. These were the main forms of relationship that were most visible and the ones that the statutes were concerned with. Yet there were many other ways in which meaningful relationships were formed and therefore a definition of retaining must stretch beyond the indenture of retainer. One Paston letter reveals the multiple ways in which bastard feudal relations could manifest themselves.[17] In June 1469 John Paston (III) wrote to his father John Paston (II) stating that neither he, Bernard nor Broom[18] had been given a gown by the duke of Norfolk. In one respect this was fortunate for them because more than 100 men were indicted for taking the duke's livery illegally the following year and Paston would certainly have been amongst the indicted had he been given the duke's livery.[19] The letter then reveals other methods by which men became bound to lords. Rather than being given a gown, Bernard and Broom along with Barney and William Calthorp were then sworn to Richard, duke of Gloucester, who was probably recruiting men in the region at this time for his brother during a period of political uncertainty.[20] Paston himself refused to swear such an oath, stating that he said to 'hym [Richard] that I was not woorthe a grootye wyth-owt yow, and therefor I wold mak no promes to no body tyll they had your good wyll first'. The letter indicates that connections between lords and men could be made via verbal agreements such as oaths and that there is no need to necessarily privilege the written word. A sworn oath or even a non-sworn verbal agreement was enough to create a meaningful relationship, as the 1468 act refers on several occasions to retaining by 'othe, writyng, indenture or promyse'.[21] This rather vague phrasing brought a whole range of connections into the law's remit, for the first time stretching beyond simply regulating the visual aspects of bastard feudalism in the form of liveries. Non-tenurial relations between lords and men were created via various means

---

[17] For the letter discussed in this paragraph see: *PL*, i, 545.
[18] The first names of both of these men are not given in the letter.
[19] Hicks, '1468 Livery Act' 24–5.
[20] Rosemary Horrox, *Richard III: A Study of Service* (Cambridge, 1989), 32–3. Horrox also noted that Sir William Calthorp is the only one of these four men who seems to have maintained any connections with the duke during the 1470s. The Pastons seem to have been close to Calthorp around this time and there is no reason to doubt the veracity of the claim made in this letter. *PL*, i, 433, 540. For Calthorp's relations with the Paston family see: Colin Richmond, *The Paston Family in the Fifteenth Century: The First Phase* (Cambridge, 1990), 149.
[21] *PROME*, xiii, 384–6.

with numerous types of rewards for servants, some of which, like oaths, may never have produced a written record.

Christine Carpenter has described how a noble affinity worked in practice, stating that it was a series of concentric circles, the closest being a lord's various councillors along with estate and household officials; then circles of those in receipt of annuities but not holding any formal office; and finally an outer circle of 'well-wishers and personal connections whose existence can usually only be inferred'.[22] The statutes were most concerned with the second circle of servants who were in receipt of fees and liveries but had no other formal connection to a lord. The first circle of servants was necessary for the operation of late medieval society and government, while the outermost circle enjoyed a relationship that could not easily be defined in law and would be impractical to prosecute. Indeed, John Maddicott has suggested for the retaining of royal justices, a change occurred after the 1390 act in the rewards given from fees and liveries to things such as 'hospitality, entertainment and favours incapable of precise definition and description'.[23] Such relations were difficult to define and prove, yet they still helped to form connections between the lord and his retainers that were created for the benefit of both parties.

Another key point to consider is why lords needed affinities at all. In essence, retainers were expected to serve a lord's various needs, which could be domestic, administrative, political or military in character. The first element of the noble affinity was the permanent members of a noble household whose primary duty was to ensure their lord's personal safety. The political instability of the fifteenth century contributed to the rise in household numbers during this period.[24] Having a large body of household retainers wearing a lord's livery *en masse* was significant because it emphasised the status and power of the lord and his household.[25] Michael Hicks highlighted the military capability of these retinues of household servants, arguing that even the lowliest of domestic servants were able-bodied men, able to bear arms and possessing the ability to engage in violent acts. Their numbers also deterred attacks on their master or burglary of his house.[26] Nobles needed retinues of servants able to bear weapons as a bodyguard for themselves and their families, with the wearing of a distinct livery helping, amongst other things, to deter attacks.

---

[22] Carpenter, 'Beauchamp Affinity', 513–17.

[23] Maddicott, 'Law and Lordship', 56.

[24] Kate Mertes, *The English Noble Household 1250–1600: Good Governance and Politic Rule* (Oxford, 1988), 136, 186–7.

[25] Noël Denholm-Young, *Seignorial Administration in England* (London, 1937), 24; C.M. Woolgar, *The Great Household in Late Medieval England* (London, 1999), 32, 173; Mertes, *English Noble Household*, 126, 132–3.

[26] Hicks, *Bastard Feudalism*, 47–8.

The militaristic character of the noble household was even more prevalent in the wider noble affinity. From at least the reign of Edward I, English kings needed nobles to retain men by various means, including indentures, in order to raise sufficient armies for their campaigns in France, Scotland and Wales. Although bastard feudalism is unlikely to have developed purely from military need, noble retaining was a key benefit to the crown.[27] The benefits were evident not only in offensive campaigns but also in the need to defend the realm, which the various laws about liveries and retaining needed to consider. The 1399 act provides an insight into social attitudes and military expediencies relating to the giving of liveries. One of the primary arguments in favour of preventing lords and nobles from being able to retain men quickly was that it could lead to local disorder, violence and even rebellion. Internally, these factors could lead to civil war. The requirements of foreign war, however, meant that being able to retain a large number of men quickly was beneficial, particularly in response to border raids or rebellion. Military expediency was expressed by the fact that the statutes exempted the constable and marshal of England. The 1399 act stated that the constables of the wardens of the march were permitted to 'use the said king's livery on the frontiers and the march of the realm in time of war'.[28] Earlier acts had not specifically stated that the wardens of the march were to be exempt. It was only after further contemplation that this proviso was included in the livery laws, which is indicative of the wider process whereby the laws were refined according to circumstances. While full-scale Anglo-Scottish warfare was rare from the 1330s onwards, border raiding and skirmishes remained a constant threat during the late medieval period. The wardens of the marches were well paid and expected to recruit men rapidly in times of war for the defence of the realm.[29] During Edward IV's reign, this proviso was also part of the 1461 and 1468 acts.[30] Edward was acutely aware of the fact that the deposed Lancastrian regime had taken refuge at the Scottish court and enjoyed much support in the north.[31] Therefore, it was useful to emphasise the need to permit his prominent northern magnates to retain men for national defence. Later, Henry VII emphasised the importance of the north for the defence of the realm, stating in his general pardon

---

[27] Michael Jones and Simon Walker (eds.), 'Private Indentures for Life Service in Peace and War', *Camden Miscellany*, xiii (1994), 15–16; McFarlane, 'Bastard Feudalism', 162–3; Michael Prestwich, *War, Politics and Finance Under Edward I* (London, 1972), 41–91.

[28] *PROME*, viii, 38.

[29] For a full discussion of the position of Warden of the Marches see: R.L. Storey, 'The Wardens of the Marches of England towards Scotland, 1377–1489', *EHR*, lxxii (1957), 593–615.

[30] *PROME*, xiii, 65, 386.

[31] On Scottish support for the Lancastrians see: Norman MacDougall, *James III*, 2nd edition (Edinburgh, 2009), 44–6.

to the north after Bosworth that part of their duty was to 'defend this land against the Scots'.[32] It was always necessary to permit those entrusted with defending the Scottish border to be able to retain and give livery to large groups of men very quickly. The statutes of livery were partly an attempt to prevent lords from raising private armies, but in the case of border raiding private armies were necessary.

Military service was one of many functions, and not necessarily the primary function, carried out by household retainers. Other factors such as professional skills were important in addition to the prestige brought to a household by those of a certain social status serving. Christopher Woolgar emphasised the importance of servants in the household of great lords in terms of their practical skills and enhancement of the prestige of the household. Servants of a higher social status were particularly vital in enhancing the reputation and prestige of a household and were, according to Woolgar, 'an ornament to the household'. Many were retained in the household for their professional skills.[33] The household was staffed by many menial servants such as cooks, maids, stable boys and others whose duty was to attend the needs of the lord. Two other examples of retaining show that others were retained by indenture not for their administrative or military talents but for their value in a courtly environment. In April 1412 Henry, Lord Beaumont, retained a trumpeter for life, granting him two messuages and two bovates in Folkingham along with 40s. rent to serve him for life.[34] Eight months later Beaumont retained a minstrel called Nicolas Duke, granting him an annuity of '40s from the issues of the lordship of Barton upon Humbre'.[35] Beaumont died the following year and the inquisition *post mortem* for his lands in Lincolnshire records these grants along with another annuity he granted in 1409 to the three-times-widowed Katherine, widow of John de Bellow Monte, Thomas Enderby and Thomas Holme.[36] Beaumont's indentures are the only examples of men being retained in this manner for their skills as entertainers to a noble household, but they do indicate the wide range of duties expected of household retainers.

Beyond the immediate household, the same balance needed to be struck between the military and administrative capabilities of a lord's wider affinity. Christine Carpenter argued that Richard Beauchamp, earl of Warwick's retainers were permanent followers and mainly came from families close to the earl, who were unlikely to have been recruited for purely military purposes.[37] Retaining helped in local politics as direct links with the county gentry could help a noble to

---

[32]   *Tudor Royal Proclamations*, ed. Paul L. Hughes and James F. Larkin (New Haven, 1964–9), i, 3–4.
[33]   Woolgar, *The Great Household*, 37.
[34]   'Private Indentures', no. 112; *CPR, 1413–16*, 137.
[35]   'Private Indentures', no. 113; *CPR, 1413–16*, 132.
[36]   *CIPM, 1 to 5 Henry V*, no. 90.
[37]   Carpenter, 'The Beauchamp Affinity', 519–20.

dominate local government in a particular county. Even the retinue of a magnate as militarily active as Edward, the Black Prince, broadened from its central military focus to include more administrative responsibilities.[38] The importance of the affinity for estate administration and local political influence is evident in the case of Edward Courtenay, earl of Devon, who used his affinity to express and consolidate his power in Devon and neighbouring counties.[39] Assisting with estate management and influencing local politics were at least as important, if not more so, than the military functions of many affinities.

Another group of servants who were exempt from many of the statutes were lawyers, or 'legal counsel',[40] an exemption made necessary by the practicalities of the legal profession as lawyers could represent multiple clients. The litigious nature of late medieval England meant that most nobles and gentry would at some point in their life become embroiled in a property dispute and nobles retained numerous lawyers regularly in their councils from at least the fourteenth century.[41] Monastic houses such as Ramsey Abbey and Christ Church, Canterbury were retaining lawyers from at least the middle of the thirteenth century, which are the earliest surviving examples identified by John Maddicott. The fact that the earliest evidence comes from ecclesiastical institutions can be explained by the better levels of surviving documentation and it is probable that secular nobles were also retaining lawyers at this time.[42] By the time that the first statute was passed in 1390, the distribution of liveries to lawyers was common, as evident in the livery roll for the earl of Devon in 1384 which shows him giving his livery to thirteen men-at-law.[43] In 1402 Elizabeth la Zouche granted her lawyer, John Bore, livery of fur along with 5 marks per annum as wages.[44] Towns also paid retaining fees and bestowed livery to various lawyers and officials.[45] Since lawyers represented multiple clients, restricting the number of people who could retain them would have seriously affected their income.

Yet it is important not to make generalisations about the nature of noble affinities based on single case studies. Simon Walker argued that John of Gaunt's

---

[38] David Green, 'The Later Retinue of Edward the Black Prince', *Nottingham Medieval Studies*, xliv (2000), 141–51.

[39] Cherry, 'The Courtenay Earls of Devon', 74–5.

[40] *PROME*, vii, 147–50; viii, 148–9; xiii, 384–6; xvi, 365–8.

[41] Christopher Given-Wilson, *The English Nobility in the Late Middle Ages* (London, 1987), 98–103.

[42] Maddicott, 'Law and Lordship', 11.

[43] BL, Add. Ch. 64320.

[44] E210/697.

[45] Nigel Ramsey, 'Retained Legal Counsel, c.1275-c.1475', *TRHS*, 5th series, xxxv (1985), 101–2, 105-6, 111; *The First General Entry Book of the City of Salisbury, 1387–1452*, ed. David R. Carr, Wiltshire Record Society, liv (2001), nos. 36, 38–9, 44, 54, 64, 71, 91, 98, 113, 140, 185, 203, 215.

retinue was primarily a military one as numerous military and diplomatic commitments meant that 'anything else would have been an expensive luxury'. An indenture of retainer with John of Gaunt was, therefore, 'an emphatically military commitment'.[46] As such the Lancastrian affinity did not dominate the politics and administration of any one county.[47] One reason for this differing interpretation is that Walker's study focused on a magnate, John of Gaunt, who had much greater military needs than most late medieval English nobles, especially in light of the fact that he claimed the crown of Castile. These commitments and his unrivalled wealth meant that Gaunt had an untypically large household, but financial constraints meant that even Gaunt could not afford to pay many fees for non-military purposes. A large affinity was expensive to maintain, as evident in the case of the earls of Northumberland. By the death of the third earl in 1461 the receivers' account indicate that between one third and one half of his gross revenues were spent on fees. By the time of the fourth earl the cost was still a major burden, as evident in the *valor* of 1489.[48] This comparatively high level of spending was probably caused by the fact the Percy family were embroiled in the upheavals of the Wars of the Roses on several occasions, coupled with higher levels of lawlessness and competition for offices in the north-east. A.J. Pollard has argued that Richard Neville, earl of Salisbury, was spending much less on retaining fees, indicating that prominent magnates did not necessarily need to spend a large proportion of their income on retaining.[49] Nevertheless, the figures indicate the extent to which retaining fees could potentially drain financial resources. Gaunt's unprecedented military commitments meant that his retine was not typical of most bastard feudal retinues. The precise characteristics of noble affinities varied depending on the specific needs of individual lords.

The Crown's Perspective

The nature of political society meant that retaining had a public as well as private function. The practicalities of pre-modern communication and the levels of government finances meant that in medieval England power could not be centralised at Westminster and therefore royal government worked by delegation to largely unpaid officials. As Gerald Harriss noted, royal government needed local elites to govern society, particularly magnates and leading churchmen who 'were a *governing* class, the king's natural counsellors, with a residual

---

[46] Walker, *Lancastrian Affinity*, 42–3.
[47] Walker, *Lancastrian Affinity*, 117–234.
[48] Bean, *The Estates of the Percy Family*, 91, 133.
[49] A.J. Pollard, 'The Northern Retainers of Richard Neville, Earl of Salisbury', *Northern History*, 11 (1976 for 1975), 64–5.

responsibility for good governance should the monarch fail'.[50] Magnates with wide-ranging responsibilities, such as the earls of Northumberland and William, Lord Hastings, had abnormally large retinues in order to assist with the governing and protection of the kingdom.[51] This was part of Edward IV's policy of creating powerful magnates in each region as a means of governing.[52] Henry VII continued this policy of promoting several great regional magnates, which is where 'the nobility really exercised authority and governance'.[53] As English kings required the cooperation of the nobility, or at least those nobles with personal preferences for a life involved in politics and administration, the noble affinity was a means through which royal government was exercised in medieval England.

In addition to needing the nobility to retain men, kings began to create their own affinities of followers throughout the later middle ages. Kings had personal connections to the knightly class during the twelfth and thirteenth centuries but these were confined primarily to the military sphere.[54] Chris Given-Wilson has noted that during the reign of Richard II a new royal policy emerged: that of creating a magnate-style affinity by retaining knights and esquires which gave Richard II a direct relationship with the county gentry, thus circumventing the higher nobility. Particularly after the crisis of 1387–8, he argues, Richard II 'wanted to be sure of a loyal core of followers in a crisis'.[55] The main duties of such members of the royal affinity changed from being primarily military to being more focused on the administration of royal government in the localities.[56] Although there were several prominent violent and bloody episodes during the later middle ages, peace was the normal state of affairs and therefore it should be expected that administration rather than military might was the key characteristic of a royal retainer.

Although the administrative abilities of royal retainers were important, it is clear that, by the standards of medieval Europe, the frequent usurpations and changes of dynasty did lead to the development of policies and laws to ensure

---

[50] Gerald Harriss, 'Political Society and the Growth of Government in Late Medieval England', *P&P*, cxxxviii (1993), 32–3.

[51] Dunham, *Lord Hastings' Indentured Retainers*; Pollard, *North-Eastern England*, 123.

[52] Charles Ross, *Edward IV* (Berkeley and Los Angeles, 1974), 333–9.

[53] James Ross, 'A Governing Elite? The Higher Nobility in the Yorkist and Early Tudor Period' in *The Yorkist Age: Proceedings of the 2011 Harlaxton Symposium*, eds. Hannes Kleineke and Christian Steer (Donington, 2013), 95.

[54] For the Anglo-Norman period see: J.O. Prestwich, 'War and Finance in the Anglo-Norman State', *TRHS*, 5th series, iv (1955), 19–34; J.O. Prestwich, 'Military Household of the Anglo-Norman Kings', *EHR*, xcvi (1981), 1–35. For the Anglo-Saxon period see e.g. Ryan Lavelle, *Alfred's Wars: Sources and Interpretations of Anglo-Saxon Warfare in the Viking Age* (Woodbridge, 2010), 107–10.

[55] Given-Wilson, *King's Affinity*, 217.

[56] Christopher Given-Wilson, 'The King and the Gentry in Fourteenth-Century England', *TRHS*, 5th series, xxxvii (1986), 87–102; Given-Wilson, *King's Affinity*, 201–57.

that there was a military presence that the king could call upon if required. After the failed Epiphany Rising to restore Richard II, Henry IV's council advised him to retain men in each county as part of a broader strategy in light of the treason of the earls of Kent and Salisbury, to ensure the king's personal safety and tighten the new regime's grip on England.[57] The importance of having men with clear military capabilities within the royal affinity was a consistent theme in affinities of several kings during the fifteenth century. One chronicler claimed that by 1458 Henry VI's mental incapacity meant that 'Englonde was oute of all good gouernaunce' and that 'the queen [Margaret of Anjou] with suche as were of her affynyte rewled the reame as her liked, gaderyng ryches innumerable'. The chronicler then claimed that Margaret feared that her son would not inherit the throne and therefore allied herself with the Cheshire gentry and made her son 'yeue lyuerey of swannys' to all gentlemen in Cheshire and in other counties too. The alleged reason was to enable Henry VI to abdicate in favour of his son.[58] This claim that Henry VI would be encouraged to abdicate in favour of his son is not credible and, as Joanna Laynesmith has argued, a Yorkist invention 'to undermine Margaret's credibility by constructing her as a traitor to her own king'.[59] However, the chronicle's reference to the distribution of liveries in Cheshire to win support is credible because the county was heavily militarised and the Lancastrian administration was exploiting the area's military and financial potential at this time.[60] The need for liveried retainers to ensure the stability of a new dynasty was evident after the Yorkist usurpation. An act from Edward IV's first parliament in 1461 prohibited the distribution of badges by those of a 'lower estate or degree' unless they had 'speciall commaundement by the kyng to reyse people for thassystyng of hym, resistyng of his ennemyes, or repressyng of riottes within his lande'.[61] In effect, such men of lesser estates were not permitted to distribute their own livery badges but were expected to distribute the king's if he need to face down a rebellion.

Henry VII was probably more acutely aware of the need to develop some sort of military base in England than any other late medieval usurper. Exiled in 1471 at the age of fourteen, Henry spent his entire adult life before becoming king abroad as a minor political figure; essentially he was a hanger-on at other people's courts.[62] Consequently, he had no natural powerbase from which to construct the

[57] *Proceedings and Ordinances of the Privy Council, Volume 1L: 10 Richard II to 11 Henry IV*, ed. Harris Nicholas (London, 1834), 107–10; Given-Wilson, *Henry IV*, 164–5.

[58] *An English Chronicle 1377–1461*, ed. William Marx (Woodbridge, 2003), 78.

[59] Joanne L. Laynesmith, *The Late Medieval Queens: English Queenship, 1445–1503* (Oxford, 2004), 166.

[60] Griffiths, *Henry VI*, 788.

[61] *PROME*, xii, 499–500.

[62] Ralph A. Griffiths and Roger S. Thomas, *The Making of the Tudor Dynasty*, revised

core of an affinity, unlike Henry IV and Edward IV who, when they ascended to the throne, were able to import a number of men from their own private bureau-cracies into royal service.[63] An act from 1487 imposed stricter penalties on royal tenants who were illegally retained and those who retained them.[64] This was part of a broader strategy of Henry VII's to ensure the loyalty of his affinity. Such tactics can also be seen in creation of the company of king's spear by Henry VII to cement his authority in the localities. Like the Order of the Garter, the company of king's spear blended chivalry with politics. The extent of its membership has been described as 'feeble' compared to the affinities of Richard II and Henry IV because membership of the king's spear was concentrated in the south-east, around the centres of royal power, while none came from Wales or the north-west. In contrast, those of Richard II and Henry IV were distributed more widely across the whole kingdom, giving those kings more direct contact with the localities. Henry VIII expanded the company, which lasted until 1515 when it was abolished as part of Wolsey's 'cost-cutting exercise' after the French war.[65] An oath on the gospel by members of the company early in Henry VIII's reign stated, amongst other promises, that they would not retain anyone without the king's 'especialle licence'.[66] The use of oaths to reinforce existing obligations was a technique Henry VII employed on several occasions, including with duchy of Lancaster officials who were made to swear oaths not to be retained by anyone else.[67] This policy was also extended to servants of the king's second son, Henry, duke of York.[68] From the perspective of the crown, noble affinities were vital for the running of government and the aristocratic strategy of granting fees and liveries to help to cement power was something that late medieval kings also adopted. Consequently, no king wanted to ban retaining but instead sought to mitigate the possible problems of it.

Liveries

The main focus of much of the legislation about retaining, and the majority of the indictments, was on the distribution of liveries. Livery was the insignia of a lord that his retainers and wider affinity wore to identify themselves as his servants.

---

edition (Stroud, 2005), 85–98.
[63] Griffiths, 'Public and Private Bureaucracies', 109–30.
[64] *PROME*, xv, 375–6 – discussed in depth in Chapter 4.
[65] For a summary of the company of king's spear see: Steven Gunn, 'Chivalry and the Politics of the Early Tudor Court' in *Chivalry in the Renaissance*, ed. Sydney Anglo (Woodbridge, 1990), 116–17.
[66] BL, Cotton MS. Titus A XIII, fol. 189.
[67] DL5/3 fols. 152d, 153. See also: McKelvie, 'Henry VII's Letter to Carlisle', 160–1.
[68] DL37/62 rot. 43.

Liveries developed from the earlier system of heraldry which stretched back to the twelfth century, when knights competing in tournament needed some means of identifying themselves.[69] Over time heraldic symbolism became increasingly elaborate and codified, as evident when Richard, first baron Scrope of Bolton, initiated a lawsuit in 1385 against the Cheshire knight Robert Grosvenor over Grosvenor's use of Scrope's arms while going on campaign to Scotland. In total 397 witnesses testified in the court of chivalry in a case lasting five years.[70] Heraldry had developed a set of laws and precedents that became increasingly complex to the point that they caused disputes within armies. Therefore, prior to Henry V's successful Normandy campaign in 1417 he ordered the sheriffs in Hampshire, Wiltshire, Sussex and Dorset to proclaim that no one was to assume any coat of arms that they did not have by right of ancestors or by gift, unless they fought with him at Agincourt. Anyone who did would not be allowed to campaign and lose all of their wages.[71] Liveries were not as regulated as heraldry and it was easier to adopt a specific symbol for a livery badge. This lack of codification enabled liveries to be adopted by a broad range of social groups including nobles, churchmen and townsmen. Yet the system of livery distribution was hierarchical, particularly in relation to gowns and cloth as opposed to badges. The amount of livery each person received depended on their social status, as evident in many lists of those given liveries by kings and nobles.[72] A letter from one of John de Vere, thirteenth earl of Oxford's servants to William Paston III makes this rule explicit: 'ye must remembre the gentilmen muste haue better than the yomen and the yomen better than the gromes.'[73]

The wearing of livery helped to create and cement a collective identity between a lord and his servants.[74] Richard III recognised the value of livery badges for fostering a sense of group identity. On 31 August 1483, in preparation for the investiture of his son as prince of Wales, Richard instructed the wardrobe of the royal household to supply him with, amongst other things, 13,000 livery badges bearing his device, the White Boar, 'for distribution to friends, well-wishers and perhaps anyone who would wear one'.[75] The extent to which Richard was associated with the White Boar is evident in William Collingbourne's seditious

---

[69] David Crouch, *Tournament: A Chivalric Way of Life* (London, 2005), 139–41; Malcolm Vale, *War and Chivalry* (London, 1981), 96–7.
[70] The testimonies are printed in: *The Scrope and Grosvenor Controversy*, ed. N.H. Nicholas, 2 vols. (London, 1832).
[71] *CCR, 1413–1419*, 433.
[72] Malcom Vale, *The Princely Court: Medieval Courts and Culture in North-West Europe, 1270–1380* (Oxford, 2004), 93–115.
[73] *PL*, ii, 497.
[74] Saul, 'Abolition of Badges', 306–7; Walker, *Lancastrian Affinity*, 96.
[75] *British Library, Harleian Manuscript 433*, ed. Rosemary Horrox and P.W Hammond, 4 vols. (Gloucester, 1979), ii, 42; Charles Ross, *Richard III* (Berkeley, 1981), 150.

rhyme against him and his close associates Francis Lovell, William Catesby and Sir Richard Ratcliffe – 'The Cat, the Rat and Lovell the Dog / Rule all England under the Hog' – for which Collingbourne was executed.[76] Another example of noble liveries being readily known relates to John of Gaunt, who used a livery collar, instead of badges, as a way of making his servants more distinct.[77] During a riot in London in 1377 one of Gaunt's knights, Sir Thomas Swinton, wished to endear himself to Gaunt and rode on horseback through the crowded streets of London wearing Gaunt's livery, 'thus inflaming the anger of the people evermore'. If the mayor was not able to rescue him, he would almost certainly have been killed by the crowd for what Walsingham described as an act of 'unadvised rashness'.[78] Gaunt's livery was known and recognizable, and the incident suggests that the crowd viewed an attack on someone wearing Gaunt's livery as a symbolic attack on Gaunt himself. The distinctiveness of such liveries should not be overstated. The foggy conditions that hindered visibility at the Battle of Barnet led to confusion within the Lancastrian army when the earl of Warwick's men reportedly attacked their own side because they mistook the earl of Oxford's livery badge for that of Edward IV.[79]

The symbolic importance of grants of livery was shared by the recipients and the grantors. For some recipients, liveries were valued and probably rarely worn except on special occasions and normally kept in a secure place. The inventory of goods stolen from the Paston family at Haylesdon in 1465 includes a reference to the king's livery which was kept in the church.[80] Livery collars, which tended to be made of more expensive material and therefore more valuable, may have been passed down as family heirlooms and only worn on special occasions.[81] Many gentry tombs included specific livery collars, particularly Lancastrian and Yorkist ones during the Wars of the Roses, which demonstrates the association between the entitlement to wear a specific livery collar and how a particular person wanted to be remembered in death.[82] In such instances liveries were a tangible link to previous generations and a symbolic outward display of a current loyalty.

During periods of rebellion or civil war liveries took on an additional significance as symbols of defiance. This was particularly the case during the reign of

[76] Horrox, *Richard III: A Study of Service*, 222.
[77] Walker, *Lancastrian Affinity*, 94–5.
[78] *The St Albans Chronicle: The Chronica Maiora of Thomas Walsingham*, 2 vols., eds. and trans. John Taylor, Wendy R. Childs and Leslie Watkiss (Oxford, 2003–11), i, 93.
[79] *Death and Dissent: The Dethe of the Kynge of Scots and Warkworth's Chronicle*, ed. Lister M. Matheson (Woodbridge, 1999), 110. This is the only account of the battle that includes this story: Ross, *John de Vere*, 66–7.
[80] *PL*, i, 325–6.
[81] Matthew Ward, *The Livery Collar in Late Medieval England and Wales: Politics, Identity and Affinity* (Woodbridge, 2016), 27.
[82] Ward, *Livery Collar*, 99–146.

Henry IV, who had deposed his cousin Richard II in 1399. Richard was subsequently killed in secret either by poisoning or starvation after the failed coup attempt against Henry known as the Epiphany Rising in early 1400 and buried at Kings Langley.[83] Nevertheless, in 1403–4 rumours circulated that Richard II was still alive and was preparing to return to England to reclaim his throne. Embroiled in the conspiracy was Maud de Vere, countess of Oxford, who was alleged to have distributed Richard II's livery badge of a white hart to garner support in December 1403.[84] Although nothing came of this particular conspiracy, the fact that livery badges were used as a means of garnering support for a particular faction further attests to the symbolic importance of livery in creating the collective consciousness necessary in acts of rebellion. Yet by the time of this conspiracy the meaning attached to the white hart badge had changed. At the battle of Shrewsbury in July 1403 the rebellious Percy army fought wearing Richard II's livery.[85] By the time of the battle of Shrewsbury, the white hart badge no longer represented a nostalgic longing for the return of the divisive and high-handed Richard II but was instead a symbol of defiance and resistance against Henry IV.

Livery was a sign of affiliation, indicating where a servant's predominant loyalty lay. After Sir William Stanley had been executed for involvement in the Perkin Warbeck conspiracy in 1495 a Yorkist livery collar was found in his residence of Holt Castle. The collar was viewed as additional proof of Stanley's continued Yorkist sentiments, though it is plausible the collar was kept for its fiscal, as opposed to symbolic, value.[86] A more serious incident occurred a generation later when Sir William Bulmer wore Stafford livery while serving as a member of the royal household. Henry VIII is reported to have said, angrily:

> that he would [have it that] none of his seruauntes should hang on another mannes sleue, and that he was aswel able to maintain him as the duke of Buckingham, and that what might be thought of his departing and what myght bee suppose be ye duke's retaining, he would not then declare.[87]

---

[83] Nigel Saul, *Richard II* (London, 1997), 424–6.

[84] *Select Cases in the Court of King's Bench Under Richard II, Henry IV and Henry V*, ed. G.O. Sayles, Selden Society, lxxxviii (London, 1971), 153. For this particular incident see: James Ross, 'Seditious Activities: The Conspiracy of Maud de Vere, Countess of Oxford, 1403–4' in *The Fifteenth Century III: Authority and Subversion*, ed. Linda Clark (Woodbridge, 2003), 25–42.

[85] *An English Chronicle*, 33.

[86] E154/2/5 fol. 13; Ward, *Livery Collar*, 28–9.

[87] *Hall's Chronicle: Containing the History of England during the Reign of Henry the Fourth and Succeeding Monarchs to the End of the Reign of Henry the Eighth* (London, 1809), 599.

Henry VIII's outburst was probably premeditated, orchestrated to emphasise the fact that he viewed Bulmer's wearing of Stafford livery as a visible sign of loyalty to Stafford rather than the king. This was a publicly staged event that countered Bulmer's public display of loyalty to Stafford.[88] The symbolic significance of wearing livery is clear: it was regarded as a visible means of displaying loyalty and contemporaries were aware of its symbolic significance, which they exploited.

Liveries were symbols of association which were designed for public display, a necessity which was taken into account in many of the provisos of exemption in various statutes. Aristocratic ideals were evident in the 1399 act which exempted 'those who wish to travel and cross the sea to lands abroad to seek honour' by allowing them to 'use the same livery in those regions'.[89] The 'honour' being referred to was clearly chivalric honour. Chivalry remained an integral facet of noble life during the later middle ages. In *The Book of Chivalry*, Geoffroi de Charny described the honour bestowed upon a knight who participated in warfare and asserted that those who travel to foreign lands for such adventure should be honoured and respected.[90] Although Charny was killed four decades earlier at Poitier, the values underpinning his book continued to be shared throughout England and France for the remainder of the fourteenth century. The international aspect of chivalric culture and the shared cross-Channel experiences of the French and English nobilities meant that Charny's views would have been shared by many in the English aristocracy during this period. According to Charny, nobles could travel to foreign lands to gain honour and demonstrate their military prowess in two ways: tournaments and foreign war, especially crusade. Both required the wearing of livery, and both were a feature of noble life and ambitions throughout the later middle ages. Crusades were military enterprises and nobles going on crusade needed to distribute their livery or coats of arms to their followers. Many early indentures of retainer included clauses that explicitly required the retained man to attend tournaments with his lord, though after 1339 this was subsumed into more general obligations to serve in times of war.[91] Tournaments required their participants to display their noble descent on their arms prior to competing in tournaments. As time progressed, simpler methods of identification were required such as a personal badge.[92] Preventing a noble from travelling outside of England wearing his livery and giving it to his attendants

---

[88] K.J. Kesselring, *Mercy and Authority in the Tudor State* (Cambridge, 2003), 139.

[89] *PROME*, viii, 38.

[90] Geoffroi de Charny, *The Book of Chivalry of Geoffroi de Charney: Text, Context and Translation*, eds. and trans. Richard W. Kaeuper and Elspeth Kennedy (Philadelphia, 1996), 87–93.

[91] 'Private Indentures', 22–3 and document numbers. 7, 11, 14–16, 28, 33.

[92] Vale, *War and Chivalry*, 96–7.

would have gone against many of the expectations of the nobility. Therefore, the chivalric ethos of the aristocratic warrior elite was taken into consideration in these exemptions from the statutes.

Cultural concerns were expressed in several statutes that led to various ceremonies and events being exempt. Spectacle and ceremony were integral to medieval life and therefore the wearing of a distinct livery to distinguish oneself or one's organisation was necessary. The 1468 act exempted livery given at the coronation of the king or queen, the enthronement of an archbishop or bishop, the inception of university clerks or when someone was made a knight or a sergeant-at-law.[93] The fact that Edward IV took steps that legally enabled the widespread use of livery at ceremonial occasions is unsurprising considering Edward's penchant for extravagant court culture. Charles Ross noted that Edward's 'awareness of the political value of display is evident from the very beginning of his reign' since at his coronation 'no expense was spared'.[94] When the Bohemian nobleman Leo of Rozmital travelled to England in 1466 his companion, Gabriel Tetzel, was suitably enough impressed by Edward's court to label it 'the most splendid court that could be found in all Christendom',[95] an impressive compliment considering they had just visited the court of Philip the Good.[96] During the festivities Edward gave all the knights in Rozmital's retinue a gold livery badge and all others a silver livery badge.[97] Liveries were integral to late medieval ceremonies and were of particular importance in the context of the royal court. Edward IV's interest in developing an elaborate royal court on a par with the duke of Burgundy is the key context which explains the exemption of certain ceremonies from the act.

Funerals were a further type of ceremony in which liveries were important as part of the mourning process. Therefore the 1504 act exempted the executors of someone's estate at their burial 'for any mornyng array'.[98] In the years prior to this statute being passed England witnessed two high-profile royal funerals, those of the queen and Arthur, Prince of Wales. In 1503, the king's mother, Margaret Beaufort, drew up a list of funeral ordinances specifying in minute detail the size and types of hood and mourning apparel to be worn.[99] In the immediate context of the 1504 act, therefore, there were incidents that are likely to have brought the issue of mourning livery to the forefront of the king's thoughts when the act was being drafted. The use of black mourning livery at funerals was well established

---

[93] *PROME*, xiii, 386.
[94] Ross, *Edward IV*, 258.
[95] *The Travels of Leo of Rosmital*, ed. Malcolm Letts, Hakluyt Society, 2nd series, cviii (1957), 45.
[96] Ibid., 26–42. On Philip the Good's court see: Vaughan, *Philip the Good*, 127–63.
[97] *The Travels of Leo of Rosmital*, 45, 53.
[98] *PROME*, xvi, 367.
[99] BL, Add MS. 45133 fol. 141.

by Henry VII's reign. At the funeral of Edward III in 1377 there were around 950 men in black mourning livery.[100] For the burial of Edward IV in 1483, William Worsley, dean of St Paul's Cathedral, paid £4 9s. for black woollen cloth in order to make livery for his servants attending the burial.[101] At Henry VII's own funeral a combined total of 18,311¾ yards of cloth was used for mourning livery.[102] Royal funerals were not, however, unique in their use of livery. As many as 900 black gowns were distributed at the earl of Oxford's funeral in 1513 and up to 1,900 liveries were distributed for the funeral of the Duke of Norfolk in 1524.[103] Guilds ensured that their members wore their livery at funerals. The weavers of London, for example, had an ordinance that on the death of one of their own all other guild members were to attend the funeral of the deceased member, with a fine of 8d. for disobeying the ordinance.[104] The will of Henry Barton, skinner, from 1436 included a provision for a livery gown to be provided to the chaplain of his fraternity for the festival of Corpus Christi and 'for the purpose of observing the obit or anniversary of any brother or sister of the same'.[105] Wearing livery at funerals was an expected aspect of late medieval life and therefore an outright ban was in direct opposition to contemporary views on acceptable livery.

The ceremonial importance of livery was deeply embedded across late medieval English society. Urban elites also used livery to distinguish themselves from the rest of the population, as at Exeter in 1483 when new red gowns were acquired for the each of the city's twenty-four council members just a year after the council passed an ordinance that the city receiver was to be distinguished from other stewards by a scarlet gown like the mayor's.[106] In London, at the elections of new mayors and sheriffs, the members of the city council were required to

---

[100] E101/397/20 mm. 30–2; E101/398/9 fol. 31–2. Discussed in Christopher Given-Wilson, 'The Exequies of Edward III and the Royal Funeral Ceremony in Late Medieval England', *EHR*, 124 (2009), 263, 268.

[101] *The Estate and Household Accounts of William Worsley Dean of St Paul's Cathedral, 1479–1497*, eds. Hannes Kleineke and Stephanie R. Hovland, London Record Society, xl (2004), 70.

[102] *L&P*, i, no. 20. For a sixteenth-century account of Henry VII's funeral describing the use of black mourning livery see: *Hall's Chronicle*, 506.

[103] Ross, *John de Vere*, 224.

[104] *Calendar of Letter-Books of the City of London, L: Edward IV to Henry VII*, ed. Reginald R. Sharpe (London, 1932), 290.

[105] *Calendar of Wills Proved and Enrolled in the Court of Husting, London: Part 2, 1358–1688*, ed. Reginald R. Sharpe (London, 1890), 477.

[106] Hannes Kleineke, 'Þe Kynes Cite: Exeter in the Wars of the Roses' in *Conflicts, Consequences and the Crown in the Late Middle Ages* ed. Linda Clark (Woodbridge, 2007) 151–2, citing Devon Record Office, Exeter receiver's acct. 1–2 Ric. III; ECA 51, f. 321. See also the illustration of the mayor-making ceremony in Bristol which depicts this type of ceremony: *The Maire of Bristowe Is Kalendar*, ed. Peter Fleming, Bristol Record Society, lxvii (2015), 60.

attend in their livery.[107] In dealings with the crown, urban governments recognised the importance of having their important citizens dressed in the appropriate
livery for royal entrance ceremonies. Royal visits were an opportunity for the
citizens and civic groups to display unity and advance their interests. The wearing
of a common livery by various civic groups was an important part of the spectacle
associated with these entries.[108] In Salisbury, the city's government took various
measures to ensure that citizens wore their liveries to create an appropriate
spectacle when the king arrived. Prior to Henry VI's visit to Salisbury in 1447,
the citizens agreed that all were 'to have a blue gown, as in the mayoralty of W.
Swan'.[109] The following year the citizens again agreed that 'all citizens and all
of enough wealth' were to have a blue gown and a red hat for the king's visit
and failure to do so would incur a fine of 13s. 4d.[110] Provisions became more
elaborate in 1451 when the stewards of all the guilds in the town were to draw up
a list of those who were obliged to wear livery, which was to be made of a green
cloth. Again, failure to wear the appropriate livery would result in a fine of 13s.
4d.[111] Royal entries were an opportunity by which both the royal household and
the civic community were able to project their group identity by wearing their
collective livery.

The symbolic importance of livery extended beyond the reciprocal relationship
between lords and their servants and, in an urban context, displayed social
cohesion and group identity. This was evident during royal entries: different crafts
wore their liveries to distinguish themselves from each other.[112] Urban groups
such as guilds and fraternities that used their livery to distinguish themselves
within their community were exempt from certain aspects of the legislation.
The 1406 act stated that guilds, fraternities and 'of those mysteries of the cities
and boroughs of the realm' were exempt from the clause which stated that 'no
congregation or company shall make for itself a livery of cloth or of hoods at
the personal expense of the same congregation or company'.[113] The Guild of
Saint Mary and All Saints in Norwich acknowledged this when they stated that
the function of their livery was so that members could 'kennen ye bretheryn
and systeryn'.[114] As Benjamin McRee has stated, 'a fraternity's annual march
was its most visible activity, affording the organization a unique opportunity to

---

[107] *Calendar of Letter-Books of the City of London, L*, 73.
[108] Neil Murphy, 'Receiving Royals in Later Medieval York: Civic Ceremony and the
Municipal Elite, 1478–1503', *Northern History*, xliv (2006), 241–55.
[109] *The First General Entry Book of the City of Salisbury, 1387–1452*, ed. David R. Carr,
Wiltshire Record Society, liv (2001), no. 411.
[110] Ibid., no. 417.
[111] Ibid., no. 441.
[112] Murphy, 'Receiving Royals', 254.
[113] *PROME*, viii, 400–1.
[114] C47/44/307.

shape its public image'. Livery therefore had the ability 'to emphasize the ties that bound their members together'.[115] The guild of St George in Norwich had ordinances that required their members to wear the livery of the guild during the procession on St George's day.[116] The guild also ordered that the aldermen and masters of the guild were to give 'no clothing to no persone in the mornyng the pryce of ye lyuery with oute consent of je xxiiij chose for the assemble'.[117] Beverley in Yorkshire provides several examples of urban groups using their livery as a means of displaying a collective group identity. The ordinances of the weavers in 1406 stated that every master was to have a suit of the brethren's livery which they were to have for two years without selling and were to wear during important feast days or when any lord or magnate visited the town.[118] The statutes of the shoemakers stated that anyone not wearing the livery of the guild when assembled at the castle against the coming of the Blessed John of Beverley was to be fined 20s., distributed equally to the guild and the community of the town.[119] The tanners and the bakers in Beverley also expected their members to wear the same suit on Monday of Rogation Week before processing 'in clothynge all of one suyt'.[120] The town took such obligations seriously: a carpenter was fined in 1446 for refusing to wear the livery of his fellowship.[121] Thus, civic groups were able to use their livery in the accustomed manner, which illustrates that it was the use of livery by the nobility, not civic groups, that was the reason for the enactment of the statutes of livery.

Conclusion

The statutes never sought to ban retaining or the granting of liveries because there were both practical and ideological barriers to this. The affinity was the key mechanism through which medieval society and government operated. Moreover, the system benefited kings who were heads of affinities in their own rights and used the affinities of the richest subjects to govern their kingdoms. Consequently, when the wearing of liveries began to become viewed as problematic at the end of the fourteenth century, the system was too engrained in medieval life to be

---

[115] Benjamin R. McRee, 'Unity or Division? The Social Meaning of Guild Ceremony in Urban Communities' in *City and Spectacle in Medieval Europe*, eds. Barbara A. Hanawalt and Kathryn L. Reyerson (Liverpool, 1994), 192.
[116] *Records of the Gild of St George in Norwich, 1389–1547*, ed. Mary Grace, Norfolk Record Society, ix (1937), 34, 37–8.
[117] Ibid., 37.
[118] HMC, *Report of the Manuscripts of the Corporation of Beverley* (London, 1900), 94.
[119] Ibid., 91
[120] Ibid., 87, 101.
[121] Ibid., 131.

abolished and was therefore restricted. Symbolism and the need for liveries at major ceremonial occasions also meant that certain occasions, not just certain groups of people, needed to be exempt from the statutes. Michael Hicks and Nigel Saul both argued that the focus of the legislation was on regulating livery and outlawing what they believed was the unacceptable use of livery.[122] This argument remains valid by this analysis but should be made stronger. The abolition of livery in both theory and practice was not, and could never be, possible in late medieval England. Livery was an important way to reward loyal servants and had symbolic importance for both lord and retainer: the lord benefited from the prestige of having servants in his livery; the retainer benefited from being associated with powerful men in their community. Moreover, there were ideological barriers to banning livery. Good lords were expected to reward their servants generously and grants of livery were part of this. In terms of both interests and ideology, livery was too engrained into society to be banned. Rather than being an unwieldy attack upon an integral feature of society, legislation against livery was targeted at specific practices deemed unacceptable by late medieval society and allowed acceptable instances of granting livery and retaining to continue.

---

[122] Hicks, '1468 Statute', 15; Saul, 'Abolition of Badges', 312–13.

2

The Early Years, 1390 to 1449

The initial laws restricting the distribution of liveries to certain categories for servants were the result of a campaign from the Commons to combat the problems associated with the unrestricted distribution of livery. These attempts are evident in a number of petitions presented by the Commons to several parliaments from the 1380s to the 1420s. The two recurrent themes in these petitions were the problem of lawlessness in the localities and the fact that previous statutes on the subject had not been properly enforced. This seems paradoxical as those MPs who called for a new law, those responsible for upholding the new law and those most likely to have been breaking them were all drawn from the same social rank, the gentry. The surviving evidence can help to address this apparent paradox.

The earliest evidence of concerns about the unrestricted distribution of liveries comes from petitions to the king in parliament from the Commons. The parliament rolls are a vital yet problematic source.[1] Unlike other medieval parliaments, the late medieval English parliament was bicameral, divided between the House of Lords and the House of Commons. The parliament rolls only record decisions and events that happened in the Commons, not in the Lords. The Lords had a more informal and direct connection with the king and therefore their discussions and decisions did not need to be formally recorded. Therefore, the surviving documents may over-emphasise the importance of the Commons in making of laws. In addition, what survives is only the final official version of the parliament and normally excludes much information on parliamentary speeches, debates and processes that the records were not intended to record. The lack of parliamentary journals for the middle ages or any records of the day-to-day proceedings also means that it is difficult to gauge what was discussed and for how long. The surviving written records only provide a glimpse of what was spoken. Despite these problems, the parliament rolls are essential for understanding the decisions made by late medieval parliaments.

Enrolled on the parliament rolls are various petitions to the crown from different groups asking the king to redress their grievances. This was the basis for the

---

[1]   For this paragraph see in particular: Chris Given-Wilson, 'The Rolls of Parliament, 1399–1421' in *Parchment and People in the Middle Ages*, ed. Linda Clark (Edinburgh, 2004), 57–72; Michael Hicks, 'King in Lords and Commons: Three Insights into Late-Fifteenth-Century Parliaments, 1461–85' in *People, Places and Perspective: Essays on Later Medieval and Early Tudor England*, ed. Keith Dockray and Peter Fleming (Stroud, 2005), 131–54.

development of the English parliament in the fourteenth century.[2] Parliamentary petitions themselves are a problematic source because they do not record the MP, or MPs, who presented the petition, nor do they give an indication of the extent to which the petition was supported. Petitions to the king from the Commons began with the generic phrase 'we the Commons pray', implying uniformity from the Commons which may or may not have existed. A.R. Myers identified several problems inherent in Commons petitions, namely: Commons petitions sometimes appear before the caption on the rolls stating '*Les communes petitions*'; some Commons petitions were not enrolled; and some were not necessarily compiled by the Commons at all.[3] Gwilym Dodd argued that during the fourteenth century Commons petitions began to incorporate what would earlier have been regarded as private grievances. The only observable link between Commons petitions was 'that each *purported* to seek change which benefited the common interest'.[4] A petition may have come from only one or two MPs, or they may have come from all the MPs in the Commons. These petitions can be juxtaposed with other contemporary records to assess the validity of the complaints. The main sources to supplement this parliamentary material are the records of the King's Bench. These records are not an adequate guide for levels of lawlessness in the localities because they show the ability or willingness of local justices to indict criminals, not the number of instances on which a particular offence was committed.[5] The records of the King's Bench provide hard data for the enforcement of the new statutes, not the number of instances of illegal livery (because instances that were not prosecuted cannot be known since they were never recorded), although they do provide an impressionistic guide. Tracking the level of enforcement provides an insight into social tensions and political attitudes and permits an analysis of the claims made in many petitions about the lack of enforcement of the statues.

Richard II's Reign

Liveries were used by Thomas, earl of Lancaster and his supporters during the civil war with Edward II when, in 1321, the baronial opposition to Edward II all wore a

---

[2] This is the central theme of G.L. Harriss, *King, Parliament and Public Finance in England to 1369* (Oxford, 1975).

[3] A.R Myers, 'Parliamentary Petitions in the Fifteenth Century', *EHR*, lii (1937), 385–404, 590–5.

[4] Gwilym Dodd, *Justice and Grace: Private Petitioning and the English Parliament in the Late Middle Ages* (Oxford, 2007), 126–55, quotation on 127.

[5] On the usefulness of the records of the King's Bench see: Griffiths, *Henry VI*, 128; Hicks, 'Bastard Feudalism: Society and Politics in Fifteenth-Century England', 10–18; Kleineke, 'Poachers and Gamekeepers', 129.

distinctive livery which they issued to their retainers.[6] The *Vita Edwardi Secundi* noted that Roger de Elmerugge, former sheriff of Herefordshire, wore the livery while holding pleas in the county as a means of insulting the king's authority.[7] In a parliamentary context the association between wearing the robes of a particular local worthy and abuses of the legal system was first made in a petition from the Lent Parliament of 1324 which complained about sheriffs taking fees, robes and pensions.[8] This was part of a more general criticism of local officials during Edward II's reign, as a petition presented at the following parliament of October 1324 included seven references to the abuses of sheriffs, their agents and other local officials.[9] These incidents did not produce any legislation about liveries during Edward II's reign and there were no known discussions about the wearing of robes or liveries during Edward III's parliaments.

The problems of maintenance, corruption and the lawlessness of noble retainers re-emerged as an important political issue at the start of Richard II's reign. During the parliament of 1377 a Commons petition noted that it was customary for those with small holdings of land or rent to keep retinues of men, including squires or other men, and to perform maintenance in lawsuits on their behalf in both reasonable and unreasonable suits.[10] The petition further stated that this problem was exacerbated by the giving of liveries to men as a means of supporting their unjust causes. The royal response stated that there were already statutes and ordinances against maintenance and that the common law also prevented such abuses. Nevertheless, proclamations were to be made across the kingdom that livery hoods were not to be given for the maintenance of lawsuits or any other confederacy. It should be noted that at no point in the petition or the response was there any reference to lords or nobles and therefore the petition cannot be interpreted as an attack on the convention of distributing livery to a large number of retainers. Similar complaints were evident in the aftermath of the Peasants' Revolt. Although they did not condone the revolt, the Commons petitioned the king to improve the governance of the kingdom, citing the excessive maintainers of quarrels and men who act like kings in their shires as reason for the recent

---

[6] Frédérique Lachaud, 'Liveries of Robes in England, c.1200–c.1330', *EHR*, cxi (1996), 295–7; Matthew Strickland, '"All Brought to Nought and Thy State Undone": Treason, Disinvesture and the Disgracing of Arms under Edward II' in *Soldiers, Nobles and Gentlemen: Essays in Honour of Maurice Keen*, eds. Peter R. Coss and Christopher Tyerman (Woodbridge, 2009), 300–2.

[7] *The Life of Edward the Second*, trans. and ed. Noël Denholm-Young (London, 1957), 202–3.

[8] SC8/108/5398. Printed in W.M. Ormrod, 'Agenda for Legislation, 1322–c.1340', *EHR*, cv (1990), 6 n. 3.

[9] Printed in Ormrod, 'Agenda for Legislation', 31–3.

[10] *PROME*, vi, 50.

great tumult.[11] Instead of targeting retaining, these complaints had a narrower focus, confined to maintenance and the corruption of justice as opposed to being a wide-ranging criticism of the practice of livery distribution.

Later in the 1380s the issue of who could distribute livery and to whom they could distribute it 'burst upon the late fourteenth century scene with surprising suddenness'.[12] These complaints differed from those in 1377 because they were directed more clearly towards the nobility as opposed to those of a lower social status. According to the *Westminster Chronicle* a dispute occurred during the parliament of April 1384 in which the Commons complained about the lawlessness and corrupt activities of those wearing the livery of peers and requested a statute to address these problems. John of Gaunt criticised this complaint for its vagueness and asserted that no statute was required on the matter because he was able to discipline his own men.[13] Gaunt's tetchy response was probably caused by other events in that parliament that furthered the deterioration of his relationship with the king. At that parliament the Carmelite friar John Latimer presented Richard II with a document detailing alleged plots by Gaunt to have Richard assassinated and claim the throne for himself. Although the friar was subsequently tortured to death by royalist knights in a bungled attempt to extract more evidence, the events left both Gaunt and Richard suspicious of each other's intentions.[14] Such tensions were likely exacerbated by the fact that Gaunt's affinity was the largest in England after the king's. The complaint was made at a time when personal relations between the king and his royal uncle were becoming strained, with many fearing a repeat of the civil war earlier in the century between Edward II and his cousin Thomas of Lancaster.[15] There is, however, no evidence that the complaints in 1384 were drawn from complaints about perversions of justice during Edward II's reign. The deteriorating personal relations between the two most powerful men in the kingdom probably focused the minds of the Commons on the necessity of limiting the size of noble affinities.

The issue of badges was raised at the Merciless Parliament of February 1388 in which the five Appellees were accused of encouraging the king to create a large retinue of followers by giving them badges, which was not a custom in England.[16] This formed part of wider criticisms of those around the young Richard II who were accused of taking advantage of royal favour and leading

---

[11] *PROME*, vi, 220.
[12] Saul, 'The Commons and the Abolition of Badges', 305.
[13] *The Westminster Chronicle, 1381–1394*, 80–4.
[14] *St Albans Chronicle*, ii, 772–7; *The Westminster Chronicle, 1381–1394*, 68–81.
[15] Given-Wilson, *Henry IV*, 36–41.
[16] *PROME*, vii, 91. The accused were Robert de Vere, earl of Oxford and duke of Ireland, Alexander, archbishop of York, Michael de la Pole, earl of Suffolk, Robert Tresilian and Nicholas Brembre.

the king astray for their own benefit to the detriment of the kingdom.[17] Richard II was the first English king to construct a magnate-style bastard feudal affinity which gave him a direct relationship with members of the county gentry, most infamously in Cheshire. Previous kings had given fees to knights who served in their households but Richard II was the first to retain knights whose main service was political rather than military.[18] Richard began retaining members of the gentry from early on in his reign. During the first two years of his reign around 240–50 men were retained by Richard, the vast majority of whom were having annuities granted to them by Edward III confirmed. Richard's policy changed around the late summer of 1387 when he began distributing his livery badge much more widely. The *Westminster Chronicle* noted that Richard was travelling around Cheshire and North Wales continually taking men into his service and sending a serjeant-at-mace into Essex, Cambridgeshire, Norfolk and Suffolk to get the more substantial members of those counties to become his men and be ready to join him armed and ready, giving them the king's livery badge in return.[19] This was essentially a 'ham-fisted' reaction to the *coup* by the Lords Appellant at Radcote Bridge.[20] The emphasis placed by the accusations at the Merciless Parliament on badges suggests that their distribution was something new and unwelcome because it was thought to strengthen the king's power in the localities at the expense of the nobility. The existence of a royal livery was not new by the late fourteenth century. From the thirteenth century it was normal for kings to distribute liveries of cloth to members of their household at major feasts such as Christmas.[21] What was new was the fact that the king was now distributing his badges like his nobility. Yet the reference to Richard's distribution of badges at the Merciless Parliament was not a pretext to enact a new law on the matter but was instead listed as one of the many crimes that his favourites had committed. To criticise the king directly for this policy would have been a step too far for the Lords Appellant. They therefore resorted to the traditional tactic of blaming the king's failings on his unpopular favourites. The criticism of Richard's retaining at the Merciless Parliament was a further charge against unpopular favourites and a criticism of royal retaining and was therefore separate from calls from the Commons in 1384 to pass new legislation on the matter.

---

[17] Saul, *Richard II*, 191.
[18] Given-Wilson, 'The King and the Gentry', 87–102. On Richard's Cheshire archers specifically see: Saul, *Richard II*, 367, 375, 393–4, 431, 440, 444–5, 460; James L. Gillespie, 'Richard II's Archers of the Crown', *Journal of British Studies*, xviii (1979), 14–29.
[19] *The Westminster Chronicle*, 187.
[20] Given-Wilson, *King's Affinity*, 213–14; Given-Wilson, 'The King and the Gentry', 92–5.
[21] Vale, *Princely Court*, 100–5.

It was not until the following parliament that there was a conscious push by the Commons, or at least some MPs, to pass a statute dealing with the issue. Specific forms of retaining became the subject of criticism in the parliament of September 1388 when one Commons petition requested the abolition of badges and all other lesser liveries such as hoods.[22] The petition finished by stating that such liveries were not to be worn or distributed 'upon the pain specified in this present parliament'. It is possible that the level of detail in this petition was in part a response to Gaunt's criticism four years earlier that complaints were presented in terms that were too general. It has been suggested that one reason why the parliament rolls were created was to create a record of previous parliaments that could be consulted in manner similar to how the crown consulted other official series, such as the patent, charter and close rolls.[23] Richard II is reported to have responded by stating that the problem would be considered at the following parliament.[24] A corresponding law seems to have been enacted at this parliament, as a petition from 1390 states that after the 1388 petition about the problem of liveried retainers, the king and lords 'ordained such a remedy'.[25] The absence of a specific law on the statute rolls suggests that this was an ordinance that was meant to be 'a provisional remedy ... which was to be in effect for a trial period until the next parliament'.[26] The petition of 1388 and the subsequent ordinance were a development of the process that began in 1377 which led to the regulation of livery.

Two years later two petitions were presented to the parliament of January 1390 complaining about the problem of badges and of liveries.[27] Thomas Walsingham's account suggests that the surviving petition may not be the original petition, stating that the Commons were continually petitioning for peers to abandon their livery badges and that the eventual legislation was essentially a compromise between the Lords and the Commons.[28] The first petition requested that livery badges should only be worn by men who 'were with the same lord for the term of his life, both in peace and war, and that by indentures sealed under their seals without fraud or ill intent'. Valets and archers would be permitted to wear livery if they dwelt in the lord's household for the full year. The second petition requested that liveries of cloth could only be distributed to a lord's 'familiars of his household, his kin and allies, his steward, his council, or his bailiffs on their

---

[22] The roll for this parliament does not survive. The petition is known from: *The Westminster Chronicle*, 354–7.
[23] W.M. Ormrod, 'On-and Off-the Record: The Rolls of Parliament, 1337–1377' in *Parchment and People in the Middle Ages*, ed. Linda Clark (Edinburgh, 2004), 49–50.
[24] *The Westminster Chronicle*, 354–7.
[25] *PROME*, vii, 149.
[26] Given-Wilson, *King's Affinity*, 239; *Stat. Realm*, ii, 55–60.
[27] For this paragraph see: *PROME*, vii, 149–50.
[28] *St Albans Chronicle*, i, 896–7.

manors'. Liveries of cloth were therefore allowed for a more select group of people, some of whom, such as bailiffs, were not continually in the presence of their lord. Badges, in contrast, could only be worn in the presence of the lord. This gave the gentry scope to continue wearing noble livery because they were the ones who held various administrative roles in noble affinities such as stewards and bailiffs. The wearing of badges, which were given to those in the lower echelons of a noble affinity, in essence restricted the wearing of livery to the ranks in society below that of the gentry who served as MPs. These complaints were, in part, 'a by-product of [the gentry's] concern for their own social position'.[29] It was always socially acceptable, and even necessary, for a lord to distribute livery to his servants, both within his household and his estate officials. Contemporary attitudes made it necessary to permit lords to give their servants livery as a part of their reward for service and it was in the interests of both lords and servants to allow this aspect of the system to continue. Those in receipt of illegal livery were to be imprisoned for a year and those who distributed illegal livery were to be fined £100. Proclamations were to be made in every city, market town and borough and all other public places.

The new legislation did not produce an immediate wave of prosecutions against those who were giving livery to men who did not fit into the legally defined categories. It is possible that the entire nobility and gentry of late fourteenth-century England began to limit those to whom they gave their livery in accordance with the statutes. Yet the limited survival of estate records for the medieval nobility, particularly any consistent set of accounts covering many consecutive years, means that it is not possible to test this assumption. However, when the focus is turned to the royal affinity, the sources become more revealing. After Richard II regained full control of government in May 1389 he began a deliberate policy of increasing the size of his affinity. In the wake of the 1390 ordinance, the king ensured his retaining practices were within the bounds of the new law by either bringing men into his household or making those knights and esquires not in his household life-long retainers.[30] Given Richard's narcissistic tendencies and exalted view of kingship it is unlikely that he was trying to set an example for the rest of the kingdom by ensuring he was distributing liveries in accordance with the new statutes.[31] Richard's retaining was most probably caused by concerns that were highlighted by the crisis in his rule in 1387–8 when a royalist army under Robert de Vere, earl of Oxford, was defeated at Radcot Bridge and government was temporarily put in the hands of the lord appellant

---

[29]   Saul, 'Abolition of Badges', 313.
[30]   Given-Wilson, *King's Affinity*, 40, 214–15, 239.
[31]   Saul, *Richard II*, 459–61; Nigel Saul, 'Richard II and the Vocabulary of Kingship', *EHR*, cx (1995), 854–77.

until Richard assumed his majority.[32] The fact that Richard was competing with many of his great nobles, especially his uncle John of Gaunt, for gentry support is unlikely to have gone unnoticed by those gentry serving as MPs. However, the fact that complaints can be detected before the first major crisis of Richard II's reign indicates that fears about resultant corruption and disorder brought about by increasingly large and unwieldy royal and Lancastrian affinities were, at best, an additional factor in the initial drive for laws restricting the distribution of noble livery.

It is, however, too simplistic to interpret these early debates as simply representing a concern about the size of the affinities of the king and the duke of Lancaster. They also represent a genuine desire from at least one section of the gentry to address lawlessness and corruption in the localities. The recurrent complaint that characterised the debates about liveries for almost four decades was that the Commons were unhappy with the lack of enforcement of the new laws. Despite the Commons' apparent desire to combat the problem of unrestricted livery distribution, the 1390 act produced no known prosecution. Consequently the Commons petitioned the king again during the 1393 parliament about liveries, claiming that the previous statutes were not being enforced.[33] This was the first petition about liveries that records a specific answer from the king, stating that no one under the rank of esquire was to wear any livery unless he was a permanent member of a lord's household staff. In addition, the statute stated that justices of the peace and assizes had the power to investigate the distribution of liveries and inform the king and Lords about any such infringements. It is unclear if there was any confusion regarding who was allowed to hear cases of illegal livery or if cases were not being prosecuted because of the uncertainty over jurisdiction. More likely, the purpose of this clause was to make the law more robust and make explicit who was responsible for hearing cases.

Repeated requests to the king that action should be taken to combat the problem of the unregulated distribution of livery did not spur on any enforcement in the localities. Only one case, involving thirty men from Yorkshire in 1393, is known for the whole of the 1390s which was different from later cases. Instead of one lord distributing livery to men who were not members of his family, legal counsel or permanent household, the indictment was against a group of men who wore the same livery 'by corrupt allegiances and confederacy, each of them maintaining the other in all plaints, true or false, against whomever should wish to claim against them or any one of them'.[34]

[32] Given-Wilson, *King's Affinity*, 214–15; Saul, *Richard II*, 148–204.
[33] *PROME*, vii, 239–40.
[34] KB27/528 rex rot. 35. Also printed in *Select Cases in the Court of King's Bench Under Richard II, Henry IV and Henry V*, 83–5.

The lack of illegal livery cases in the King's Bench records at this time shows that statements in petitions that claimed the statutes were not being enforced reflected a reality about law enforcement and the difficulties of enforcing new statutes. Therefore, these complaints in the petitions cannot be interpreted as fiction created for rhetorical purposes.

Towards the end of Richard II's reign the problem of livery became inextricably bound with the criticisms of Richard's reign and his supposed tyranny. The records of the parliament of January 1397 again indicate that the Commons were unhappy about the enforcement of the statutes. According to the parliament rolls, Richard II summoned his Lords, both spiritual and temporal, to him at Westminster. Richard then stated that he had heard that the Commons had been speaking to the Lords the previous day about 'various matters, some of which it seemed to the king were contrary to his regality and estate and his royal liberty'. A four-point petition was presented to Richard, drafted by the cleric Thomas Haxey. The third point made in the petition was that the Commons wished for the statutes of livery to be upheld and enforced, which is consistent with the lack of cases found in the surviving records.[35] As a result of this petition Richard II issued a rather short statute preventing those from below the rank of esquire from taking the livery for any lord unless they were a menial servant or an official on their estates. The statute did little to develop the law and essentially restated previous statutes on the matter. The real significance is that the issue of liveries was listed as one of four main problems that informed wider criticisms of Richard II's kingship. The petition also requested that royal officials should be of sufficient standing and hold office only for a year, which by this point had been repeated on several occasions over the previous century.[36] A more serious concern was expressed about Scottish raiding in violation of the truce. The final matter was that the king's household should be reduced. Over the fourteenth century the size of the royal household had continually grown and had become a source of criticism for Richard II.[37] The inclusion of the problem of the enforcement of the statutes of livery in this complaint to Richard indicates that the problem of livery was regarded as one of many problems of Richard's government. Liveries during Richard II's reign were therefore not an isolated issue, but were bound up with many other criticisms of his kingship.

[35] *PROME*, vii, 313–14. The petition itself has become known as Haxey's Petition after the clerk who allegedly drafted it; see especially: A.K. McHardy, 'Haxey's Case, 1397: The Petition and its Presenter' in *The Age of Richard II*, ed. James L. Gillespie (Stroud, 1997), 93–114.
[36] Saul, *Richard II*, 369.
[37] Given-Wilson, *King's Affinity*, 39–41, 278; Saul, *Richard II*, 259, 367–9, 439.

Henry IV's Reign

The two years that followed Haxey's petition witnessed the breakdown in Richard's relations with several of his leading nobles, most importantly his cousin Henry Bolingbroke who usurped him in 1399. It was in the context of Richard II's 'tyranny' that a further act that had a distinct emphasis on royal livery was passed in the first Lancastrian parliament of 1399.[38] The act was a response to the activities of Richard II's retainers, particularly his Cheshire archers, described by Adam Usk as 'men of the upmost depravity who went about doing as they wished, assaulting, beating, and plundering his subjects with impunity … committing adulteries, murders and countless other crimes'.[39] Richard II's supporters amongst the peerage were also accused of creating large affinities to the detriment of public order. The forfeitures of the dukes of Aumale, Surrey and Exeter in 1399 include a clause stating that they should not give 'livery of badges, or create a retinue of men except of necessary officers within their households, and of necessary officers outside their households to govern their lands and possessions'.[40] No indictments for illegal livery against any of these dukes survive in the records of the King's Bench. Nevertheless, the inclusion of livery in their forfeiture implies either that they had been distributing illegal livery but were never indicted, or at least that it was believed by contemporaries that their retaining practices were causing public order problems. It was also reported in January 1400 that an esquire of the earl of Huntingdon, Raulyn Govely, wore the earl's livery and refused to remove it 'in spite of all who would speak against it'.[41] There is, however, no known indictment against Govely for illegal livery. The clear impetus for this legislation at Henry IV's first parliament was the various criticisms of Richard II's use of his retinue of Cheshire archers and their crimes, which was the fourth of the thirty-three charges for which he was deposed.[42]

The 1399 act was the first livery act, and the only one prior to 1461, for which there was no corresponding petition. This suggests a degree of royal initiative in the passing of this act that did not occur again until Edward IV's reign. The act permitted the king to give livery to any peer whom he pleased. Below the level of the peerage, the king could only give livery to those knights and esquires who were in his household or who were in receipt of an annual fee from him. Those knights and esquires in receipt of the royal livery were only allowed to wear it in

---

[38] For the next three paragraphs, unless stated otherwise, see: *PROME*, viii, 38.
[39] *The Chronicle of Adam Usk, 1377–1421*, ed. and trans. Christopher Given-Wilson (Oxford, 1997), 49.
[40] *PROME*, viii, 11–12.
[41] *Calendar of Inquisitions Miscellaneous, 1399–1422* (London, 1968), no. 88.
[42] *Chronicles of the Revolution, 1397–1400: The Reign of Richard II*, ed. Christopher Given-Wilson (Manchester and New York, 1993), 174.

his presence and were explicitly prohibited from wearing the royal livery in their own localities. Any knight or esquire who contravened the statute was to permanently lose his right to wear the royal livery and receive a retaining fee. A further clause prevented yeomen from taking royal livery on pain of imprisonment and a fine, payable to the king. Lords of all ranks were banned from distributing livery badges to any knight, esquire or valet, although presumably they were permitted to distribute other types of liveries such as robes, collars and hoods. In an attempt to define the law more stringently, this was also the first act to explicitly state that archbishops, bishops, abbots and prelates were bound by the statute, although earlier acts had referred to lords both spiritual and temporal.

Two exceptions to this act were the constable and marshal of England on the king's frontiers and those travelling abroad in search of honour. In theory this reduced those who could wear the king's livery in England to peers of the realm, those present at the royal court, soldiers on the Scottish and Welsh borders and presumably the English soldiers in Ireland and France. This clause was probably included because of deteriorating Anglo-Scottish relations at the time, the opportunistic raiding in the north of England by the Douglas family and Henry IV's more assertive policy toward English overlordship over Scotland and his stated intention in November 1399 to lead an army north.[43] The necessity of border warfare meant that those nobles charged with defending the border with Scotland needed to retain large numbers of men in order quickly to repeal any invasion.

Livery remained a problem which the Commons were keen to address during several of Henry IV's early parliaments. One petition from around 1400 claimed that the introduction of livery badges into England had resulted in divisions and maintenance.[44] The most forcefully worded of all the Commons petitions regarding the distribution of livery was presented to the 1401 parliament.[45] The petition requested the wholesale abolition of 'all types of liveries and badges' with the exception of the king's livery. Even then there were only three categories of people permitted to wear the king's livery. The first category was 'all the king's sons, dukes, earls, barons and bannerets', who could wear the king's livery collar anywhere. The second category was an undefined group of other knights and squires who were permitted to wear the king's livery but only in the king's presence. Presumably, this would have restricted the occasions in which they were allowed to wear livery to royal ceremonies, again emphasising the fact that parliament did take account of ceremony and visual display when drafting legislation. The Commons also requested that the king should be allowed to give his livery to only 'his household servants, his officers, his counsellors, justices of one

---

[43] Alastair J. MacDonald, *Border Bloodshed: Scotland, England and France at War, 1369–1403* (Edinburgh, 2000), 133–7.

[44] SC8/100/4985. Printed in Saul, 'Abolition of Badges', 314–15.

[45] For this paragraph see: *PROME*, vii, 148–9.

bench and the other, his clerks of the chancery, the barons of the exchequer, and other people of his council learned in the one law or the other'. The emphasis on the king's livery may have been a response to the proliferation of the Lancastrian collars of Esses, the number of which may have been as high as 1,000.[46] In keeping with the existing legislation, the petition requested that all spiritual and temporal lords and those of lesser estates (presumably the gentry) could still give livery to their permanent household servants and lawyers. This clause appears rather conservative but an incident from the parliament of 1404 suggests that certain sections of the Commons may have wished the legislation to go further. The speaker, Sir Arnold Savage, who had also been speaker in 1401, denied in his opening address that he had requested the total abolition of liveries during the 1401 parliament, and maintained that he only requested that lords adhere to the statute.[47] Although no such request was recorded in the official parliamentary records, the fact that the speaker later had to deny making such a request suggests that some MPs were keen for the total abolition of livery badges, although not necessarily the abolition of other forms of livery such as gowns and hoods.

In reality, such a wide-ranging attack on the use of livery was unlikely to succeed because social conventions and structures prohibited the abolition of all liveries. If there was such a radical petition in 1401 to abolish all livery badges, it may be an indication of an increased confidence in the Commons in their ability to pass new radical laws. Alternatively, such a request may have been deliberately extreme and used by the petitioners as the starting point for negotiation. Petitions were part of a wider conversation that took place between the king and his subjects.[48] Starting from an extreme position could have allowed room for negotiation regarding the terms of any specific law. The fact that they wished greater enforcement of the existing law is clear enough in their request that JPs were to have the power of *oyer et terminer* in matters regarding livery which would have given them greater powers to deal with those contravening the statutes. Henry IV was evidently sympathetic to this wish, as the resultant act gave local justices the power of *oyer et terminer* in cases which, in theory, strengthened the procedures for the enforcement of the statutes. Another clause in the petition requested that anyone suing on behalf of the crown should obtain half the resultant fine (which was not made law until the 1406 act); this suggests an element of self-interest from the petitioners. However, there was much in the petition to suggest that the problem of livery was something the Commons wanted remedied and the inclusion in the petition cannot be dismissed as simply a desire to profit from the

[46] Given-Wilson, *Henry IV*, 393–4.
[47] *PROME*, viii, 230. See also: Given-Wilson, *King's Affinity*, 240.
[48] W. Mark Ormrod, 'Voicing Complaint and Remedy to the English Crown, c.1300–c.1460' in *Medieval Petitions: Grace and Grievance*, eds. W. Mark Ormrod, Gwilym Dodd and Anthony Musson (York, 2009), 135–55, especially 155.

law. The Commons were likely aware of the inability of the statutes to produce prosecutions and wanted the situation remedied.

The resultant act of 1401 relaxed the terms of the 1399 act in regard to royal retaining in two ways. First, the knights and esquires who were retained by the king could wear the king's livery when travelling to and from the royal household and in their own county, as well as in his presence. Minor adaptations of legislation like this were a response to practical difficulties: in this instance, difficulties experienced by royal household members going to and from the royal household, or by local justices attempting to enforce the statutes. Alternatively, they acknowledged an opinion that the 1399 act was over-zealous in its wholesale attack against royal retainers. The 1399 act was relaxed by a further clause that permitted 'dukes, earls, barons and bannerets' to wear their livery 'in their county and elsewhere'. By 1401 the problem of livery, and particularly the king's granting of liveries, does not seem to have been the contentious political issue it had been in 1399 and therefore the statutes were partially relaxed.

Second, the act permitted the Prince of Wales to give his livery to his gentle-born servants, while lords were able to wear the Prince's livery of the swan as they would the king's. Richard II's lack of an adult heir meant there was no imperative to legislate for one during his reign. It was only with the Lancastrian usurpation that it became necessary to explicitly state in law that the Prince of Wales was permitted to distribute his livery to whomever he pleased. Yet this clause did more than simply tidy up the legislation. The clause was not part of the Commons' petition but is included in the response. This suggests that it was part of a dialogue between the Commons, or at least a section of the Commons, and the king. Part of this dialogue seems to have included Henry IV making it clear that he wanted the Prince of Wales to be allowed to distribute his livery to any member of the gentry. The reason for this clause was part military, part dynastic. Prince Henry was fourteen or fifteen when this act was passed[49] and was expected to play an active military role in suppressing the Glyn Dŵr uprising in Wales. Henry IV wrote to his son, probably a few months after the parliament in June 1401, stating that Conway Castle had been lost because of the negligence of one of the prince's officers and that the prince himself was responsible for retaking the castle.[50] Henry IV wanted his son to create a larger affinity than other lords to ensure that he was able to fulfil his duties as Prince

---

[49] For the uncertainty about whether Henry V was born in 1386 or 1387 see: Christopher Allmand, *Henry V* (London, 1992), 7–8. Allmand suggests that 1386 is more the likely year because Henry is known to have been born in Monmouth Castle and his parents are known to have been in Monmouth during the summer of 1386.

[50] *Royal and Historical Letters During the Reign of Henry the Fourth, Volume 1, 1399–1404*, ed. F.C. Hingeston (1860), 71–2. For the dating of his document see: Allmand, *Henry V*, 27.

of Wales and because it could help to ensure dynastic security by providing the prince with his own support base. Despite the continued discussion of the issues in parliament, there are no known prosecutions brought by the crown at this time. Henry IV was not ambivalent about illegal livery but rather used other methods to force compliance, communicating with nobles directly on the issue. In 1403 Henry IV ordered John, Lord Welles to stop granting liveries and gathering unlawful assemblies in order to avoid the king's wrath. The letter stated that the king had been informed that Welles had been granting liveries illegally.[51]

One case that is known is that of Henry Percy, earl of Northumberland, who appeared before parliament on 8 February 1404 to plead for mercy for the various crimes he had committed. Included in this plea was a confession that he had not kept many of the king's laws and statutes 'especially by gathering power and giving liveries'.[52] The previous July, Northumberland was conspicuous by his absence at the Battle of Shrewsbury, at which a rebel army led by his son, Henry Percy, 'Hotspur', and Northumberland's brother the earl of Worcester were defeated by the new Lancastrian regime. Hotspur was killed during the fighting and Worcester was summarily beheaded soon after.[53] One chronicler noted that the rebels at Shrewsbury wore the livery of Richard II.[54] The belief that the Percies had given illegal livery led to that being one of the accusations against the earl of Northumberland in parliament. Despite his being accused in parliament, no corresponding indictment has been identified from the surviving King's Bench files because a parliamentary trial negated the need for any case before the King's Bench.

It was the second major Yorkshire rising against Henry IV that provided the context for the further development of the law during the Long Parliament of 1406 which, once again, began with a Commons petition.[55] The petition has an unusual focus on the retaining practices of ecclesiastical lords, beginning by stating that no archbishops, abbots, priors or any other church men 'or temporal person' were to grant livery to anyone except their household servants, estate officials or lawyers. Thereafter the petition stated that, contrary to the previous statutes, lords were still illegally distributing livery, claiming that in some instances this was to as many as 300 followers. This was not the known complaint about livery being distributed by an ecclesiastical magnate. In 1388 various clerics of the church of

---

[51] *CCR, 1402–1405*, 109.
[52] *PROME*, viii, 231–2.
[53] For contemporary accounts see: *An English Chronicle*, 32–4; *Chronicle of Adam Usk*, 168–71; *Chronica Maiora of Thomas Walsingham*, 326–9. For the most recent secondary account see: Given-Wilson, *Henry IV*, 218–32.
[54] *An English Chronicle*, 33.
[55] For the next three paragraphs see *PROME*, viii, 400–1.

St John of Beverley claimed that in a dispute in 1381 with the previous archbishop of York, Alexander Neville, Richard II had taken them into his protection. When Robert Rous and Richard Hembrigge were sent to Beverley to proclaim this they were prevented from doing so because the archbishop had procured a large group of supporters all wearing his livery caps.[56] The lack of knowledge about who presented the petition, the failure to name a specific lord and the absence of any known cases mean it is uncertain if the petitioners were discussing a specific incident, or exaggerating the problem for rhetorical effect. The emphasis on the retaining practices of ecclesiastical lords was probably alluding to the failed rebellion led by Richard le Scrope, archbishop of York in 1405, which led to the archbishop's beheading. Yet none of the chroniclers make any reference to Scrope or any of his supporters wearing any specific livery.[57] Either the chroniclers were not interested in recording such facts or the rebellion was used by the Commons to further their objectives on the issue of liveries.

The petition was successful, leading to a further act about liveries. Part of the petition's success can be attributed to the fact that it linked the concern the Commons had about lawlessness exacerbated by the unrestricted distribution of livery with problems facing Henry IV, showing that both king and Commons had a mutual interest in developing the law further. Medieval petitions were 'artful constructs designed to get something done', not simply 'the outpouring of real-life, hard-luck stories'.[58] This is not to argue that such petitions were purely fictitious or that they had no basis in reality: for a petition to have a chance of becoming law, the complaints to which it alluded needed to be credible. Many of the petitions during the reigns of Richard II and Henry IV appealed to the royal prerogative, stating that the reason for the petition was that earlier law – i.e. the king's laws – were being habitually broken. Appeals to royal interests and the incorporation of livery into the vocabulary used to decry widespread lawlessness was the rhetoric used by petitioners in order to ensure legislation was passed regulating the distribution of livery. The emphasis on ecclesiastical lords was a means of drawing a connection between the concern the Commons had regarding unregulated livery and the two rebellions that Henry IV had recently suppressed.

The 1406 act largely reiterated previous legislation but introduced larger fines. Those illegally distributing livery were to be fined 100*s*. for each person to whom they had given livery, and those who received livery were to be fined 40*s*.

---

[56] SC8/20/992.

[57] *An English Chronicle*, 35–7; *Chronica Maiora of Thomas Walsingham*, 336–9; *St Albans*, ii, 440–51; *Chronicle of Adam Usk*, 203; *The New Chronicles of England and France by Robert Fabyan*, ed. Henry Ellis (London, 1811), 572.

[58] W. Mark Ormrod, 'Introduction: Medieval Petitions in Context' in *Medieval Petitions: Grace and Grievance*, eds. W. Mark Ormrod, Gwilym Dodd and Anthony Musson (York, 2009), 11.

The large discrepancy in fines between those granting and those receiving illegal livery acknowledges two important aspects about the lord–servant relationship: first, the differing economic backgrounds between those giving and receiving illegal livery, since it was the wealthier lords who would face much larger fines; second, by fining those distributing livery illegally, for each person illegally given livery, it was possible to levy larger fines on those who distributed illegal livery. This had the potential to damage their finances, and therefore local standing, as well as their ability to continue retaining. The focus was therefore directed towards those distributing the livery more than those receiving it. In addition to the increased punishment, reporting the crime was incentivised by giving anyone who wished to bring about a suit on behalf of the king half of the fine 'for his labour'. To ensure prosecutions, penalties were not to 'in any way be pardoned'. An attempt was made to limit the amount of livery being made, with the statute stating that 'no congregation or company' was to 'make for itself a livery of cloth or of hoods at the personal expense of the same congregation or company'. The punishment for anyone breaking this was a fine of 40*s*. The 1406 act therefore increased both provisions for enforcing the statutes and the fines for contravening the statute which 'were by no means low' and therefore gave kings 'a weapon' against lawless nobles.[59] After a petition similar to that of 1406 the statutes were again reiterated in 1411.[60]

Henry V and the Eventual Enforcement

While the Commons were successful in getting new laws passed, they were unsuccessful in ensuring the enforcement of the statutes. During Henry IV's reign the only identifiable case was in Derbyshire when twenty-four men were charged with offences against the statutes under a private suit in 1410.[61] The private suit in Derbyshire in 1410 may indicate that prior to Henry V's accession, the King's Bench only dealt with private suits which the 1401 act permitted.[62] Even if there were other private suits during Henry IV's reign, it would not account for the lack of cases before the 1401 act enabled private suits.

It is during Henry V's reign that the first sustained effort to indict people for illegal livery can be identified. The first significant cluster of illegal livery indictments was recorded by an *oyer et terminer* commission in Staffordshire in

---

[59] Quotations from: Bean, *From Lord to Patron*, 208.
[60] *PROME*, viii, 547–8.
[61] KB27/596 plea rot. 76. Printed in *Select Cases in the Court of King's Bench Under Richard II, Henry IV and Henry V*, 192–4.
[62] *PROME*, viii, 148–9.

1414 which produced twenty-one indictments for illegal livery.[63] One further case can be identified from Staffordshire the following year.[64] In total, Staffordshire accounted for 71 per cent of all cases of illegal livery during the reign of Henry V (22/31). A further five cases can be identified from the *coram rege rolls* from Shropshire in 1414.[65] To this one case from Cheshire in 1415 can be added.[66] These cases were part of Henry V's attacks against lawlessness in the localities early in his reign, which he had to undertake before he could mount a military campaign abroad.[67] The most obvious threat he needed to combat was the Lollard rebellion led by John Oldcastle in 1414.[68] Henry did not just react to rebellion but also took the initiative to attempt to improve public order by making widespread changes to the personnel involved in law enforcement throughout England. Soon after his coronation Henry V had issued new commissions of the peace for all counties and replaced his Chief Justice of the King's Bench, William Gascoigne, with William Hankford.[69] The cases in Staffordshire and Shropshire occurred during a period of violent local feuding that had been ongoing since the early years of Henry IV's reign.[70] Two of the main culprits in 1414, Edmund Ferrers and Hugh Erdeswyk, had each petitioned parliament in April 1414 complaining that the other had gathered a large group of men together and attacked their respective properties.[71] The cases were picked up at the time in which justices were travelling across the midlands dealing with instances of unrest and local disturbances. Despite the fact that cases are only known in three counties, it is clear that the first major clusters of cases arose when the new king, Henry V, was attempting to eradicate, or at the very least minimise, local disorder, before undertaking his military campaigns in France.

Towards the end of Henry V's reign cases became infrequent, although there continued to be a steady stream of indictments during the early years of Henry VI's minority. From 1421 until 1423 four further cases of illegal livery are known: one from Shropshire in 1421[72] and three from Yorkshire between 1421

---

[63] KB29/53 rot. 24; KB9/113 mm. 2, 11, 28, 40–3. Calendared in 'Extracts from the Plea Rolls of the Reigns of Henry V and Henry VI', ed. George Wrottesley, William Salt Archeological Society, xvii (London, 1896), 6–7, 9–10.
[64] KB27/617 rex rot. 16.
[65] KB27/613 rex rott. 39–40.
[66] CHES25/25 m. 14.
[67] Powell, *Kingship, Law and Society*, 168.
[68] See e.g. Powell, *Kingship, Law and Society*, 141–67.
[69] *CPR, 1413–16*, 416–16. For a contemporary account see: *Chronicle of Adam Usk*, 244–7; *Chronica Maiora of Thomas Walsingham*, 394–5.
[70] Powell, *Kingship, Law and Society*, 208–24.
[71] 'Extracts from the Plea Rolls of the Reigns of Henry V and Henry VI', 3–4.
[72] KB27/640 rex rot. 7; KB27/642 rex rot. 7.

and 1423.[73] In this respect there was a clear continuity between the reigns of Henry V and Henry VI. Thereafter, there was a lull of five years until the next cluster of cases can be identified from Cheshire in 1428, when fourteen occurred in the palatinate.[74] The sporadic nature of the enforcement of the livery laws was consistent throughout the fifteenth century. From 1415 onwards, there was a decline in the number of cases because the statutes were enforced only when it was deemed necessary.

The cases from Cheshire are significant because they throw light upon both the nature of the enforcement of the statutes and the development of the 1429 Livery Act, which was the final act to have its origins in a Commons petition as opposed to royal initiative.[75] After 1411, the issue of liveries is not recorded as being discussed during another parliament until 1427 when, after a petition from the Commons, it was stated that the existing statutes were to be upheld.[76] The petition went on to request that justices should have the power to award writs of attachment and distraint against those alleged to have contravened the statutes. These truncated procedures which, in theory, 'shifted the advantage to the prosecution'[77] would enable justices of the peace to arrest suspects, interrogate them and convict them without resort to a jury. It was also requested that the laws should be enforced in the palatinates of Cheshire and Lancashire. Finally, certain people were to be exempt from the act, including mayors while in office, sergeants and those entering the universities. This petition was unsuccessful and no new statute was passed.

Two years later, in 1429, a further petition was more successful in expanding the legislation.[78] The ease with which this petition became law is suggested by the fact that the surviving bill is a verbatim copy with no annotations of what appears in the parliament roll.[79] The statute was the first to state that the statutes were to be enforced in the palatinates of Cheshire and Lancashire and that women were bound by them. Previously it was believed that the 1429 act extended the legislation to the palatinate counties[80] but when the indictments for Cheshire are examined, it is clear that nothing new came from this statute. The palatinates of Cheshire and Lancashire had never been exempt from the statutes, as is evident

---

[73] KB27/642 rex rot. 31; KB27/645 rex rot. 8; KB29/56 rot. 25; KB29/57 rot. 5.
[74] CHES25/12 mm. 16–17.
[75] The act and the broader context in which it was passed are discussed in detail in: McKelvie, 'The Livery Act of 1429', 55–65.
[76] *PROME*, ix, 354–5. This, however, was not recorded on the statute roll: *Stat. Realm*, ii, 240–1.
[77] Hicks, '1468 Statute of Livery', 16.
[78] For the next two paragraphs, unless stated otherwise, see: *PROME*, ix, 402–3.
[79] C49/19/8.
[80] Griffiths, *The Reign of Henry VI*, 134; Tim Thornton, *Cheshire and the Tudor State, 1480–1560* (Woodbridge, 2000), 2 n. 5, 120 n. 3.

from the fact that a case of illegal livery from Cheshire can be identified from 1415[81] along with a further fourteen cases from 1428,[82] although none can be identified for Lancashire.[83] Similarly, Elizabeth, lady Neville, daughter-in-law of Ralph, first earl of Westmorland, had been indicted for giving livery illegally to three yeomen in 1423.[84] The 1429 act did not extend the scope of the law to cover women or the palatinate counties because they were already bound by the statute. Rather than extending the jurisdiction of the law, the 1429 act formalised existing practice and clarified the precise terms of the statutes.

In addition, the 1429 act included more stringent measures for enforcement and punishment. Fines were imposed per offence, rather than per item of livery distributed or received, which remained at 100s. for distributing illegal livery and 40s. for receiving illegal livery. Anyone purchasing cloth and fraudulently making their own copies of a noble's livery for the purpose of maintenance in a lawsuit was to be convicted under the terms of the statute, echoing the problems addressed by the 1377 act. It was under this clause that cases from the Tudor era in which men fraudulently wore the livery of someone who was not their lord were prosecuted.[85] In a similar vein, lords were prohibited from giving livery to, or keeping in their household, known felons. Lords were required to abandon such men 'without delay', thus attempting to ensure that they could be brought to justice. Finally, provisions were made for more rigorous enforcement of the statutes. Justices were given the power 'to award writs of attachment and distraint' against those contravening the act. This was to be given to the sheriff and if returned '*capias* and *exigent*' was to be awarded against them in the same manner it was against those who committed trespass against the king's peace with force and arms. These measures were both a statement of intent and an attempt to obtain more prosecutions for illegal livery.

In the decade following the passing of the 1429 act there was continued enforcement of the statutes, notably one indictment of a fowler in Sussex in 1429,[86] which was followed by a three-year gap in which no cases can be identified. There then seems to have been some initiative from Henry VI's minority government to tackle the problem of illegal livery. During the 1430s the geographical location of the cases expanded, with twenty-four cases occurring over eight counties between 1432 and 1440. The first two of these cases were

---

[81] CHES25/25 m. 14.
[82] CHES25/12 mm. 16–17.
[83] It should be noted that only two plea rolls survive for Lancashire prior to 1429: PL15/1–2. This is also true of the palatinate of Durham, although it should be noted that only three rolls survive between 1390 and 1429: DURH13/224–6.
[84] KB29/56 rot. 25.
[85] KB9/390 mm. 47; KB9/434 mm. 18, 21; KB9/436 mm. 7–9, 14; KB27/1013 rex rot. 8.
[86] KB29/62 rot. 3.

in Cheshire in 1432[87] followed by two in Somerset in 1433.[88] Other cases are known from Kent in 1435,[89] Warwickshire in 1436[90] and Sussex in 1437.[91] The largest number of cases during the 1430s was in Derbyshire when in 1434 an *oyer et terminer* commission identified thirteen cases of illegal livery in the county connected to lawlessness in the county.[92] These cases were followed by three further cases in 1439–40, one of which came from London;[93] another from Yorkshire;[94] and one from Oxfordshire.[95] In May 1441 writs were sent to each sheriff in England ordering them to proclaim the 1401 statute of livery.[96] Yet this order did not produce further prosecutions for illegal livery as after 1440 there was another nine-year gap in which no cases can be identified. The next known case occurred in 1449 when Sir Robert Hungerford allegedly gave a livery cap and gown to John Rooley, gentleman of Andover on 21 September 1448.[97]

In summary, the 1430s was a decade in which cases of illegal livery were beginning to arise in more counties, although, like Staffordshire in 1414, the majority of cases occurred in a single county that was experiencing local disorder. The absence of cases in both 1423–8 and the 1440s is consistent with the broader chronological distribution of cases prior to the reign of Henry VII: there were short periods in which many cases arose followed by long periods in which the records indicate that no charges were made against anyone illegally distributing or receiving livery.

New Laws in Late Medieval England

The discussion thus far has indicated that medieval statutes were enforced sporadically and the fact that a new law was passed did not mean it would be enforced. Yet the continual petitioning about liveries by the Commons indicates that MPs were concerned about liveries and sought sufficient remedies. If this hypothesis is correct, it means that there was an inherent contradiction in relationship between the passing of legislation about liveries and the enforcement of such legislation: those who were calling for the new laws were from the same class of people

---

[87]   CHES25/12 mm. 25.
[88]   KB29/66 rot. 28; KB29/67 rot. 4.
[89]   KB29/68 rot. 11.
[90]   KB29/69 rot. 19.
[91]   KB29/70 rot. 16.
[92]   KB9/11 mm. 15, 17; KB29/68 rott. 4–5, 9–10, 17, 20.
[93]   KB29/72 rot. 30.
[94]   KB29/72 rot. 22.
[95]   KB29/74 rott. 3, 14.
[96]   *CCR, 1435–1441*, 480–1.
[97]   KB27/764 rex rot. 24; KB27/765 rex rot. 8.

who were responsible for upholding them but were also the same class who were breaking the law, i.e. the county gentry.

The apparent inability to implement decisions made in parliament and enforce newly passed legislation was noted by contemporaries. Reporting on the Cambridge Parliament of 1388, Thomas Walsingham refused to waste either time or parchment reciting most of the statutes passed 'for the very good reason that those same statutes were often enacted before this, but had hitherto not been observed'.[98] Although chroniclers were, in general, poorly versed in the technicalities of parliamentary procedure, they are a valuable source for gauging contemporary opinions that are not always apparent from administrative records.[99] Walsingham's claim that it was not worth his time recording for posterity unimportant and irrelevant laws that were not going to be enforced is given some justification by the surviving records, particularly in relation to new laws. This problem continued beyond the medieval period. The Lord Keeper's speech at the close of parliament on 8 May 1559 told MPs that he should not need to remind them 'how small purpose good lawes doe serve being not daylie and diligently executed'.[100] Statements reminding MPs of the importance of enforcing the laws they had just made when they were back in their counties acting as JPs were a common feature of many speeches in Elizabethan parliaments.[101] The implication is that in medieval and early modern England laws were not enforced simply because they were on the statute book. Yet to note the initial lack of enforcement of the statutes of livery as symptomatic of a broader problem in pre-modern law enforcement does not explain why the statutes of livery were eventually enforced. The lack of regular enforcement of the statutes of livery in the years after the initial legislation was passed needs to be considered in the broader context of the effectiveness of new laws passed by various English parliaments during the later middle ages. The new laws against which illegal livery need to be compared are those which can be regarded as 'period specific'. Such 'period-specific' laws are those relevant in particular societies with specific concerns and technologies, as opposed to laws relating to acts such as murder or theft which have been prohibited in almost all known human societies.

A lack of enforcement was evident in the 1401 *De Heretico Comburendo* which prescribed the death penalty, by burning, for heresy.[102] The significance,

---

[98] *Chronica Maiora of Thomas Walsingham*, i, 859.
[99] On chronicle descriptions of parliamentary events see: Christopher Given-Wilson, *Chronicles: The Writing of History in Medieval England* (London and New York, 2004), 174–6, 188; Antonia Gransden, *English Historical Writing, c.1307 to the Early Sixteenth Century* (London, 1982), 111.
[100] *Proceedings in the Parliaments of Elizabeth I: Volume 1, 1558–1581*, ed. T.E. Hartley (Leicester, 1981), 49.
[101] Ibid., 49–51, 71, 82, 111, 171, 191, 417, 464, 469, 495.
[102] For this act see: *PROME*, viii, 122–5.

and even the necessity, of passing this act are unclear. Lollards were viewed as a threat to public order and the act was almost certainly part of Henry IV's need to bolster his authority in the early years of his reign.[103] Heresy had always been a crime in England and the first secular legislation in Western Europe since antiquity against heretics was incorporated into the Assize of Clarendon by Henry II in 1166.[104] Heretics had been subject to forfeiture and were burned on several occasions in England during the thirteenth and fourteenth centuries.[105] *De Heretico Comburendo* was the first parliamentary statute that ensured lapsed heretics were burned but this did not lead to any mass executions of Lollards. Between 1401 and 1414 only two men were executed for heresy: William Sawtre on 2 March 1401 (curiously, before the act itself was passed[106]) and John Badby, in 1410 after a trial that was 'manifestly opportunistic', relating more to the immediate concerns of Archbishop Arundel than any legal niceties.[107] There was no great religious fervour to begin the mass execution of heretics because the campaign against heresy was primarily against the intellectual aspect of Lollardly, with the drive being predominantly against wayward preachers, books and scholars. It was only after the attempted Lollard *coup d'état* in early 1414, led by John Oldcastle, that there was a mass execution when 113 Lollards were executed as part of the suppression of the rebellion.[108] Thereafter the investigation of heresy again became an issue primarily addressed by ecclesiastical courts as opposed to secular ones.[109] Two points should be made about *De Heretico Comburendo* when comparing it to the statutes of livery. First, as was the case with illegal livery, in the early years of his reign Henry V began enforcing certain laws with more rigor than it appears his predecessors did. Second, *De Heretico Comburendo* was only rigorously enforced once Lollardy had become disruptive

---

[103] A.K. McHardy, '*De Heretico Comburendo*' in *Lollardy and the Gentry in the Later Middle Ages*, eds. Margaret Aston and Colin Richmond (Stroud, 1997), 112–23; Given-Wilson, *Henry IV*, 186.

[104] R.I. Moore, *The First European Revolution, c. 970–1215* (Oxford, 2000), 160–4.

[105] P.R. Cavill, 'Heresy, Law and the State: Forfeiture in Late Medieval and Early Modern England', *EHR*, cxxix (2014), 274–5.

[106] The writ, dated 26 February 1401, ordering the mayor and sheriff to proceed with the burning of Sawtre for heresy is recorded in: *PROME*, viii, 108–9. Although 2 March is generally accepted as the date of execution it should be noted that this information is only recorded in chronicles, not the parliament rolls: McHardy, '*De Heretico Comburendo*', 118. For a discussion about how the burning was presented by Henry IV as a clear part of the new king's own political programme see: Paul Strohm, *England's Empty Throne: Usurpation and the Language of Legitimation, 1399–1422* (New Haven and London, 1998), 43–5.

[107] Given-Wilson, *Henry IV*, 374–5.

[108] Figures taken from Powell, *Kingship, Law and Society*, 151, 156–7. For a reappraisal of this uprising see: Strohm, *England's Empty Throne*, 65–86.

[109] Ian Forrest, *The Detection of Heresy in Late Medieval England* (Oxford, 2005), 47.

to public order and associated with treason and an open rebellion that directly challenged Henry V's sovereignty. In the case of livery it was in order to deal with lawlessness in the localities as opposed to the direct threat to his sovereignty which Oldcastle's Revolt represented.

The inability to implement parliamentary decisions at a local level was not confined to statutes relating to criminality. A petition from the May 1421 parliament requesting that those practising medicine should be properly trained was approved in parliament but never implemented, despite the fact that four of the petitioners had direct ties to Humphrey, duke of Gloucester's household. They failed because of their reliance 'upon elite patronage without having any means of putting policy into practice'.[110] Decisions taken in parliament needed to be practical and enforceable for any new law to have an effect. The necessity for laws to be practical is evident in the Sumptuary Laws passed by Edward III's parliament. The Sumptuary Laws passed in the parliament of 1363 which regulated the types of clothes people could wear according to their social status were repealed by the parliament of 1365 because the legislation had led to an increase in prices.[111] This legislation was particularly unusual because the 1363 act included a clause that allowed the legislation to be withdrawn if it was found to be inoperable. The act itself was part of a broader campaign by the Commons in favour of protectionist measures to address the problem of rising prices in the wake of the Black Death. It has been suggested that Edward III and his council 'wedded to the general principles of the free market' desired such an outcome.[112] The Sumptuary Laws were viewed as impractical and unenforceable and there was no desire to ensure a new workable law was enacted. In this case the Commons accepted the limitations of parliamentary laws. The fact that they continually raised the issue of liveries during the late fourteenth and early fifteenth centuries suggests that the problem of unrestricted livery distribution was thought to be too serious to ignore.

The notable exception to the general rule that new laws were not immediately enforced in late medieval England was the labour laws of the mid-fourteenth century that attempted to restrict peasant wages after the demographic catastrophe of the Black Death. Bertha Putnam demonstrated that the statutes were enforced almost immediately after being passed and it is also known that 7,556 people in Essex were fined for taking excess wages in 1352.[113] This may not necessarily

---

[110] Justin Colson and Robert Rally, 'Medical Practice, Urban Politics and Patronage: The London "Commonalty" of Physicians and Surgeons of the 1420s', *EHR*, cxxx (2015), 1104.

[111] *PROME*, v, 164–8, 182.

[112] W. Mark Ormrod, *Edward III* (London, 2011), 475–6.

[113] Bertha Putnam, *The Enforcement of the Statutes of Labourers During the First Decade after the Black Death, 1349–1359* (New York, 1908), 170–4. See also: Christopher Given-Wilson, 'Service, Serfdom and English Labour Legislation, 1350-1500' in

demonstrate the effectiveness of the law in impacting upon social practice, as people were clearly ignoring the labour laws, but it does indicate that when there were clear economic advantages, those entrusted with enforcing new laws could begin enforcement almost immediately.

It may appear that the activities of parliament rarely impinged upon daily life in late medieval England, with the probable exceptions of taxation and labour laws. In one sense this vindicates J.M.W Bean's argument that during the late medieval period a statute 'could not be viewed as a piece of absolute law that must always be enforced with total rigor'. The enforcement of a particular statute depended 'upon the king's will at any given time'.[114] On its own this interpretation is unsatisfactory as it exaggerates the king's role in the day-to-day running of law enforcement, although Bean's point about the sporadic nature of the enforcement of certain statutes is beyond dispute. The fact that there was an apparent lag between a law being passed in parliament and being enforced in the localities suggests MPs did not simply go back to their boroughs and shires after a parliament armed with new laws which they were eager to enforce. The conclusion from all of this evidence must be that new laws needed a catalyst to be enforced at first. For economic legislation such as the Statutes and Ordinances of Labourers, those entrusted with enforcing the legislation, the local gentry, had an economic imperative to begin immediate enforcement. Other legislation required something more dramatic. The lack of executions under the 1401 act against Lollardy until after the Lollard Rising suggests that it was the secular problem of rebellion rather than religious zealotry that led to those executions. With regard to illegal livery, many members of the gentry retained men by grants of livery and therefore it was not in their interest to begin rigorous enforcement. Despite continual complaints during the reigns of Richard II and Henry IV it was Henry V's campaign to restore order in the localities that provided the catalyst for the enforcement of the statutes. The new laws about Lollardy and livery were only enforced after they became entangled within larger problems relating to widespread lawlessness and/or rebellion. To respond to Walsingham's complaint about the Cambridge Parliament of 1388: the statutes were not observed because there was yet to be a catalyst for their enforcement.

Concepts and Patterns of Service in the Later Middle Ages, eds. Anne Curry and Elizabeth Matthew (Woodbridge, 2000), 24.

[114] Bean, *From Lord to Patron*, 217.

3

The Later Years, 1449 to 1520

The statutes lay dormant for most of the 1440s and re-emerged as a key political issue towards the end of the decade, with new legislation about livery emanating from the crown as opposed to the Commons in parliament. The period examined in this chapter encompasses the violent upheavals of the Wars of the Roses and the development of the 'New Monarchies' of the Yorkists and Tudors. These events helped to shape the development and enforcement of the law. A key point to stress throughout this discussion is that no king wanted to destroy the independent power of the English nobility, including Henry VII, whom previous generations of historians believed did have such ambitions. There were more cases from the second half of the fifteenth century, many of which coincided with events of national significance. As with the previous chapter, the focus here remains the relationship between the development of the law in parliament and its enforcement in the localities.

The 1450s

At the Winchester sessions of the 1449 parliament John, Lord Stourton, stated that the problem of liveries along with 'murders and ryottes don ageinst the peace' necessitated the issuing of commissions of *oyer et terminer* throughout England.[1] There is no record of the discussion on the parliament roll because it was part of a discussion in the Lords as opposed to the Commons. Stourton's comments are recorded in a report about 'a frank and open debate among lords in Parliament itself' that survives in two seventeenth-century copies that appear to be genuine.[2] The reason why liveries were included along with murders and riots is uncertain, as there were no large-scale private feuds at this point akin to those a few years later between the Percy and the Neville families or the Courtenay and Bonville families. Shortly before this session, there had been the

---

[1] *EHD*, iv, 468–9.
[2] Ralph Griffiths, 'The Winchester Session of the 1449 Parliament: A Further Comment', *Huntingdon Library Quarterly*, xlii (1979), 181–91, quotation on 186. See also A.R Myers, 'A Parliamentary Debate of the Mid-Fifteenth Century', *Bulletin of the John Rylands Library*, xxii (1938), 402–3; William H. Dunham, 'Notes from the Parliament at Winchester, 1449', *Speculum*, xiii (1942), 402–4; A.R Myers, 'A Parliamentary Debate of 1449', *BIHR*, li (1978), 81–3.

first known case of illegal livery in England for nine years. During Easter 1449, Sir Robert Hungerford was indicted in Hampshire for giving illegal livery to John Rooley, gentleman, from Andover the previous September.[3] Although the Hungerfords were a prominent southern family and the crime was committed close to the location of that parliament, it is unlikely that such a minor case sparked Stourton to claim this.

The man who raised the issue of liveries, John, Lord Stourton, was a noted member of the Lancastrian government, and was treasurer of the royal household from November 1446. Despite this close proximity to the Lancastrian inner circle, he avoided becoming identified too closely with the duke of Suffolk's faction during the 1440s and remained relatively detached from much of the political upheaval of the 1450s.[4] The fact Stourton raised this concern is suggestive of broader concerns about the problem of livery. The previous month Margaret of Anjou wrote to the town of Leicester claiming that she had heard that 'certeyn persones in Leycestre had taken clothyng of diuverses persones ayenst the forme of the statut', notably from Viscount Beaumont and Lord Ferrers. It was therefore ordained that 'for the pease and wele of our tenauntes' no one was to 'geve any clothyng or lyverey to any persone dwellyng within our said lordship'.[5] The honour of Leicester was part of Margaret's dower when she became queen[6] and therefore the phrase 'within our said lordship' refers to the honour, not just the town, of Leicester. An inquisition returned to chancery by the sheriff of Leicestershire reported six instances of illegal livery being given to various artisans from Leicester in the town itself. Thomas de Ferrers was alleged to have given livery to six men from Leicester who were not his servants or lawyers and therefore against the terms of the statute. There is, however, no indictment against Viscount Beaumont for distributing illegal livery.[7] Margaret was only nineteen years old when the letter was sent and therefore it is uncertain if the letter was written of her own volition or if she was advised to issue the letter. Either way, it is clear that there was a concern within Lancastrian circles about illegal livery in the queen's lands. Margaret's letter is indicative of a broader change from the

---

[3] KB27/764 rex rot. 24.
[4] G.L. Harriss, 'Stourton Family (*per*, c.1380–1485)', *ODNB*, lii, 975.
[5] For this paragraph see: *Records of the Borough of Leicester, Volume 2: 1327–1509*, ed. M. Bateson (London, 1901), 256-7.
[6] Eric Acheson, *A Gentry Community: Leicestershire in the Fifteenth Century, c.1422–c.1485* (Cambridge, 1992), 4, 99.
[7] *Calendar of Inquisitions Miscellaneous, 1442–1485* (London, 2003), no. 213. These instances are reported in a returned inquisition before the sheriff and escheator of Leicestershire but no corresponding references to such offences appear in the records of the King's Bench. The offences were only reported but those alleged to have contravened the statutes were never indicted.

Commons in parliament being those most concerned about widespread livery distribution to the crown being the main driver of new legislation.

Despite the discussion between the lords in 1449, in the early years of the 1450s only a few minor cases of illegal livery were prosecuted: Derbyshire in 1450,[8] Hampshire in 1451,[9] Huntingdonshire in 1452[10] and Shropshire in 1453.[11] The political tensions of the duke of Suffolk's murder, Jack Cade's rebellion and the return to England of Richard, duke of York at the head of a large retinue of men produced no cases of illegal livery in 1450. There is no reason to suppose that the judicial murder of Suffolk or Cade's popular rebellion would necessarily have used or distributed liveries illegally. Both were instances of popular anger and unrest and were not openly associated with a particular noble. In contrast, the return of York from Ireland in September 1450 and his subsequent march to Westminster was an instance in which the military power of a particular noble did cause concerns about the stability of the kingdom. Although the event was not an attempt to cajole the king, the large retinue he had with him would certainly have caused concern.[12] Yet there is no evidence that those accompanying York received illegal livery, presumably because there was no opportunity to assemble and distribute liveries. Even if there were any illegal retainers, the specific context of this incident and the professed desire by Henry and York to demonstrate their cordial relations mean that any proceedings against York would have been dangerously antagonistic, as any prosecution of such a prominent noble and critic of the court circle was, first and foremost, a political decision.

During the 1450s there were several large clusters of cases connected to events of more national prominence. Henry VI's mental breakdown on hearing about the loss of Gascony in August 1453 witnessed one particularly tense occasion in which concerns about liveries were facilitating the escalation of political tensions. This happened at the time of the parliament of 1454 which saw Richard, duke of York appointed Protector. The newsletter sent by John Stodeley to the duke of Norfolk on 19 January 1454 reported that numerous prominent nobles were coming to a parliamentary session at Westminster with large numbers of heavily armed men. Stodeley further noted that the duke of Buckingham had 2,000 of his livery badges (the Stafford knot) made to distribute widely.[13] The reliability of this source for the activities of the nobles is uncertain, as some of the claims were probably speculative. Stodeley did not know the contents of one the articles

---

[8]   KB29/82 rot. 7.
[9]   KB29/83 rot. 2.
[10]   KB9/42/1 m. 11.
[11]   KB29/84 rot. 5.
[12]   Ralph Griffiths, 'Duke Richard of York's Intentions in 1450 and the Origins of the Wars of the Roses', *Journal of Medieval History*, i (1975), 187–209.
[13]   *EHD*, iv, 272–3.

in Margaret of Anjou's bill to transfer kingly power to herself, which suggests the information was known from hearsay, rumour and possible conjecture. Such rumours are in themselves revealing because they indicate a genuine concern within London about large noble affinities at this time.

Once made Protector, York needed to address various private feuds that built up throughout the early years of the 1450s. The most significant challenge to York's authority during his first protectorate was a minor, easily quashed rebellion led by his son-in-law Henry Holland, duke of Exeter, who believed he had a better hereditary claim to the protectorate. In a letter warning the young duke of Exeter about his actions and arrogant behaviour Richard ordered him, amongst other things, to stop gathering men from far parts of the land.[14] The letter is silent on whether or not Exeter was distributing liveries at all and there is evidence the duke was indicted. Yet the letter does indicate a further concern about lords opportunistically gathering large groups of men in times of political uncertainty.

A more serious problem was the two private wars that were engulfing Yorkshire and its neighbouring counties, and the south-west, respectively. The Percy–Neville and Courtenay–Bonville feuds were the two largest of the 1450s. Yet only the Percy–Neville feud produced any cases of illegal livery as part of a judicial commission in the country in 1453 in which illegal livery was one of the offences that the commissioners were required to investigate.[15] Despite the fact that most of those named on the commissions were neither Percy nor Neville adherents, there were enough Neville adherents 'to weight the investigation in their favour', with Richard, duke of York, a close ally of the Nevilles, also hearing the cases.[16] The commission indicted Henry Percy, earl of Northumberland's two sons, Thomas and Richard, on five occasions between them for illegal livery.[17] The commission indicted no known Neville adherents. The key point about indictments against Percy adherents is that they indicate the use of illegal livery as a means of conducting a feud that gained a wider significance in national politics.

In contrast, the private war that occurred in the south-west between the Bonville and Courtenay factions produced no instances of illegal livery, despite several commissions of *oyer et terminer*, which produced a large number of other prosecutions, being issued to address the feud. The most dramatic of these events

[14] The letter has been published twice: T.B. Pugh, 'Richard, Duke of York and the Rebellion of Henry Holland, Duke of Exeter in May 1454', *Historical Research*, lxiii (1990), 248–62; Carole Rawcliffe, 'Richard, Duke of York, the King's "Obesiant Liegeman": A New Source for the Protectorates of 1454 and 1455', *Historical Research*, lx (1987), 232–9.

[15] *CPR, 1452–61*, 121–3.

[16] Ralph Griffiths, 'Local Rivalries and National Politics: The Percies, the Nevilles, and the Duke of Exeter, 1452–55', *Speculum*, xliii (1968), 594–5.

[17] KB9/148/2 mm. 31, 38, 54–5; KB9/149 mm. 20–1, 49, 53.

was in 1451 when Thomas Courtenay, earl of Devon, raised a force of between five and six thousand men to besiege Taunton Castle.[18] Although no one was indicted for illegal livery in connection with this feud, William Bonville received a pardon for illegal livery and several other offences on 19 February 1452, the same day that his ally James, earl of Wiltshire received a similar pardon.[19] Both men supported the royalists at the Dartford incident while Thomas, earl of Devon was the only prominent noble supporting the duke of York at this time. The earl's position diminished after this event but, again, there is no evidence that Henry VI felt any need to indict him for illegal livery. Violence erupted once again in 1455, culminating with the indecisive battle at Clyst Bridge between the two factions in December that year, but there is no indication that anyone was wearing livery they were not entitled to at this battle. The large amounts of land held by both Courtenay and Bonville combined with large quantities of royal patronage available to them from the duchy of Cornwall perhaps meant that they had suffi-cient numbers of legal retainers to perpetrate various crimes. Although neither Bonville nor Courtenay is known to have distributed illegal liveries, it is clear that their own private powerbases were being used to wage a violent local feud.

The most politicised illegal livery cases from the 1450s were the two clusters in Herefordshire in 1452 and 1457.[20] An *oyer et terminer* commission sent to the county in August 1452 identified three instance of illegal livery.[21] Two of those indicted for distributing illegal liveries were retainers of the duke of York: Walter Devereux, who allegedly gave livery to thirty-one men on 5 January 1452; and Henry ap Griffiths, an esquire from the Welsh Marches, who gave livery to a corvesor in April 1452.[22] The indictment against Devereux is suggestive as it was a month before the duke of York held an armed demonstration at Dartford protesting against Henry VI's favourites, in particular Edmund Beaufort, duke of Somerset. The duke of Somerset was one of the members of the commission and it is probably this that gave the commission a 'partisan spirit', also evident in

---

[18]   For a discussion of this feud see: Cherry, 'The Struggle for Power', 123–40; R.L. Storey, *The End of the House of Lancaster*, 2nd edition (Gloucester, 1986), 84–92, 165–75.

[19]   *CRP, 1446–52*, 525.

[20]   For the broader contexts in which cases arose see: Alisa Herbert, 'Herefordshire, 1413–61: Some Aspects of Public Disorder' in *Patronage, The Crown and The Provinces in Later Medieval England*, ed. Ralph A. Griffiths (Gloucester, 1981), 103–22.

[21]   All three indictments are on KB9/34/1 m. 5.

[22]   For Devereux's connections to York see: Johnson, *Duke Richard of York*, 230–1. For Griffiths see: Adam Chapman, '"Dug fi at y Dug o Iorc" [He took me to the Duke of York]: Henry Griffith, a "Man of War"' in *'Gwalch Cywyddau Gwŷr': Essays on Guto'r Glyn and Fifteenth Century Wales*, eds. B.J. Lewis and D.F. Evans (Aberystwyth, 2013), 103–34.

the fact that around one third of the crimes heard were perpetrated by Henry ap Griffiths or his associates.[23]

The political tinge evident in the 1452 indictments in Herefordshire was relatively minor when compared to a further second commission of *oyer et terminer* in 1457 which identified ten further instances of illegal livery in Herefordshire between 1 June 1455 and 12 June 1456. Although connected to events of national importance, none of the offences were committed during York's Second Protectorate.[24] The commission, issued on 8 March, was a response to acts of lawlessness by the Yorkist faction in the region and included many prominent peers such as the duke of Buckingham, the earls of Arundel, Shrewsbury and Wiltshire along with chief justice Fortescue.[25] The most notable of the Yorkist crimes was in August 1456 when Devereux and Sir William Herbert gathered a force of around 2,000 men from the duke of York's lands and laid siege to Carmarthen Castle to retake it for the duke. The king's half-brother, Edmund Tudor, earl of Richmond was imprisoned but died probably from plague, shortly after his release in November 1456. Both Devereux and Herbert were subsequently imprisoned for their role in these events.[26] These cases seem to have prompted royal government to take a more active interest in addressing the problem of liveries. Soon after this commission sat, on 12 April 1457, the sheriffs across England were ordered to proclaim that any man giving badges or liveries contrary to the statutes was to be subject to the 'pains and forfeitures' laid down in the statutes.[27]

Another case from this period with apparent political overtones is known from the records from Edward IV's reign. During Michaelmas 1461 Edward Neville, Lord Bergavenny, John, Lord Clinton, Edward Brooke, Lord Cobham and eight others in Kent were ordered to appear before the sheriff regarding instances of illegal livery.[28] The case is only known from an entry in the controlment roll for 1 Edward IV (March 1461–2), but the indictments against Edward Neville and John Clinton must have originated towards the end of Henry VI's reign given that Edward Neville was the uncle to both Edward IV and the earl of Warwick. Although he was not as active as other members of his family he 'could not escape involvement in the civil war'.[29] This is plausible because the only known

[23] Herbert, 'Herefordshire, 1413–61', 115.
[24] KB9/35 mm. 6, 67–9. York was named Protector for a second time by Parliament on 11 November 1455. *PROME*, xii, 348–56. The precise date when the Protectorate ended is unclear, although P.A Johnson notes that it was no later than 25 February 1456: Johnson, *Duke Richard of York*, 137.
[25] *CPR, 1452-61*, 348–9; Herbert, 'Herefordshire, 1416–61', 115.
[26] KB935 m. 24. Discussed in Storey, *End of the House of Lancaster*, 179–80.
[27] *CCR, 1454–1461*, 205.
[28] KB29/92 rot. 13.
[29] T.B. Pugh, 'Edward Neville, first Baron Bergavenny', *ODNB*, xl, 488–9.

case involving any of the men named in this writ refers to Lord Cobham giving illegal livery to five men at Maidstone in 1455. The initial indictment was heard on 10 June 1456 by a commission of the peace headed by John Fortescue.[30] There is no further evidence of any action against Edward Neville or John Clinton, presumably because there was no need to continue the prosecution.

Although instances of illegal livery were prosecuted throughout the 1450s, the problem itself was never discussed in any parliaments until the full outbreak of hostilities between Yorkist and Lancastrian factions in the first phase of the Wars of the Roses. This occurred at the decisively anti-Yorkist parliament of November 1459, later dubbed 'the Parliament of Devils' by Yorkist propagandists because of the passing of a bill of attainder against Yorkist nobles.[31] In addition to the attainders passed against Yorkist lords, one petition complained about the lawlessness of men who wore the livery of certain lords.[32] This was part of a larger petition about the violent and lawless activities throughout England that named twenty-five gentry and yeomen who were particularly responsible for such crimes. This petition was different from earlier petitions because it did not request a new law in relation to the granting of liveries. The list included four men from Herefordshire who had been indicted earlier on in that decade for illegal livery.[33] Prior to this parliament two cases of illegal livery can be identified from the previous Easter and Trinity terms in Dorset and Leicestershire respectively.[34] Moreover, three writs of *venire facias* had been sent to some of those men from Yorkshire who had not appeared before the King's Bench after their indictments in 1454–5,[35] indicating that there was an interest in ensuring the statutes were enforced. By 1459 the problem was not, as it had been earlier in the century, that the laws were not being properly enforced. Instead, the illegal livery was part of the broader rhetoric of the petition, emphasising its potential to facilitate disorder.

Yorkist England

Two more cases can be identified from the final year of Henry VI's first reign: one in Hertfordshire where a local esquire, Alexander Marshall, gave illegal

[30] The case is only known from the pardon given to Cobham in 1463, which recites the earlier indictment. The commission of the peace in Kent had been given on 5 May 1456 – *CPR, 1452–1461*, 668.
[31] *PROME*, xii, 448, 453–61.
[32] *PROME*, xii, 499–500.
[33] The four men were: James Baskerville, George Monyngton, Thomas Monyngton (all KB29/87 rot. 15, 18) and Hugh Shirley (KB9/35 m. 6).
[34] KB29/88 rott. 33, 35; KB29/89 rott. 3, 5–6, 32
[35] KB29/89 rott. 3, 5–6, 32.

livery to seven yeomen and a piper[36] and one in Warwickshire where John Holt, esquire, distributed illegal livery to twelve men, including four from neighbouring Staffordshire.[37] There is no evidence linking either of these cases to the Lancastrian–Yorkist civil war that raged for eighteen months between September 1459 and March 1461.[38] Those fighting in the seven battles between Blore Heath on 23 September 1459 and Towton on 29 March 1461 presumably wore some form of insignia or livery to identify them with their commanders. The Londoner Robert Bale described the various liveries worn by those supporting Edward, earl of March, before the Second Battle of St Albans when the troops were being arrayed.[39] Bale was not the only chronicler to note the proliferation of liveries at this time. Gregory's chronicle states that men were wearing their lords' liveries to recognise each other in battle while a contemporary poem about the Battle of Towton identified the combatants by their livery badges.[40] On 3 February 1461 proclamations were ordered to be made in Middlesex and Hertfordshire prohibiting men from wearing any livery badges except those whose retinues were joining the king in the lead-up to the Second Battle of St Albans.[41] Although liveries were a key issue at this time and were used as a means for recruiting troops, there were no prosecutions of illegal livery connected to this phase of the Wars of the Roses. This is not to say that everyone who wore liveries to these battles was entitled to under the statutes, but rather that no one was indicted for these illegal activities. The reason for the absence of cases in the aftermath of this period of civil war is that the nature of the war, and the need for reconciliation afterwards, meant it that would be unrealistic to expect prosecutions for such a minor offence compared to more serious offences of homicide and treason.

Despite few prosecutions for illegal livery occurring during the first phase of the Wars of the Roses, the problems of lawlessness and feuding that it exacerbated were something the young new king Edward IV needed to address. The repeated failure of the Lancastrian administration during the 1450s to maintain

---

[36] KB29/89 rot. 24. A further writ was issued regarding this case four years later: KB29/93 rot. 4.

[37] KB29/89 rott. 24, 30.

[38] John Holt is listed in Christine Carpenter's directory of the Warwickshire gentry in the fifteenth century, though discussion of him in her study relates to earlier and later events. Carpenter's discussion does not link Holt to any of the broader political machinations in the county – Carpenter, *Locality and Polity*, 110, 183, 408, 410 n. 38, 415, 429 n. 126, 430, 657.

[39] Hannes Kleineke, 'Robert Bale's Chronicle and the Second Battle of St Albans', *Historical Research*, lxxxvii (2014), 745–6, 749–50.

[40] *The Historical Collections of a Citizens of London in the Fifteenth Century*, ed. J. Gairner, Camden Society, new series, vii (1876), 212; F. Madden, 'Political Poems of the Reigns of Henry VI and Edward IV', *Archaeolgia*, xxix (1842), 344–7.

[41] *CPR, 1452–1461*, 658.

public order was one of the main causes of the Wars of the Roses.[42] The first parliament of the new reign passed an act relating to the distribution of badges which also reiterated the terms of the previous statutes.[43] The act commanded that 'noo lord nor other persone of lower estate or degree, spirituell or temporell' was to distribute 'any lyveree of signe, marke or token of compaignie' unless commanded to by the king to assist him in repressing rebellions and riots. The act is vague about the meaning of 'lower estate or degree' because it does not say if it was only members of the peerage who could distribute badges or if 'lower estate' referred to those below the rank of gentry. Furthermore, it was only the distribution of badges, as opposed to robes, gowns, collars or caps, which the act restricted. The events of the 1450s made the new king, and those around him, acutely aware of the potential problems caused by large retinues created in a short space of time. As badges were cheaper to make and mass-produced they were the form of livery most suited to creating a large faction of men who were unified by wearing a common insignia. It was therefore in the king's interests to attempt to limit this practice.

Although writs ordering people to appear to answer allegations of illegal livery were issued during the early years of Edward IV's reign, it is uncertain if these relate to offences committed during this period or relate to offences that occurred during Henry VI's reign. As stated, a writ of *venire facias* was issued to the sheriff of Kent in 1461 ordering him to compel Edward Neville, Lord Bergavenny, John, Lord Clinton, Edward Brooke, Lord Cobham and eight others to appear, though the further details of the livery offences are unknown.[44] The following year a writ was issued ordering one yeoman from Upton in Herefordshire to appear before the sheriff in response to an accusation of illegal livery,[45] while a similar writ was issued to John Nicholl, yeoman from Northfield, Worcestershire in 1463.[46] In all of these instances, the date and place of offence were not recorded and it can be presumed that the offence itself was relatively minor.

Towards the end of the 1460s, the problem of liveries once again became a prominent issue. In part this was caused by the growing tensions between Edward IV and his brother George, duke of Clarence and Richard, earl of Warwick (Warwick the Kingmaker). There is some suggestion that measures to curb retaining were taken in the years leading up to the passing of a new act in 1468. John Warkworth noted that after the dismissal of Warwick's brother, George Neville, as chancellor in late 1467 'the erle of Warwyke toke to hym in fee als many knyghtes, squires, & gentilemen as he might to be strong' and that the

---

[42] This is the central argument of Storey, *End of the House of Lancaster*.
[43] *PROME*, xii, 499–500.
[44] KB29/92 rot. 13.
[45] KB29/93 rot. 16.
[46] KB29/94 rott. 1, 6.

king 'did that he myght to feble the erles power'. Warkworth also noted that the two never loved each other after this time.[47] On 23 September 1467, Londoners were prohibited from receiving the livery of any magnate. Anyone who broke this ordinance would permanently lose his office. This ordinance was probably related to Warwick's growing isolation around this time and concerns about him retaining men in the capital.[48]

It was in this wider atmosphere of distrust that the statute concerning the wearing of liveries was passed in May 1468, during the third session of the 1467–8 parliament. The law was extended beyond the visual manifestation of such relationships to restricting the actual relationships themselves by including retaining by indenture.[49] Unlike the majority of earlier acts, the impetus for this development in the law came from the king, not the Commons. The preamble stated that the king was mindful about the previous statutes regarding the distribution of livery but that nevertheless many people 'not dredyng thoo peynes nor forfaitours, daily offenden' against the existing statutes. Prior to the passing of this statute, there had been twelve cases of illegal livery during the previous two years. There had been a case in Derbyshire in 1466[50] followed by three in Surrey[51] and one in Cornwall in 1467.[52] The most significant cases were the six prosecuted up by an *oyer et terminer* commission in Derbyshire in Easter 1468.[53] Like many of the cases from the 1450s, those in Derbyshire came from an *oyer et terminer* commission triggered by the violent feuding in the county. The most serious incident was the murder of Roger Vernon, brother of Henry Vernon of Netherhaddon, by men in the service of Lord Grey of Codnor. Among the indicted was John Talbot, third earl of Shrewsbury. In total fifty-six offences were recorded, twenty-three of which were committed several years earlier. Although several leading gentry and magnates, and their men, were involved in many of the offences, most of the connections were legal under the existing livery laws.[54] Before 1468, the statutes restricted only the distribution of liveries and therefore these cases may have highlighted the need to address retaining by other methods, such as indentures and fees, which were not readily visible but still created serious problems. It was likely these disturbances, along with Warwick's retaining practices, that gave Edward the impetus to introduce a new statute on the matter which now sought to limit other categories of retaining,

---

[47] *Death and Dissent*, 95.
[48] *Calendar of Letter-Books of the City of London, L*, 73, and 73 n. 1; William H. Dunham, *Lord Hastings' Indentured Retainers*, 81.
[49] For the next three paragraphs, unless stated otherwise, see: *PROME*, xiii, 384–6.
[50] KB29/97 rot. 29.
[51] KB29/98 rott. 8, 19.
[52] KB29/98 rot. 20.
[53] KB9/13 mm. 11, 19–23, 53, 63.
[54] Hicks, '1468 Statute of Livery', 17–20.

including indentures of retainer. The inclusion of prominent councillors such as the king's brothers, the dukes of Clarence and Gloucester and earl Rivers in the commission[55] suggests that the king was informed by close associates about the problems associated with illegal livery that had occurred in Derbyshire. As the commission was held between the second and third sessions of parliament, the act was likely an immediate reaction to these broader events as opposed to being planned legislation when the parliament was initially summoned.

The resultant statute was the biggest extension of the law since the first act in 1390. The most radical aspect of the statute was the inclusion of retaining by indenture, not just retaining by livery, stating that no one was to 'gyve eny such lyveree or signe, or reteigne eny persone … by oothe, writyng or promysse, or retenaunce by indenture', except lawyers, household servants and estate officials. The reference to 'writyngs' and promises is rather vague and ill defined. A 'promyse' in such circumstances must have referred to a binding verbal agreement but unlike an oath, one not sworn on the gospel. This gave the law a rather flexible definition of retaining but one that was clearly meaningful to contemporaries. The act declared that all existing indentures contrary to this statute were void but still permitted retaining men for 'lawful service'. Lord Hastings, for instance, continued to enter into indentures of retainer after 1468 that were legal because of the 'lawful service' clause.[56] In addition, larger fines were introduced for those who received livery illegally or fees. Those receiving livery or fees were to be fined 100s. per offence, the same as those distributing illegal livery. Considering those with an income of 40s. were deemed to be of sufficient standing to vote in shire elections,[57] such large financial penalties would have been a major financial burden for many, suggesting that those being retained were being targeted along with those doing the retaining. This policy was a development from earlier legislation in which financial penalties were more stringent against those distributing illegal liveries, presumably to act as an additional deterrent.

In order to ensure more prosecutions, judges were given discretion regarding what evidence they could accept. Connected to the increase in judges' powers was the fact that the statute repeated a clause from the 1406 statute which gave half of the fine to anyone who brought forth a case on the king's behalf. The number of courts that could hear the cases was also increased. As well as JPs, *oyer et terminer* commissions, gaol delivery and the king's justices in the palatinates of Cheshire and Lancashire, jurisdiction was given to ecclesiastical courts, namely

---

[55]   *CPR, 1467–1477*, 69–70.
[56]   Dunham, *Lord Hastings' Indentured Retainers*, 119–20. It should be noted, as Michael Hicks has highlighted, that Hastings' retinue was unique throughout England since it was 'essentially the king's'. Michael Hicks, 'Lord Hastings' Indentured Retainers?' in *Richard III and his Rivals*, 245.
[57]   *PROME*, x, 405–6.

the archbishop of York's court in Hexhamshire[58] and the Bishop of Durham's court and all the incorporated towns, cities, boroughs and ports. Again, these clauses formalised existing practices. Earlier royal charters to towns had given the right to hear and determine livery cases to Norwich in 1452,[59] Canterbury in 1453,[60] Derby in 1459,[61] Rochester in 1462[62] and Colchester in 1462.[63] This was part of the broader process of tightening up the legislation by making what was implicit in earlier acts now explicit.

Cases were prosecuted soon after the act was passed, though these only covered the wearing of liveries as opposed to other forms of retaining. Forty men from Devon were summoned to answer charges of illegal livery during Trinity term 1468.[64] However, it was the twelve cases from Suffolk in 1469 that were the most prominent of Edward IV's reign.[65] The cases from Suffolk are atypical because members of the peerage, the dukes of Norfolk and Suffolk, were indicted, which was connected to the context in which the indictments occurred. Edward IV was in East Anglia at this time on pilgrimage to Bury St Edmunds and Walsingham, soon after a commission of *oyer et terminer* was issued for the whole country.[66] The king himself did not sit on the commission, but close allies did, including his father-in-law, earl Rivers, his chamberlain William, Lord Hastings, and his chief justice Thomas Billing. The earl of Warwick was also on this commission. The presence of the king and several of his key courtiers may well have emboldened the local jury to indict East Anglia's two most prominent nobles.[67] Both magnates were at that time embroiled in disputes with the Paston family. In 1465, the duke of Suffolk had pulled down the family's lodge at Hellesdon[68] while later that summer the duke of Norfolk laid siege to Caister Castle as part of an ongoing dispute with the Paston family over the will of John Fastolf.[69] These indictments fit a broader pattern of enforcement because they occurred when the king was taking an active interest in addressing problems of local lawlessness.

Furthermore, the cases from East Anglia are the only ones that occurred around the time of the second phase of the Wars of the Roses (1469–71) and

---

[58]   Part of Northumberland since 1572.
[59]   *Calendar of Charter Rolls Preserved in the Public Record Office, Volume VI, 1427–1516* (London, 1927), 115.
[60]   Ibid., 124.
[61]   Ibid., 132.
[62]   Ibid., 151.
[63]   Ibid., 179.
[64]   KB27/829 rex rot. 31–2; KB27/829 rex rot. 21d.
[65]   KB29/99 rott. 31–2.
[66]   *CPR, 1467–77*, 170.
[67]   Hicks, '1468 Statute of Livery', 23–4.
[68]   *PL*, i, 544–5.
[69] *PL*, i, 340, 344–6, 406, 550; ii, 557–9, 587.

relate to localised violence as opposed to wider political events. The lack of cases connected to the Second War should not imply that liveries were not distributed at this time. One account of the Battle of Empingham, as part of the Lincolnshire Rebellion, described how there were many men on the field wearing the duke of Clarence's livery and chanting 'A Clarence! a Clarence! a Warrwike!' One rebel, Robert Wells, was apprehended after the battle carrying various bills that incriminated Warwick and Clarence and confessed to his part in the treason provoked by Warwick and Clarence before he was executed.[70] As with the first phase of the wars, there were no indictments relating to illegal liveries. Clarence's reconciliation with his brother made any prosecution politically problematic, as indicting those wearing Clarence's livery would have been viewed as trivial, petty and antagonistic.

After Edward IV's second usurpation in 1471, there were no immediate cases of illegal livery, though he remained concerned about the problem. Edward wrote to the mayor and sheriffs of Coventry in February 1472 ordering that no one in the town was to give or receive livery contrary to the statutes.[71] Illegal livery and retaining was something that Edward IV clearly associated with rebellion early in his second reign. In 1472 commissions of *oyer et terminer* given in London, Oxfordshire, Essex and Middlesex included illegal livery and illegal retaining among the crimes for the commissions to investigate along with various treasons, rebellions, insurrections and other felonies.[72] Although the commissions identified no instances of illegal livery, the inclusion of the offence in such writs indicates that the king was interested in ensuring the statutes were upheld.

The final cluster of cases during Edward IV's reign occurred between 1476 and 1480, when nineteen cases arose. Edward's interest in illegal retaining at this time is evident in two ordinances for the duchy of Lancaster from August 1476. The first ordinance, addressed to Halton in Cheshire, forbade illegal retaining within the borough. The second stated that two members of the local gentry William Bryerton, knight and John Daviport, esquire were not to retain any of the king's tenants.[73] Yet there is no clear link between the enacting of these ordinances in the crown's private estates and the prosecution of illegal livery at this time because the cases did not arise in Cheshire. Indictments were confined predominantly to the southern counties. Ten of these cases occurred in Kent during Trinity 1478,[74] while four others arose in Sussex (three in 1476 and one

[70] *Chronicle of the Rebellion in Lincolnshire, 1470*, ed. John G. Nicholas, Camden Society (London, 1847), 10–11.
[71] *The Coventry Leet Book or Mayor's Register, 1420–1555*, ed. M.D. Harris, Early English Text Society (London, 1907–13), i, 374.
[72] KB9/76 mm. 5–7, 15–16.
[73] DL5/1 fol. 136. Printed in A.R. Myers, *Crown, Household and Parliament in Fifteenth Century England* (London, 1985), 327.
[74] KB29/108 rot. 12.

in 1480),[75] one in Hampshire (1476),[76] two in Shropshire (1477 and 1480),[77] one in Oxfordshire (1478)[78] and one in Coventry (1480).[79]

After 1480, there were no more cases of illegal livery during Edward IV's reign, which is consistent with wider trends regarding the enforcement of the legislation: there are clusters of cases over a short period of a few years followed by periods of several years in which no charges occur. Edward IV's first reign continued a trend that began during the latter years of Henry VI's first reign in which the statutes of livery were being more widely enforced than they had been. The number of cases and the clusters in 1460–3, 1467–70 and 1476–80 show the statutes of livery were enforced on certain occasions during the reign of Edward IV.

The pattern continued during Richard III's reign, in which there were no cases of illegal livery. This included Buckingham's Rebellion in 1483, after which no one was indicted for liveries or retaining, which fits with a broader pattern in the aftermath of many rebellions and uprisings during the Wars of the Roses when such indictments were probably seen as unnecessarily petty and punitive. Unlike several previous rebellions in Yorkist England, particularly the period 1469–71, there is no other evidence suggesting the widespread distribution of liveries. Richard, however, continued his brother's policy of writing to specific towns and lordships regarding retaining and the granting of liveries. Richard's surviving signet book includes eight letters to urban governments and royal officials warning them not to retain or be retained illegally.[80] Unacceptable forms of retaining was something that Richard III addressed in his letters to various local authorities, but such concerns from the crown did not translate into cases of illegal livery or retaining in the King's Bench. In all, Richard III's reign was part of a broader pattern of sporadic enforcement that was evident since the reign of Henry V.

Henry VII

Henry VII's reign was the apex for the enforcement of the livery and retaining statutes. In total, 150 cases (44.6 per cent of all cases) arose during his reign – more than double the number found in any other reign examined in this study, and more than treble every other reign except that of Henry VI, which was much longer. At first, this may appear to strengthen the older argument that Henry VII

[75] KB29/106 rott. 11, 28; KB29/110 rot. 12.
[76] KB29/106 rot. 24.
[77] KB29/107 rot. 12; KB29/110 rot. 16.
[78] KB27/908 rot. 5 rex.
[79] KB29/110 rot. 17.
[80] *Harleian 433*, ii, 10, 19, 69–70, 81, 162–3, 166–7; HMC, *11th Report, Appendix, Part 3: The Manuscripts of the Corporations of Southampton and King's Lynn* (London, 1887), 16.

used retaining laws to rein in noble power. This view has a long tradition. Writing in the seventeenth century, Francis Bacon recounted a story that when Henry VII was visiting John de Vere, thirteenth earl of Oxford, the earl was entertaining him 'nobly and sumptuously'. After discovering that in order to put on a suitable spectacle, Oxford had given livery to yeomen and gentlemen who were not his permanent retainers or household servants, Henry fined him immediately.[81] No formal indictment against the earl of Oxford survives in the records of the King's Bench and Oxford's biographer found no evidence of the earl paying any fines for illegal livery.[82] Bacon himself prefaced the story, stating that 'there remaineth to this day a report',[83] suggesting his own uncertainty regarding the truth of the story. The origin of Bacon's story was probably an oral tradition that is likely to have stemmed from three cases in 1505 in which three men were indicted for wearing the earl's livery even though they were not in his service.[84] Bacon's story was probably a misinterpretation of these indictments that turned into legend and then accepted fact. In essence, the story reveals an important aspect of Henry VII's posthumous reputation – that he was dogmatic in ensuring that his laws were upheld. Understanding the relationship between the passing of parliamentary acts about retaining and their enforcement is therefore vital for fully understanding the nature of Henry VII's reign.

Henry VII's reign witnessed the most sustained enforcement of the statutes but when Henry became king, he was content with the law as it stood. Henry made the attending secular and ecclesiastical lords at his first parliament swear an oath that they would not harbour any known felons or retain anyone contrary to the statutes.[85] The key objective for Henry was that lords would adhere to and enforce the existing legislation, as opposed to desiring new legislation. His desire to see the law enforced is evident in a letter to the mayor and JPs of Coventry in January 1486 reminding them not to permit any retaining contrary to the statutes.[86] It is clear that he saw unrestricted retaining as a means of facilitating disorder and raising troops for rebellions. After a minor uprising in Yorkshire in 1486 Henry wrote to the city's government reminding them to uphold the statutes regarding retaining.[87]

Despite his not wishing to extend the scope of the legislation at the start of his reign, retaining was a more pressing concern for Henry VII after his usurpation

[81] Francis Bacon, *The History of the Reign of King Henry VII and Selected Works*, ed. Brian Vickers (Cambridge, 1998), 177–8.
[82] Ross, *John De Vere*, 141–3.
[83] Bacon, *Reign of Henry VII*, 177.
[84] KB9/436 mm. 7, 9, 14.
[85] *PROME*, xv, 131–2.
[86] HMC, *The Manuscripts of Shrewsbury and Coventry Corporations [Etc] Fourth Report*, Appendix: Part X (London, 1899), 120.
[87] *The York House Books, 1461–1490*, 2 vols., ed. Lorraine Attreed (Stroud, 1991) ii, 521.

than it had been for either Henry IV or Edward IV. The first Lancastrian and Yorkist parliaments addressed the issue of unregulated retaining and livery distribution that were thought to have facilitated outbreaks of disorder, but there was an added concern at the start of Henry VII's reign, namely the first Tudor king's lack of a powerbase in England. While Henry IV and Edward IV had bases from which to draw their support, Henry VII spent his formative years in France and had little direct experience of the English polity.[88] More importantly, he had no natural affinity from which to draw the support that was necessary for the governing of the country. Several measures taken during his reign indicate a concern about maintaining a support base. An act passed at Henry's second parliament in 1487 imposed stricter penalties on royal tenants who were unlawfully retained and those who retained them. The reference to being unlawfully retained indicates that it was still possible to legally retain the king's tenants. The preamble stated that the act was passed because of the negligence and corruption of royal officials, which had contributed to many lawless acts and problems managing royal estates. Royal tenants who were illegally retained were to forfeit their copyhold.[89] In many respects, the act expanded ordinances made by Edward IV and Richard III forbidding illegal retaining within duchy of Lancaster lands to all of the king's lands. Yet the situation in 1487 meant that the specific reasons for passing the act were twofold. First, the act sought better management of royal estates, presumably as a means of ensuring that they were profitable. Second, the act was intended to ensure Henry VII could rely on his own tenants to fight for him if he needed to face further rebellions. It was passed shortly after the Battle of Stoke, which reminded Henry of the precarious situation he was in as a usurper, attempting to ensure the loyalty of his new subjects. This precarious situation is suggested by the fact it was that the earl of Oxford's vanguard that did most of the fighting at Stoke with large sections of the Tudor army not actually engaging in any fighting.[90] Although the rebels struggled to recruit men from the north-east, they did manage to recruit one duchy official, Sir Edmund Hastings of Roxby, steward of Pickering, to their cause.[91] The military realities facing Henry, along with a desire to ensure the profitability of crown lands, were the motivation for the 1487 act. Stiffer penalties for those illegally retaining his tenants, and for the tenants themselves, were an attempt by Henry to shore up his support base and remind people of their obligations to him.

Henry VII took care to ensure that his tenants, particularly in the duchy of Lancaster, adhered to the statute. Between 13 March 1488 and 26 May 1501, Henry sent at least eleven letters to various duchy of Lancaster officials stating

---

[88] Griffiths and Thomas, *The Making of the Tudor Dynasty*, 85–98.
[89] *PROME*, xv, 375–6.
[90] Sean Cunningham, *Henry VII* (London, 2007), 58; Ross, *John de Vere*, 124.
[91] Pollard, *North-East England*, 375–8.

that only the king could retain them and that they were not to retain others illegally, which implicitly referred to this act.[92] For instance, in a letter to the steward of his lordship of Sutton in Lincolnshire on 16 February 1489 Henry stated that all his estate officials and their deputies were to inform him and his counsel of instances of illegal retaining 'uppon payne of forfator of oure offices'.[93] This was part of a broader policy of ensuring the loyalty of duchy officials which was also evident in two oaths recorded around Easter 1497 taken by various duchy of Lancaster officials stating that they would only be retained by the king, the queen 'or my lord prince'.[94] Such oaths indicate that obligations of loyalty extended beyond Henry VII to the royal family more generally. Henry's letter to the steward of Pontefract in 1492 stated that the king's tenants could only be retained 'with us and oure derest sonne the prince', a reference to his eldest son Arthur.[95] Although aged only five in 1492 Arthur was set up in his own household at Ludlow, far away from the centres of royal power, where he may have been vulnerable if Henry faced rebellion.[96] Henry VII extended this policy to his second son. Attached to patent roll for the duchy of Lancaster for Henry VII's reign is an oath for unspecified persons, presumably duchy officials, that they owed their service 'unto Henry duke of York the kinges second son to serve the king at all tymes for the conserucaion of his peax and defence of this his roialme'.[97] The document is undated but sewn in the roll between various entries from around May 1501, one year before Arthur died, when Henry was the second in line to the throne. The implication is that Henry VII was trying to ensure that his second son also built up an adequate support base.

Such records indicate that Henry VII's policy towards retaining at the time of the 1487 act was not simply concerned with indicting more men. Illegal livery and retaining were two of the reasons given for the passing of two further acts during Henry VII's reign, though neither act was a new livery law as such. The 1487 parliament, which passed an act about royal tenants, also passed the Star Chamber Act enabling six or seven councillors to determine certain cases including illegal livery and retaining.[98] Two remarkably similar bills, which were never merged into a single act, were presented to the 1495 parliament about unlawful assemblies and rioting, one from the Commons and one from the king. Both bills sought to address failure to enforce statutes relating to rioting and unlawful assemblies by allowing JPs to proceed by bills as well as indictments

---

[92] DL37/62 rott. 4, 5, 6d., 14, 17d., 19, 21, 30d., 41, 43, 42d. See Appendix 5.
[93] DL37/62 rot. 6d.
[94] DL5/3 fol. 152d.
[95] DL37/62 rot. 14d.
[96] Sean Cunningham, *Prince Arthur: The Tudor King Who Never Was* (Stroud, 2016), 62–82 passim.
[97] DL37/62 rot. 43 (attached to the roll).
[98] *PROME*, xv, 370.

against those accused of such crimes. The bill from the Commons placed illegal retaining as one of the causes of such rioting while the king's bill included illegal retaining in a host of crimes to be dealt with in this manner.[99] A further act passed against perjury in 1495 included unlawful retaining as one of the causes of that crime.[100] These acts did not redefine what was, and what was not, illegal but focused on the procedures by which the statutes were enforced. The specific emphasis in these bills echoes concerns about liveries a century earlier, about the corruption of justice. The key difference by the late fifteenth century was that the king was the person articulating this concern, which is particularly evident in 1495, when the Commons were concerned primarily with rioting and the king's remit was broader and included liveries. Furthermore, the emphasis in this legislation on corruptions of the legal system evident in royal bills is additional evidence that Henry VII did not simply view illegal retaining as a means of attacking the political power of his nobles.

Although Henry was keen to remind his subjects to adhere to the statutes from the start of his reign, there were no known cases for three years. The first known case during Henry VII's reign was in 1488 when nine esquires, two gentlemen, two yeomen, a canon and a shoemaker were indicted for receiving the livery of George Talbot, earl of Shrewsbury on 4 September 1488.[101] This was followed by twenty-one cases in 1489: fifteen in Warwickshire,[102] two in Norfolk,[103] two in Northamptonshire,[104] one in Hertfordshire[105] and one in Yorkshire.[106] The number of cases reduced to three in 1490,[107] but rose again to twenty-one in 1491.[108] After 1488, there was at least one case each year, with the exceptions of 1497 and 1506. The sustained enforcement was a clear change from previous reigns when the enforcement of statutes was more sporadic. In a letter to Viscount Wells on 16 February 1489 Henry boasted that 'we dayly execute … the penalte of our seid lawes in that behalf in euery part thorough this our reyme and entend to do so'.[109] From 1491 until the 1504 act the number of cases per annum remained lower than ten with the exception of 1499. During this period there was: one case in 1492;[110]

---

[99] *PROME*, xvi, 239–40, 245–7.
[100] *PROME*, xvi, 273–4.
[101] KB9/379 m. 5. The wording of the indictment is ambiguous as to whether or not the earl himself was indicted.
[102] KB29/119 rot. 10; KB29/120 rott. 1, 11–13, 16, 28.
[103] KB29/119 rott. 12, 14; KB29/120 rot. 13.
[104] KB29/120 rot. 3.
[105] KB29/119 rot. 17.
[106] KB29/119 rot. 18.
[107] KB29/120 rott. 15, 19, 28; KB29/121 rot. 2.
[108] KB29/121 rott. 11, 15–16, 24, 27–8; KB29/122 rott. 4–5, 7.
[109] DL37/62 rot 6d.
[110] KB29/123 rot. 5.

two in 1493;[111] two in 1494;[112] two in 1495;[113] one in 1496;[114] none in 1497; one in 1498;[115] 22 in 1499;[116] seven in 1500;[117] five in 1501;[118] three in 1502;[119] and five in 1503.[120] There were not large clusters of politically sensitive cases at this time. Instead, the law was enforced more consistently than in previous reigns.

The final parliament of Henry VII's reign witnessed the most far-reaching legislation on retaining.[121] The 1504 act built on precedents built up since 1390 and, like all legislation, attempted to ensure more prosecutions via a combination of stricter definitions of the rules, more varied methods of enforcement, financial incentives for informers and punishment for those failing to enforce the statutes. It began by confirming all previous statutes on the matter and declaring that they were to be upheld. Like the 1468 act, any existing indentures that contravened the act were declared void. The act was to take effect from 'after Whitsun next' (26 May 1504) and was to last only for the life of the king. In a further attack on those retaining and being retained illegally, fines were made more severe. Fines now took account of how long the illegal retaining had been occurring. The fine for illegally giving livery was set at 100s. per each person illegally retained for every month that they were retained illegally. Similarly, those who were illegally retained were given the severe penalty of 100s. for each month that they had been retained or worn the livery that they were not entitled to. These larger fines were part of Henry VII's broader policy of maximising his legitimate profits from the legal system.

In addition, the statute covered those pretending to be retained by a lord or buying the livery of a lord when they were not his servant. This addressed the problem of former servants continuing to wear their old lord's livery after being dismissed from his or her service and using it as a shield against various crimes, as well as the problem of people making their own livery for the same purposes which repeated a clause from the 1429 act. To ensure that the statutes were enforced, the law was extended to punish local justices and juries who failed to convict those breaking the terms of the statute by fining them £10 every time that 'such jurer be sworne'. Concealing evidence or giving false evidence likewise resulted in a fine of 6s. 8d. or imprisonment. At the centre, the chancellor or

---

[111] KB29/123 rott. 22–3; KB29/124 rot. 13.
[112] KB29/125 rot. 6.
[113] KB29/126 rot. 4.
[114] KB29/127 rot. 7.
[115] KB29/129 rot. 2.
[116] CHES25/18 mm. 7–9, 11–14, 17, 21, 26, 28, 33–4; KB29/129 rot. 22.
[117] KB29/130 rott. 14, 16; KB29/131 rott. 2–3.
[118] KB29/131 rott. 15, 19–20.
[119] KB29/132 rot. 33.
[120] KB29/133 rot. 27.
[121] For the next three paragraphs see: *PROME*, xvi, 365–7.

keeper of the privy seal was allowed to hear cases in the Star Chamber. The intention was presumably to make it easier to prosecute members of the peerage when they were illegally retaining large groups of men who could potentially overawe sessions of the local court and intimidate local jurors and justices of the peace. As was the case with earlier acts, informers were to be rewarded, although rather than promising half of the fine they were to have a 'resonable reward'. Any costs incurred by an informer were to be recouped from the person convicted. This clause was part of Henry VII's wider fiscal policy, which attempted to bring more money into the crown via the legal system.[122] The lack of precision over the amount due to an informer permitted the crown to keep a higher share of the original fine. The informer's overall amount of money would not have been affected if they could gain enough money from the person prosecuted who would, effectively have ended up being fined even more money for illegally retaining.

The 1504 act was not an attack on noble power or an attempt to end bastard feudalism. Although penalties had become stricter and there was a greater incentive to inform on illegal retaining, the act permitted certain nobles to expand their affinities as a means of bolstering the crown's support base. The act states that no one was to retain by any means 'other then suche as he giffeth houshold wages unto without fraude or colour, or that he be his manuell servaunt or his officer or man lerned in the <one> lawe or in the othe'. It was therefore perfectly legitimate to retain as many people as one wanted, provided they fitted within one of those categories. Mervyn James suggested that Henry, fifth earl of Northumberland, simply increased the number of estate officials he had in order to remain within the terms of the statutes.[123] The act further stated that the law was not to apply to those who 'by the vertue of the kynges plagart or writyng signed with his hand and sealed with his prevy seale or signet, shall take, appoynt or indent with any persons to do and <to> be in a redynes to do the kyng service in warre, or otherwyse at his commaundment'. Therefore, nobles could increase the size of their affinities as long as the king permitted it by giving them a licence. There are only two known licences from Henry VII's reign: one for the king's mother, Margaret Beaufort, alongside a pardon for illegal retaining[124] and one for Sir Thomas Lovell permitting him to retain 1,365 men.[125] Lovell's finances are

---

[122] See e.g. Cavill, *English Parliaments of Henry VII*, 92–100.
[123] Mervyn James, *Society, Politics and Culture: Studies in Early Modern England* (Cambridge, 1986), 51.
[124] KB27/976 rex rot. 3.
[125] HMC, *Report 24: Manuscripts of His Grace the Duke of Rutland*, iv (1908), 559–66. Steven Gunn, 'Sir Thomas Lovell (c.1449–1524): A New Man for a New Monarchy?' in *The End of the Middle Ages? England in the Fifteenth and Sixteenth Centuries*, ed. John L. Watts (Stroud, 1998), 119 n. 12 and Cameron, 'Giving of Livery and Retaining', 24, both note that this is the only known extant list of retainers under the 1504 act.

likely to have been insufficient to enable legal retaining of men on a permanent basis on this scale, as the previous statutes demanded. It has been speculated that close associates of Henry VII such as the earl of Oxford as well as Edmund Dudley and Richard Empson must have been in possession of a licence that is now lost.[126] The 1504 act gave the crown more scope for controlling retaining within England because it enabled the crown to build up the affinities of trusted royal servants, thus avoiding them being legally retained by those whom the crown distrusted. By increasing the fines for illegal retaining and introducing more stringent methods of enforcement it was also part of a broader strategy by Henry VII to maximise the crown's profits from penal statutes and the legal system.

The 1504 act produced another upsurge in the number of cases, with fifty-one cases occurring between 1504 and the death of Henry VII in 1509.[127] The average number of cases per annum also increased at this point. There are ninety-eight known cases between 1488 and 1503, giving an average of 6.13 cases per annum. In contrast, there are fifty-two known cases between 1504 and 1509, which gives an average of 8.7 cases per annum. These figures, however, remain low and indictments for illegal livery were not a common feature of many quarter sessions. The real change after the 1504 act was passed which differentiated this cluster from earlier clusters was the geographic diversity of cases. Earlier clusters normally had many cases in one area with miscellaneous cases in other counties. Most cases after 1504 were in two counties, Yorkshire and Cambridgeshire, in which many cases were concentrated in 1504–5, fourteen in Yorkshire[128] and thirteen in Cambridgeshire.[129] However, there are a large number of cases from various other counties. Thirteen further cases from 1505 can be identified over eight counties: Sussex,[130] Berkshire,[131] Derbyshire,[132] Hampshire,[133] Staffordshire[134] Hertfordshire,[135] Huntingdonshire[136] and Worcestershire.[137] After the initial cluster of cases, eleven more occurred during Henry VII's reign: four in 1507 spread

---

[126] Steven Gunn, 'The Accession of Henry VIII', *Historical Research*, lxvi (1991), 286; Ross, *John de Vere*, 142.
[127] Cavill, *English Parliaments of Henry VII*, 77–8.
[128] KB29/134 rott. 26–7; KB29/135 rot. 12.
[129] KB9/436 mm. 9, 13–14, 42.
[130] KB29/135 rot. 6.
[131] KB9/436 m. 16.
[132] KB9/437 m. 17.
[133] KB9/436 mm. 13; KB29/135 rot. 13.
[134] KB29/135 rot. 10.
[135] KB29/135 rot. 11.
[136] KB9/436 m. 8.
[137] KB29/135 rott. 12, 20.

across Kent,[138] Sussex[139] and Hertfordshire;[140] and seven in 1508 spread across Yorkshire,[141] Berkshire[142], Hertfordshire,[143] Bedfordshire,[144] Shropshire[145] and Wiltshire.[146] Included in these cases are the two indictments against George Neville, Lord Bergavenny from 1507 for illegally retaining 471 men. It was the final years of Henry VII's reign that witnessed the most sustained and rigorous enforcement of the statutes of livery. The upsurge in cases immediately after the 1504 act, along with the act itself ,marked the reign of Henry VII as the most important for the regulation of retaining and the enforcement of the statutes.

Henry VIII's Early Years

The 1504 legislation was only to last for the life of Henry VII. When illegal retaining was prosecuted during the early years of Henry VIII's reign the 1504 act was not cited. For instance, two husbandmen in Rutland were indicted in 1510 for illegally wearing the livery of the earl of Surrey under the 1429 act rather than the 1504 act which also prohibited this practice.[147] The 1504 act no longer carried legal weight, but the clause that those in receipt of a licence could retain beyond the accepted categories seems to have remained in practice as licences to retain survive from the rest of the sixteenth century.[148] The most likely reason for this is that such licences were permitted and acceptable for years before the 1504 and that the act had formalised the existing lawful practices.

The young Henry VIII and his council were keen to ensure that statutes continued to be upheld. After hearing that men had started illegal retaining in the guise of preparing themselves for a possible French invasion, Henry VIII issued a proclamation against illegal retaining on 3 July 1511.[149] Enforcement early in Henry VIII's reign followed a similar pattern to the later years of Henry VII's reign. During the first three years of Henry VII's reign eight cases can be identified,

---

[138] KB29/136 rott. 16–17.
[139] KB29/137 rot. 1.
[140] KB29/137 rot. 1.
[141] KB29/137 rot. 17.
[142] KB29/137 rot. 36; KB9/444 m. 80.
[143] KB29/137 rot. 27.
[144] KB29/137 rot. 27.
[145] KB29/137 rot. 36.
[146] KB29/138 rot. 5.
[147] KB27/1013 rex rot. 8.
[148] For surviving licences see: HRO, 5M53/150; Dunham, *Lord Hastings' Indentured Retainers*, 67–89; Bean, *From Lord to Patron*, 148–57. A list of those given licences during the reign of Queen Mary and the early years of Elizabeth I survives in: BL, Lansdowne, 14, fol. 2.
[149] *Tudor Royal Proclamations*, i, no 62.

over a wide geographical range in the town of Nottingham and the counties of Northamptonshire, Rutland, Yorkshire (all in 1510), Hampshire (1511) and Kent (1512).[150] It was four years until the next cases in 1516 when four members of the peerage were indicted: George Neville, Lord Bergavenny was again indicted in Kent for illegally retaining eighty-five men;[151] the earl of Arundel in Sussex;[152] and the Marquis of Dorset and Lord Hastings (created earl of Huntingdon in 1529) in Leicestershire.[153] The following year there were twenty-two cases of illegal retaining in Worcestershire and Gloucestershire against members of the Savage family who were prominent in those counties[154] and a further case in Herefordshire in 1518.[155] A few months before this cluster of cases started in Leicester in 1516 Thomas Wolsey was appointed lord chancellor in December 1515. Central to Wolsey's law enforcement policy was the view that the law was to be applied to everyone regardless of economic or social position. He ordered the assize justices to report about 'misdemeanours' they encountered: 'that is to say, who be retainers or oppressors or maintainers of wrongful causes'.[156] If Wolsey's words were to be taken seriously it was necessary for him to show early in his chancellorship that he would indict peers who committed crimes. The illegal retaining of the four peers in 1516, along with other disturbances carried out by the marquess of Dorset and Lord Hastings[157] at this time, gave Wolsey the necessary opportunity.

The latter history of retaining laws is obscure and, given the sporadic nature of enforcement, the number of cases is impossible to estimate. Writs were issued to six men from Norfolk in 1522 ordering them to appear to answer charges of illegal livery, which are the only instances of illegal livery recorded in the King's Bench between 1518 and 1530.[158] Retaining and the distribution of liveries continued throughout the Tudor period and later Tudor monarchs were concerned about the problems associated with retaining.[159] Royal procla-

---

[150] KB29/140 rott. 26, 31; KB29/142 rott. 7, 24; KB29/143 rott. 24, 41; KB29/143 rot. 23.
[151] KB29/148 rott. 17–18.
[152] KB29/148 rott. 12, 40.
[153] KB29/148 rot. 16.
[154] KB29/148 rott. 50–1, 53–4.
[155] KB29/150 rott. 21–2.
[156] John A. Guy, 'Wolsey and the Tudor Polity' in *Cardinal Wolsey: Church, State and Art*, eds. Steven J. Gunn and Philip G. Lindley (Cambridge, 1991), 70–2, citing Henry E. Huntingdon Library, Ellesmere MS 2655, fol. 13; Peter Gwyn, *The King's Cardinal: The Rise and Fall of Thomas Wolsey* (London, 1991), 130.
[157] KB29/148 rot. 23.
[158] KB29/154 rot. 32.
[159] See in particular: Simon Adams, 'Baronial Contexts? Continuity and Change in the Noble Affinity, 1400–1600' in *The End of the Middle Ages? England in the Fifteenth and Sixteenth Centuries*, ed. John L. Watts (Stroud, 1995), 155–98; J.P. Cooper, 'Retainers in Tudor England' in *Land, Men and Beliefs: Studies in Early-Modern*

mations were made by Elizabeth I regarding the enforcement of the statutes of retaining in 1572 and 1583.[160] The continued importance of the nobility for the functioning of local government meant that retaining was still a key facet of political life in early modern England and therefore the crown still kept an eye on the practice. James I referred to unlawful retaining twice in his instructions to the President and Council of the North in June 1603, and again to the giving of liveries to the king's tenants in his instructions to the President and Council of Wales in 1617.[161] Despite this apparent interest in Jacobean England, in 1628 parliament repealed the statutes, apparently with little or no discussion.[162] By this time, it is likely that the statutes themselves had fallen into disuse or were no longer considered necessary.

History, eds. G.E Aylmer and J.S. Morrill (London, 1983), 78–96; Peter Roberts, 'Elizabethan Players and Minstrels and the Legislation of 1572 against Retainers and Vagabonds' in *Religion, Culture and Society in Early Modern Britain*, eds. Anthony Fletcher and Peter Roberts (Cambridge, 1994), 29–55.

[160] *Tudor Royal Proclamations*, ii, nos. 582, 664.

[161] *Select Statutes and other Constitutional Documents Illustrative of the Reigns of Elizabeth and James I*, ed. G.W. Prothero, 4th edition (Oxford, 1919), 377, 382, 386.

[162] *Stat. Realm*, v, 27–30.

4

Outcomes and Enforcement

In a discussion between the justices at Blackfriars soon after Henry VII's first parliament in 1485, chief justice William Hussey stated that 'the law would never be carried out properly until the lords spiritual and temporal are of one mind for the love and fear they have of God, or the king, or both, to carry them out effectively'. Hussey then recalled that when he was an attorney during Edward IV's reign, various lords had sworn in Star Chamber not to illegally retain but that less than an hour later he witnessed lords retaining men 'by oath, and swearing, and doing other things contrary to the above mentioned promises and oaths'.[1] If accurate, the report suggests that many of the problems related to the enforcement of the law already examined were recognised by contemporaries. The law was enforced sporadically but a fuller understanding of the effectiveness of the statutes needs to account for how cases were, or were not, resolved. This chapter therefore explore the outcomes and the legal processes of the cases to develop a fuller understanding of the enforcement of the statutes.

Who Heard the Cases?

Ninety-nine cases are known from *oyer et terminer* files, while the rest in the King's Bench were presumably initiated by local JPs. In theory, *oyer et terminer* commissions had the advantage that they imported into a locality powerful nobles and judges who were independent of the county's internal power structures, making them 'the most powerful instrument the king possessed'.[2] Such commissions either arose from a private request or were initiated by the crown after reports of disorder in a particular county or counties. Yet some commissions of *oyer et terminer* could be biased in favour of a certain faction within the county. John Watts has stated that '*oyer et terminer* commissions to local notables were entirely ineffective as a means of asserting central authority' because 'most of the commissioners with muscle were already belligerents; those without were soon drawn in'.[3] Not all commissions of *oyer et terminer*, however, were one-sided affairs. The Staffordshire cases of 1414 arose from a commission resulting from

[1]   *EHD*, v, 532–3.
[2]   J.G. Bellamy, *Crime and Public Order in England in the Later Middle Ages* (London, 1973), 99.
[3]   Watts, *Henry VI and the Politics of Kingship*, 301.

parliamentary petitions from both Hugh Erdeswyk and Edmund Ferrers about the lawless activities of the other. The subsequent indictments against Ferrers, Erdeswyk, their retainers and others in the county were a result of their own complaints.[4] In contrast, the cases that arose in Derbyshire in 1468 came from a crown initiative caused by Edward IV's 'alarm' at the violence occurring in the county after the murder of Roger Vernon. The incident prompted Edward to issue a powerful *oyer et terminer* commission that included the king's two brothers, the dukes of Clarence and Gloucester, earl Rivers and the earl of Warwick.[5]

JPs, in contrast, were drawn primarily from the local gentry, although peers were given commissions that were normally honorific. JPs were embedded within the county where they heard cases and were part of the wider political and social structures of the county, hearing a wide range of cases of illegal livery. JPs were normally drawn from the gentry and rarely had the clout to indict those of a higher rank. Consequently, peers were normally indicted by commissions of *oyer et terminer*, particularly before the reign of Henry VII. One notable exception was Edward Broke, Lord Cobham, who was indicted by the local JPs in Kent in 1456.[6] The reign of Henry VII marked a change in this respect as local justices indicted peers such as John Grey, Lord Wilton[7] and Edward Grey, Viscount Lisle.[8] Lord Bergavenny's indictment by local justices for illegally retaining 471 men almost certainly enjoyed royal backing.[9] In addition to the indictments of peers, the fifteen cases of illegal livery in Warwickshire in 1489 were identified by JPs, in contrast to an *oyer et terminer* commission in the county two years earlier that yielded no cases of illegal livery.[10] In this instance a writ from Henry VII to the local JPs and other prominent gentry to investigate instances of lawlessness, rioting and illegal livery in the county must have given the local justices the confidence to indict these men.[11] In this respect Henry VII's reign differed from earlier reigns because larger clusters of cases were also brought up by local JPs as opposed to *oyer et terminer* commissions, which is indicative of the more wide-ranging enforcement of law during that reign.

It was not just royal influence, however, that encouraged the enforcement of the statutes by local sessions of the peace. Thomas Savage, archbishop of York, heard cases of illegal livery in early May 1504 in which men were fraudulently wearing the livery of Henry Percy, fifth earl of Northumberland and various other

---

4   'Extracts from the Plea Rolls of the Reigns of Henry V and Henry VI', 3–4; KB9/113 mm. 2, 11, 28, 40–3.
5   *CPR, 1467–1477*, 69–70; Hicks, '1468 Statute of Livery', 18
6   KB27/808 rex rot 36. See also p. 000.
7   KB9/417 m. 119.
8   KB27/912 rex rot. 4.
9   KB27/985 rex rott. 7–8.
10   KB9/380 m. 41. For the earlier commission see: KB9/138.
11   KB9/380 m. 45.

lords.[12] Later that month, on 23 May 1504, a brawl occurred at Fulford between servants of the earl of Northumberland and the archbishop of York which was the culmination of a local rivalry between the two factions. R.W. Hoyle has stated that although 'the earl *was* able to intimidate the archbishop through the use of force, the latter was able to strike at the earl through indictments'.[13] This is a clear interest of local politics and interests influencing the enforcement of the statutes in a particular locality.

The involvement of bishops and archbishops in hearing cases of illegal retaining was part of their role in local government. Archbishop Savage was involved in the prosecution of other cases of illegal retaining in Yorkshire at this time. An entry in Henry VII's household books states that on 22 July 1504 'tharchbisshope of yorke sent a rolle of parchment by master magnus wherin er compiled certyrn endictments made aygents master Stanley concerning his reteyndors'.[14] The indictment is probably that against Sir Edward Stanley for illegal retaining in Yorkshire at this time.[15] Around this time Savage, although not officially Lord President of the Council of the North, had assumed a position very similar to the position that came into being later in the sixteenth century.[16] As archbishop of York, Savage was the prominent ecclesiastical lord in the north of England and was expected to take part in the enforcement of the law. A similar example of a prominent cleric hearing cases of illegal livery came from Hampshire in 1505 when Richard Fox, bishop of Winchester, took the unusual step of personally attending the quarter session that indicted Sir William Sandys for illegal livery and other crimes related to feuding with the Lisle family, which indicated 'the gravity of the event'.[17] The Hampshire bench was dominated by the bishop of Winchester but, like many great lords, it was unusual for him to attend in person. Instead the bench was staffed by lawyers who were usually 'the bishop's hand-picked servants'.[18] A bishop or an archbishop attending a quarter session in person was as significant as a duke or an earl attending in person, and thus indicates the seriousness of the cases against Sandys and Stanley.

By Henry VIII's reign, commissions of *oyer et terminer* were no longer the most effective means of prosecuting illegal livery as other mechanisms were being developed. In 1516, Cardinal Wolsey ordered Lord Hastings and the marquis of Dorset to appear before him in Star Chamber to answer charges of

---

[12] KB9/434 mm. 18, 20–2.
[13] R.W. Hoyle, 'The Earl, the Archbishop and the Council: The Affray at Fulford, May 1504' in *Rulers and Ruled in Late Medieval England*, eds. Rowena E. Archer and Simon Walker (London, 1995), 239–56, quotation on 245; E163/9/27.
[14] BL, Add MS. 21,480 fol. 189.
[15] KB29/134 rot. 26.
[16] Rachel R. Reid, *The King's Council in the North* (London, 1921), 85.
[17] KB9/436 m. 16; Luckett, 'Crown Office and Licensed Retinues', 231.
[18] J.R. Lander, *English Justices of the Peace, 1461–1509* (Gloucester, 1989), 159.

illegal retaining, which was part of his attempts to deal with disorder and 'demonstrate an even-handed application of justice'.[19] In 1519 a case against the Welsh knight Sir William Griffith was heard in Star Chamber as part of a broader attack on Griffith's abuses connected to his dominance in north Wales at this time.[20] The case related to events in north Wales which did not return indictments to King's Bench, meaning that this mechanism was not open to Charles Brandon, duke of Suffolk, when he was trying to reform the government of the region at this time. Commissions of *oyer et terminer* were an opportunity to deal with local disorders and indict leading men of the county for several crimes, including illegal livery. Henry VII's reign, while continuing to have cases of illegal livery arising from commissions of *oyer et terminer*, witnessed more cases arising from ordinary sessions of the peace.[21]

Outcomes

Resolving legal cases during the middle ages was an arduous task and most cases were never fully resolved. Outcomes can only be identified for 1,057 of the 3,733[22] occasions on which people were indicted for illegal livery (28.3 per cent). The biggest barrier to resolving a case was getting people to appear before the King's Bench. Some cases could take decades to be resolved and the *coram rege rolls* contain an abundant corpus of returned writs from sheriffs stating that the accused had not appeared. An extreme example is that of Thomas Shirwood, gentleman, of Coventry. During Michaelmas 20 Edward IV a writ was sent out ordering him to appear before the local justices to respond to charges of illegal livery.[23] Seven writs were returned by the local sheriffs between 1 Richard III Easter and 15 Henry VII Trinity stating that Shirwood had not appeared.[24] The

---

[19] Mary L. Robertson, 'Court Careers and County Quarrels: George Lord Hastings and Leicestershire Unrest, 1509–1529' in *State, Sovereign and Society in Early Modern England*, eds. Charles Carlton and Arthur Joseph Slavin (Stroud, 1998), 158–9; KB27/1021 rex rott. 22–3; KB29/148 rot. 16; *L&P*, ii, no. 2018.

[20] STAC2/28/76. For context see: Steven Gunn, 'The Regime of Charles, Duke of Suffolk, in North Wales and the Reform of Welsh Government, 1509–25', *Welsh History Review*, xii (1985), 470–8.

[21] E.g. Surrey in 1491: KB9/390 mm. 44,47, 52–3.

[22] It should be noted that included in this figure are the 476 men indicted in Cheshire. The palatinate of Cheshire does not have an equivalent to the controlment rolls that provide evidence of things such as outlawry.

[23] KB29/110 rot. 17.

[24] 1 Richard III Easter – KB27/891 rex rot. 20; 2 Henry VII Easter – KB27/903 rex rot. 6; 6 Henry VII Easter – KB27/ 919 rex rot. 25; 8 Henry VII Trinity – KB27/928 rex rot. 11; 11 Henry VII Michaelmas – KB27/ 937 rex rot. 20; 13 Henry VII Hilary – KB27/946 rex rot. 9; 15 Henry VII Trinity – KB27/956 rex rot. 12.

case was never resolved and Shirwood was outlawed. Other cases were resolved after many years. For instance, in 1511 the Yorkshire knight Sir Thomas Darcy obtained a pardon for an indictment from 1500, for giving livery illegally to ten men at Templehurst on 4 July 1498.[25]

In many cases, only some of the men involved obtained a pardon, or were fined, as evident in the indictment against Thomas Waryn of Brook in Hampshire, esquire, for giving illegal livery to four men at Brook on 31 March 1452. Two writs of *venire facias*, one in 34 Henry VI Michaelmas[26] and the following Hilary,[27] illustrate the difficulty involved in compelling indicted men to appear in court. The initial writ stated that Waryn had been outlawed, but the second writ states that he was eventually pardoned. Only three of the five men involved appeared in court several years later. Waryn appeared before the King's Bench on 8 February 1456 to obtain his pardon[28] while two of the men who took his livery, William Martindale, a merchant from Newport[29] and John Jaye, a husbandman from Brook, appeared two years later on 18 April 1458 with a pardon.[30] In addition to illegal livery, Waryn was indicted for several assaults in August 1455 along with various unknown others.[31] Given that Waryn had illegally distributed livery three years before committing the assaults and that he only retained four men illegally while being accused of committing various crimes with between seven and ten unknown others, it is impossible to say if any, all or some of those illegally retained were involved in Waryn's other illegal activities. The implication is that Waryn only sued for a pardon for illegal livery after he was indicted for more serious crimes.

Those who distributed the liveries or fees were more likely to take the initiative to bring their case to a resolution, usually by obtaining a pardon. When William Birmingham was indicted in Staffordshire in 1414 for illegally giving livery to one carpenter and two yeomen at Easter 1413,[32] he obtained a pardon whereas those who received the livery never had their case resolved.[33] Walter Blount, Lord Mountjoy, was indicted in 1468 for giving illegal livery to ten men,[34] yet only one of those men, John Bonnington, esquire, obtained a pardon[35]

[25] KB27/1002 rex rot. 13; KB29/130 rot. 14.
[26] KB29/86 rot. 1.
[27] KB29/86 rot. 11.
[28] KB27/779 rex rot. 23.
[29] KB27/788 rex rot. 7.
[30] KB27/788 rex rot. 2..
[31] KB27/779 rex rot. 23.
[32] KB9/113 m. 11.
[33] KB27/617 rex rot. 18.
[34] KB9/13 m. 22.
[35] KB27/830 rex rot. 47.

in addition to Blount.[36] The same pattern was evident in Henry VII's reign when the acts were enforced with more vigour. Sir William Lucy was indicted in Warwickshire in 1489 for giving illegal livery to three yeomen,[37] only one of whom, John Somerlane of Warwick, also obtained a pardon.[38] In these two cases the men who received illegal livery obtained their pardon after those who had given them liveries. In the case of Somerlane, who obtained his pardon in 1499, it was a decade after Sir William Lucy. There were, of course, exceptions to this trend. Indictments against Sir Thomas Cokesey, Edward Grey and Robert Throgmorton, for illegal livery in Warwickshire, in 1489, were settled within a year of the original indictments, with those who received illegal livery also obtaining pardons.[39] However, these cases were rare, even within this cluster, since some cases were not resolved at all or took a longer time to be resolved, such as that against Thomas Shukburgh, esquire, in 1489, which was not resolved until 1497.[40] It was usually those distributing the livery, rather than those receiving it, who were more proactive in obtaining a resolution to their indictment.

Cases that involved members of the peerage illegally retaining large numbers of men tended to be resolved relatively quickly. George Neville, Lord Bergavenny, was indicted in Hilary 22 Henry VII 1507 for illegally retaining[41] and his fine was recorded in the rolls for Michaelmas the following year.[42] The recent imprisonment of Edmund de la Pole, earl of Suffolk, and Henry VII's dynastic concerns after the death of Prince Arthur suggest wider problems and concerns about the security of the Tudor dynasty. Consequently, any powerful magnate with a large retinue comprising many illegal retainers that could easily turn into a private army aroused government suspicions.[43] Edward Grey, Viscount Lisle, who was indicted in 1489 was also pardoned soon after, along with the two husbandmen and two yeomen who were accused of receiving illegal livery from him.[44] In contrast, the cases against John Grey, Lord Wilton petered out, although some of the men in receipt of their livery obtained a pardon.[45] The vast majority of cases, however, did not involve the peerage illegally distributing fees and/or livery to

---

[36] KB27/831 rex rot. 13.
[37] KB9/380 m. 41B.
[38] KB27/913 rex rot. 20; KB27/928 rex rot. 3; KB27/951 rex rot. 5.
[39] The three indictments are found at: KB9/380 m. 41. For Cokesey's pardon see: KB27/913 rex rot. 19. For Grey's pardon see: KB27/912 rex rot. 4. For Throgmorton's pardon see: KB27/913 rex rot. 18.
[40] KB9/380 m. 41B; KB27/942 rex rot. 27.
[41] KB29/136 rott. 16–17.
[42] KB27/985 rex rott. 7–8.
[43] Cameron, 'The Giving of Livery and Retaining', 31–3.
[44] KB27/912 rex rot. 4.
[45] KB27/952 rex rot. 7.

yeomen. Instead, they involved members of the gentry illegally retaining, or giving livery to, a small number of men of a lower rank.

Others were acquitted because of insufficient evidence and because legal technicalities, such as poorly drafted indictments, could see a case being thrown out of court. This happened in the case against Hugh Peshale, esquire, in Shropshire, for illegally giving livery to fourteen men on 10 August 1476. Those accused promptly appeared in court after being indicted and through their attorney stated that the indictment was insufficient in law, since it failed to state the quantity of livery given to them.[46] Indictments in Worcestershire in 1501 against Robert Throgmorton[47] and in Surrey in 1491[48] were similarly thrown out for being insufficient. These instances were, however, rare. Unless prompted by other concerns, most indictments were ignored and therefore the accused was less likely to go to the trouble and expense of having their indictment declared insufficient in law.

There was one case in which the fragmented documentation suggests that parliamentary activity may have encouraged someone to seek a resolution to an outstanding indictment. In 1457 the Dorset 'courtholder' Simon Raule was indicted for giving illegal livery to a labourer but did not obtain a pardon for the offence until Trinity term 1468, a few months after the passing of the 1468 statute of livery.[49] This case seems to be unusual because it may have been resolved on the prompting of a new statute being introduced. The likely reason for this is that parliamentary activity and cases did not match up neatly for there to be any evident correlation between the two. Nevertheless, the fact that in this case the person in question waited eleven years to obtain a pardon suggests that the new act was influential in his decision making.

Pardons

There were 392 pardons for illegal livery recorded in the records of the King's Bench. Pardons were widely available and could be obtained for virtually any crime, regardless of its severity, because clemency and forgiveness were integral to the operation of law and the conception of royal justice. General pardons, in particular, were a useful tool to help enhance the aura and authority of a king. Helen Lacey has argued that 'the strategic issue of a general pardon allowed the political community to symbolise reconciliation and demonstrate their support

---

[46] KB27/865 rex rot. 2. See also Dunham, *Lord Hastings' Indentured Retainers*, 83–4, 146–7.
[47] KB29/131 rot. 15.
[48] KB29/121 rot. 27.
[49] KB27/829 rex rott. 6, 13; KB29/88 rot. 35; *PROME*, xiii, 384–6.

for the regime'.[50] Pardons were also a source of revenue since a fee of 18s. 4d. needed to be paid to Chancery to obtain a copy of a pardon,[51] which was cheaper than the majority of fines prescribed by various statutes. Nearly 3,000 people bought copies of the general pardon issued by Henry VIII at his accession within the first year of his reign with a further 300 purchasing pardons over the following three years.[52] Pardons therefore needed to be wide-ranging and include as many crimes as possible, including illegal livery or retaining. Politically, a wide-ranging pardon could encourage more people to obtain them, and thus acknowledge the legitimacy of the sovereign.

General pardons possessed significant political symbolism and therefore needed to cover a wide range of crimes to allow as many people to acknowledge the king's authority as possible. At the parliament summoned for November 1414 a general pardon specifically for illegal livery that occurred before 8 December 1414 was issued.[53] This coincided with the first significant wave of enforcement of the statutes that year in Staffordshire and Shropshire. In October 1416 this pardon was extended until Michaelmas 1417.[54] General pardons were meant to symbolically usher in a new era, such as the general pardon of 1437 which occurred at the parliament that marked the end of Henry VI's minority.[55] In theory, this was when the young king was supposed to begin taking active control of government. The pardon, however, only covered offences up to 21 September 1431, five and a half years prior to the pardon being issued.[56] In this instance the pardon only covered older crimes, which ensured that any recent crimes could be prosecuted. The general pardon of 1455 included illegal livery.[57] Again, it was at a time when the government was attempting to signify a new era of reconciliation, this time between the Lancastrian and Yorkist factions in the aftermath of the First Battle of St Albans. Reconciliation was the key aspect of a general pardon and thus the more crimes included the more people that could partake in this process. The clearest example of this comes from the final days of Henry VII's reign, when the dying king offered a general pardon to his subjects in order to help ease the transition of power to his young son.[58] The pardon, however, was only to last

---

[50] Helen Lacey, *The Royal Pardon: Access to Mercy in Fourteenth-Century England* (York, 2009), 92.
[51] Paul Cavill, 'The Enforcement of the Penal Statutes in the 1490s: Some New Evidence', *Historical Research*, lxxxii (2009), 486.
[52] Kesselring, *Mercy and Authority*, 58, 69. Figures produced from C67/56–61.
[53] *PROME*, ix, 80–1.
[54] *PROME*, ix, 181–2.
[55] Ibid., xi, 220–2. A copy of this pardon survives in the archives of the city of Exeter: HMC, *Report of the Records of the City of Exeter* (London, 1916), 9.
[56] *PROME*, xi, 220–2.
[57] Ibid., xii, 346–7.
[58] Gunn, 'Accession of Henry VIII', 281.

for the life of the king, and the new king, Henry VIII, promptly issued a new, more wide-ranging general pardon that included 'all unlawful retainers'.[59] The general pardon helped Henry VIII rehabilitate those who had fallen foul of royal government during the latter years of Henry VII's reign, demonstrating a clear break from the old unpopular regime.[60]

Pardons were also given in return for military service. The first occasion was during Edward I's Gascon campaign in 1294.[61] Although controversial in the fourteenth century as it was thought to condone criminal behaviour, it was used throughout the Hundred Years' War by several kings, for instance Edward III who used the process to increase his naval strength.[62] Several pardons issued during Henry V's reign for illegal livery also had a clear military dimension, such as the pardon to Thomas Stanley, who was indicted for giving livery illegally to thirteen men in Staffordshire.[63] The king was 'informed that the said Thomas gave livery to no other purpose than to serve the king's kinsman the earl of Warwick and cross with him on the king's service to the town of Calais' and consequently pardoned him.[64] Similarly, Edward Powell argued that Henry V's letter to his chief justice ordering the pardon of William and John Mynors for various offences in Staffordshire was a display of favour to them. William Mynor even went on to serve with Henry V at Agincourt and therefore the pardons were part of Henry's wider process of reconciliation and law enforcement in the years prior to his French campaigns.[65] John Mynors had been indicted for illegal livery in Staffordshire in 1414[66] but neither Henry's letter to his chief justice, on 6 June 1414, nor the pardon produced by the Mynors mentioned illegal livery.[67] The pardon was presumably for all offences that Mynors had committed.

Not every instance in which illegal livery was included in a pardon equated to an indictment for illegal livery as several pardons include illegal livery, yet

---

[59] *Tudor Royal Proclamations*, i, 81–3.
[60] Helen Miller, *Henry VIII and the English Nobility* (Oxford, 1986), 7–9.
[61] Lacey, *Royal Pardon*, 100.
[62] Craig L. Lambert, *Shipping in the Medieval Military: English Maritime Logistics in the Fourteenth Century* (Woodbridge, 2011), 16–18. See also: W.M. Ormrod, *Edward III* (London, 2011), 106, 218, 250, 264, 380; Nicholas A. Gribit, *Henry of Lancaster's Expedition to Aquitaine, 1345–46: Military Service and Professionalism in the Hundred Years War* (Woodbridge, 2016), 46–8.
[63] KB9/113 mm. 11, 41.
[64] *CPR, 1413-1416*, 403.
[65] Powell, *Kingship, Law and Society*, 213–14.
[66] KB9/113 m. 42.
[67] KB27/612 rex rot. 24. KB145/5/2/1, unnumbered document. The writ is torn with most of the left-hand side missing but the absence of any mention of illegal livery in the pardon suggests that was not included in the original writ. The two men who took his livery failed to appear in court in Hilary 1416 which is the last record of the case: KB27/619 rex rot. 9.

no case is known. For instance, a letter patent dated 19 February 1452 pardoned James, earl of Wiltshire, for 'all trespasses, offences, misprisions, contempts and impeachments against the statutes of liveries prior to 20 December [1451]'.[68] Despite this pardon, there is no evidence that the earl of Wiltshire was indicted for illegal livery. Eighteen pardons recorded in the patent rolls between 1452 and 1461 included illegal livery as one of the crimes committed, although those pardoned are not known to have been indicted.[69] Such practices were common at this time. For instance, the general pardon given in the wake of Jack Cade's Revolt in 1450 was purchased by many not involved in the revolt but who procured a pardon for legal protection in other crimes, though not illegal livery.[70] The reason for this is that 'for many, the purchase of a pardon might have been regarded as protection against malicious accusation[s] which never in fact materialised'.[71]

The pardon for Margaret Beaufort is illustrative of the fact that pardons did not necessarily mean that an offence had been committed. Henry VII had enrolled in the *coram rege rolls* for 20 Henry VII Trinity a signet letter in which he pardoned his mother, Margaret Beaufort, for any offences against the statutes of livery, and permitted her to continue retaining as she was.[72] Unlike licences given to others, there was no limit on the number of people she was permitted to retain.[73] Michael Jones and Malcolm Underwood only refer to the letter as a licence for the king's mother to retain whomever she saw fit to retain.[74] Clearly this was a licence to retain, but this is only one aspect of the document's significance. There were indictments in Cambridgeshire and Huntingdonshire during Hilary 1505 against men fraudulently wearing Margaret Beaufort's livery.[75] Although the case was only against the gentleman Robert Mace for wearing Margaret's livery and not against Margaret for distributing it, the signet letter pardoning Margaret must be

---

[68] *CPR, 1446–52*, 525.
[69] *CPR, 1452–1461*, 17, 110–12, 469, 478, 485, 498, 537, 540, 545, 569, 575, 599, 625, 628, 629, 633. It should also be noted that two of the pardons cover the same person, Edmund Blake, usher of the chamber, on 13 September 1458 and 10 February 1459 respectively: *CPR, 1452–1461*, 469, 478. For a later example see Richard Haye, who was pardoned by Henry VII for his involvement in rebellion in Warwickshire and Worcestershire. Illegal livery was included in his pardon, although he was never indicted for illegal livery: KB27/909 rex rot. 20.
[70] Griffiths, *Henry VI*, 619–23. On the composition of this pardon roll see: I.M.W. Harvey, *Jack Cade's Rebellion of 1450* (Oxford, 1991), 192–9.
[71] Lacey, *The Royal Pardon*, 91.
[72] KB27/976 rex rot. 3.
[73] A licence from 1540 permitted Thomas Wrothesley to retain up to forty men. Presumably, it would have been an offence for him to retain more; HRO, 5M53/150.
[74] Michael K. Jones and Malcolm G. Underwood, *The King's Mother: Lady Margaret Beaufort, Countess of Richmond and Derby* (Cambridge, 1992), 81. The letter is, however, described as a pardon in: Ross, *John de Vere*, 142.
[75] KB9/436 mm. 8, 14.

regarded as additional protection against any, albeit unlikely, indictment against her. Margaret's licence to retain was dated 1 June 1505 at Richmond Palace, just a few months after the indictments in Cambridgeshire. Margaret Beaufort's pardon was a necessary formality to prevent any potential indictment, while the licence ensured that there could never be a case against her.

As well as individuals, urban and clerical communities obtained general pardons which must have been intended to cover the entire community. Pardons which included illegal livery were obtained by civic governments and survive within local civic records such as those given to the city of Carlisle in 1425 and the mayor, bailiffs and commonality of Exeter in 1437 which included offences against the statutes of livery.[76] In 1416 the mayor, bailiffs and community of Lancaster obtained a general pardon granted for breaches of the statutes of livery.[77] The Dean and Chapter of Wells ensured they obtained general pardons which included offences against the statutes of livery in 1415, 1437, 1458 and 1468.[78]

Pardoning was integral to the late medieval legal system. The fact that many of the cases of illegal livery ended with a pardon is therefore unsurprising. This is not to say, however, that no one was ever prosecuted, found guilty and punished by the medieval legal system. Many cases went to King's Bench because those indicted wanted them moved to a higher court in order to obtain a pardon, a verdict that could only be overturned by an act of parliament.[79] Coupled with the fact that few indictments ever reached a resolution, it is clear that in many instances people were able to ignore their indictments for illegal livery. They only obtained pardons due to pressure from the legal system or as a safeguard against future, potentially burdensome fines and indictments.

Outlawries

Another possible outcome of an indictment of illegal retaining was that the accused was outlawed. Outlawry was supposed to happen after someone accused of a crime failed to appear at four successive county courts, a process that normally took between six and twelve months. In theory, the consequences were severe with the outlawed person having no legal protections, their goods confiscated and facing the death penalty if captured. In practice, however, the

[76] CRO, Ca1/8; HMC, 'The City of Exeter: Commissions, Pardons etc.' in *Report On the Records of the City of Exeter* (London, 1916), 9.
[77] *A History of the County of Lancaster: Volume* 8, eds. William Farrer and J. Brownbill (London, 1914), 43.
[78] HMC, 'Liber Albus II: Fols. 172–200' in *Calendar of the Manuscripts of the Dean and Chapter of Wells: Volume 1* (London, 1907), 404–5, 407, 424.
[79] Blatcher, *Court of the King's Bench*, 1.

system was slow, complex and prone to abuse or inefficiency from local officials, and by the fifteenth century many of those outlawed were able to function in society without hindrance. Outlawry had become 'an empty sanction' that failed to compel people to appear in court.[80] It has been suggested that 'by the later fifteenth century to be outlawed was much less of a calamity than it had been a century before'.[81] The figures relating to illegal livery in many ways confirm this picture as 430 men indicted for illegal livery were outlawed.

There was a significant regional variation in where such men were outlawed, with 184 out of 430 coming from Yorkshire. A further 110 came from Shropshire, forty-five were from Suffolk and twenty-three were from Surrey. The remaining seventy-two came from thirteen other counties. The fact that Yorkshire had the largest number of men who were outlawed is unsurprising considering the large number of cases that occurred in Yorkshire and the size of the county. The fact that this constituted 55.9 per cent of the men indicted in Yorkshire is indicative of the fact that most of the Yorkshire cases, and also most of the outlawries, occurred during the reign of Henry VII. The cases that occurred in Yorkshire in 1504 resulted in seventy-nine men being declared outlaws[82] but others not outlawed obtained pardons soon after.[83] The number of outlawries in this case happened after the retaining act of 1504 when the statutes were enforced with greater vigour. The 1504 act increased the scale of outlawries in Yorkshire but earlier cases from the county that resulted in outlawries had a similar pattern to many cases in which pardons were obtained. Nine of the ten men given illegal livery by Sir Thomas Darcy in 1498 were outlawed, although Darcy himself obtained a pardon in 1511.[84] Similar examples can be found elsewhere: five yeomen given illegal livery at Rowner by Henry Bruyn, who was later pardoned, in January 1451 were outlawed[85] and six yeomen in Herefordshire were outlawed in 1491.[86]

These examples highlight a further point, namely that it was predominantly those of lower social standing who received illegal livery that were outlawed. Out of the 430 men outlawed for illegal livery, thirty-one were from the gentry: one knight, Sir William Littleton,[87] eight esquires and twenty-two gentlemen. This equates to approximately 5.5 per cent of those knights, esquires and gentlemen indicted for illegal livery. In contrast, approximately 7.2 per cent of yeomen indicted for illegal livery (145 out of 2,025) were outlawed. Members of the

[80] A.J. Pollard, *Imagining Robin Hood: The Late Medieval Stories in Historical Context* (London and New York, 2004), 105–6.
[81] Bellamy, *Crime and Public Order*, 105.
[82] KB29/134 rott. 26–7.
[83] KB27/976 rex rot. 8; KB27/988 rex rot. 19.
[84] KB27/1002 rex rot. 13; KB29/130 rot. 14.
[85] KB29/83 rot. 2; KB29/93 rot. 10.
[86] KB29/122 rot. 7.
[87] KB29/135 rot. 20.

gentry were more likely to get their case resolved via the purchase of a pardon. One reason may be financial, since they were wealthier, but general pardons were relatively inexpensive and most yeomen could have afforded one if they so wished. Another plausible explanation is that the gentry were the main target of prosecution and the various legal activities they engaged in meant that they could not afford politically, economically and socially to be outlawed to the same extent that yeomen could.

Outlawries for illegal livery can almost entirely be identified for cases that began during the reigns of Edward IV (194, which averages at 8.8 per year) and Henry VII (210, which averages at 8.75 per year), with the other outlawries occurring in Henry VI's reign (twenty-two, which averages at 0.6 per year) and the first decade of Henry VIII's reign (twenty-two, which averages at 2.2 per year). The fact that Henry VII's reign witnessed the highest number of outlawries for illegal livery is unsurprising given the king's rigorous attempts to have the statutes enforced. However, those indicted in Edward IV's reign, which had fewer cases, were more likely to be indicted. Many of the early cases during the reign of Edward IV resulted in outlawries, many against those receiving illegal livery such as in Kent in 1462,[88] Worcestershire in 1463[89] and Surrey in 1466.[90] The largest case during the reign of Edward IV, however, came from Shropshire in 1480. Out of the 117 men indicted for illegal livery in Shropshire in 1480, 110 are recorded on the controlment roll as being outlawed.[91] The remaining seven, including Gilbert Talbot, esquire, who distributed the livery, obtained a pardon in 1488.[92] It should also be noted that the reigns of Edward IV and Henry VII had approximately the same number of outlawries per annum. Therefore, the legal system during Edward IV's reign was more likely to outlaw someone indicted for illegal retaining than it was under Henry VII. In regard to outlawries, Edward IV's government was as efficient in enforcing the statutes as Henry VII's government.

Fines

Fines were an unusual outcome in many late medieval legal cases. For instance, only one out of 704 people indicted in the Midlands in 1414 for rape, larcenery, robbery, arson and burglary is known to have paid a fine.[93] The 10s. fine paid by Richard Dyne, yeoman of Maidstone, in Hilary term 1463 after an indictment

---

[88] KB29/92 rot. 13.
[89] KB29/94 rott. 1, 6.
[90] KB29/98 rott. 8, 19–20.
[91] KB29/110 rot. 16.
[92] KB27/908 rex rot. 19.
[93] Powell, *Kingship, Law and Society*, 279.

for illegal livery during Michaelmas term 1461 is a rare example of someone paying a fine. Dyne was the only one of the ten men in receipt of illegal livery from Edward, Lord Cobham, to pay such a fine.[94] Bringing criminals to heel, particularly those of considerable social standing or those with powerful patrons, was an arduous and at times impossible task. The legal system needed to work within these limitations. 'A careful monarch, such as Henry VII', Marjorie Blatcher noted, 'could take steps to make some pardons more expensive, at least to procure, and thereby more nearly approximate to a fitting punishment for the wrong-doing which they erased.'[95] The rate at which pardons were purchased for illegal livery changed little during the period under examination, although the number of cases and the number of persons indicted did increase, particularly during the reign of Henry VII. Fines were not necessary in many cases because the payment of a pardon constituted an acceptable financial penalty for the crime committed, even if the penalty was not as severe as the law prescribed. Pardons needed to be purchased and that was the means by which someone was financially penalised for illegal livery.

Many of the fines known to have been paid were by those indicted by commission of *oyer et terminer*, which tended to pick up the more serious or politically sensitive cases. During Michaelmas term 1415, seventeen men who were illegally given livery by Edmund Ferrers at Christmas 1413 paid fines of 40s. to the King's Bench.[96] Similarly, the *oyer et terminer* commission in Herefordshire in 1457 produced several fines. Three men who illegally received livery from Hugh Shirley at Leominster paid fines of 5s. during Trinity 35 Henry VI,[97] although Shirley himself obtained a pardon during the previous legal term.[98] An entry in the patent rolls indicates that at least two men who received illegal livery from Sir Walter Devereux paid their fine. On 8 November 1459 Robert Chambre, page of the King's buttery, was granted 'two sums of 40s' that had been forfeited by Robert Cook, husbandman, and William Aldern, yeoman, for illegally receiving a gown of livery from Sir Walter Devereux.[99] There may have been many unidentified fines paid to sheriffs, JPs or town courts that were recorded in the now lost records of local government. For instance, fines for thirteen men from York for receiving illegal liveries can be found in the city's chamberlain's accounts for 1455, in connection with indictments relating to the Percy–Neville feud.[100] However, this is the only known instance of such

[94] KB27/807, fines; KB27/808 rex rot. 36.
[95] Blatcher, *Court of King's Bench*, 84.
[96] KB27/618 fines. For the original indictment see: KB9/113 m. 41.
[97] KB27/785 fines. For the original indictment see: KB9/35 m. 6.
[98] KB27/784 rex rot. 18; *CPR, 1452–1461*, 353.
[99] *CPR, 1452–1461*, 530–1.
[100] *York City Chamberlain's Account Rolls, 1396–1500*, ed. R.B. Dobson, Surtees Society, cxcii (1980 for 1978/9), 87–8.

payments being made. The fact that most people obtained either pardons or no resolution can be identified for their case implies that the laws were not enforced stringently enough to compel people into paying fines. That the payment of fines is evident in the 1414 Staffordshire cases and those in Herefordshire in 1457 is a product of the politicised nature of those cases. The Staffordshire cases occurred as part of Henry V's campaign against lawlessness in the localities. The indictments had themselves come about after complaints in parliament by Ferrers and Erdswyke about violence being perpetrated on them by the other's affinity. The Herefordshire cases were linked with both local disorder and, more importantly, Lancastrian–Yorkist quarrels during the 1450s and therefore there were no guaranteed immediate pardons.

It was Henry VII's reign that witnessed the most prominent fines for illegal retaining. Successive acts had increased the severity of fines including the 1504 act which set a fine of 100s. per person illegally retained.[101] The largest known fine was against James Stanley, bishop of Ely, who was fined £145,610 for illegal retaining while his retainers were fined £58,644 between them.[102] Sean Cunningham noted that this 'impossibly large fine' permitted Henry VII to 'load the leading Stanleys and their chief servants with recognisances and obligations that kept more swingeing fines at bay'.[103] A similar tactic was evident in the fine of £70,650 issued to George Neville, Lord Bergavenny in 1507[104] 'which no one at the time could possibly have paid' and meant that 'bargaining began'.[105] Henry's measures against Bergavenny were punitive, as the fine was far greater than the capital value of all his English estates and he was never in possession of his Welsh marcher lordship of Abergavenny which left him 'at the king's mercy'.[106] Bergavenny was placed under several bonds in December 1507, one of which was for £5,000 and barred him from entering the counties of Kent, Surrey, Sussex and Hampshire without royal consent. A further bond for £5,000 obliged him to be 'true in his allegiance'. The almost unprecedented amount of Bergavenny's fine is implied in a bond in which Henry VII 'graciously contented at his suit for avoiding the extremity of the law to accept as parcel of the debt the sum of £5000 payable over ten years'; the bond was rather vague on the precise amount

---

[101] *PROME*, xvi, 365–6.

[102] *L&P Hen. VIII*, i, no. 309.

[103] Sean Cunningham, 'St Oswald's Priory, Nostell v Stanley: The Common Pleas of Lancaster, the Crown, and the Politics of the North-West in 1506' in *Foundations of Medieval Scholarship*, ed. Paul Brand (York, 2008), 153.

[104] KB27/985 fines, rex rott. 7–8.

[105] J.R. Lander, 'Bonds, Coercion and Fear', 344.

[106] T.B. Pugh, 'Henry VII and the English Nobility' in *The Tudor Nobility*, ed. G.W. Bernard (Manchester, 1992), 70. E36/214 fol. 263 records payments due on Candlemas 1508 from Bergavenny for his debts to the crown, which must have included his fine for illegal retaining.

of Bergavenny's fine, stating it was '£100,000 or thereabouts'.[107] These fines were not concerned with revenue raising, nor were they necessarily about punishing the offenders for past offences. Instead they were used to exert additional pressure on James Stanley and Lord Bergavenny by preventing any future breaches of the statutes, hence why they were placed under various bonds. In short, these large fines for illegal retaining were never expected to be paid in full but instead were used to erode the autonomy of potentially rebellious members of the nobility by placing them in debt to the crown and thus at the king's mercy. Henry VII used the retaining laws tactically to weaken, both politically and financially, those whom he distrusted.

The fines against James Stanley and Lord Bergavenny are indicative of Henry VII's hardening attitude towards the enhancement of private power by magnates whose loyalty was not fully trusted. After Henry VII's death Henry VIII began a process of reconciliation with members of the nobility and Bergavenny's fine was eventually cancelled after Henry VIII pardoned him and restored him to the royal council. Bergavenny later participated in Henry VIII's military expedition to France in 1513, being involved in the capture of Tournai.[108] Yet the policy was not uniform as no similar pardon seems to have been given to James Stanley. Henry VIII's regime did not relax the financial burdens previously placed on members of the nobility by Empson and Dudley, and in the early years of Henry VIII's reign the Stanley family as a whole still owed the crown substantial sums of money.[109]

Bonds

Fines were only one of many options kings had to control the behaviour of their richest subjects and indeed not necessarily the most efficient one, since a crime needed to be committed before a fine could be levied. One option was to place subjects under bonds which covered a wide range of stipulations ranging from specific offences to rather vague requirements of good behaviour, which became most apparent towards the end of Henry VII's reign.[110] This was not a Tudor innovation as Lancastrian and Yorkist kings made use of bonds and recognisances in order to curb aristocratic violence and ensure the good behaviour of their

---

[107] The three bonds are found on *CCR, 1500–1509*, no. 825.
[108] Hawkyard, 'George Neville', *ODNB*, xl, 495–7; *L&P Hen. VIII*, i, no. 438 [p. 234].
[109] Barry Coward, *The Stanleys, Lord Stanley and the Earls of Derby: The Origins, Wealth and Power of a Landowning Family*, Chetham Society, 3rd series, xxx (Manchester, 1983), 147–8.
[110] Cunningham, *Henry VII*, 215–23.

subjects.[111] Bonds were intended to be guarantees for future good behaviour as opposed to punishment for specific offences, and were effectively warnings to the individuals placed under such obligations. Illegal livery was one of many crimes for which Henry VII placed his subjects under bonds, although he was not the first king to warn specific subjects about their retaining practice. In 1403 Henry IV warned John, Lord Welles to stop distributing illegal liveries and Edward IV in 1476 ordered William Bryerton, knight, and John Daviport, esquire, not to retain any of the king's tenants.[112] Henry VII also wrote to some of his tenants directly to warn them not to illegally retain, including George Talbot, earl of Shrewsbury in 1501, along with the inhabitants of the honour of Tickhill.[113] Henry VII's bonds about retaining were more formal than those of his predecessors, including specified penalties. The earliest such example was in December 1488 when John Eggerton was bound under £300 not to be retained in any way.[114] Similarly, William Molyneux was placed under an obligation of £40 after being pardoned for illegal retaining.[115] Yet no indictments for either man for illegal retaining are known. Indeed, the records of the King's Bench indicate that many of those placed under bonds for illegal retaining had not been indicted for committing the offence before being placed under a bond.

One type of obligation that was placed on several subjects has been dubbed 'composite recognisances' which involved several individuals, all of whom faced financial penalties if just one person broke the terms of the agreement.[116] Several examples suggest that Henry VII used such bonds as part of his policy towards retaining.[117] Six gentlemen from Derbyshire were bound together on 3 July 1489 for £100 to be 'prepared to serve in the company of the seneschal of Tutbury and of no other' and not to act against the form of the statutes.[118] This has to refer to the 1487 act against retaining the king's tenants. Other bonds were limited in scope to a specific location such as the one made on 20 May 1490 between two dyers, a mercer and a draper, all from Beverley in Yorkshire, who were bound for

[111] J.R. Lander, 'Bonds, Coercion and Fear: Henry VII and the Peerage' in *Florilegium Historiale*, eds. J.G. Rowe and W.H. Stockdale (Toronto, 1971), 327–67.

[112] *CCR, 1402–1405*, 109; DL5/1 fol. 136.

[113] DL637/62 rot. 42. For a full list of similar letters see Appendix 5.

[114] C255/8/4 no. 119. I am grateful to Dr Sean Cunningham for sharing his unpublished calendar of this roll with me.

[115] BL, Lansdowne 127, fol. 43.

[116] Lander, 'Bonds, Coercion and Fear', 343.

[117] Sean Cunningham, 'The Establishment of the Tudor Regime: Henry VII, Rebellion and the Financial Control of the Aristocracy' (unpublished PhD thesis, Lancaster University, 1995), 107.

[118] *CCR, 1485–1500*, no. 386. The same men were placed under a similar bond a year later on 3 June 1490 – *CCR, 1485–1500*, no. 456.

£500 to take no liveries contrary to the law as long as they lived in Beverley.[119] Presumably, if any of these men moved elsewhere they were no longer financially liable under this bond and could only be fined the amount set out in the statutes. The bond between Sir Robert Cheyney and Roger Cheyney and Henry VII from January 1499 explicitly prohibited them from retaining anyone from Newbury or its lordship in Berkshire 'by word, sign, badge, or livery'.[120] There is no evidence that either man was indicted for distributing illegal livery. Moreover, the earliest case of illegal livery in Berkshire was in 1505.[121] Presumably, if either man illegally retained someone not from Newbury or its lordship in Berkshire then they would only be fined as per the statute. On 7 December 1506 Sir Piers Edgecombe was bound in a recognisance worth 1,000 marks with the earl of Devon that they 'would make noo retaynors contrarie to the statute'.[122] There is no evidence that either Edgecombe or the earl of Devon was ever indicted for illegal retaining. The purpose of many bonds was not to punish men for illegal retaining but to discourage future behaviour.

The specific reason behind the decision to place many under such bonds is difficult to decipher, as little context is given in the actual bonds themselves. One clear case in which the wider context allows such inferences comes from September 1491 when Henry VII placed two Herefordshire knights, Ralph Hakluyt and Thomas Cornewall, under two separate bonds of £500 each not to retain anyone from the town of Leominster.[123] The bonds were a response to wider gentry feuding in Herefordshire that stretched back to the 1480s. A riot in Leominster in June 1487 was connected to a dispute over the manor of Brymfield between Thomas Cornewall and Richard Croft, at that time steward of Leominster. Those placed under this bond were intimately bound up with this feuding. Richard Croft and his son Edward acted as guarantors for Hakluyt's bond while Cornewall had Henry VII's close ally Rys ap Thomas along with Thomas Vaughan as his guarantors. The need to deal with such feuding was exacerbated by the fact that the Welsh Marches was where Henry VII decided to set up a household and powerbase for his first-born son Arthur. Until such feuding could be curbed, the prince and his household would not be able to dominate the region.[124] This use of bonds was designed to address a particular problem of urban retaining in an area of the kingdom that was closely bound to Henry VII's long-term dynastic ambitions.

[119] *CCR, 1485–1500*, no. 492.
[120] *CCR, 1485–1500*, no. 1108.
[121] KB9/436 m. 16.
[122] BL, Lansdowne 127, fol. 34.
[123] C255/8/5 nos. 8–9.
[124] Cunningham, *Prince Arthur*, 93–101.

There were instances, however, in which someone's illegal retaining activities was why they were placed under a bond, such as Lord Bergavenny to ensure he paid his fine.[125] Others were placed under bonds to ensure their good behaviour after purchasing a pardon. Sir Edward Stanley, who was indicted for illegally retaining fifty-two men in Yorkshire in 1504, obtained a pardon on 23 March 1506 but was placed under an obligation of £200 by Edmund Dudley.[126] Members of the Stanley family were placed under several bonds and obligations by Henry VII in order to ensure their good behaviour.[127] Another placed under a similar agreement was Sir William Sandys, who was indicted for illegal retaining in Hilary 1505 and was bound in a recognisance with two other knights and a merchant on 1 October 1505.[128] Sandys was likely under some financial pressure when he was placed under this bond, as a rather terse entry in the records of the council learned in law for Easter 1505 noted that he was indebted to the crown by £24.[129] He eventually obtained a pardon in 1509 as part of the general pardon issued by Henry VIII at the start of his reign.[130] These are rare instances in which men were placed under bonds for illegal retaining after they had been indicted, as opposed to being bound to prevent future behaviour.

The use of bonds was a means by which Henry VII was able to exert pressure on his richest subjects. A similar mechanism used by Henry VII and his government was the council learned in law, which pursued the crown's rights and prosecuted various offences that may have ended in fines.[131] There was one known instance in which the council investigated an instance of illegal retaining. In Easter 1505 Peirs Newton was ordered by the council learned in law to provide details on 'divers enditements of reteynors ayenst the lord Dudley Sir John Savage [and] Sir Robert Thorgmerton'.[132] Cases of illegal retaining can be found against all three men. Sir John Savage was indicted in Worcester in 1502 for giving illegal livery to six men.[133] Robert Thorgmerton was indicted on two occasions before this: once in Worcestershire in 1502[134] and once in Warwickshire

---

[125] *CCR, 1500–1509*, no. 825. See above.
[126] BL, Lansdowne 127, fol. 17; KB29/134 rot. 26.
[127] E36/214 fol. 186, 226, 227, 246, 248.
[128] For the indictment see: KB9/436 m. 13. For the relevant bonds see: E36/214 fol. 189, 194–5.
[129] DL5/4 fol. 48.
[130] KB27/993 rex rot. 12.
[131] R. Somerville, 'Henry VII's "Council Learned in the Law"', *EHR*, liv (1939), 427–42; Steven Gunn, *Henry VII's New Men and The Making of Tudor England* (Oxford, 2016), 54, 80.
[132] DL5/4 fol. 53.
[133] KB29/132 rot. 33.
[134] KB29/131 rot. 15.

in 1489, although he had been pardoned for this offence by 1505.[135] These were recent cases and there is little evidence of an ulterior motive in pursuing the cases against Savage and Thorgmerton.

In contrast, the other case does suggest that this was part of a conscious policy by the council learned in law to purse revenues due to the crown from the legal system. In 1505, Edward Sutton, Lord Dudley, was indicted for giving illegal livery to a yeoman and a husbandman as far back as 1491.[136] He was also indicted for illegally retaining two further men at Dudley on 1 November 1504, soon after the passing of the 1504 act.[137] Lord Dudley was the cousin of the notorious Edmund Dudley, one of Henry VII's new men. According to Steven Gunn, Lord Dudley was one of the few members of the peerage with whom Edmund Dudley had any 'traction'.[138] The case was alluded to several years later by Edmund Dudley while imprisoned in the Tower of London. In August 1509 Edmund Dudley petitioned the young Henry VIII, listing all the men who had been harshly treated by Henry VII's government, with the various bonds and debts members of the nobility had been placed under. Among the complaints was one stating that 'the Lord Dudley payed 1000*li*: vpon a light surmyse'.[139] C.J. Harrison suggested that the order to provide further details of Dudley's retaining indictment may have been a veiled reason for the king to claim some of Lord Dudley's lands in 1506, for which Dudley paid the king £1,000.[140] Lord Dudley was not pardoned until Easter 1510, presumably taking advantage of the general pardon issued by Henry VIII at the start of his reign.[141] Lord Dudley was not illegally retaining a large number of men like Bergavenny and did not have the regional hegemony of the Stanleys. Therefore, the decision to pursue such a minor case for an offence committed fourteen years earlier, along with the more recent offence in 1504, should be viewed as an example of royal government's use of the law as a means of raising revenue towards the end Henry VII's life.[142]

---

[135] KB9/380 m. 41C; KB27/319 rex rot. 18.

[136] KB27/976 rex rot. 13.

[137] KB27/995 rex rot. 15.

[138] Gunn, *Henry VII's New Men*, 197; *The Complete Peerage of England, Scotland, Ireland, Great Britain and the United Kingdom*, ed. Vicary Gibbs, new edition, 6 vols. (London, 1910), ii, 480–1. For the most recent discussion of Edmund Dudley's actions towards the end of Henry VII's reign see: James Ross, '"Contrary to the Ryght and to the Order of the Lawe": New Evidence of Edmund Dudley's Activities on Behalf of Henry VII in 1504', *EHR*, cxxvii (2012), 24–45.

[139] C.J. Harrison, 'The Petition of Edmund Dudley', *EHR*, lxxxviii (1972), 88.

[140] Ibid., 93 n. 25. See also: BL, Lansdowne 127, fols. 19, 24.

[141] KB27/995 rex rot. 15.

[142] For the legal system in the last few years of Henry VII's reign see for example: Cunningham, *Henry VII*, 153–5; Thomas Penn, *Winter King: Henry VII and the Dawn of Tudor England* (London, 2011), 147–70, 261–82.

Royal Intervention

Another option open to the king in the legal process was to intervene in proceedings against someone. Instead of the accused appearing in court and producing a pardon, the king could instead issue a writ, usually under the privy seal, to his justices ordering them to cease the proceedings against the defendant.[143] These were not pardons, but rather a halt to the legal proceedings, which could be restarted at a later date if deemed necessary by the king. Henry VII exercised this option on the last day of his second parliament in 1487 when he reopened all of the cases suspended by Edward IV and Richard III 'for suche interest and profite as be longeth unto us'.[144] Henry VII did not object to this process as he issued similar writs himself, the earliest of which came after he reopened suspended cases related to a case of illegal livery. On 14 February 1488 Henry VII ordered the suspension of legal proceedings against three labourers, a miller and a tailor from Kent who were indicted by a commission of *oyer et terminer* in 1478 for receiving illegal livery from Walter Roberd of Cranbrook, esquire, on 4 December 1477.[145] Roberd himself had recently purchased a pardon and therefore did not require his case to be halted.[146] Such writs are examples of 'prerogative' instructions that Edmund Dudley later counselled against in *The Tree of Commonwealth* as these privy seal letters were used 'in stopping of justice'.[147] However, Dudley's criticism is an isolated example as the there is no evidence that others objected to this use of the royal prerogative which was used in several cases of illegal livery and retaining.

One key benefit of this process was that it was relatively quick and enabled the king to show favour to trusted servants. The personal nature of such a procedure is exemplified in Edward IV's letters to the chief justice of the King's Bench, dated 23 November 1468, which stopped proceedings against Sir William Brandon, and the six men alleged to have been in receipt of his livery, at Southwark on 10 July 1465.[148] Edward stated that Brandon and the men that he was alleged to have illegally retained had been wrongfully accused of illegal livery, and therefore proceedings against them were to cease.[149] The king clearly knew Brandon and was familiar with his practices, and was reported to have said to Brandon that

---

[143] This process is discussed in more detail in: Gordon McKelvie, 'Kingship and Good Lordship in Practice: Henry VII, the Earl of Oxford and the Case of John Hale (1487)', *Journal of Medieval History* xl (2019), 504–22.

[144] KB27/906 rex rot. 7; KB145/9/3 unnumbered document.

[145] KB145/9/3 unnumbered document. For the initial writ see: KB29/108 rot. 12.

[146] KB27/901 rex rot. 8.

[147] *The Tree of Commonwealth: A Treatise Written by Edmund Dudley*, ed. D.M. Brodie (Cambridge, 1948), 35. Also printed in *EHD*, v, 624.

[148] KB29/98 rot. 8; KB27/908 rex rot. 8.

[149] PSO1/33/1742.

'thou can beguile the duke of Norfolk' but 'thou shalt not do me so for I understand thy false dealing well enough'.[150] The letter was dated June 1469 when Edward IV was in East Anglia and six months after he had intervened on behalf of Brandon to prevent his prosecution for illegal livery. Brandon and his family were subsequently loyal servants to Edward IV, although he abandoned the Yorkist regime after Richard III's usurpation. He was indicted for seditious activities for treasonable words said against Richard III on 2 November 1484 and fought alongside Henry Tudor at Bosworth; his son was killed by Richard himself.[151] Previously, Brandon's son had been knighted by Edward IV and was attainted after being implicated in the duke of Buckingham's rising in October 1483, although Brandon himself was not attainted.[152] Yet Brandon's case highlights the temporary nature of such writs because fighting for Henry at Bosworth and losing a son did not necessarily protect him from future legal trouble. After Henry VII ordered his chief justice to resume all cases suspended by this mechanism Brandon obtained a pardon for illegal livery and his seditious activities during Richard III's reign.[153] Brandon was protecting himself from any future action because royal intervention was no absolute legal guarantee and could only last for the life of the king intervening.

The ability of this mechanism to help the king show favour to specific servants is evident in a privy seal writ dated 26 November 1471 which ordered the cessation of all processes against those indicted for taking the liveries of the dukes of Norfolk and Suffolk two years earlier.[154] During the Readeption, Norfolk had appeared before the King's Bench on 8 February 1471 along with Sir William Calthorp to obtain a pardon for their indictment for illegal livery[155] while Suffolk had appeared two days earlier to obtain a pardon.[156] However, both men aided Edward in regaining his throne, with *The Arrivall* reporting that Norfolk was one of the men who sat in judgement on the leading Lancastrians after the Battle of Barnet.[157] Michael Hicks has stated that the 'divers great consideracions' that caused these writs to be issued were clearly political and by that point the two dukes had proven themselves to be trustworthy servants.[158] Although the case

[150] *PL*, i, 544; Ross, *Edward IV*, 305–6.
[151] KB27/908 rex rot. 8; Ross, *Richard III*, 224.
[152] Josiah C. Wedgwood, *History of Parliament: Biographies of the Members of the Commons House, 1439–1509* (London, 1936), 102–3.
[153] KB27/908 rex rot. 8.
[154] KB145/7/11, unnumbered membrane.
[155] KB27/839 rex rot. 31.
[156] KB27/839 rex rot. 32.
[157] *Historie of the Arrivall of Edward IV in England and the Final Recouerye of his Kingdomes from Henry VI. A.D. M.CCC. LXXI.*, ed. John Bruce, Camden Society (London, 1838), 31.
[158] Hicks, '1468 Statute', 26.

against the two dukes had been resolved, the cases against those in receipt of their livery remained live.

Other writs halting cases of illegal livery were issued by Edward IV, two of which came from the cases from Derbyshire in 1468 which demonstrate a different way in which kings could employ this malleable legal mechanism. The first, dated 25 January 1469, regards the earl of Shrewsbury and twenty of the twenty-two men to whom he gave illegal livery[159] and states that Edward 'of oure grace espiall' ordered his chief justice to halt all procedures. The second, dated 3 February 1469, concerns John Pole, esquire who was one of the ten men indicted for receiving illegal livery from Walter Blount by the *oyer et terminer* commission at Derby in 1468, and orders a similar halt to proceedings.[160] Blount and one of the men he allegedly illegally retained, John Bonnington, esquire, had already appeared before the King's Bench to produce pardons for their offences.[161] In both writs Edward IV ordered his chief justice to stop proceedings 'unto suche tyme as shal pleas us'.[162] This was a clear attempt by Edward IV to ensure good behaviour of these men in the same manner that kings at this time employed other legal mechanisms like acts of attainder and resumption to manipulate the behaviour of their richest subjects.[163]

The use of such writs in the process of reconciliation was evident in the only occasion in which Henry VI is known to have ordered a halt to proceedings against someone indicted for illegal livery. On 11 August 1452 Henry VI issued a writ under his signet which ordered a halt to proceedings against Sir Walter Devereux.[164] The writ is brief, omits any elaborate address clauses and is much shorter than other similar writs, suggesting that it may have been drafted in haste, although what survives may only be a draft. Devereux's livery offence is not explicitly mentioned but instead the writ refers to all of the offences he had committed, including leading the Yorkist demonstrations in the city of Hereford which had triggered the commission. The *oyer et terminer* file thereafter contains pardons for those men who were illegally in receipt of Devereux's livery.[165] Halting the legal proceedings against Devereux was a quick means of reconciling members of the Yorkist affinity in the county with the Lancastrian government.

---

[159] KB9/13 m. 23. The two men named in the indictment but not in the letter are two yeomen of Bakewell, Derbyshire.

[160] KB9/13 m. 22.

[161] KB27/830 rex rot. 47; KB27/831 rex rot. 13.

[162] KB145/7/8. Note: the documents in this file are not numbered, although the writ regarding Pole does immediately follow the letter regarding Shrewsbury.

[163] Michael Hicks, 'Attainder, Resumption and Coercion, 1461–1529', *Parliamentary History*, iii (1984), 15–31.

[164] KB9/34/2 m. 33.

[165] KB9/34/2 mm. 34–8, 40. See Chapter 10 for a full discussion of these events.

Henry VII also interceded in the legal process in a writ to his chief justice on 15 November 1491 relating to a livery case in Surrey, which differs from other royal interventions in livery cases. The first difference is that the writ suspended proceedings against eleven men of a lower social status: three yeomen, three brewers, two tailors, one innholder, one smith and one skinner. These men, along with two other men, a yeoman and a tailor, were indicted by an *oyer et terminer* commission in Surrey, in 1491, for illegally wearing the livery of the earl of Arundel on 30 September 1490.[166] The second, and crucial, difference is the reason for Henry's intervention. Instead of stating that they had been wrongly accused, Henry stated that his chief justice was to halt proceedings because 'suche fynes as the said persones haue forfauted unto us in this partie been paied unto oure cofers'.[167] The two men who were not named in Henry VII's writ were pardoned because in the controlment roll entry for this case has the phrase '*sine die*' inserted above their names.[168] The relatively obscure status of these eleven men means that little else can be said about them with any certainty. In the context of Henry VII's reign, the fact that he diverted cash from his chief justice to his own coffers fits with the image of the avaricious Henry VII profiteering from the legal system.

Conclusion

These interventions in legal proceedings by kings highlight an apparent contradiction in the late medieval legal system: it was the king's duty to uphold justice in a manner that was not arbitrary but the king reserved final judgement on all legal cases that came before his courts. The process in which kings intervened in legal cases by issuing a privy seal writ to the chief justice was the malleable legal instrument that permitted them to reopen cases at a later date. In general, however, there were various options for the crown such as placing someone under a bond, allowing an individual to purchase a pardon or issuing general pardons. Henry VII used bonds regularly in his reign, though he was not the only king to issue specific warnings or adopt malleable legal instruments when livery or retaining cases arose. In many ways Henry VII adapted the methods employed by earlier kings, particularly Edward IV in the enforcement of the legislation. The main problem faced by the late medieval legal system was its inability to compel people to appear in court and therefore many cases were never resolved. For many of the cases discussed here an additional pressure needed to be placed

---

[166] KB9/390 m. 47.
[167] KB145/9/7 no. 95. Transcribed in: McKelvie, 'Legality of Bastard Feudalism', 213–14.
[168] KB29/121 rot. 27.

on the accused for them to have their case resolved. Such pressures ranged from political insecurity in the case of Lord Bergavnney to indictments for other acts of lawlessness as in the case of Thomas Waryn. The outcomes of the cases and the nature of the legal processes involved in bringing cases of illegal livery to a resolution, or failing to, are indicative of both the apparent inefficiencies of the late medieval legal system and the specific context of many of the cases.

5

The Identity of the Indicted

Although this book takes its core data from the records of the King's Bench, the potential of the material extends far beyond simply tracking levels of lawlessness and law enforcement. Legal records cannot be detached from the society that created them and therefore they are an indispensable source for understanding the structure of late medieval English society, which can be characterised as a 'bastard feudal' society. This book shares one of the professed aims of Andrew Spencer's recent study of earls during Edward I's reign, which was to 'perform a little historical necromancy' by reviving the use of the term bastard feudalism. Spencer noted that historians have used two definitions of bastard feudalism: a narrow definition in which bastard feudalism was the method by which nobles altered the way they obtained service by using grants of cash as opposed to the 'feudal' grant of land as rewards; and a broader definition in which the nobility dominated localities in a corrupt and intimidating manner.[1] The focus of this chapter is the narrow definition that views bastard feudalism as primarily a method of obtaining service.[2]

Studies of late medieval affinities have concentrated on the surviving private records, most notably indentures of retainer which K.B. McFarlane described as the 'peculiar instrument of bastard feudalism'.[3] The large corpus of surviving indentures of retainer from John of Gaunt in the late fourteenth century and William, Lord Hastings, during Edward IV's reign have enabled detailed studies of those particular affinities.[4] Others have identified the composition aristocratic affinities from a range of private estate papers such as valors, deeds and wills in conjunction with references in the records of central government.[5] Consequently, the topic has been approached from the perspective of those peers who retained men of local standing and prominence. Previous chapters have noted that the statutes permitted livery to be distributed by those below the level of the peerage, provided it was to family members, household servants, legal counsel and estate officials. There is, however, not the same richness in

[1]   Spencer, *Nobility and Kingship*, 100–9, quotation on 100.
[2]   A broadly similar definition is given in: Hicks, *Bastard Feudalism*, 1–4, 43–68.
[3]   McFarlane, 'Bastard Feudalism', 164.
[4]   Dunham, *Lord Hastings' Indentured Retainers*; Walker, *Lancastrian Affinity*.
[5]   Bean, *The Estates of the Percy Family*; Bean, *From Lord to Patron*; Carpenter, 'Beauchamp Affinity', 205–37; Cherry, 'The Courtenay Earls of Devon', 71–97; Hicks, *Clarence*; Johnson, *Duke Richard of York*; Ross, *John de Vere*; Carole Rawcliffe, *The Staffords*.

private estate records for the gentry compared to the peerage. This is in part an accident of survival and in part because the administrations of estates of the peerage were more sophisticated and on a larger scale. Consequently, these estates produced more documents and developed more sophisticated methods of record keeping. This makes indictments for illegal livery valuable sources for understanding the nature of social relationships because they provide an alternative perspective on bastard feudalism, as they predominantly focused on the retaining practices of the gentry who are less well documented than their counterparts in the peerage.

This chapter examines the social status and occupations of those indicted for illegally distributing livery and retaining fees as well as those in receipt. There were 3,733 occasions on which someone was indicted for illegal livery. This figure includes those who are counted on multiple occasions such as George Neville, Lord Bergavenny who was indicted in 1507[6] and 1516[7] and the Herefordshire knight Walter Devereux who was indicted in 1452[8] and 1457.[9] Identifying the social status of each person is simplified by the 1413 statute of additions which ensured that every person named in a legal document had to have their rank or occupation listed.[10] A consideration of the social status and occupations of those indicted for illegal livery casts a flood of light on the nature of bastard feudalism and demonstrates that the 'magnate–gentry' model based on the indenture of retainer only reveals one aspect of bastard feudal relations. Biographies of the Suffolk knight John Hopton and the Cheshire gentleman Humphrey Newton have shown how members of the gentry obtained service from those of a lower rank.[11] Yet the gentry's links with those of a lesser rank are rarely illuminated by private records. The records of the King's Bench afford a unique opportunity to examine these links. Exploring such links demonstrates why governments needed to permit those below the ranks of the peerage to retain men in order to ensure the proper operation of local government. Finally, an examination of those clergy, women and townsmen indicted demonstrates that bastard feudalism needs to be viewed in broader terms, not simply the traditional model that was focused on secular male peers.

---

[6] KB29/136 rott. 16–17.
[7] KB29/148 rott. 17–18.
[8] KB9/34/1 no. 5; KB9/34/2 no. 142.
[9] KB9/35 mm. 6, 69.
[10] *PROME*, ix, 20–1.
[11] Colin Richmond, *John Hopton: A Fifteenth Century Suffolk Gentleman* (Cambridge, 1981); Deborah Youngs, *Humphrey Newton (1466–1536): An Early English Gentleman* (Woodbridge, 2008), 78–81.

The Peerage

Twenty-two members of the peerage were indicted in the King's Bench for distributing illegal livery or retaining illegally between 1390 and 1520. This figure does not include those who were promoted to the peerage after their indictment for illegal livery, such as William Herbert, who was a knight when he was indicted in 1457 but was subsequently raised to the title of earl of Pembroke by Edward IV.[12] The first member of the peerage known to have admitted to distributing illegal livery was Henry Percy, the first earl of Northumberland. In the wake of the Battle of Shrewsbury, the earl pleaded for mercy in parliament in 1404 and stated that he had distributed livery to his followers during the Percy Revolt.[13] As this was a plea for mercy in parliament and not an official indictment in the King's Bench, it is not possible to know those in receipt of illegal livery from him. The first indictment in the King's Bench against a member of the peerage occurred in 1422 when a peeress, Elizabeth, Lady Neville, the daughter-in-law of Ralph, earl of Westmorland, was indicted.[14] In 1434 Henry, Lord Grey of Codnor, became the first male peer indicted in the King's Bench when he was accused of giving illegal livery to two knights, two esquires, three gentlemen, three yeomen and one smith.[15] Neither of these cases is connected to any desire from the crown or local law enforcement to curb the retaining practices of an entire class of society. Indeed, when the social status of those indicted for illegal livery is considered in its proper context, it is clear that this was never the intention of the statutes.

The importance of illegal retaining prosecutions against the peerage has been most extensively discussed for Henry VII's reign. Traditional interpretations emphasised the importance of the reign for reining in the independent power of private nobles, which enabled the expansion of royal, and by implication state, power under the Tudors.[16] For Henry VII's reign, there are ambiguities in the records of the King's Bench which make it difficult to provide an exact number of peers indicted for illegal livery. Two indictments that name the earl of Shrewsbury in 1488 and the earl of Northumberland in 1504 are unclear as to whether those earls were indicted or it was simply the people receiving their livery who were indicted. Most cases of illegal livery note that someone had given (*dedit*) liveries to a group of men. In contrast, the indictment that named the earl of Shrewsbury

---

[12] KB9/35 m. 69; Ralph Griffiths, 'William Herbert, First Earl of Pembroke (c.1423–1469)', *ODNB*, xxvi, 729–31.

[13] *PROME*, viii, 231–2.

[14] KB27/645 rex rot. 8; KB29/56 rot. 25d.

[15] KB9/11 m. 15.

[16] E.g. S.T. Bindoff, *Tudor England* (Harmondsworth, 1950), 29; Anthony Goodman, *The New Monarchy: England, 1471–1534* (Oxford, 1988), 52 – 'The larger aim of Henry VII's policy seems to have been to discipline the magnates'.

only stated that fifteen men received the earl's livery (*recepit*).[17] The indictment that named the earl of Northumberland listed twenty-seven men who had taken (*capitur*) the earl's livery without his permission against the form of the 1399 and 1401 statutes.[18] Neither earl was named in the respective writs of *venire facias* recorded in the controlment rolls, indicating that they were not ordered to appear before the local justices for any such offence.[19] In both cases they would have been breaking the law if they themselves distributed the livery. It may have been the case that one of their agents distributed the relevant liveries, but this would mean that the agent should have been indicted as opposed to the earl in question. There is no reference to any such agents in either of these indictments. Other indictments for illegal livery from this period name the earls of Derby, Essex, Northumberland and Oxford as well as the king's mother, Margaret Beaufort. In these cases the peers themselves were not indicted but others were indicted for wearing their livery despite not being members of their household or one of their permitted officials.[20] In such cases the peers in question were not named on writs of *venire facias* ordering them to appear before the local justices, indicating that they were not indicted themselves.[21] Therefore it is probable that none of those peers were themselves indicted for distributing illegal livery but rather people were indicted for wearing their livery.

The number of unambiguous indictments against peers for distributing illegal liveries shows that no king viewed the statutes as a weapon with which to break the independent power of the secular nobility. Three lords, John Grey, Lord Wilton,[22] George Neville, Lord Bergavenny[23] and Edward Sutton, Lord Dudley,[24] along with one viscount, Edward Grey, Viscount Lisle[25] were indicted for illegal livery during Henry VII's reign. This contrasts with two dukes[26], one earl[27] and six lords[28] who are known to have been indicted for illegal retaining during the reign of Edward IV's reign. Included in the figure for Edward IV's reign are two

---

[17] KB9/379 m. 5.
[18] KB9/434 m. 22.
[19] For Shrewsbury: KB29/119 rot. 2; for Northumberland: KB29/134 rot. 17.
[20] KB9/390 m. 47; KB9/434 mm. 18, 21; KB9/436 mm. 7–9, 14; KB27/925 rex rot. 6.
[21] KB29/121 rot. 27d; KB29/134 rott. 27d, 33.
[22] KB9/417 m. 119.
[23] KB29/133 rot. 27, KB29/136 rot.
[24] KB27/976 rex rot. 13; KB27/995 rex rot. 15; KB29/135 rot. 12
[25] KB27/912 rex rot. 4.
[26] Norfolk and Suffolk in 1470: KB29/99 rott. 31–2.
[27] John Talbot, third earl of Shrewsbury in 1468, KB9/13 mm. 26
[28] Edward Brooke, Lord Cobham in 1461, KB29/92 rot. 13; John, Lord Clinton of Ash in 1461, KB29/92 rot. 13; Edward Neville, Lord Bergavenny in 1461, KB29/92 rot.13; Walter Blount, Lord Mountjoy in 1468, KB9/13 mm. 11, 63; Henry, Lord Grey of Codnor in 1468, KB9/13 m. 20; John Brooke, Lord Cobham in 1478, KB29/108 rot. 12.

lords, Edward Neville, Lord Bergavenny and John, Lord Clinton of Ash, for whom there is only a writ of *venire facias* ordering them to appear before local justices about allegations of illegal livery, and not a full indictment detailing to whom they gave illegal livery along with where and when the act occurred.[29] In short, seven peers are known to have been indicted during Edward IV's reign and a further two were probably indicted. Similarly, more peers were indicted during the initial decade of Henry VIII's reign than that of Henry VII. The earls of Arundel and Huntingdon[30] were indicted along with the marquess of Dorset[31] and, once again, George Neville, Lord Bergavenny.[32] When the two widowed peeresses who were indicted during Henry VI's reign are counted then even his government, often viewed as lax in relation to the lawlessness of the aristocratic affinities, indicted more peers than Henry VII, with six in total, although Henry VI's reign was significantly longer.[33]

One reason why fewer peers were indicted during Henry VII's reign than his historical reputation suggests is the lack of adult males among the higher nobility during his reign. Henry VII became king after thirty years of intermittent civil war in which many peers, who 'were bound to get caught up in events more deeply than others', were killed.[34] For his first parliament in November 1485 Henry VII summed two dukes, ten earls, two viscounts and twenty barons, in total thirty-four out of the fifty-five temporal lords in England.[35] Of the twenty living barons four were minors while many were 'time-serving nonentities or political lightweights'.[36] By the end of Henry VII's reign there were forty-one noblemen in England, a reduction caused by a combination of natural extinction in the male line and Henry VII's reluctance to create new peers as Edward had done.[37] Put simply, there were fewer politically active peers during Henry VII's reign to commit illegal retaining. Yet this does not mean that Henry VII's government was reluctant to indict peers when they retained illegally. One of the most politically active, Lord Bergavenny, was indicted for illegally retaining 471 men.

---

[29] This was in the same writ as Edward Brooke, Lord Cobham – KB29/92 rot. 13. However, the record of the case in the *coram rege* rolls only refers to Cobham's illegal livery offence – KB27/808 rex rot. 36.

[30] KB29/148 rott. 12, 16 40.

[31] KB29/148 rot. 16.

[32] KB29/148 rot. 18.

[33] Elizabeth Neville in 1422 – KB29/56 rot. 25d; Henry, Lord Grey of Codnor, Ralph, Lord Cromwell and Joan Beauchamp in 1434; Thomas Percy, Lord Egremont in 1452 – KB9/148/2 mm. 31, 38, 54; James, Lord Audley in 1457 – KB9/35 m. 69.

[34] Colin Richmond, 'The Nobility and the Wars of the Roses', *Nottingham Medieval Studies*, xxi (1977), 83.

[35] *CCR, 1485–1500*, no. 57; Pugh, 'Henry VII and the English Nobility', 78, 106–10.

[36] Ross, *John de Vere*, 114–15.

[37] Pugh, 'Henry VII and the English Nobility', 78–9.

Furthermore, prominent local knights, who were later promoted to the peerage, were indicted for illegal livery during Henry VII's reign, such as Edward Stanley, later first baron Monteagle[38] and William Sandys, later Lord Sandys of Vyne as reward for his service to Henry VIII.[39] There were more indictments during Henry VII's reign but the overwhelming majority of those indicted for illegal retaining were members of the gentry. Henry VII was willing to have some of richest and most powerful subjects indicted but peers were not the main targets of the indictments for illegal retaining during his reign.

The indictments against most of these peers during the reigns of Henry VI, Edward IV and Henry VIII occurred at times when the peers in question were implicated in other instances of lawlessness. For instance, the dukes of Norfolk and Suffolk were indicted due to events surrounding the siege of Caister Castle and the uncertain loyalty of both dukes at that time.[40] George, Lord Hastings, and the marquise of Dorset were indicted in 1516 as part of a long-running feud between the two lords in the midlands.[41] Likewise, the indictments against peers during Henry VI's reign occurred in a context of more general local disorder. The indictments against Lord Egremont in Yorkshire[42] and Lord Audley in Herefordshire[43] during the 1450s were connected to the feuding in those counties during that decade. Two earlier indictments from Derbyshire against Lord Grey of Codnor and Lord Cromwell were part of a wide-ranging commission of *oyer et terminer* that indicted many of the prominent men of the county for various crimes. Joan Beauchamp, widow of William Beauchamp, was also indicted for illegal livery by the commission.[44]

Peers were indicted for distributing illegal livery at various points during the fifteenth and sixteenth centuries. It was not the case that the statutes of livery were used by Henry VII to victimise the peerage. The distribution of the indictments against peers indicates that the statutes regarding retaining should not be viewed as a means by which kings attacked the military or political power of the nobility. In fact the statutes left a wide range of methods by which nobles could retain men legally. Some nobles, such as Henry, fifth earl of Northumberland, were able to increase the number of estate officials they had in order to keep within the terms of the statutes.[45] This option was open to the nobility to a far greater extent than

[38] KB29/134 rot. 26; Gervase Phillips, 'Edward Stanley, First Baron Monteagle (c.1460–1523)', *ODNB*, lii, 174.
[39] KB9/436 m. 13; Ronald H. Fritze, 'William Sandys, First Baron Sandys (c.1470–1540)' *ODNB*, xlviii, 935–6.
[40] Hicks, '1468 Statute of Livery', 24–6.
[41] Robertson, 'Court Careers and County Quarrels', 153–70.
[42] KB9/148/2 mm. 31, 38, 54.
[43] KB9/35 m. 69.
[44] KB9/11 m. 15.
[45] James, *Society, Politics and Culture*, 51.

the gentry because of their greater individual wealth. Kings needed to utilise the wealth and resources of the nobility in order to reign successfully. For the king noble affinities were crucial for them being able to uphold their various duties and fulfil what was expected of them in terms of law and order and good governance, because 'England could not be governed without them'.[46]

Gentry and Peasants

It was members of the gentry who were most likely to be indicted for distributing illegal livery. There were eighty-four occasions on which a knight was indicted, seventy-eight occasions on which an esquire was indicted and forty-nine occasions on which a gentleman was indicted for distributing illegal liveries. The statutes consistently included various clauses which permitted livery to be given to household staff, estate officials, lawyers and family members. The number of indictments against the gentry for illegal retaining indicates that the gentry need to be thought of as potential bastard feudal lords as well as retainers of magnates. Rees Davies argued that it would be 'a distortion' to interpret the actions of magnate retainers simply in terms of their vertical relations to their lord since many of them were men of prominent standing in their own right.[47] The only surviving indenture of retainer in which a member of the gentry retained someone of a lower rank was made on 17 January 1468 when Thomas Sandforth, esquire, retained the yeoman William Bradley of Knipe for life.[48] Yet other sources show that members of the gentry acting as bastard feudal lords, at a lower level. Michael Hicks cited the example of William Plumpton, who as well as being a servant of the earls of Northumberland, had requests from many lower down the social scale for his good lordship.[49] Further examples of gentry lordship are evident in the accounts of the Cheshire gentleman Humphrey Newton, whose income placed him at the lower end of gentry society. Although his accounts make no mention of reeves, bailiffs, stewards or any other officials commonly recorded in the records of larger secular and ecclesiastical estates, they do show that he had a 'counsel' to assist him in drawing up his rentals and when property was transferred between tenants. His lack of a large administrative structure meant that 'a select few' of

[46] Sean Cunningham, 'Henry VII, Sir Thomas Butler and the Stanley Family: Regional Politics and the Assertion of Royal Influence in North Western England' in *Social Attitudes and Political Structures in the Fifteenth Century*, ed. Tim Thornton (Stroud, 2002), 241; Ross, 'A Governing Elite?', 95–115.
[47] R.R. Davies, *Lords and Lordship in the British Isles in the Middle Ages*, ed. Brendan Smith (Oxford, 2009), 210.
[48] 'Private Indentures', no. 149.
[49] Michael Hicks, *English Political Culture in the Fifteenth Century* (London, 2002), 141–2, 154–6.

his servants 'took on managerial' roles which in larger estates would have been specialised.[50] Proofs of age similarly indicate that gentry landowners retained servants for various purposes, some of whom even had their own council. The difference between the households, and broader groupings of servants that are best described as an 'affinity', was 'in numbers, not in functions'.[51] The statutes of livery and their resultant cases provide an additional glimpse into gentry lordship and indicate that it was perfectly legitimate for the gentry to retain, provided they adhered to the terms of the statutes.

As well as distributing illegal livery, members of the gentry were indicted for being in receipt of it. There were thirty occasions on which a knight was indicted for receiving illegal livery, 155 occasions on which an esquire was indicted for receiving illegal livery and 174 occasions on which a gentleman was indicted for receiving illegal livery. As would be expected from a society with an acute sense of social hierarchy and in which livery was a symbol of dependence, most people received illegal livery from someone of a higher social status. One exception to this general rule was in Warwickshire in 1489 when John Arden of Alspath, gentleman, was indicted for giving illegal livery to five men including a fellow gentleman, Henry Purfrey of Saltby.[52] Such exceptions aside, members of the gentry were normally indicted for receiving illegal livery from peers, as was the case when the dukes of Norfolk and Suffolk were indicted in 1470. Amongst those given illegal livery by John de la Pole, duke of Suffolk, were four knights, nine esquires and gentlemen[53] while John Mowbray, duke of Norfolk gave illegal livery to four knights, twenty-one esquires and one gentleman.[54] A similar pattern was evident in 1516 when George Hastings was indicted in Leicestershire for illegally retaining four knights, twenty-three esquires and seventeen gentlemen along with 141 other men whose rank or occupation was not recorded.[55] Thomas Grey, marquess of Dorset, was indicted at the same time for illegally retaining three knights, twenty esquires and six gentlemen along with 130 men whose status was not recorded.[56] The gradations within the gentry meant that members of the gentry illegally retained gentry of a lower rank, as would be expected. For instance, in Cheshire in 1428 Ralph Maynwarynge, esquire, was indicted for illegally retaining seven gentlemen

---

[50] Youngs, *Humphrey Newton*, 76–81.
[51] Michael Hicks, 'Retainer, Monks and Wine: Three Insights into Everyday Life' in *The Later Medieval Inquisitions Post Mortem: Mapping the Medieval Countryside and Rural Society*, ed. Michael Hicks (Woodbridge, 2016), 179–81.
[52] KB9/380 m. 41C.
[53] KB29/99 rott. 31–2.
[54] KB27/839 rex rot. 31; KB29//99 rot. 32.
[55] KB27/1021 rex rot 23; KB29/148 rot. 16.
[56] KB27/21 rex rot. 22; KB29/148 rot. 16.

along with twenty-three yeomen.[57] The gentry's place in the lower echelons of nobility while being men of prominent standing locally meant that they were both the receivers and distributors of illegal livery.

The vast majority of those indicted for receiving illegal livery were members of the peasantry. On 2,064 occasions a yeoman was indicted for being retained illegally while a husbandman was indicted on 121 occasions and a labourer on ninety occasions. There was one case in which a yeoman is known to have distributed illegal livery. In Staffordshire, in 1414, John Mynors of Uttoxeter gave illegal livery to two other yeomen.[58] John Mynors, along with his brothers William and Thomas, came from an old gentry family in Staffordshire that were part of the affinity of Thomas of Lancaster but had fallen into obscurity during the fourteenth century.[59] The Mynor family had fallen from membership of the gentry to membership of the sub-gentry class that historians have dubbed the 'middling sort' who formed the upper peasantry that worked with members of the gentry in various capacities. This 'middling sort' included the forty-shilling freeholders who were electors in parliamentary elections and served on local juries. These were the men who were members of Thomas Lovell's Oxfordshire affinity in the early sixteenth century and 'were bound into local circles of feoffees, witnesses and executors' with members of the gentry.[60] The indictment against Mynors highlights the fact that demarcations between certain ranks in society were somewhat artificial, even though such distinctions were recognised by contemporaries. Greater knights had incomes of over £100 per annum; lesser knights £40–100; esquires £20–39; gentlemen £10–19; and yeomen £5–9.[61] An esquire with an income of £20 per annum had more in common, in economic terms, with a gentleman on £19 per annum than with a fellow esquire on £39 per annum. This argument equally applies to the peasantry who, like the nobility, were not a homogenous group but were instead 'a markedly stratified class'.[62] The fact that John Mynor was described in his indictment as a yeoman does not necessarily mean he was an impoverished peasant. In all likelihood he was a member of

---

[57] CHES25/12 rot. 16.

[58] KB9/113 m. 42.

[59] J.R Maddicott, *Thomas of Lancaster, 1307–1322: A Study in the Reign of Edward II* (Oxford, 1970), 42, 43, 339; Powell, *Kingship, Law and Society*, 209–10.

[60] Gunn, 'Sir Thomas Lovell', 145; Matthew Holford, '"Thrifty Men of the County"? The Jurors and Their Role' in *The Fifteenth Century Inquisitions Post Mortem: A Companion*, ed. Michael Hicks (Woodbridge, 2012), 214–18; Simon Payling, 'The Widening Franchise: Parliamentary Elections in Lancastrian Nottinghamshire' in *England in the Fifteenth Century*, ed. Daniel Williams (Woodbridge, 1987), 174–5.

[61] Gerald Harriss, *Shaping the Nation: England, 1360–1461* (Oxford, 2005), 138; Payling, *Political Society*, 2–3.

[62] Rodney Hilton, 'Reasons for Inequality Among Medieval Peasants', *Journal of Peasant Studies*, v (1978), 271.

the upper peasantry whose economic resources were only slightly below those towards the bottom end of the income scale for a gentleman. When John Mynor distributed illegal livery he was continuing the traditional role his family played, despite their decline in wealth and status.

The statutes did not, and could not, completely ban the nobility or the gentry from retaining because they were crucial for the operation of medieval government. Most of the work of medieval government was undertaken by unpaid officials, usually members of the nobility and gentry. Those indicted in Hampshire in 1503 for receiving illegal livery from William Sandys stated that they had been retained to do the king's work.[63] Those indicted for illegal livery could find themselves holding local office shortly after their indictment, which was consistent throughout the fifteenth and early sixteenth centuries. On 6 July 1415, Hugh Erdeswyk was appointed to the commission of the peace in Staffordshire[64] even though he had been indicted on two counts of illegal livery the previous year.[65] In Derbyshire, in 1434, Sir Richard Vernon was indicted for illegal livery[66] yet he was named on the subsequent nine commissions of the peace for Derbyshire between 1437 and 1449.[67] Vernon had also been named on the five commissions of the peace immediately preceding his indictment for illegal livery between 1423 and 1431.[68]

In addition to law enforcement, military expediency dictated that during times of war or potential foreign invasion it was necessary to enlist the help of the nobility and gentry to raise troops. The regular threat of war with Scotland meant that the wardens of the march towards Scotland were exempt from the statutes.[69] Similarly, an indictment for illegal retaining did not exempt those accused from performing military service. When faced with a possible French invasion, Henry VII issued a commission of array to seventeen men in Warwickshire, on 5 May 1491, of whom four knights and one esquire had been indicted for illegal livery just two years earlier.[70] In February 1513, Henry VIII gave commissions of array in light of a threatened French invasion to eight men across Somerset, Dorset, Hampshire and Wiltshire,[71] of whom four

[63] KB9/436 m. 13; KB27/993 rot. 12.
[64] *CPR, 1413–1416*, 423.
[65] KB9/113 mm. 2, 40.
[66] KB9/11 mm. 15, 17.
[67] *CPR, 1436–1441*, 581; *CPR, 1441–1446*, 469; *CPR, 1446–1452*, 588.
[68] *CPR, 1422–1429*, 561; *CPR, 1429–1436*, 615.
[69] *PROME*, vii, 313–14; viii, 38; xiii, 65, 386.
[70] *CPR, 1485–1494*, 356–7. Those indicted were: Sir William Lucy, Sir Thomas Cokesay, Sir Simon Mountford, Sir Edward Raleigh and Robert Throgmorton, esquire – KB29/119 rot. 10; KB29/120 rott. 11–13.
[71] *L&P Hen. VIII*, i, no. 1662 (27).

knights had been indicted for illegal retaining: William Sandys[72] and John Lysle in Hampshire;[73] and Walter Hungerford[74] and Edward Darell in Wiltshire.[75] The importance of noble power at this time is further evident in the lead-up to the Battle of Flodden on 9 September 1513. In August 1513 Henry VIII gave commissions across all the counties of England 'to seize the property of all born subjects (except ecclesiastics) of the King of Scots ... selling such as cannot be kept and making inventories of the property &c'.[76] Several knights who were given this commission had previously been charged with illegal livery, including William Say (in Hertfordshire),[77] Edward Darell (in Wiltshire)[78] and Walter Griffith (in Yorkshire).[79] The precise scale of this task is difficult to judge as there are no reliable figures for the number of Scots living in England at this time.[80] The nobility and gentry needed to be allowed to recruit men for the purposes of running local government. Even if they had a history of retaining unlawfully, the nature of local government and raising troops for the purposes of defence meant they could not be permanently barred from office.

In addition to positions in local government, members of the gentry acted as estate officials for magnates and there are several examples of members of the gentry being indicted for illegal retaining and holding offices of magnates who were not connected to their livery indictments. Sir William Say was connected to the affinity of John de Vere, thirteenth earl of Oxford in 1486 and 1487,[81] and was indicted for illegal livery four years later in 1491.[82] Sir Henry Willoughby, indicted in Warwickshire in 1489, was steward, overseer and governor of four of John, Lord Clinton's manors in Warwickshire.[83] Richard Broun, gentleman of Repton was indicted for receiving illegal livery from three different lords in 1434 (Ralph Cromwell, Sir Richard Vernon and Joan Beauchamp) but also had

---

[72] KB9/436 m. 13.
[73] KB29/143 rot. 24.
[74] KB29/138 rot. 5.
[75] KB9/436 m. 16.
[76] *L&P Hen. VIII*, i, no. 2222 (16).
[77] KB9/391 m. 33; KB29/122 rot. 4.
[78] KB9/436 m. 16.
[79] KB29/142 rot. 7.
[80] The 'England's Immigrants database' includes thirty-five references to Scots. www. englandsimmigrants.com. An earlier study by J.A.F. Thomson did note the chrono-logical spread of Scots across England in the fifteenth century and the pattern was presumably the same in 1513: J.A.F. Thomson, 'Scots in England in the Fifteenth Century', *Scottish Historical Review*, lxxix (2000), 1–16.
[81] Ross, *John de Vere*, 122, 162, 188, 190, 196, 236.
[82] KB9/391 m. 33; KB29/122 rot. 4.
[83] *IMP, 1–12 Hen VII*, no. 331. For Willoughby's indictment for illegal livery in 1489 see: KB9/380 m. 41; KB29/133 rot. 16.

custody of the park of Bretby which the duke of Norfolk granted him in 1432.[84] Ecclesiastical estates provide similar examples. Sir John Legh and Sir William Sandys, both indicted in Hampshire in 1505 and 1511 respectively,[85] held offices in the bishopric of Winchester.[86] The fact that some retainers of ecclesiastical establishments were indicted for illegal livery should be unsurprising since ecclesiastical lords required service and retainers in much the same way as their secular counterparts.[87] These cases illustrate that those gentry indicted for illegal livery, and therefore lords in their own right, also looked for their own lords higher up the social scale to obtain fees and offices.

Clergy

Although most indictments were for members of the gentry giving livery illegally to those of a lower rank, contemporaries did not believe these were the only sections of society engaged in this practice. Members of the clergy and their household servants could become embroiled in violent disputes with the affinities of prominent lay magnates, as was the case in May 1504 when a brawl ensued at Fulford, Yorkshire, between servants of Thomas Savage, archbishop of York, and Henry, fifth earl of Northumberland.[88] The broader networks of ecclesiastical servants, which can be referred to as an affinity, could also be a threat to public order and ensured that members of the clergy were bound by livery and retaining laws. The 1399 act stated explicitly that the statutes should apply to ecclesiastical lords[89] while a petition presented to the 1406 parliament drew particular attention to the retaining practices of ecclesiastical lords.[90] The King's Bench records show that members of the clergy were indicted for both receiving and distributing illegal livery. In total, twenty-two members of the clergy were indicted in the King's Bench: fourteen clerics, six chaplains and one canon.

The majority of cases involving the clergy occurred during the early Tudor era, when more cases of illegal livery happened. Most indictments for members of the clergy illegally distributing livery were low key. The cleric indicted was Henry Willaboy in Cheshire, who allegedly distributed illegal livery to two men

---

[84] *CIPM, 1432–1437*, no. 108; KB9/11 m. 15.
[85] For Sandys see: KB9/436 m. 13. For Legh see: KB29/143 rot. 24.
[86] R.A. Brown, 'Bastard Feudalism and the Bishopric of Winchester, c.1280–1530' (unpublished PhD thesis, University of Winchester (Southampton), 2003), 304, 306.
[87] Note similar point made about the bishops of Durham: Christian D. Liddy, *The Bishopric of Durham in the Late Middle Ages: Lordship, Community and the Cult of St Cuthbert* (Woodbridge, 2008), 104.
[88] Hoyle, 'The Affray at Fulford', 239–56.
[89] *PROME*, viii, 38.
[90] *PROME*, viii, 400–1. Discussed in detail in Chapter 3.

on 27 December 1434[91] while in 1478 the rector of Queen's College Oxford, John Parson, obtained a pardon for an indictment for giving illegal livery six years earlier.[92] The most prominent case against a member of the clergy for illegal retaining was against James Stanley, the future bishop of Ely, who was indicted twice in 1499 for distributing livery to thirty men at Chester on 10 October 1496 and to eighteen men at Knutsford on 30 September 1494.[93] He was again indicted in Yorkshire in 1500 for illegally distributing badges five years earlier as part of a larger cluster of cases in Yorkshire at that time.[94] It is also likely that he was indicted again in 1506, since a list of outstanding recognisances and debts owed to Henry VIII early in his reign records debts of £145,610 for Stanley and £58,644 for his retainers.[95] Given the fact that Lord Bergavenny was fined £70,650 for illegally retaining 471 men between June 1504 and December 1506, Sean Cunningham has speculated that Stanley's illegal retinue may have consisted of as many as 1,000 men, assuming that he was illegally retaining for around the same amount of time that Bergavenny was.[96]

James Stanley's indictment for distributing illegal livery was a consequence of secular, not ecclesiastical concerns. Like his secular counterparts, James Stanley was able to advance his career after being indicted for illegal livery and became bishop of Ely in 1506.[97] Other members of the Stanley family were indicted for illegal retaining around the same time, namely Sir William Stanley twice in Cheshire in 1499[98] and Edward Stanley in Yorkshire in 1500.[99] Henry VII was concerned about potential power of the Stanley family in the north-west. The family had helped him secure his throne at Bosworth but they were notoriously circumspect. Their loyalty was called into question by Sir William Stanley's defection to the cause of Perkin Warbeck. The reason for the indictments against members of the Stanley family in 1499 and 1500 was political and came from Henry VII's concern about the family's retaining practices, similar to the indictment against Lord Bergavenny.[100]

Although the most prominent cases involving a member of the clergy were connected to secular concerns, surviving records show that bishops and abbots acted as bastard feudal lords too. Indeed, the earliest examples that John

---

[91] CHES25/12 m. 30.
[92] KB27/908 rex rot. 5.
[93] CHES25/18 mm. 13–14.
[94] KB8/3/1 m. 5.
[95] *L&P Hen. VIII*, i, no. 309.
[96] Cunningham, 'St Oswald's Priory, Nostell v Stanley', 153.
[97] D.G Newcombe, 'James Stanley (c.1465–1515)', *ODNB*, lii, 221–2.
[98] CHES25/18 m. 11.
[99] KB29/134 rot. 26.
[100] For a full account of the relationship between Henry VII and the Stanley family see: Cunningham, 'Henry VII, Sir Thomas Butler and the Stanley Family', 220–41.

Maddicott cited in his study on the retaining of royal justices were based on lists of fees paid by monastic institutions from the 1240s.[101] The tendency of ecclesiastical documents to have better survival rates than their secular counterparts accounts for this fact. Nevertheless, it is clear that ecclesiastical institutions were paying fees to gentry and lawyers from at least the mid-thirteenth century. Matthew Holford similarly traced how the bishops of Durham in the thirteenth and fourteenth centuries were a prominent source of patronage and good lordship in the palatinate of Durham, showing that they consistently retained and paid fees to officials in various positions.[102] Bishops of Winchester were also bastard feudal lords who used annuities occasionally to retain people for particular services, in particular lawyers. They also had households and various stewardships and bailiwicks to manage their vast estates and, by the early fifteenth century, retained members of the local gentry.[103] Yet the limited studies of ecclesiastical affinities have shown that they were not simply copies of those of the secular peerage. Clerics in the bishop of Durham's household, for instance, had a greater influence and prominence than clerics in the households of secular nobles. Christian Liddy has shown that the household and affinity of successive bishops of Durham changed, depending on the background and character of the respective bishops.[104] Ecclesiastical lords constructed affinities for the running of their estates and did not have the same military expectations as their secular counterparts, with the notable exception of the bishop of Durham who had an important role in defending the north of England in times of possible invasion.[105]

Most clergy, however, were indicted for being retained illegally. Noble households included clerics for the running of religious ceremonies for the lord and his household, the number of which increased with the size of the noble household.[106] In 1384–5 the earl of Devon gave livery to two canons, one prebendary and five parsons[107] while Edward, the Black Prince, granted livery to the clerks of his chapel in 1355.[108] From Henry VII's reign onwards, there are instances of members of the clergy being illegally retained by members of the peerage and gentry. One canon, Richard Shirburn of Lichfield, was indicted in 1488 along with nine esquires, two gentlemen, two yeomen and a shoemaker for illegally receiving the earl of Shrewsbury's livery,[109] while three clerics were

---

[101] Maddicott, 'Law and Lordship', 4–7.
[102] Holford and Stringer, *Border Liberties and Loyalties*, 96–171.
[103] Brown, 'Bastard Feudalism and the Bishopric of Winchester', 289–91.
[104] Liddy, *Bishopric of Durham*, 107–17.
[105] Ibid., 106, 110–11.
[106] Woolgar, *The Great Household*, 176–8.
[107] BL, Add. Ch. 64320.
[108] *Register of Edward, The Black Prince, IV, 1351–1365* (London, 1933), 132–3.
[109] KB9/379 m. 5; KB29/119 rot. 2.

indicted in 1506 for being illegally retained by Lord Bergavenny[110] and another in Lincolnshire in 1504 who was indicted for illegally wearing the livery of Sir Giles Daubeney.[111]

One cluster of indictments against members of the clergy can be connected to a growth in anti-clerical feeling during the early years of Henry VIII's reign. The case in which the largest number of clerics was indicted for being illegally retained was in Worcestershire in 1517 when five clerics and four chaplains were indicted for being illegally retained by John Savage VI, under the 1468 statute.[112] These indictments occurred at a time in which benefit of clergy was being restricted and sanctuary was under attack. E.W. Ives argued that the removal of John Savage VI from the priory of St John of Jerusalem in Clerkenwell in connection with the murder of John Pauncefote 'certainly belongs to the destruction of sanctuary'.[113] This is not to argue that there was a conscious decision made to include these nine clerics in the indictments against the Savage family because the issue of sanctuary had arisen in these cases. Nor can it be argued that the anti-clericalism and the attacks on benefit of clergy and sanctuary meant that there was any conscious initiative to indict members of the clergy for illegal retaining. Anti-clericalism was not a factor in indicting clerics for being illegally retained, which indicates that there was no significant opposition to clerics being part of a noble household since they were needed for the religious case of the noble's affinity.

Women

Four cases of illegal livery involved women, three of which were indictments against widows for distributing illegal livery. In many cases involving women it is difficult to identify the specific social and political contexts surrounding those involved since women rarely appear in surviving records. In theory, women did not hold offices in local government or lead troops into battle and therefore did not need to retain for those purposes. Conversely, since women did not hold positions such as steward or bailiff there were few instances in which they would

---

[110] KB29/136 rott. 16–17.
[111] KB9/435 m. 11.
[112] KB27/1028 rex rot. 33; KB29/148 rott. 50, 53. The numbering of the members of the Savage family and the biographical information is taken from Tim Thornton, 'Savage Family', *ODNB*, xlix, 63–6.
[113] Eric W. Ives, 'Crime, Sanctuary and Royal Authority under Henry VIII: Exemplary Sufferings of the Savage Family' in *On the Laws and Customs of England*, eds. Morris S. Arnold et al. (Chapel Hill, 1981), 303. Tim Thornton has similarly commented that the issues around this indictment 'provided the occasion for a radical reinterpretation of the laws of sanctuary'. Tim Thornton, 'Savage Family', *ODNB*, xlix, 63–6.

be retained. Women did however hold land, usually as widows who were entitled to a third of their dead husband's estates, although Jennifer Ward argued that noblewomen had a role in developing retinues, citing Elizabeth de Burgh, Lady de Clare, Isabella Morely, Joan Beauchamp and Anne, countess of Stafford as examples of women who had their own retinues.[114] Queens and noblewomen had their own households that were predominantly male. Although late medieval society, and the records it produced, did have a strong gendered bias in favour of men, women did have a role in estate management and land ownership, for instance Thomasine Hopton, second wife of John Hopton.[115]

Three of the four cases of illegal livery in which women were indicted involved widows illegally distributing livery. The first occurred in Yorkshire in 1422 when Elizabeth, Lady Neville, was indicted for illegally distributing livery to three yeomen on 2 December 1420. The offence occurred at Kirkby Moorside where Elizabeth Neville is recorded to have resided.[116] She died shortly after on 1 January 1423 and her inquisition *post mortem* indicates that Yorkshire was one of ten counties in which she held land.[117] One of the yeomen illegally retained, John Flesshewer, later served on an inquisition jury for William de Lokton on 1 April 1426.[118] This suggests that at least one of the men that Elizabeth Neville illegally retained possessed at least some measure of local standing.[119]

The last known widow who was indicted was Joan Pelham, who was indicted in Sussex in 1437 for giving illegal livery to two yeomen.[120] She obtained a pardon on 1 November 1439.[121] The absence of any plea in the surviving legal records means that little can be said about the connection between Joan Pelham and her illegal retainers. However, other records indicate that Joan Pelham's case was similar to that of many men charged with illegal livery. She was the wife of Sir John Pelham, who became a key figure in the government of Henry IV and the leading knight in Sussex through 'opportune service to the house of Lancaster'.[122] Prior to his death, he gave warranty of all his moveable goods to his wife Joan, his bastard son and heir John and Bishop Langley.[123] Little is known about Joan Pelham to suggest that this particular indictment was part of any broader legal difficulties she was encountering at that time.

---

[114] Jennifer C. Ward, *English Noblewomen in the Later Middle Ages* (London, 1992), 129–42, especially 133–6.
[115] Richmond, *John Hopton*, 97, 115–20, 183.
[116] KB27/645 rex rot. 8; KB29/56 rot. 25.
[117] *CIPM, 1422–1427*, nos. 144–54, 355.
[118] *CIPM, 1422–1427*, no. 750.
[119] Holford, '"Thrifty Men of the County"?', 214.
[120] KB29/70 rot. 16.
[121] *CPR, 1436–1441*, 343; KB27/707 rex rot. 9.
[122] *History of Parliament, 1386–1421*, iv, 39–44, quotation on 40.
[123] *CCR, 1422–29*, no. 388.

It is the second indictment against a widow that most illustrates the potential political power of widows in late medieval England. Joan Beauchamp, lady Abergavenny, widow of William Beauchamp, labelled 'that second Jezebel' by Adam Usk,[124] was indicted for giving illegal livery to two gentlemen from Derbyshire, Thomas Maceworth and Richard Broun, the previous April.[125] Her activity in Derbyshire is difficult to decipher and her inquisitions *post mortem* do not include any land in Derbyshire, despite her widespread holdings in twenty counties and the City of London.[126] Out of the three widows indicted for distributing illegal livery, she is the only one known to have held local office. Joan Beauchamp was named on several commissions to raise loans: in Worcestershire, Warwickshire and Gloucestershire in 1426;[127] in Leicestershire in 1428;[128] and in Warwickshire and Leicestershire in 1431.[129] Christine Carpenter noted that it is 'remarkable' that she held any local office at all.[130] It was indeed unusual that she held office but Carpenter's description does not explain why she was appointed. Local government in the middle ages only functioned effectively when the king delegated to members of the nobility and gentry who were responsible for running local government on his behalf. In turn those nobles looked to their own affinities and networks to find men to carry out these dry, but necessary, administrative tasks. For this to work effectively, those appointed to such commissions needed to possess an element of local power and influence. Yet despite the financial resources that many widows enjoyed, few were named on local government commissions, presumably as there were no expectations from medieval society that they would be involved in local government. Joan Beauchamp was appointed because she had the necessary resources and willingness to execute such commissions.

The fact that widows were the only women who were indicted for distributing illegal livery is consistent with other sources that reveal aspects of female lordship in late medieval England since widows 'enjoyed an unusual degree of independence'.[131] One woman who, more than most, enjoyed a significant degree of independence was Henry VII's mother, Margaret Beaufort. After two

---

[124] *Chronicle of Adam Usk*, 133. Note: this is the only reference to her by Usk.
[125] KB9/11 mm. 15. It should also be noted that the only reference to her in Susan M. Wright's study of fifteenth-century Derbyshire regards her indictment for illegal livery: Wright, *Derbyshire Gentry*, 131.
[126] *CIPM, 1432–1437*, nos. 412, 500–19.
[127] *CPR, 1422–1429*, 354.
[128] *CPR, 1422–1429*, 481.
[129] *CPR, 1429–1436*, 126.
[130] Christine Carpenter, 'William Beauchamp V', *ODNB*, iv, 608–9.
[131] Monika Simon, 'Of Lands and Ladies: The Marriage Strategies of the Lords Lovell (c.1200–1487)', *Southern History*, xxxiii (2011), 21.

men had been indicted for wearing her livery fraudulently,[132] Henry VII gave his mother a pardon which included a licence to retain an unlimited number of men.[133] Although the king's mother was a special case, the licence does indicate that it was accepted that women would retain various officials for various reasons. Moreover, widows had the financial capability to do this because they benefited from the increasing use of jointure, enfeoffment and conveyance, usually to the financial detriment of their husband's heir. These developments led Rowena Archer to comment that 'the best years of a woman's life in the later middle ages were those of her widowhood'.[134] Widows were the heads of households that distributed livery, as was the case with Elizabeth de Burgh who gave livery to 338 people in 1343.[135] Her household and estate records show that she had a broader affinity of servants who received her fees and liveries for performing various legal and administrative tasks. For instance, the receiver's accounts for 1342–3 show that her steward, John de Hertford, received a fee of £20 from the Clare estates while her receiver Henry de Neuton was in receipt of £6 13s. 4d. Sir Andrew de Bures was given £2 9s. 2d. expenses for an eight-day trip to London on 'the Lady's business concerning Caerleon and Weymouth'.[136]

The final case involving women occurred in Southwark in 1491 when five women and two men were indicted for illegally wearing livery that they were not permitted to wear throughout January and February 1492.[137] Unlike the previous indictments, this case did not involve a widow continuing her dead husband's retaining practice, but rather women illegally wearing livery. Four out of the five women were spinsters, while the fifth, Katherine Turner, was married but her husband, John Turner, was not indicted. Since these women were of a lower social status, it is not possible to identify any definitive or meaningful traces of them in the surviving sources. Although little else can be said about this specific case, it serves as a further example of women wearing the livery of great lords. Women were not prominent in noble households or affinities but there are occasional references that show that, although it was uncommon in the late medieval period, women were involved at some level in noble households.[138] The livery roll of the earl of Devon from 1384 shows that three damsels received livery from the earl[139]

---

[132] KB9/436 mm. 8, 14.
[133] KB27/976 rex rot. 3.
[134] Rowena E. Archer, 'Rich Old Ladies: The Problem of Late Medieval Dowagers' in *Property and Politics: Essays in Later Medieval English History*, ed. Tony Pollard (Gloucester, 1984), 19.
[135] E101/92/23.
[136] *Elizabeth de Burgh, Lady of Clare (1295–1360): Household and Other Records*, ed. Jennifer Ward (Woodbridge, 2014), 104.
[137] KB9/390 m. 52.
[138] Woolgar, *The Great Household*, 34
[139] BL, Add. Ch. 64320.

while *The Black Prince's Register* lists twenty-seven women of the household who received liveries of cloth and fur in 1357.[140] These numbers are small in comparison to the number of men receiving livery. In total Edward Courtney distributed livery to 127 men, meaning women only accounted for 2.3 per rcent of the total number receiving livery. Even in the households of noble women there was only ever a minority of female servants,[141] as evident in the livery roll of Lady de Clare, in which only eleven women received livery compared to 227 men.[142] The surviving Kalendars show that four women were living in the household of John Fastolf when he was at war in 1431–2[143] and ten women were in the household of the countess of Warwick in 1420–1.[144] The household of Lady Joan Dinham was exceptional with regard to number of women in her household, even being served by a female reeve, Joan Hurding, in her manor of Matford.[145] The only instance in which a woman is known to have been retained by indenture was in 1419, indicating that William de Hesilton and his wife Katherine were retained by William de Burgh, esquire. It should be noted, however, that the agreement only allowed for William Hesilton to receive the livery of William de Burgh.[146] Women were part of the late medieval household as domestic servants and ladies-in-waiting, but they were small in number and are unlikely to have filled any administrative roles in a noble affinity or partook in many crimes such as riot that were usually associated with illegal livery.

Rather than there being a social bar against distributing livery to women, it is clear that a small number of women did receive livery. Cases of illegal livery against women were not the conscious product of gender biases preventing women from receiving livery or distributing it. Women gave and received livery, but on a much smaller scale than men, which meant that they only had a minority of opportunities to retain, or be retained, illegally. When cases involving women did arise, the contexts were not distinct from cases in which men were charged. Office-holding was rarely an avenue open for women to retain or be retained, but connections could be formed as a result of land ownership. Therefore, the lack of opportunities for women to give and receive livery in general translated into only four cases in which women were charged with offences against the statutes of livery.

[140] *Register of Edward, The Black Prince*, iv, 227.
[141] Ward, *English Noblewomen*, 53.
[142] E101/92/23.
[143] Magdalen College, Fastolf Paper 8.
[144] Magdalen College, GDIII/66/1, 8–9.
[145] Hannes Kleineke, 'Lady Joan Dinham: A Fifteenth-century West-country Matriarch' in *Social Attitudes and Political Structures*, ed. Tim Thornton (Stroud, 2002), 73–4.
[146] 'Private Indentures', no. 115.

Townsmen

The most problematic group of people indicted for illegal livery to define is townsmen because a precise definition of who constituted a townsman is elusive. Even the definition of what constituted a town is problematic. The lack of adequate population data, particularly for small towns, discounts population as a satisfactory indicator, while other criteria such as the right to return two MPs to parliament or possession of an urban charter exclude many of the small towns that were scattered across England. The most satisfactory working definition of a town is a trading centre 'where employment was heavily dependent on non-agrarian activities'.[147] Defining a town as a place where most people made a living primarily by means other than agriculture does not mean that a townsman can be defined as anyone below the grant of gentleman described as something other than a 'yeoman', 'husbandman' or 'labourer' in the records. Numerous indictments include men from places that, by any definition, were towns who were described as a 'yeoman'. In York, yeomen were indicted for illegal livery in 1423,[148] 1455[149] and 1504,[150] while thirty yeomen from Rochester were indicted in 1507 for being illegally retained by George Neville, Lord Bergavenny.[151] Similarly, eleven of the twenty-four yeomen that Sir John Fortescu was accused of giving illegal livery to in 1491 were from St Albans and one was from Hertford.[152] To this can be added: two yeomen from Chester who were indicted in 1428,[153] seven yeomen from Derby who were indicted in 1468[154] and five yeomen from Devizes who were indicted in 1508.[155] It may be that in these cases the men being referred to were born in the countryside and had moved to towns, or were employed in agriculture just outside the town in which they lived. During the fifteenth century there was fluidity between town and county, with people moving between them. Such people were valuable to their new communities because of the 'training and experience' they brought.[156] Yet these yeomen

---

[147] Richard Britnell, 'Town Life' in *A Social History of England, 1200–1500*, eds. Rosemary Horrox and W. Mark Ormrod (Cambridge, 2006), 134. See also: Samuel K. Cohn, *Popular Protest in Late Medieval English Towns* (Cambridge, 2013), 18–19.
[148] KB27/696 rex rot 19; KB27/737 rex rot. 1; KB29/57 rot. 5.
[149] KB9/149/1 m. 21; KB29/89 rot. 3.
[150] KB29/134 rot. 27.
[151] KB27/985, fines, rex rot. 7; KB39/136 rot. 16.
[152] KB9/391 m. 34; KB27-995 rex rot. 13; KB29/122 rot 4.
[153] CHES25/12 rot. 16.
[154] KB9/13 mm. 11, 20, 63.
[155] KB27/990 rex rot. 4; KB29/138 rot. 5.
[156] Christopher Dyer, 'England's Economy in the Fifteenth Century' in *The Fifteenth Century XIII: Exploring the Evidence: Commemoration, Administration and the Economy*, ed. Linda Clark (Woodbridge, 2014), 209.

were inhabitants of towns and therefore should be defined as townsmen. In what follows a 'townsman' is classed as someone whose primary occupation was not in agriculture or who was a yeoman, husbandman or labourer who lived in a town. There was a variety in the number of men from any one town who were indicted for illegal livery and there were several prominent towns which had no one indicted for illegal livery, including Bristol, Carlisle, Exeter and Southampton. The only cases of illegal livery that were returned to the King's Bench from towns rather than counties were in York in 1454,[157] Coventry in 1480[158] and Nottingham in 1510.[159] All of these cases were small in scale and involved either someone wearing the wrong livery or a lord giving illegal livery to one person. The possibility that there were cases that were heard by city courts and not returned to King's Bench is suggested by the fact that cases were heard in the borough of Nottingham in 1483,[160] though such examples are rare. Despite it being the largest and most populous city in England, only one case is recorded in the King's Bench as having occurred in the city of London, involving a gentleman from Scarborough in 1439. Even in this case a writ was sent out at the same time to the justices in Yorkshire regarding the same offence.[161] On two occasions someone from London was indicted outside London: John Dek, dyer in Kent in 1435[162] and Henry Haydon in 1478, also in Kent.[163] Yet this figure is somewhat deceptive as Southwark, just next to the city of London, was the place in which the largest number of people indicted for illegal livery lived. In total, seventy men from Southwark were indicted for illegal livery. England's second largest city, York, had only a few men indicted for illegal livery. John Johnson, yeoman of York, was indicted in 1423 along with six other yeomen and one gentleman for illegally receiving livery from Sir Ralph Greystoke.[164] Thomas Percy, Lord Egremont, gave illegal livery to one fletcher from York and seven other men from the surrounding countryside in York on 4 February 1454.[165] In 1504, four yeomen and two merchants from York were ordered to appear before the local justices for violations of the statutes of livery.[166]

Although several major towns had no one indicted for illegal livery, several middle-ranking towns did have a large number of indictments for illegal livery.

---

[157] KB9/148/2 mm. 31, 38, 54–5.
[158] KB29/110 rot. 27.
[159] KB29/140 rot. 31.
[160] *Records of the Borough of Nottingham, Vol 2: 1399–1485*, ed. W.H. Stevenson (Nottingham, 1883), ii, 330–1.
[161] KB29/72 rott. 22, 30.
[162] KB29/68 rot. 11.
[163] KB29/108 rot. 12.
[164] KB29/57 rot. 5.
[165] KB9/149/1 m. 53.
[166] KB29/134 rot. 27.

After Southwark, the towns with the largest number of people indicted were Hereford (fifty-seven), Lichfield (fifty-three), Maidstone and Whitchurch (forty-eight in each). Derby, where twenty-one men indicted for illegal livery resided, clearly demonstrates the potential urban–rural connection with regard to illegal livery – in particular, the cluster of cases in 1434 when several leading members of the gentry were indicted for distributing illegal livery to men from Derby as well as the surrounding countryside.[167] Richard Vernon was indicted on three occasions for giving illegal livery between Christmas 1429 and 1 December 1431. On the first occasion he gave illegal livery to three men from Derby in Derby. On two subsequent occasions the location of the offence was his principal residence of Haddon, in which only one man out of twenty-two was from Derby in Easter 1431 and one draper and two souters from Derby out of five men on 1 December 1431. Similarly, Lord Grey of Codnor had given livery illegally to two yeomen and one smith from Derby out of a total of eleven men at Easter 1433. Henry Booth, gentleman, gave illegal livery to one yeoman from Derby and two others at Easter 1431. One yeoman, William Orme, was indicted twice for receiving livery from both Lord Grey of Codnor and Sir William Vernon. The cases themselves were entangled with broader factional feuding throughout the county.[168] Presumably, those lords who were distributing illegal livery were concerned with increasing the number of men they could call upon as opposed to specifically targeting townsmen.

Although there was a link in some areas between rural gentry and townsmen, there is no evidence to suggest that any noble or gentry sought to retain extensively from any particular urban occupation. Excluding those labels denoting membership of the nobility and gentry, or people described as yeomen, husbandmen and labourers, there were seventy-nine occupations recorded as having at least one person indicted for illegal livery. The most numerous of these were tailors. There were seventy occasions in which a tailor was indicted for illegal livery. The other most numerous urban occupations were butchers (thirty-three), shoemakers (twenty-four), smiths (twenty-two), weavers (twenty-one) and carpenters (twenty). In general, those from urban occupations were not illegally retained in bulk. For instance, the twenty carpenters indicted for being illegally retained were scattered across nineteen different cases.[169] Similarly, the eight glovers who were indicted were all indicted in different cases.[170] There are a few

---

[167] For the Derbyshire indictments of 1434 see: KB9/11 mm. 15, 17.

[168] Wright, *Derbyshire Gentry*, 128–33.

[169] KB9/34/1 m. 5; KB9/35 mm. 6, 68-9; KB9/113 m. 11; KB9/342 m. 36; KB9/380 m. 41C; KB9/390 mm. 44, 47, 53; KB29/120 rot. 3; KB29/121 rot. 27; KB29/123 rot. 22; KB29/126 rot. 4; KB29/130 rot. 16; KB29/131 rot. 15; KB29/135 rott. 6, 11; KB29/148 rot. 50.

[170] KB9/34/1 m. 5; KB9/35 m. 6; KB9/380 m. 4; KB27/908 rex rot. 19; KB27/1002 rex rot. 12; KB27/1028 rex rot. 34; KB29/121 rot. 15; KB29/133 rot. 27.

cases in which a small number of men from the same occupation were given illegal livery by the same lord, though the highest number of men from the same profession was four, when four butchers from Hereford were indicted in 1452 for taking illegal livery from Sir Walter Devereux.[171] The general pattern of illegally retained townsmen suggests that nobles did not seek to illegally retain a large number of men from any one occupation in particular.

Instances of illegal retaining by townsmen were rare. Indeed, the only instance in which a top-ranking civic official was indicted for illegal livery was in Chester in 1428 when the town's mayor John Hope was indicted for giving illegal livery to a baker and a yeoman from Chester on 4 November 1426 in the town.[172] Previously he had been sheriff of Chester from 1412 until 1415 and he spent seven terms as the mayor of Chester between 1419 and 1428.[173] At the same time, another former mayor of Chester, John Whitmore was also indicted for giving illegal livery to five men in November 1423.[174] Whitmore was also a member of the city's ruling elite and was mayor during the period in which Hope was sheriff.[175] The exemption given to mayors while in office by the 1429 act explains why there were no other indictments against serving mayors. Indeed, the act itself may have been influenced by this and other indictments in Cheshire in 1428.[176]

The general pattern in which only a few townsmen are known to have been illegally retained by members of the nobility is matched with the surviving documents that record legitimate bastard feudal relations. There are only two known indentures of retainer between a magnate and a townsman, the earliest of which was drawn up on 24 June 1461 when Richard Neville, earl of Warwick, as warden of the West March, retained John Faucon of Carlisle, gunner, for life. The indenture stated that Faucon would array men to ride with Warwick and give the earl one third of any spoils of war.[177] The reason why this particular indenture deviates from the traditional magnate–gentry model was Carlisle's location on the edge of the Scottish border, which meant it was at a greater risk of raiding and therefore needed to be more militarised than most English towns. Warwick's position as warden of the Marches meant that he was expected to retain men in this area to contribute to the defence of the realm.[178] The only other such indenture

---

[171] KB9/34/1 m. 5; KB9/34/2 m. 142.

[172] CHES25/12 m. 16.

[173] *A History of the County of Chester: Volume V Part 2, The City of Chester, Culture, Buildings, Institutions,* eds. C.P. Lewis and A.T. Thacker (London, 2005), 309–10; Jane Laughton, *Life in a Late Medieval City: Chester, 1275–1520* (Oxford, 2008), 119.

[174] CHES25/12 m. 16.

[175] *Victoria County History Cheshire,* v 60 (1), 309 (2).

[176] McKelvie, 'The Livery Act of 1429', 55–65.

[177] 'Private Indentures', no. 140.

[178] The wardens of the Marches were permitted to retain as many men as they required under the law regarding retaining: *PROME,* viii, 38; xiii, 65, 386.

was between Warwick's successor as warden, Richard, duke of Gloucester and another prominent citizen of Carlisle, Henry Denton in 1473 who went on to be mayor in 1478 and 1480.[179] These indentures of retainer may be representative of a broader shift in the military use of towns towards the end of the fifteenth century. English towns were, in general, not as militarised as their continental counterparts. During the Hundred Years' War the main contribution towns made to the defence of the realm was financial, such as by loans, though they did on occasion contribute ships.[180] Afterwards, during the Wars of the Roses and Henry VIII's French expeditions towns were increasingly expected to provide troops as well as money for the king's armies in the face of rebellion and to wage foreign war.[181] Towards the end of the fifteenth century there seems to have been an increase in the likelihood of magnates to retain those dwelling in urban areas for military purposes, if only as a supplement to their rural support base.

Indentures of retainer were primarily concerned with the military dimension of bastard feudal relations, whereas other sources that give a more rounded view of noble affinities indicate that nobles were willing to incorporate townsmen into their broader affinity. In 1384–5 thirteen men with connections in the city of Exeter were in receipt of the earl of Devon's livery along with three men with connections in Tiverton. Included in the list was Robert Winford, esquire, who, along with John Grey 'dominated the city of Exeter in the 1370s'.[182] Around 120 years later, the list of men retained by Sir Thomas Lovell under the 1504 statute includes men from Lichfield, Walsall, Derby, St Albans and Oxford.[183] The high status of some of the men retained is indicated by the fact that four former mayors and three future mayors of Walsall were retained by Lovell.[184] Rosemary Horrox has alluded to the attractiveness of such service to townsmen, suggesting that with the scarcity of purchasable land, royal and aristocratic service was one of the best means of social advancement for townsmen.[185] The evidence from various

---

[179] 'Private Indentures', no. 153; Henry Summerson, *Medieval Carlisle: The City and the Borders from the Late Eleventh to the Mid-Sixteenth Century*, 2 vols. (Kendal, 1993), 463.

[180] Liddy, *War, Politics and Finance*, 29–42; Lorraine Attreed, *The King's Towns: Identity and Survival in Late Medieval English Boroughs* (New York, 2001), 190–2.

[181] Steven Gunn, David Grummitt and Hans Cool, *War, State and Society in England and the Netherlands, 1477–1559* (Oxford, 2007), 51–6; Neil Murphy, 'Henry VIII's First Invasion of France: The Gascon Expedition of 1512', *EHR*, cxxx (2015), 34–5.

[182] BL, Add. Ch. 64320. Figure are taken from Martin Cherry, 'The Crown and the Political Community in Devonshire, 1377–1461', (unpublished PhD thesis, University of Wales (Swansea), 1981), 332–7, quotation on 373. For these figures 'connections' is defined as anyone described as a citizen, canon or MP of Exeter or anyone stated to have owned property in the city.

[183] HMC, *Manuscripts of His Grace the Duke of Rutland*, 559–66.

[184] Gunn, 'Sir Thomas Lovell', 119.

[185] Rosemary Horrox, 'The Urban Gentry in the Fifteenth Century' in *Towns and*

indictments, estate records and urban records indicates that although bastard feudalism was primarily concerned with those living in a rural environment, there was an urban element to the noble affinity, though it was only a minor element.

Conclusion

This chapter has demonstrated two key points, fundamental to understanding the broader social structures of bastard feudalism that influenced the ways in which the relevant acts of parliament were enforced. First, that the construction of affinities was not the preserve of the secular male peerage, as members of the gentry, clerics and widows have all been shown to have created networks and affinities of retainers and supporters wearing their liveries. People from all sections of society were able to enter into bastard feudal relations, either as lords or servants, provided these were within the terms of the statutes. Second, that the records of the King's Bench are an important source for understanding the nature of late medieval society, particularly when used in conjunction with other documents, because they reveal social relations and connections not necessarily captured in the private records of noble families. The remaining chapters go on to examine the ways in which these connections were formed, where they were formed and how they were used.

Townspeople in the Fifteenth Century, ed. John A.F. Thomson (Gloucester, 1988), 22–44.

6

The Geography of the Cases

To fully understand the enforcement of the statutes it is necessary to examine where cases occurred as well as when they occurred and who was indicted. The use of counties for understanding social history can be problematic because many were artificial constructs, created for administrative ease. Christine Carpenter has shown that these artificial constructs did not necessarily determine social, political and economic connections as many people regularly formed such connections that crossed county boundaries.[1] The concept of the 'county community' is more appropriate to the early modern period than the late medieval period but the county is nevertheless the appropriate unit at which to discuss levels of law enforcement. England was divided into separate counties and justice was administered at this level with JPs having jurisdiction in one county. Gerald Harriss noted that judicial business was one of the few areas in which the whole shire routinely functioned as a political institution.[2] The arrangement of records by county is beneficial for an examination of the efficiency of local law enforcement because it allows a comparison of the ways in which separate county administrations enforced the statutes.

The numerous local studies of late medieval English society and landholding have shown that no two counties had an identical socio-political character as each county had its own idiosyncrasies. Differing patterns of landholding are evident in the *Nomina Villarum* returns from 1316.[3] In Somerset 77 per cent of vills were held by the gentry while 20 per cent belonged to the church, 2 per cent to the crown and 1 per cent to the greater magnates. In contrast, in Kent the crown held 14 per cent of the vills, while the church held 46 per cent, the magnates held 7 per cent and the gentry held 33 per cent. Sussex similarly had a different composition with the magnates holding 25 per cent of the vills, the gentry holding 45 per cent, the church holding 26 per cent and the crown holding 4 per cent. For Devon, the extensive landholding of Edward Courtenay, earl of Devon, made him the most significant political figure in the county.[4] In contrast,

---

[1] Christine Carpenter, 'Gentry and Community in Late Medieval England', *Journal of British Studies*, xxxiii (1994), 340–8.

[2] Harriss, *Shaping the Nation*, 188.

[3] The following figures relating to Kent, Somerset and Sussex are taken from: Toby Scott Purser, 'The County Community of Hampshire, c.1300–c.1530, with Special Reference to the Knights and Esquires' (unpublished PhD thesis, University of Winchester (Southampton), 2001), 47.

[4] Cherry, 'The Courtenay Earls of Devon', 75–6.

counties such as Nottinghamshire, Leicestershire, Cheshire and Lancashire had few resident magnates with landed income, leading historians of these counties to regard the gentry in them as being more independent.[5] Different counties could therefore have radically different structures of landholding which affected the exercise of power.

Other chapters have examined the law enforcement attempts of the crown and concerns about the Commons in parliament about retaining. In contrast, this chapter focuses on enforcement patterns in the localities to sketch out a fuller picture of the enforcement of the statutes. This analysis takes the county as its unit of comparison, rather than looking at regional variations, because there is no simple correlation in which specific regions, as opposed to counties, were more susceptible to illegal livery. In the east midlands, for example, there were twenty-two cases in Derbyshire compared with one in the neighbouring county of Nottinghamshire and one in the town of Nottingham. Similarly, in the south, Hampshire had six cases of illegal livery compared to one each in Wiltshire and Dorset.[6] Such discrepancies between neighbouring counties mean that a regional or multi-county approach to these cases would fail to produce any meaningful analysis and therefore this discussion is based on differences in enforcement patterns at the level of the county. In order to do so, counties are grouped together here according to the number of cases of illegal livery that occurred in them. Although the groupings are somewhat arbitrary, they nevertheless illuminate the variations in the enforcement of the statutes at a local level.

High Number of Cases

Yorkshire was the county that returned the highest number of cases to the King's Bench.[7] In total, thirty-six cases from Yorkshire and one from the city of York are known between 1393 and 1510. The earliest case identified in this study involved thirty men from Yorkshire in 1393.[8] Thereafter, there were no further cases until the early 1420s when three cases occurred in 1421, 1422 and 1423.[9] A subsequent single case then appears in the controlment roll for Easter 17 Henry VI (1439).[10] There were five cases of illegal livery between 1454

---

[5]   Acheson, *A Gentry Community*, 28; Bennett, *Class, Community and Careerism*, 76; Payling, *Political Society*, 18.
[6]   See Appendix 2.
[7]   More cases occurred in Cheshire, but the King's Bench had no jurisdiction in the county. See below.
[8]   KB27/528 rot. 35 rex. Also printed in *Select Cases in the Court of King's Bench Under Richard II, Henry IV and Henry V*, 83–5.
[9]   KB27/56 rex rot. 25; KB27/57 rex rot. 5; KB27/462 rex rot. 21; KB27/645 rot. 8.
[10] KB29/72 rot. 22.

and 1455 relating to the Percy–Neville feud.[11] There was then a lull in cases from Yorkshire until 1489 when twelve men from Cottingham were indicted,[12] followed by one case in 1491[13] and two in 1494.[14] The largest cluster of cases arose between 1500 and 1505. Six cases arose in 1500[15] followed by fourteen in 1504, three of which were for wearing the livery of a noble fraudulently[16] and one in 1505.[17] Two further cases occurred in 1508[18] and 1510[19] respectively. Larger clusters of cases occurred in other counties, but these clusters were more isolated, occurring over a shorter chronological period. Yorkshire, in contrast, had numerous clusters distributed throughout the long fifteenth century.

The high number of cases in the county fits with general views of the county's violent and lawless nature. Ralph Griffiths characterised fifteenth-century Yorkshire as having 'an unusually large number of magnate and gentry families consumed with mutual jealousies that frequently erupted in feuding and violence'.[20] Such characterisations were frequently made by contemporaries, particularly southern chroniclers such as the two continuators of the Crowland chronicle who were prejudiced against northerners across the fifteenth and sixteenth centuries.[21] It was during the reign of Henry VII that most of the cases from Yorkshire, twenty-nine in total, occurred. Tudor commentators noted the problems faced by Henry VII with regard to governing Yorkshire and the rest of the north. Polydore Vergil stated that 'the folk of the North' were 'savage and more eager than others for upheavals'[22] and Henry VII needed to deal with uprisings and disturbances in Yorkshire in both 1485–6 and 1489.[23] Although Henry had to deal with rebellion in other regions, Yorkshire posed 'a unique challenge' because that was where the man he deposed, Richard III, 'had his roots'.[24] Yet

[11] KB9/148/2 mm. 31, 38, 54–5; KB9/149 mm. 20–1, 49, 53. The cases relating to the Percy–Neville feud are discussed in depth in Chapter 9.
[12] KB29/120 rot. 16
[13] KB29/122 rot. 5.
[14] KB29/125 rot. 6.
[15] KB29/130 rot. 14; KB29/131 rott. 2–3.
[16] KB29/134 rott. 26–7; KB29/135 rot. 12.
[17] KB29/135 rot. 12.
[18] KB29/137 rot. 17.
[19] KB29/142 rot. 7.
[20] Griffiths, *Reign of Henry VI*, 132.
[21] On Crowland see: Michael Hicks, 'Crowland's World: A Westminster View of the Yorkist Ages', *History*, xc (2005), 178–9.
[22] *The Anglica Historia of Polydore Vergil, AD 1486–1537*, ed. and trans. Denys Hay, Camden Society, lxxiv (London, 1950), 11.
[23] Ibid. On the risings themselves see e.g. Pollard, *North-Eastern England*, 380–3; Michael Hicks, 'The Yorkshire Rebellion of 1489 Reconsidered', *Northern History*, xxii (1986), 39–62.
[24] Pollard, *North-Eastern England*, 368.

the uprisings in 1485–6 and 1489 did not lead to cases of illegal livery in the county and there is no evidence that Richard III's livery badge was used as a sign of anti-Tudor sentiments in the way that Richard II's livery badge was used by those opposing Henry IV at the start of the fifteenth century. Moreover, it was rare for uprisings that directly challenged royal authority to produce cases of illegal livery. Large clusters of cases were normally connected to local disputes related to the internal politics of a county, which were frequent in Yorkshire throughout the later medieval period. For instance, fourteen of the cases in the county related to men wearing the liveries of nobles whose livery they were not entitled to wear that were heard on 2 May 1504. These indictments occurred as part of the increased tension in the county between Thomas Savage, archbishop of York and Henry, fifth earl of Northumberland which culminated in a brawl between the servants of both men at Fulford on 23 May 1504.[25] There were several prominent feuds in Yorkshire during the fifteenth century which drew in several regional magnates. Not every outbreak of disorder prompted a high number of cases but the high number of livery cases in the county is consistent with the general picture that enforcement was linked to instances of widespread disorder.

There were six counties with between nineteen and twenty-six cases of illegal livery. Five of these counties are in the west midlands and the Welsh Marches – Worcestershire, Staffordshire, Derbyshire, Herefordshire and Warwickshire – while one is in the south, Kent. The prominence of cases of illegal livery in the midlands coincides with much discussion of lawlessness in the region, although it should be noted that some counties such as Nottinghamshire and Lincolnshire had few cases of illegal livery. The primary characteristic of these counties is that most of the cases that occurred in these counties did so in clusters, except for a few miscellaneous cases.

Twenty-two cases of illegal livery from Derbyshire are found on the crown side of the King's Bench records between 1434 and 1505. There were two main clusters of cases in Derbyshire in 1434–5[26] and 1468,[27] along with three other cases in 1450,[28] 1466[29] and 1505.[30] There was also a private suit in the county when William Vernon, son of Richard Vernon, was indicted in 1410.[31] Derbyshire had a record of disorder during the fifteenth century. Prior to the cluster of cases in 1434–5, in 1433 a large number of men were charged for various offences

---

[25] Hoyle, 'The Affray at Fulford', 239–56; E163/9/27 contains several bills and articles relating to this event.
[26] KB9/11 mm. 15, 17; KB29/68 rott. 4, 5, 9, 10, 17, 20.
[27] KB9/13 mm. 11, 19–23, 53, 63.
[28] KB29/82 rot. 7.
[29] KB29/97 rot. 29.
[30] KB9/437 m. 20.
[31] KB27/596 plea rot. 76.

such as unlawful maintenance, conspiracy, mayhem and extortion.[32] The cluster of cases in 1468 was heard by an *oyer et terminer* that resulted from disorder in the county which included the murder of Roger Vernon.[33] Bordering Yorkshire, Derbyshire displays similar characteristics in terms of a reputation for disorder and the existence of multiple clusters of cases, but is on a much smaller scale. Twenty-two cases can be identified in Derbyshire, compared to thirty-six in Yorkshire. Derbyshire also has a lower total number of cases than either Warwickshire or Staffordshire (discussed below). Derbyshire does, though, have more clusters of cases and the cases are spread out more consistently over a long chronological period.

A similar trend can be detected in two other midland counties, Warwickshire and Staffordshire, as both counties had large clusters of cases along with a few other cases scattered across the century. In 1414 an *oyer et terminer* commission found twenty-one cases in Staffordshire.[34] Another case, apparently unconnected, arose the following year.[35] Afterwards, no cases arose until 1488,[36] with two more occurring in 1501[37] and 1505.[38] Warwickshire had a broadly similar distribution pattern to Staffordshire. The largest cluster of cases in Warwickshire was in 1489 when fifteen cases can be identified in the county.[39] To this can be added four individual instances of illegal livery in 1436,[40] 1460,[41] 1492[42] and 1493.[43] In both counties there were very large clusters of cases which incorporated all but a few of the cases of illegal livery in these counties, with the exception of a few scattered cases at other periods.

Herefordshire also had numerous cases of illegal livery. In total, twenty cases can be identified from the county, the earliest of which was in 1452 when a commission of *oyer et terminer* included three indictments for illegal livery.[44] A second commission in 1457 prosecuted ten cases of illegal livery[45] to which can be added three further cases identifiable from the controlment rolls.[46] Four

[32] KB29/67 rot. 14.
[33] Hicks, '1468 Statute', 18.
[34] KB9/113 mm. 2, 11, 28, 40–3; KB29/53 rot. 24.
[35] KB27/617 rex rot. 16.
[36] KB29/119 rot. 2.
[37] KB29/131 rot. 19.
[38] KB29/135 rot. 10.
[39] KB9/380 m. 41; KB29/119 rott. 10–11; KB29/120 rott. 11–13, 16, 28.
[40] KB29/69 rot. 19.
[41] KB29/89 rot. 30.
[42] KB29/123 rot. 5.
[43] KB29/123 rot. 23.
[44] KB9/34/1 m. 5; KB9/34/2 mm. 42, 142.
[45] KB9/35 mm. 6, 67–9.
[46] KB29/87 rott. 15, 18.

further cases can be identified from the county in 1461,[47] 1490,[48] 1491[49] and 1518.[50] Many key marcher lords who became embroiled in the Wars of the Roses held lands in the county and the wider region. Although they themselves were not indicted, men with a close connection to them were. Richard, duke of York, held large amounts of land in the neighbouring region of South Wales and retained several members of the leading gentry in the county. Other prominent peers such as the duke of Buckingham and the earl of Shrewsbury similarly had retainers in the county.[51] This combination of magnate influence and proximity to the Welsh border made Herefordshire a county in which the excesses of bastard feudalism could thrive.

The neighbouring county of Worcestershire too had cases that involved prominent members of local society. One cluster of cases arose in 1517 when members of the Savage family, Sir John, and his son also called John, were indicted for various offences against the statutes of livery.[52] Other cases had arisen in Worcestershire prior to these charges. There had been two previous clusters of cases in Worcestershire: three cases had arisen in 1463[53] and a further eight between 1501 and 1505.[54] Three further cases arose in 1517–18, not involving the Savages.[55] Gloucestershire has similarities with Worcestershire that are appropriate to highlight here because the Savages had connections and influence that cut across county boundaries. Both John Savage Sr and John Savage Jr were each indicted twice for illegal livery in 1517,[56] meaning that in that year they were charged a total of eleven and nine times respectively. Gloucestershire differs from Worcestershire with respect to other cases that arise. Only three further cases can be identified in Gloucestershire, all of which are in the period 1517–18.[57] The fact that Worcestershire and Gloucestershire border each other and that the same knights were indicted in both counties suggests two things. First, that there was a concerted effort by justices in both Worcestershire and Gloucestershire to curb the power of the Savage family in that area. This was a consequence of family's

[47]   KB29/93 rot. 16.
[48]   KB29/120 rot. 15.
[49]   KB29/119 rot. 11; KB29/122 rott. 3, 7.
[50]   KB29/150 rott. 21–2.
[51]   Herbert, 'Herefordshire, 1413–61', 105; Johnson, *Duke Richard of York*, 1–27; 228–41, passim. *CIPM, 1422–1427*, nos. 510–12 lists the lands York inherited from his uncle, Edmund, earl of March, in Herefordshire and the adjacent March of Wales in 1425.
[52]   KB29/148 rott. 50–1, 53.
[53]   KB29/94 rott. 1, 2, 6.
[54]   KB27/995 rex rot, 15; KB29/131 rott. 15, 20; KB29/132 rot. 33; KB29/135 rott. 12, 20.
[55]   KB29/149 rot. 7; KB29/150 rot. 5; KB29/151 rot. 25.
[56]   KB29/148 rot. 54.
[57]   KB29/148 rot. 54; KB29/150 rot. 16.

involvement in the murder of the Worcestershire JP John Pauncefote in 1516. The Savages, and their wider affinity, had a reputation for lawlessness before and after their charges of illegal retaining.[58] Second, illegal retaining practices could stretch beyond county borders.

The southern county in which the highest number of illegal livery cases occurred was Kent. There were twenty-one cases of illegal livery, although the cases in Kent did not confine themselves to large clusters like Warwickshire or Staffordshire. Instead, Kent had one large cluster of cases in 1478, a smaller cluster in 1503 along with other cases spread out over a period of time. Kent had the *cause célèbre* of illegal livery cases when, in 1507, George Neville, Lord Bergavenny, was indicted for illegally retaining 471 men.[59] Bergavenny was indicted again in 1516 for illegally retaining eighty-three men.[60] His grandfather, Edward Neville, was ordered to appear before the justices in Kent, along with ten others, in 1461.[61] However, the largest number of separate cases to cluster together was in 1478 when ten cases arose.[62] Another cluster occurred in 1503 when there were five cases of illegal livery, including an earlier indictment against Bergavenny for illegal retaining.[63] A further case can be identified from 1512.[64] In summary, the distribution pattern in Kent was one major cluster of different cases in 1478, a smaller cluster in 1503, along with several other larger individual cases involving prominent nobles.

Medium Number of Cases

Six counties had between ten and fourteen cases, with similar distribution patterns to many counties which had a larger number of indictments. Suffolk followed a similar pattern to Warwickshire and Staffordshire, but on a smaller scale. Twelve cases occurred in 1470,[65] in addition to a further case in 1491.[66] While the number of cases is fewer than Warwickshire and Staffordshire, Suffolk is similar because there was one large cluster of cases that accounted for the vast majority that arose in the county and a smaller number of cases that occurred independently. These three counties display broadly similar characteristics in terms of cases of illegal livery: the vast majority were confined to very large

---

[58]   Discussed fully in: Ives, 'Crime, Sanctuary and Royal Authority', 296–320.
[59]   KB29/136 rott. 16–17.
[60]   KB29/148 rott. 17–18.
[61]   KB29/92 rot. 13.
[62]   KB29/108 rot. 12.
[63]   KB29/133 rot. 27.
[64]   KB29/144 rot. 23.
[65]   KB29/99 rott. 31–3.
[66]   KB29/121 rot. 11.

clusters, in addition to a few other miscellaneous cases. The cases that occurred in Suffolk are consistent with the broader pattern of enforcement of the statutes, as the majority of the cases were connected to widespread magnate lawlessness. Thirteen cases in 1469 were picked up by a commission dealing with instances of disorder that centred on the siege of Caister Castle. Similarly, the 1491 case occurred during a period in which there was widespread enforcement of the statutes in the early years of Henry VII's reign.

There was one large cluster of cases in Cambridgeshire when, in 1505, all thirteen cases from the county arose. Only fourteen men were indicted in Cambridgeshire for fraudulently wearing the livery of prominent nobles, namely the earl of Oxford, the duke of Buckingham and Margaret Beaufort, mother of Henry VII as well as a local knight, Robert Cotton.[67] These peers were not themselves indicted for illegal livery but people were indicted for illegally wearing their livery. The broader regional context at this time explains the peculiarities of this particular cluster of cases. During 1505 similar indictments were made in the neighbouring counties of Essex[68] and Huntingdonshire[69] when the liveries of the earl of Oxford and the king's mother were being worn without their permission. Given the pattern of land ownership in Cambridgeshire at this time it is clear why cases such as these occurred. John de Vere, earl of Oxford, had extensive landholdings across East Anglia, including eight manors in Cambridgeshire and forty-five in Essex.[70] Margaret Beaufort likewise held land in both Cambridgeshire and Essex[71] while the duke of Buckingham held land in Essex.[72] Cambridgeshire was a county in which several prominent nobles and royals owned land; it was in that county that men who were either former servants or impersonating their servants were indicted for fraudulently wearing their livery. As each of these nobles had lands, and therefore servants, in the counties where people were fraudulently wearing their livery, it is likely that the livery was easily recognisable to locals. Presumably such liveries were also readily available or recognisable enough that they could be replicated or forged.

A similar type of case was also prevalent in Surrey. All fourteen of the cases from Surrey were confined to two clusters, the first three of which all happened in 1467.[73] There were eleven cases in 1491, seven of which were for the wearing of livery of various leading nobles: the earls of Oxford, Arundel, Essex, Shrewsbury, the bishop of Winchester, Sir Thomas Bourchier, Sir John Turbervyle and

---

67 KB9/436 mm. 9, 14, 42.
68 KB9/436 m. 7
69 KB9/436 m. 8.
70 Ross, *John De Vere*, 92–3.
71 Jones and Underwood, *King's Mother*, 262–7.
72 Rawcliffe, *The Staffords*, 191, 193.
73 KB29/98 rott. 8, 19–20.

Margaret Beaufort.[74] Six of these seven offences occurred in Southwark and the other in Wandesworth. As these were boroughs next to London it may be assumed that the liveries of such prominent magnates were well known in the capital. Again such liveries were either readily available in the area or it was possible to find someone who knew the liveries enough to be able to produce replicas.

There were also fourteen cases in Hertfordshire, the first of which was in 1460.[75] No further cases can be identified in Hertfordshire until the reign of Henry VII when the remaining cases arose. The thirteen cases from Henry VII's reign in Hertfordshire were spread out between 1489 and 1508 with: one case in 1489;[76] three cases in 1491;[77] two cases in 1495;[78] one case in 1499;[79] one case in 1500;[80] two cases in 1502;[81] one in 1505;[82] one case in 1507;[83] and a final case in 1508.[84] Sussex differed from Hertfordshire and Surrey because, although the statutes were enforced on a similar scale in all three counties, the majority of cases from Sussex did not occur during the reign of Henry VII. Ten cases can be identified from Sussex. Two 'mini-clusters' of three cases each can be seen to arise in 1476[85] and 1505–7[86], with further isolated cases arising in 1480[87] and 1516[88] in addition to two earlier cases from 1429[89] and 1437.[90]

The final county discussed in this section is Shropshire, which was remote from the centres of power at Westminster but had fewer cases than the other marcher counties of Cheshire and Herefordshire. The ten cases in Shropshire were from one cluster of cases in connection with major local disturbances, along with other miscellaneous cases. Five cases occurred in 1414 as a result of Henry V's campaign against disorder that produced twenty-one cases in the neighbouring county of Staffordshire.[91] The King's Bench visited Shropshire immediately after

---

[74]   KB29/127 rott. 27–8.
[75]   KB29/89 rot. 24; KB29/93 rot. 16.
[76]   KB29/119 rot. 11.
[77]   KB29/120 rot. 3
[78]   KB29/126 rot. 4.
[79]   KB29/129 rot. 22.
[80]   KB29/130 rot. 16.
[81]   KB29/132 rot. 33.
[82]   KB29/135 rot. 11.
[83]   KB29/137 rot. 1.
[84]   KB29/137 rot. 27.
[85]   KB29/106 rott. 11, 28.
[86]   KB29/135 rot. 6; KB29/137 rot. 1.
[87]   KB29/110 rot. 12.
[88]   KB29/148 rott. 12, 40.
[89]   KB29/62 rot. 3.
[90]   KB29/70 rot. 16.
[91]   KB27/613 rott 39–40 rex; KB27/617 rott. 31, 40 rex; KB27/618 rot. 14 rex; KB27/619 rott. 5, 18, 24.

visiting Staffordshire. The initial petition complaining about lawlessness and the suppression of the Glyndŵr revolt by 1414 suggests that internal politics and feuding were the cause of the visit.[92] Another five cases can be identified from the county over the following century during periods in which the statutes were being enforced in other counties, in 1421,[93] 1453,[94] 1477,[95] 1480[96] and 1508[97] respectively. Moreover, it should be noted that there was no obvious Welsh element to the indictments in Shropshire, although the evidence is insufficient to state whether there was any general avoidance of giving liveries to Welshmen in this region at this point. Instead, the cases of illegal livery in Shropshire were related to wider instances of illegal livery and/or disorder in the midlands.

Low Number of Cases

Nineteen counties had between one and seven cases of illegal livery, many of which occurred in isolation. This was evident in the south-west where, despite the region's reputation for lawlessness, banditry and violence, there were few cases of illegal livery. Cornwall only had one case of illegal livery, in 1467, when seven men were indicted for illegally receiving livery from John Vivian.[98] The activities of other members of the Cornish gentry and their retainers were noted by contemporaries but no further cases of illegal livery are known. Richard Tregoys, a notorious lawbreaker in Cornwall, was said to have kept a liveried retinue of malefactors but was never indicted for illegal livery.[99] In Cornwall the problems of livery and retaining occurred but this did not produce cases for illegal livery. A similar lack of cases is evident in Somerset which had only two cases of illegal livery, both occurring in 1433 with four and six men being indicted in each case.[100] There were only four cases of illegal livery in Devon. During Easter 1491 there were three indictments against Sir William Courtenay and

---

[92] It should be noted that the cases from this period were not included in the justice of the peace rolls that have been identified and edited for the county. *Shropshire Peace Roll, 1400–1414*, ed. E.G. Kimball (Shrewsbury, 1959); Edward Powell, 'Proceedings before the Justices of the Peace at Shrewsbury in 1414: A Supplement to the Shropshire Peace Roll', *EHR*, xcix (1984), 541–50.
[93] KB27/640 rex rot. 7; KB27/642 rex rot. 7.
[94] KB29/84 rot. 5.
[95] KB29/107 rot. 12.
[96] KB29/110 rot. 16.
[97] KB29/137 rot. 36.
[98] KB29/98 rot. 20.
[99] C1/42/108. For Tregoy's career see: Kleineke, 'Why the West was Wild', 75, 78, 83–93; Kleineke, 'Poachers and Gamekeepers', 134–6.
[100] KB29/66 rot. 28; KB29/67 rot 4.

ninety-two others, eight of whom were from Somerset, for illegal livery,[101] which coincides with riots in the county.[102] This reputation for lawlessness and violence, however, rarely translated into cases of illegal livery. The only other known case comes from a returned sheriff's writ from Trinity 1468 which stated that Thomas Cokeyn, esquire, Henry Rolstone, esquire, two gentlemen and thirty-six yeomen had failed to appear in court.[103]

In terms of the pattern of enforcement Devon was most similar not to a fellow county in the south-west, but to Leicestershire. Two cases arose in Leicestershire in 1516 in which 343 men were indicted for offences against the statutes of livery.[104] Only one other case from Leicestershire can be identified, from 1459.[105] As in Devon, the high number of cases in Leicestershire happened in the same year that a large number of people were also indicted for rioting.[106] These disturbances were connected to feuding in the county between two peers, Thomas Grey, marquess of Dorset and George, Lord Hastings. The disturbances attracted some contemporary attention. In a letter to the earl of Shrewsbury, Thomas Alen wrote that 'there is great trouble between the Marquis [of Dorset], Lord Hastings and Sir Ric[hard] Sacheverell' and that both sides were 'bound to appear' in Star Chamber.[107] Indictments for rioting occurring with those for illegal retaining in Devon and Leicestershire fits with the broader picture that cases arose in connection to wider local disputes.

In contrast, Hampshire's seven cases occurred in isolation rather than clusters. The first cases from Hampshire were in the late 1440s and 1450s, the same time as cases were becoming more common across England, and again during the reign of Henry VII, which was the reign with the largest concentration of cases. The first three cases occurred during a six-year span in 1449,[108] 1451[109] and 1455[110] respectively. A further case arose in 1476 when Thomas Grenefield, gentleman, was indicted for illegally giving livery to one tailor.[111] There was then a gap of twenty-nine years without a case in Hampshire until 1505, when

---

[101] KB29/121 rott. 15–16.
[102] KB29/121 rot. 14.
[103] KB27/829 rex rot. 21.
[104] KB29/148 rot. 16.
[105] KB29/88 rot. 33.
[106] For Devon KB29/121 rot. 14. For Leicestershire: KB29/148 rot. 23.
[107] *L&P Hen. VIII*, ii, no. 2018. Discussed fully in: Robertson, 'Court Careers and County Quarrels', 153–70.
[108] KB27/764 rex rot. 24.
[109] KB29/83 rot. 2.
[110] KB29/86 rott. 1, 11.
[111] KB29/106 rot. 24.

there were two cases,[112] followed by a final case in 1511.[113] Hampshire differed from many other counties in terms of landholding because the church was the dominant power in the county. Hampshire had a large number of monastic institutions and contained the seat of the bishopric of Winchester, the largest and wealthiest bishopric in England. Consequently, no secular magnate had a strong landed base in Hampshire and the county was not seriously affected by forfeitures and appointments to office resulting from political change at the centre.[114] Nevertheless, there were cases of illegal livery in the county, but unlike counties such as Yorkshire, Warwickshire and Staffordshire there was no large cluster of cases in Hampshire.

There were three cases in Norfolk heard by the King's Bench: two in 1489[115] and an additional one in 1496.[116] To this can be added one case against William Skipwith, gentleman, for giving liveries to three other men at Fordham in 1504 which was heard in the Exchequer.[117] Soon after the period that this study focuses on, six further men from Norfolk were sent writs of *venire facias* for alleged offences against the statutes of livery in 1522.[118] This is in contrast to its neighbouring county of Suffolk which had several prominent cases of illegal livery including the indictments against the dukes of Norfolk and Suffolk in 1469. Twelve men from Norfolk, including one knight and eight esquires, were indicted for illegal livery in 1469 along with the duke of Norfolk.[119] The fact that members of the gentry from both Norfolk and Suffolk were indicted at the same time for illegal livery is evidence that some members of the East Anglian gentry had horizons that looked beyond their home county and had more a regional perspective. This is also evident in Gloucestershire, where the six cases of illegal retaining were connected to other various offences committed by the Savage family in Worcestershire.[120]

Lincolnshire also had no cases of illegal livery until the reign of Henry VII, during which all three cases occurred, with two cases in 1490–1[121] and one in 1504.[122] The absence of cases during the Lancastrian era is indicative both of the low levels of enforcement of the statutes prior to the 1450s and that, during

---

[112] KB9/436 m. 13; KB29/135 rot. 13.
[113] KB29/143 rot. 24.
[114] Purser, 'The County Community of Hampshire', 276, 280, 286.
[115] KB29/119 rott. 12, 14; KB29/120 rot. 13.
[116] KB29/127 rot. 7.
[117] E159/282 rott. 7, 17.
[118] KB29/154 rot. 32.
[119] KB29/99 rott. 31–2.
[120] KB29/148 rot. 54; KB29/150 rot. 16; Ives, 'Crime, Sanctuary and Royal Authority', 296320.
[121] KB29/120 rott. 19, 28; KB29/121 rott. 2, 19.
[122] KB9/435 m. 11.

the Lancastrian period, gentry violence in Lincolnshire 'would appear to have been at a reasonably low and, in medieval terms, generally acceptable level'.[123] The absence of cases before the reign of Henry VII is evident in several other counties that only experienced a handful of illegal livery cases. In Berkshire the three cases that arose in the county occurred in the space of three years between 1505 and 1508.[124] In the neighbouring county of Northamptonshire there was a cluster of three cases of illegal retaining between 1488 and 1491[125] and a further case early in Henry VIII's reign in 1510.[126] This trend is evident in many of the counties that had only a few cases of illegal livery, such as Bedfordshire. In 1498 John, Lord Grey of Wilton was indicted for giving illegal livery to three men of Dunstable.[127] This was followed by a case heard by the Exchequer in 1505 against William Parker, gentleman for illegally retaining three other men in the county[128] and one further case heard in King's Bench involving one labourer in 1508.[129] In Essex the two cases of illegal livery occurred in 1493 when nine men were indicted[130] and in 1505 when one smith was indicted for fraudulently wearing the livery of the earl of Oxford.[131] The absence of cases of illegal livery in many counties until the reign of Henry VII is indicative of the more widespread and rigorous enforcement of the statutes that occurred during his reign. In this respect Oxfordshire is atypical because the only two identifiable cases arose before the reign of Henry VII: in 1440 when two men were indicted[132] and again in 1478 when the rector of Queen's College Oxford was indicted for giving illegal livery to one man.[133] Similarly, in Somerset the only two cases occurred during the reign of Henry VI in 1433.[134]

Several counties only had one case of illegal livery. The only known case from crown side of the King's Bench in Nottinghamshire was in 1456 when twelve men were indicted.[135] There was also a private suit in Nottinghamshire in 1451 when Sir John Talbot brought a suit against Sir John Stanhope for illegally distributing livery in January 1450 in connection with a parliamentary election

---

[123] Jonathan S. Mackman, 'The Lincolnshire Gentry and the Wars of the Roses' (unpublished D.Phil thesis, University of York, 1999), 142.
[124] KB9/436 m. 16; KB9/444 m. 80; KB29/137 rot. 36; KB29/142 rot. 7.
[125] KB29/120 rot. 3.
[126] KB29/140 rot. 26.
[127] KB9/417 m. 119; KB29/129 rot. 2.
[128] E159/284 rott. 3, 46.
[129] KB29/137 rot. 27.
[130] KB29/123 rot. 22; KB29/124 rot. 13
[131] KB9/436 m. 7.
[132] KB29/74 rott. 3, 14.
[133] KB27/908 rex rot. 5.
[134] KB29/66 rot. 28; KB29/67 rot 4.
[135] KB29/86 rot. 27.

dispute.[136] Given the connection between illegal livery and wider instances of lawlessness, this evidence is consistent with Simon Payling's argument that, during the Lancastrian period, 'the index of aristocratic disorder in the county was low'.[137] Although no study of gentry violence has been conducted for Nottinghamshire during the Yorkist and Tudor periods, the absence of cases of illegal livery suggests that Nottinghamshire continued to have a low index of aristocratic disorder. Only one further case occurred in the county, which was from the town of Nottingham itself when one man was indicted in 1510.[138] Other counties in which only one case can be identified have not been the subject of similar studies of gentry violence. One case occurred in Dorset when, in 1459, Simon Raule, 'courtholder', was indicted for illegally giving livery to one labourer.[139] Rutland was on a similar scale with two men, Robert and Nicholas Greenham, both husbandmen, being indicted in 1510, which is the only identifiable case in the county.[140] Wiltshire likewise had only one case of illegal retaining: it arose in 1508 when Sir Walter Hungerford illegally gave livery to seven men from Devizes.[141] The lack of cases from Dorset, Wiltshire and Rutland and the relatively small number involved suggests a low level of gentry violence on a similar scale to Nottinghamshire.

Counties with No Cases

There were some counties in which there were no cases of illegal livery, but this does not mean that people from those counties were never indicted. Men from Buckinghamshire and Middlesex were indicted for offences against the statutes of livery but had no cases of illegal livery in the counties themselves. Instead, men from these counties were charged with breaking the livery laws in neighbouring counties: Bedfordshire in the case of John Grey, Lord Wilton, in 1498;[142] Hertfordshire in the case of two husbandmen and a yeoman from Middlesex in 1495.[143] Buckinghamshire and Middlesex neighbour London, but this was not necessarily the reason for the lack of cases of illegal livery in them, since other counties such as Hertfordshire, Kent and Surrey had cases of illegal livery throughout the period discussed. Indeed, in some circumstances a noble with a large retinue of men close to the capital may help to provoke an enforcement of

---

[136] CP40/763 rot. 483; CP40/769 rot. 138; Payling, *Political Society*, 162–4.
[137] Payling, *Political Society*, 214.
[138] KB29/140 rot. 31; KB29/143 rot. 41.
[139] KB29/88 rot. 35.
[140] KB29/142 rot. 24.
[141] KB29/138 rot. 5.
[142] KB29/129 rot. 2.
[143] KB29/126 rot. 4.

the statutes, such as Lord Bergavenny in 1507 when he was indicted for retaining 471 men in Kent.[144] The absence of cases in Buckinghamshire and Middlesex was a product of the sporadic nature with which the statutes were enforced. The fact that men from Buckinghamshire and Middlesex were indicted for illegal livery in neighbouring counties despite no cases occurring in their own county is evidence that, although the law operated on a rigid county structure, society did not.

Three counties had no cases of illegal livery, nor was anyone from them charged with illegal livery in a different county. These were the three most northern counties: Cumbria, Westmorland and Northumberland. The absence of cases in the northern counties of England is a result of the fact that the wardens of the marches were exempt from the livery statutes because armed liveried retainers were required for the purposes of protecting the Anglo-Scottish border.[145] Another reason for the absence of cases from these counties is that they were sparsely populated. These counties are poorly documented compared with the more populous areas and there has been no study of landed society in these counties for the later middle ages. In the neighbouring Lordship of Richmond elements of the old feudal settlement remained strong during the fifteenth century and 'retained their relevance'.[146] It may be that the practice of retaining was not as prevalent in these large, thinly populated northern counties. Alternatively, the lack of cases of illegal livery may be indicative of either problems associated with law enforcement in the region or the problems of travelling to London from such far-flung areas.

Cheshire

The county that experienced the largest number of cases of illegal livery was Cheshire, where thirty-nine cases arose. Cheshire, as a palatinate county, had a different administrative structure from the rest of the kingdom.[147] This palatinate status cannot be viewed as the reason for the higher number of cases because one

---

[144] As suggested in: Gwyn, *King's Cardinal*, 187.
[145] *PROME*, xiii, 65; xiii, 386.
[146] Melanie Devine, 'The Lordship of Richmond in the Later Middle Ages' in *Liberties and Identities in the Medieval British Isles*, ed. Michael Prestwich (Woodbridge, 2008), 110.
[147] The most comprehensive study of the administration of medieval Cheshire is: Dorothy J. Clayton, *The Administration of the County Palatine of Cheshire, 1442–85* (Manchester, 1990). For a discussion of attempts to maintain law and order in fifteenth-century Cheshire see: Dorothy J. Clayton, 'Peace Bonds and the Maintenance of Law and Order in Late Medieval England: The Example of Cheshire', *BIHR*, lviii (1985), 133–48.

of the other palatinates, the bishopric of Durham, had no cases of illegal livery.[148] Lancashire, the other palatinate, only had one known case of illegal livery but this was a private suit in 1429.[149] In many ways, this fits the broader trend of several northern counties such as Cumbria, Westmorland and Northumberland where statutes on illegal livery seem to have been barely enforced. Men from Lancashire were, however, indicted in other counties for illegal retaining. Three men from Lancashire were indicted in Yorkshire in three separate cases: Richard Radcliff, gentleman in 1491;[150] James Stanley, the future bishop of Ely in 1500;[151] and Sir Edward Stanley in 1504.[152] In these cases the King's Bench was not operating in Lancashire; rather, the men in question were breaking the livery laws in Yorkshire.

The higher number of cases in Cheshire was not simply the product of a different means of enforcing law and order in the county because the different methods in Lancashire and the bishopric of Durham produced similar enforcement patterns to other northern counties. Instead, the higher number of cases in Cheshire was connected to the social, political and military composition of the county. Cheshire was heavily militarised and was prone to prolonged periods of violence and lawlessness.[153] The heavily militaristic aspect to this county society was why Richard II built up a retinue of men from the county during the 'tyranny' of the final years of his reign in an attempt to 'convert the earldom into a bastion of royal power'.[154] The activities of Richard II's Cheshire archers and their crimes were a source of serious criticism during Richard's final years and the acts of 1399 and 1401, both of which had an emphasis on royal retaining practices, were influenced by the activities of men from Cheshire during Richard II's final years.[155]

When these cases are viewed in the broader context of enforcement across England, it is clear that Cheshire followed a broadly similar pattern to the rest of the kingdom. The first case to arise in Cheshire was in 1415 when seven men

---

[148] DURH13/1, 224–30.
[149] PL15/2 rot. 2.
[150] KB29/122 rot. 5.
[151] KB29/131 rot. 2. This case is discussed in depth on p. 000.
[152] KB29/134 rot. 26.
[153] It was for this reason that Philip Morgan regarded Cheshire as an 'ideal choice' for examining the impact of military service on a community, although he acknowledges that these local variations made the county atypical of the rest of England. Philip Morgan, *War and Society in Medieval Cheshire, 1277–1403*, Chetham Society, 3rd series, xxxiv (Manchester, 1987), 1–2, 8.
[154] Bennett, *Community, Class and Careerism*, 168. On Richard II's Cheshire archers see also: Saul, *Richard II*, 367, 375, 393–4, 431, 444–5, 460; Gillespie, 'Richard II's Archers of the Crown', 14–29.
[155] *PROME*, viii, 11–12, 148–9.

were indicted.[156] This can be viewed as part of the first major cluster of cases of illegal livery which occurred at the start of Henry V's reign when he was attempting to eradicate lawlessness in the localities. Thereafter, fourteen cases of illegal livery occurred in 1428.[157] These cases are of particular significance in a parliamentary context because they shed light on the workings of parliament and the development of parliamentary legislation. In 1429 a new act was the first to state explicitly that the statutes were to be upheld in the palatinate counties of Cheshire and Lancashire,[158] which indicates that parliament was essentially formalising legislation rather than expanding it. There were then two further cases in 1432[159] and one in 1434.[160]

After the 1434 case there was a gap of over six decades until the next cluster of cases when an *oyer et terminer* commission identified twenty-one instances of illegal retaining in 1499.[161] These cases coincided with Prince Arthur's first visit to the county in August 1499 after being created earl of Chester on 29 November 1489 and the eyre at this visit represented 'increased financial, judicial and political oversight'. According to Tim Thornton, 'the intention behind the eyre was clearly financial and political gain'.[162] Two members of the Stanley family were indicted by the commission: Sir William Stanley on three occasions[163] and James Stanley, rector of Manchester college, twice.[164] The Stanleys were the pre-eminent family of the north-west during this period and were influential in Henry VII's victory at Bosworth and defecting to his side, subsequently becoming 'the military backbone of the new régime'.[165] They were related to the new king via the marriage of Thomas Stanley, earl of Derby, and the king's mother Margaret Beaufort. There were, however, problems and mistrust between Henry and his step-family which were most evident in 1495 when Sir William Stanley was executed for treason after he became embroiled in the Perkin Warbeck conspiracy and defected to his cause in 1493. When considered in conjunction with the fact that James Stanley[166] and Edward Stanley were indicted for illegal livery in Yorkshire in Michaelmas 1500,[167] it is clear that the Stanley

---

[156] CHES25/25 m. 14.
[157] CHES25/12 mm. 16–17.
[158] *PROME*, ix, 402–3; McKelvie, 'The Livery Act of 1429', 55–65.
[159] CHES25/12 m. 25.
[160] CHES25/12 m. 30.
[161] CHES25/18 mm. 7–9, 11–14, 17, 21, 26, 28, 33–4.
[162] Thornton, *Cheshire and the Tudor State*, 71, quotations on 185.
[163] CHES25/18 mm. 8, 11.
[164] CHES25/18 m. 13. The case against James Stanley is discussed in depth on p. 000.
[165] For this discussion of the Stanleys see: Cunningham, 'Henry VII, Sir Thomas Butler and the Stanley Family', 220–4, quotation on 223.
[166] KB8/3/1 m. 5.
[167] KB29/134 m. 26.

family was the target of many illegal livery prosecutions at this time. To view these indictments purely as an attack upon the Stanley family, however, would be simplistic. Members of other prominent Cheshire families such as Sir William Booth, Sir John Legh, Sir Peter Legh, Ewan Carrington, esquire, Sir John Warren, Sir Thomas Pole, William Davenport, esquire and William Brereton, esquire were also indicted for illegal livery.[168] Therefore, these cases from 1499 were an attack upon illegal livery in Cheshire which coincided with attempts by Henry VII to assert more control over the county.[169]

The fact that Cheshire had the largest number of cases of illegal livery, and a different legal system which did not return cases to King's Bench, could be interpreted as representing a microcosm of patterns of enforcement throughout England at a local level, where records of local quarter sessions do not survive. J.G. Bellamy and Alan Cameron both stated a concern that the loss of local records means there is no way of ascertaining how many cases of illegal livery there were.[170] Yet when the pattern and nature of cases is considered it is clear that Cheshire was not different in terms of the enforcement of the statutes of livery, but followed a similar pattern to the rest of England. Cases of illegal livery were not an annual occurrence in the palatine of Cheshire. The pattern of short periods of enforcement producing large clusters of cases followed by lengthy periods in which the statutes were seemingly not enforced – sixty-five years between the indictments of 1434 and 1499 – is consistent with the pattern experienced in many other counties. Similarly, there were no cases in the records of the other palatinate counties. Only one case has been identified from Lancashire, which was a private suit, not a case brought by a royal official.[171] Furthermore, no cases are known in Middlesex, the county for which the King's Bench was the first court. Only one case of illegal livery is evident in the surviving justice of the peace proceedings, which was in Hampshire in 1476 against Thomas Grenefield, and also appears in the records of the King's Bench.[172] This evidence suggests that palatinate counties did not differ from the rest of England in enforcing the statutes of livery. The large number of cases in Cheshire cannot be attributed to a differing administrative system for which better records survive. Instead, the pattern in Cheshire is broadly similar

---

[168] 'Prominent' families taken from Tim Thornton's list of thirty-nine elite Cheshire gentry families between 1480 and 1560: Thornton, *Cheshire and the Tudor State*, 30–1. For indictments see: CHES25/18 mm. 9, 13–14, 26, 28, 33.

[169] Consider, in particular, Thornton's argument that 'Henry VII's policy in Cheshire was therefore to use the palatine to his own purposes, not to destroy it and replace it with subjection to central institutions'. Thornton, *Cheshire and the Tudor State*, 186.

[170] J.G. Bellamy, *Bastard Feudalism and the Law* (London, 1989), 4; Cameron, 'The Giving of Livery and Retaining', 26 n. 8.

[171] PL15/2 rot. 2.

[172] *Proceedings Before the Justices of the Peace*, 249–50; KB29/106 rot. 24.

to many other counties from the midlands and the north such as Yorkshire, Staffordshire and Derbyshire in which cases of illegal livery arose sporadically, in clusters, usually in conjunction with wider lawlessness.

Conclusion

The evidence presented here provides no simple correlation between landholding or geographical region and the propensity for places to have cases of illegal livery. The social and political character of many counties helps to explain some of these variations, but not all of them. Indeed, the evidence of illegal livery reinforces the need not to over-generalise from the example of one county or region. Cases of illegal livery tended to coincide with other instances of disorder, particularly larger clusters of cases. Therefore the fact that the two counties with the highest number of cases, Cheshire and Yorkshire, were heavily militarised and had reputations for violent feuding fits with this broader picture. Yet other counties with violent reputations, such as Devon and Cornwall, only had a few cases of illegal livery. Similarly, a regional approach is not appropriate because although counties and certain regions such as the south-west and the far north shared the common traits of having few or no cases of illegal livery, other regions such as the midlands and the home counties saw significant variations in the number of cases between neighbouring counties. There were illegal retaining links that crossed county borders, which is most evident in the fact that seventy-nine men were indicted for illegal livery in a county they did not reside in, but in each case they were indicted in a neighbouring county. The discrepancies between counties are in many ways a symptom of the sporadic enforcement of the statutes and the specific social and political characteristics of individual counties.

7

Networks and Localities

While previous chapters have explained who was indicted and where such indictments occurred, this chapter explores how such connections were formed. Most of the surviving records are formulaic, which means that the precise connections that led to someone receiving an annuity, entering into an indenture of retainer or benefitting from 'good lordship' are obscure. The reasons why someone entered the service of a particular lord must normally be inferred from the surviving documentation. Although the precise reasons are not always clear, men did enter into the service of those of a higher rank, and therefore recruitment into the service of a great lord, or even a minor member of the gentry, must have been one of the various activities in which medieval affinities engaged. Consequently, an understanding of the ways in which people came into the service of a lord further illuminates the inner workings of medieval affinities. There broadly two interpretations about how medieval affinities operated in practice. Christine Carpenter's work has emphasised the importance of vertical ties between a particular magnate who was the head of the affinity and the members of his affinity, noting that the affinity was 'a series of concentric circles' around the particular noble.[1] In contrast, Simon Walker emphasised the horizontal connections and links between members of a noble affinity which gave the affinity a greater element of coherence.[2] Neither interpretation is fully satisfactory because these positions take two opposing perspectives: Carpenter adopts a 'top-down' perspective in which the lord is at the centre of everything while Walker's 'bottom-up' approach risks minimising the significance of the leader of the affinity. The evidence examined here approaches the topic from a different perspective: that of those who entered into an illegal retaining relationship with a particular member of the nobility or gentry. Rather than examining a particular affinity or the workings of patronage in a locality, this chapter uses the 334 cases of illegal livery and retaining to highlight broader patterns about the nature of illegal affinities. It provides additional insights into the business of retaining in late medieval England by examining the nature of connections between those indicted together for illegal retaining, employing both the 'top-down' perspective of landholding and the 'bottom-up' perspective of familial connections between those illegally retained.

---

[1] Carpenter, 'Beauchamp Affinity', 515.
[2] Walker, *Lancastrian Affinity*, 94–116.

Landholding

In medieval society, land was the predominant source of wealth and political power which, in turn, influenced the area where a lord retained men. Landholding affected appointments to local offices and commissions, the development of a noble's military power and how bastard feudal connections were formed. The effect of landholding on local lawlessness differed from county to county and from noble to noble depending on patterns of land ownership. A key feature of English elite society was the tendency for nobles to have their lands scattered across the kingdom as opposed to having large consolidated territorial blocks. One extreme example that illustrates this was George, duke of Clarence, who held lands as far apart as Yorkshire and Cornwall.[3] Although lands were dispersed, most nobles had areas where they had a large number of manors constituting their principal estates and residences, but not on the scale of the consolidated power blocks that many aristocrats in other parts of Europe enjoyed.[4] The implication of such disparate landholdings was that great land owners in England could not actively run all of their estates. Retaining men across a wide geographical area for the purposes of estate management was the only feasible way to run large estates, though such domestic practicalities could evolve into political influence if desired. Patterns of landholding determined where a lord needed to retain men. The key question posed here is to what extent did landholding influence where men retained illegally? The first point to note is that most cases discussed here relate to members of the gentry as opposed to members of the peerage. Members of the gentry had less landed wealth than the aristocracy, which meant their lands tended to be more compact over fewer counties. The second point to note is that the surviving sources do not necessarily provide a full picture of the estates that members of the gentry held. This is most apparent in the main corpus of material for this study, the records of the King Bench, which state the place of residence of the indicted but provide no details on their other holdings. Other records, particularly inquisitions *post mortem*, can help reconstruct the landholding of a member of the gentry. However, such inquisitions *post mortem* do not exist for every person indicted for illegal livery, meaning that such additional records can only be used qualitatively. Despite these concerns, the surviving documentation is sufficient to provide an indication of the importance of landholding for the creation of illegal retaining relationships.

---

[3]   Hicks, *Clarence*, 187–197.
[4]   Christopher Given-Wilson, 'Rank and Status among the English Nobility, c.1300–1500' in *Princely Rank in Late Medieval Europe: Trodden Paths and Promising Avenues*, eds. Thorsten Huthwelker, Jörg Peltzer and Maximilian Wemhöner (Ostifildern, 2011), 97–8.

In certain cases, the indictments explicitly show that the men were being given illegal livery by lords who were local landholders. For instance, in 1476, the Sussex gentleman John Lyle of Pulborough was indicted for the illegal gift of livery to three husbandmen, one fuller and one carpenter, all from Pulborough, two years earlier at Pulborough.[5] The case highlights the very localised nature of many illegal livery cases. Yet the geographical scope of many cases was normally broader than this, with only some of the men who were illegally retained coming from the same place as their lord, since most cases involved men being retained illegally from several places. In 1489 William Hugford, an esquire from Warwick, was indicted for giving illegal livery to five men from Warwick along with seventeen other men from Warwickshire.[6] There were only sixty occasions in which at least one of the people who were illegally retained was recorded in the indictment as coming from the same place as the person illegally retaining them. The reason for this low number is that if a person lived on their lord's manor, they were tenants, or could claim to be permanent servants of his, which therefore entitled them to wear his livery. The localised nature of such cases and the possible influence of an offending member of the gentry may also have made local justices reluctant to prosecute such instances or feel no requirement to do so if there were not broader problems. Consequently, the King's Bench records rarely show lords illegally retaining men from where they themselves lived. Additional evidence is thus required for most cases in order to examine the link between illegal retaining and land ownership.

Although those retaining and being retained were rarely listed as residing in the same place, on most occasions the lord doing the illegal retaining was listed as residing in the same county as those being illegally retained. In only nineteen cases was the lord distributing illegal livery listed as coming from a county other than the one where he was indicted. In some cases peers who held land in several counties were indicted, such as John Talbot, third earl of Shrewsbury, who was indicted in Derbyshire in 1468, where the family had made various acquisitions during the fifteenth century.[7] Ralph Greystoke of Barnard Castle in the palatinate of Durham was indicted for distributing livery illegally to seven yeomen and one gentleman from Yorkshire in August 1423.[8] A familial connection to Yorkshire is evident in the fact that the manor of Slinsby in Yorkshire was held by Sir Alexander Metham from baron Greystoke, at that time Ralph's father

---

[5]   KB9/342 m. 36.
[6]   KB9/380 m. 41C.
[7]   KB9/13 m. 63; A.J. Pollard, 'The Family of Talbot, Lord Talbot and the Earls of Shrewsbury in the Fifteenth Century' (unpublished PhD thesis, University of Bristol, 1969), 413.
[8]   KB27/696 rot. 19 rex; KB27/737 rot. 1 rex.

John Greystoke, illustrating a familial connection.[9] There are others for whom it is difficult to identify their landed estates. The inquisition *post mortem* for John Grey, Lord Wilton, indicates that he only held land in Buckinghamshire[10] yet he was indicted for giving livery to three men in the neighbouring county of Bedfordshire.[11] Moreover, in the instances in which someone received livery illegally in another county, they were always from the neighbouring county. In Devon, in 1491, seven yeomen and one shoemaker from Somerset were indicted for receiving illegal livery from Sir William Courtenay of Powderham, in Devon.[12] In Warwickshire Sir Edward Raleigh was indicted for illegally giving livery to one husbandman from Oxfordshire in addition to another from Warwickshire in September 1488.[13] Likewise, in 1414, Thomas Tailor, yeoman of Cheshire, was indicted along with five men from Stafford for illegally receiving livery from Robert Erdeswyk, gentleman.[14] When someone was indicted for receiving illegal livery in a county they were not from, then they were from the neighbouring county. This illustrates how such socio-political networks crossed administrative county boundaries in the same way that has been shown in Warwickshire and its neighbouring counties during the fifteenth century.[15]

During the reign of Henry VII, similar circumstances are evident with members of the Stanley family. Three members of the Stanley family, all listed as coming from Lancashire, were indicted in Yorkshire and Cheshire for illegal livery between 1499 and 1504.[16] Since the Stanley family were major landholders in the palatinate counties of Cheshire and Lancashire,[17] the fact that they were retaining men in the neighbouring county of Yorkshire suggests they had influence there too. In the north-west there was 'a considerable degree of social intercourse between the Cheshire and Lancashire gentry' that was ensured by the independence of the two counties and their remoteness from the centre.[18] The connection between the men of these northern counties is further evidenced by the fact that Sir Thomas Assherton and Alexander Radcliff, esquire, were both

---

[9]   *CIPM, 1 to 5 Henry V*, no. 497; *Complete Peerage*, ii, 196–7.
[10] *CIPM, 1504–1509*, no. 882.
[11] KB9/417 m. 119.
[12] KB29/121 rot. 15.
[13] KB9/380 m. 41B.
[14] KB9/113 m, 2.
[15] Carpenter, *Locality and Polity*, 281–346.
[16] Sir Edward Stanley in Yorkshire in 1504: KB29/134 rot. 26; Sir William Stanley twice in Cheshire in 1499: CHES25/18 m. 11; and James Stanley, later bishop of Ely in twice Cheshire in 1499 and twice in Yorkshire in 1500: CHES25/18 m. 13–14, KB29/131 rott. 2–3, KB8/3/1 m. 5.
[17] See e.g. Coward, *The Stanleys*, 111–26.
[18] Bennett, *Community, Class and Careerism*, 15.

Lancashire gentry indicted in 1499 for distributing illegal livery in Cheshire.[19] Similarly, in 1491 the Lancashire gentleman Richard Radcliff was indicted for giving illegal livery in Yorkshire.[20] The cases in these northern counties are a clear example of how such socio-political relationships crossed county boundaries. This was particularly true in the case of powerful families, like the Stanleys, whose influence was spread over several counties, albeit to varying degrees between counties.

The scale of their regional power made the Stanley indictments an exceptional instance of prosecutions for illegal livery because they were part of a concerted effort by the crown to attack the local influence of one family. The only other comparable case, in which the crown sought to undermine the local influence of a particular noble, during Henry VII's reign was against George Neville, Lord Bergavenny, in 1507.[21] Most cases of illegal livery were against members of the gentry who traditionally provided the backbone of county administration and therefore needed to retain men to perform the duties expected of them in the areas where they were important landholders. The case of the Hampshire knight, Sir William Sandys, created Lord Sandys of Vyne by Henry VIII in 1523,[22] illustrates the connection between land ownership, office-holding and illegal retaining. Sandys was indicted in 1505 for illegally retaining men across Hampshire, including four in Andover, one in Winchester, one in Clatford and one in Amport.[23] The inquisition *post mortem* for his father indicates that Sandys inherited a considerable amount of land in Hampshire, including the manor of 'Aylyvys' in Andover,[24] along with two manors in Surrey.[25] His prominent landed wealth in the county made him a natural person for the crown to appoint as a local law enforcer. Consequently, he was given ten commissions of the peace in Hampshire and Wiltshire between 1498 and 1504[26] and also named in an *oyer et terminer* commission for Hampshire in 1501.[27] Prior to his indictment, Sandys had been the beneficiary of crown patronage. In 1499 he was made steward of the manors of Christchurch and Ringwood, bailiff of Christchurch and constable of Christchurch Castle.[28] Thereafter, he was made ranger of Chute Forest in 1501[29] and given the manors of 'Peryton' and 'Westrandon' forfeited by Lord Audley

---

[19] CHES25/18 mm. 7, 18.
[20] KB9/391 mm. 13–14.
[21] KB27/985 rex rott. 7–8.
[22] Ronald H. Fritze, 'William Sandys', *ODNB*, xlviii, 935–6.
[23] KB9/436 m. 13.
[24] *CIMP, 1–12 Hen VII*, no. 1246.
[25] Ibid., no. 1245.
[26] *CPR, 1494–1509*, 625, 665.
[27] Ibid., 287.
[28] Ibid., 187.
[29] Ibid., 354.

in 1504.[30] It was Sandys' landholdings, most of which were in Hampshire, that led to him being named on these commissions and given various stewardships. Those indicted for being illegally retained by Sandys pleaded that they had been lawfully retained since Sandys had given them livery of a red rose (a Lancastrian and Tudor symbol) in order to serve the king.[31] Sandys' office-holding and landholding were the means by which he came into contact with those whom he had illegally retained.

Family Connections

In addition to the formal, horizontal relationships created by geography and landholding, society operated via vertical and informal personal relationships such as family and friendship that contributed to the creation of these relationships. The most informal of these was friendship. Despite friendship being one mechanism through which society functioned, the sources for late medieval England render any discussion of its workings elusive. Colin Richmond commented about John Hopton that: 'If it is true that you can tell a man by his friends, then another way of coming at John Hopton is through a study of his. There is one snag: we do not know who were his friends.'[32] Similar problems of evidence are apparent in Philippa Maddern's discussion of friendships within the Norfolk gentry of the fifteenth century. Her evidence is derived from both literary sources and surviving records such as deeds, witness lists and who acted as feoffees, attorneys etc. Although people would have acted in conjunction with those whom they considered to be their friends, many witnesses to deeds may well have been passing acquaintances. Written documentation of this kind says little about the notion of friendship among yeomen, who formed the bulk of the illegal retainers.[33] The surviving records prohibit any meaningful discussion of the influence of friendship since such informal relationships are not readily recorded in the prosaic records of the King's Bench.

A more fruitful method of inquiry into the informal relations that bound members of an affinity together is to study members of the same family. Familial connections were a means by which many entered the service in the households of nobles and gentry, occupying the more menial roles such as cooks and stable

[30] Ibid., 425.
[31] KB9/436 m. 13; KB27/993 rot. 12.
[32] Richmond, *John Hopton*, 159.
[33] Phillippa Maddern, '"Best Trusted Friends": Concepts and Practices of Friendship among Fifteenth-Century Norfolk Gentry' in *England in the Fifteenth Century*, ed. Nicholas Rogers (Stamford, 1992), 100–17.

boys.[34] The records of the King's Bench enable an examination of the extent to which family ties coincided with bastard feudal connections, albeit illegal ones. John Maddicott suggested that family ties were important for the 'vigour of the retinue' of Thomas of Lancaster and that 'family feelings thus reinforced the link between lord and retainer'.[35] In total, eighty-seven out of the 334 cases identified (26 per cent) have at least one surname repeated, although the number of times multiple members of the same family were illegally retained by the same person is likely to have been higher due to other familial relationships in which surnames were not shared, such as in-laws and relations on the maternal side. In certain cases the records explicitly state the nature of the familial relationship. Richard Oates, a labourer from Halifax, for example, was described as son of William Oates who was also indicted in the same case in 1500. John Oates, yeoman from Halifax, was also indicted at the same time but there is no indication what, if any, relation he was to either Richard or William Oates. In the same case, nine men with the surname Kay were indicted in 1500, one of whom, John Kay, was described as the son of Henry Kay, although no Henry Kay was indicted.[36] Presumably the nine Kays were all related, but *how* they were related was not recorded. On other occasions the phrases 'junior' and 'senior' were used to distinguish between members of the same family, such as in Leicestershire in 1516, when John Harrington, senior, and his son John Harrington, junior, both esquires, were both indicted for being illegally retained by Lord Hastings.[37] The surviving records, however, rarely explicitly state any family connection, meaning that a degree of speculation is required by assuming that those people with the same surname from the same area were related. For instance, John Woode, Henry Woode and Humphrey Woode, all from Dunstable in Bedfordshire, were indicted for illegally receiving liveries of cloth and badges from John, Lord Grey of Wilton on 12 June 1498. Although the records do not state the nature of any familial relationship – i.e. brothers, cousins, father and sons, uncles and nephews etc. – they were almost certainly related.[38] The records seldom reveal the precise nature, or even existence, of any familial relationships. Nevertheless, it is a reasonable assumption that whenever a surname was shared by various men illegally retained by the same lord, they were in some way related. Despite these limitations, indictments for illegal livery shed light on the link between family connections and bastard feudal relationships, albeit illegal ones.

Many cases of illegal livery occurred in conjunction with instances of feuding between rival families. Feuding was very much a family affair, in part

---

[34] Mertes, *English Noble Household*, 63–5.
[35] Maddicott, *Thomas of Lancaster*, 60.
[36] KB29/131 rott. 2–3.
[37] KB29/148 rot. 16.
[38] KB9/417 m 119; KB27/952 rex rot. 7; KB29/129 rot. 2.

because feuds often originated in disputes about land in which the complexities of the English legal system made a satisfactory resolution almost impossible to achieve.[39] The fact that those with kinship ties tended to join together in supporting one particular side in a local dispute should be unsurprising. As Alexander Grant noted, in England, 'as elsewhere, [feuding] meant that *honourable* use of arms in defence of family interests'.[40] Consequently, some clusters of cases produced several instances of indictments for illegal livery being brought against men who shared the same surname. In Staffordshire, in 1414, for instance, six out of the twenty-one cases involved several members of the same family.[41] There were instances in Staffordshire during Henry IV's reign of multiple members of the same family working in conjunction with each other and other families. John Myners, who was indicted for illegally distributing livery to two yeomen, was involved in several assaults, along with his two brothers, against prominent Lancastrians in the county. They were also involved with Hugh Erdswyke in a raid upon the house of John Pasmere of Uttoxeter, a Lancastrian servant, in February 1409. Erdswyke himself gave illegal livery to several members of the same family.[42] Edmund Ferrers similarly distributed illegal livery in Staffordshire to members of the same families, such as John and William Pas of Chartley, Thomas and Richard Sturdy of Ruggeley and John and Richard Cooper of Abbots Bromley.[43] Familial relations in Staffordshire helped to create social ties that were manifest in instances of illegal retaining and public disorder.

The importance of family connections in the waging of feuds is evident in the cases from Herefordshire in the 1450s, many of which can be linked to the increased factionalism and lawlessness of the decade that was one of the major causes of the Wars of the Roses.[44] Three men indicted for distributing illegal livery in 1457 were related and members of Richard, duke of York's affinity in the county: Sir Walter Devereux; his son, Walter Devereux, esquire (later Lord Ferrers of Chartley, when he inherited his father-in-law's title); and Sir William Herbert (promoted to the earldom of Pembroke by Edward IV) who married Anne Devereux in 1449, making him son-in-law and brother-in-law to the two Devereuxs.[45] In this situation three leading members of the gentry, connected via

[39] Harriss, *Shaping the Nation*, 197–202.
[40] Alexander Grant, 'Murder Will Out: Kingship, Kinship and Killing in Medieval Scotland' in *Kings, Lords and Men in Scotland and Britain, 1300–1625*, eds. Steve Boardman and Julian Goodacre (Edinburgh, 2014), 209.
[41] KB9/113 mm. 2, 11, 41–3.
[42] KB9/113 mm. 2, 42, 46–7; Powell, *Kingship, Law and Society*, 209–14.
[43] KB9/113 m. 41.
[44] The political significance of these cases is discussed in greater depth on pp. 194–200.
[45] For the relevant indictment see: KB9/34/1 m. 5 and KB9/35 mm. 6, 69 for Devereux senior; KB9/35 m. 67 for Devereux junior; KB9/35 m. 69 for Herbert. For the biographical information on these men see: Ralph Griffiths, 'Walter Devereux, First

familial ties and service to a major regional magnate, were distributing illegal liveries across the county, almost certainly in a coordinated effort to obtain supporters. However, they did not necessarily give liveries to large numbers of men from the same family, as there is only one case in which several men with the same surname were indicted for receiving illegal livery from one of the Devereuxs. Four members of the Monyngton family – Thomas Monyngton, of Sarnesfield, esquire, along with Richard, George and Henry, all gentlemen from Lawton – were indicted for receiving illegal livery from Walter Devereux, knight, on 1 April 1456 at Leominster.[46] At the same time men from the March of Wales were indicted for illegal livery by the *oyer et terminer* commissions in the county. In 1452, Henry ap Griffith, esquire, was indicted for illegally giving livery to a shoemaker from Hereford on 6 April 1452.[47] His son, John ap Harry, was indicted in 1457 for giving illegal livery to eight men the previous April.[48] There is no evidence of either of these men holding any land in Herefordshire. Their connection to the county was probably the product of its proximity to Wales and through the Devereux–Herbert faction in Herefordshire at a time of local political instability.[49] Other familial relations are evident in indictments against men with no obvious connection to Richard, duke of York. Henry Oldcastle, esquire, gave illegal livery to three men, including two butchers, Richard Butcher and John Butcher, on 6 August 1455 in Hereford.[50] As in Staffordshire a generation earlier, familial connections were a way in which men became entangled in wider local disputes and were one of the causes of becoming attached to particular feuding parties.

When considering the wider significance of familial connections in the creation of affinities, comparisons can be made with evidence of the distribution of legal livery, particularly the few surviving livery rolls of magnates. The livery roll of Edward Courtenay, earl of Devon, from 1384 shows that he gave livery to 143 people, including five other Courtenays. Granting livery to multiple members of one family, however, was an uncommon occurrence. On only four occasions can multiple persons from the same family be identified on the Courtenay livery roll.[51] There are only two examples of shared surnames from the 338 people

---

Baron Chartley (c.1432–1485)', *ODNB*, xv, 969–71; Ralph Griffiths, 'William Herbert, First Earl of Pembroke (c.1423–1469)', *ODNB*, xxvi, 729–31.

46 KB9/35 m. 6.
47 KB9/34/1 m. 5. Henry ap Griffith's origins are opaque since he is referred to as coming from various parts of Wales, the March of Wales and Herefordshire in official documents: Chapman, 'Henry Griffith, a "Man of War"', 103–34.
48 KB9/35 m. 69.
49 Chapman, 'Henry Griffith, a "Man of War."'
50 KB9/35 m. 69.
51 BL Add. Ch. 64320. The roll is also discussed in McFarlane, *Nobility of Later Medieval England*, 111.

named on the livery roll of Elizabeth de Burgh, lady de Clare in 1434.[52] The Kalendar of the inner household of Richard Beauchamp, earl of Warwick, for 1420–1 implies few familial connections between members of this household. The only familial relationship that can be positively identified is a mother–daughter relationship between two women of the chamber: Agnes, 'wife of Adam' and Agnes, 'daughter of Adam'.[53] Likewise, the Kalendar of the absent John Fastolf's household indicates that the only familial relationship in the household was between Milicent Fastolf and her daughter Alice.[54] A similar pattern is evident in the household books of Robert Dudley, earl of Leicester, from the late sixteenth century that includes a few examples of men with shared surnames serving the earl in various capacities.[55] The indication from this material is that the nobility did take multiple members of the same family into their service but this was not necessarily standard practice.

Similar patterns appear in the various lists of retinues, servants and affinities drawn up for members of the higher nobility. The affinities of John of Gaunt, Richard, duke of York and John de Vere, thirteenth Earl of Oxford have all been shown to have included multiple members of the same family.[56] William, Lord Hastings indentured three members of the Meverell family in 15 Edward IV – Thomas, Thomas junior and Nicholas – as well as Robert and Richard Eyre in 16 Edward IV. During 21 Edward IV, he also indentured Henry and Ralph Longford and Nicholas and Thomas Ruggeley.[57] The royal affinity created more opportunities for its members to bring their relatives into the fold. Three hundred and forty out of 860 known members of the royal affinity between 1360 and 1413 shared a surname with at least one other member.[58] Larger royal affinities afforded greater opportunity for membership than those of even the wealthiest peer. Even in this situation, the majority of retainers, officials and servants were not related to each other and only a small percentage were related in all of these examples.

Christine Carpenter described bastard feudal affinities of the later middle ages as 'a series of concentric circles' with the lord at the centre.[59] This was how affinities worked when considered from the centre. When considered from the perspective of members of an affinity, it is clear that the strength of the

---

[52] E101/92/23.
[53] Magdalen College, GDIII/66/1, 8.
[54] Magdalen College, Fastolf Paper 8.
[55] *Household Accounts and Disbursement Books of Robert Dudley, Earl of Leicester*, ed. Simon Adams, Camden fifth series, vi (Cambridge, 1995), 423, 427–8, 431, 435–6, 438.
[56] Johnson, *Duke Richard of York*, 228–41; Ross, *John de Vere*, 228–40; Walker, *Lancastrian Affinity*, 262–84.
[57] Dunham, *Lord Hastings' Indentured Retainers*, 119–20.
[58] Given-Wilson, *King's Affinity*, 217, 282–90.
[59] Carpenter, 'The Beauchamp Affinity', 515.

connections between members of each concentric circle varied. Members of Richard II's household were able to secure positions in the royal household for their kin. Simon Burley, Richard's under-chamberlain, was able to secure his brother John a position as Richard's chamber knight and his nephew William a post as an esquire of the household.[60] The three Burleys were not in the same 'concentric circle' around the king, but the connection between them was as strong, and likely stronger, than with others in the same 'concentric circle' as them. Similar influences are likely to have been at work further down the social scale, and probably influenced gentry retaining policy. Illegal livery cases indicate that family connections were a factor in the recruitment of bastard feudal affinities. Such patterns are also evident in the lists of retinues, annuitants and servants drawn up in the appendices of various studies, which show that while family relations did occur, they were rare. In this instance, there is a clear parallel between legal and illegal bastard feudal affinities. Family relations had a role in the formation of both legal and illegal retaining relationships: it was a factor in some cases, but it was not a routine feature.

Conclusion

This chapter has examined the creation of illegal retaining relationships via the 'top-down' perspective of vertical ties based on landholding and the 'bottom-up' horizontal connections evident in familial connections as evident in the sharing of surnames. There were plenty of other ways in which people came into the service of a lord but these are the two manners most frequently recorded in the indictments and can therefore be examined in a more quantitative manner. Landholding was a clear influence in determining where a lord retained men for lawful and unlawful purposes. Illegal retaining normally occurred in a county where a peer or member of the gentry held land, though it was unusual for them to retain someone from their own place of residence. In many cases those who lived nearby could claim to be legitimate servants, or the local justices may have been unlikely to indict. Such reluctance may be explained by a fear of the relevant lord doing the retaining but could also be explained by the lackadaisical enforcement of the statutes discussed previously. This could be particularly prevalent when there were no additional crimes that prompted justices to indict men for illegal livery, for instance local feuding. Although the motivations of local justices can only be speculated upon, the point here is that men normally illegally retained from other places in the counties where they held land, or neighbouring counties, rarely from their own lands. Society also operated on many informal levels that did not necessarily leave traces in the written record, which means little can be said about

[60] Given-Wilson, *King's Affinity*, 217–18.

them. One exception to this is family connections as surnames were recorded in the indictments. Family connection, while present in legal retinues, households and affinities, was a feature of only a small percentage of the majority of late medieval affinities. The cases examined in this study have one crucial difference in comparison with previous studies: instead of focusing on the higher nobility retaining the gentry, they are predominantly focused on the gentry retaining those of lower social status such as yeomen and husbandmen. With respect to family connections, this evidence suggests that the legal and illegal retaining practices of the gentry were similar to the legal and illegal retaining practices of the peerage, albeit on a smaller scale. Although the records do not allow any firm conclusions based on quantitative data, an examination of landholding and family connections shows that the vertical relations relating to landholding differed between legal and illegal retaining because people rarely illegally retained from lands they held directly, unlike legal retaining, but that the horizontal connections relating to family relationships operated on a similar manner for legal and illegal retaining.

8

Livery and Disorder

Bastard feudalism could be a force for cohesion in late medieval England and the nobility are no longer viewed as a self-interested, socially disruptive class continually undermining royal power. K.B. McFarlane argued that civil disorder was really the product of inadequate kingship, such as that of Henry VI, and therefore 'the abuse of lordship and the prevalence of corruption were merely signs that England lacked a ruler'.[1] Consequently, problems of disorder were a symptom of a lack of leadership as opposed to any inherently violent tendencies of the aristocracy and their followers. Nevertheless, retaining remained a means of recruiting men for rebellious and lawless purposes and, particularly during the Wars of the Roses, many leading nobles were able to exercise a disproportionate influence on national politics.[2] As Philippa Maddern pointed out: 'a lord was expected to be attended by a retinue which could serve him honourably in time of war; the problem was to tell when a retinue was unjustifiably warlike'.[3] The usurpations of Henry IV, Edward IV (twice), Henry VI, Richard III and Henry VII all depended, to varying extents, on either the ability of the usurper and his allies to mobilise their followers, or the inability of the deposed king to mobilise support from the nobility and the gentry. Retaining was a method of recruiting military support that led to many of fifteenth-century England's usurpations, which ultimately gave the English the unenviable reputation in late fifteenth-century Europe as a nation of king killers.[4] England's record for usurpations made Tudor kings sensitive about large gatherings of noble retainers, as most dramatically witnessed in 1521 when Henry VIII had Edward, duke of Buckingham, executed after he suddenly asked for permission to raise an armed bodyguard to visit his Welsh troops. According to Carole Rawcliffe the duke was genuinely afraid for his own security when visiting Wales, but his family's history of rebellions had raised Henry's suspicions.[5]

Although rebellion was clearly a concern for many kings who sought to limit retaining, the key problem that was connected to the widespread distribution of

[1] McFarlane, *Nobility of Later Medieval England*, 121.
[2] Michael Hicks, 'Bastard Feudalism, Overmighty Subjects and the Idols of Multitude during the Wars of the Roses', *History*, lxxxv (2000), 386–403.
[3] Philippa C. Maddern, *Violence and Social Order: East Anglia, 1422–1442* (Oxford, 1992), 108.
[4] P.S. Lewis, *Essays in Later Medieval French History* (London, 1985), 191–2.
[5] Rawcliffe, *The Staffords*, 42–3, 100.

liveries was maintenance. The phrase 'livery and maintenance' is commonly used in the historiography of bastard feudalism, notably by William Stubbs who viewed them as 'two great sources of mischief'.[6] The connection between livery and maintenance is not an anachronistic term devised by later scholars because it was commonly used in the fourteenth and fifteenth centuries. For instance, the first act dealing with liveries in 1377 stated that liveries were not to be given for the purposes of maintenance and imposed no restrictions on categories of servants who could wear liveries.[7] When the law did begin to restrict the categories of servants entitled to wear liveries, maintenance was a key element in this debate. One of the professed aims of the 1399 act was 'to abolish maintenance, and to nurture love, peace and tranquillity everywhere in the realm'.[8] Such objectives were common in numerous petitions about liveries which referred to the problem of maintenance, suggesting the giving of liveries and maintenance were linked in the minds and language of late medieval petitioners.[9] Nigel Saul has suggested that throughout the fourteenth century 'maintenance was on the increase'.[10] Despite this, there was no correlation between prosecutions for illegal livery and prosecutions for illegal maintenance during the later middle ages. One reason is that, like the distribution of liveries, certain forms of maintenance were legal and acceptable to contemporaries.[11] Another reason is that livery and maintenance were not necessarily linked in practice other than being products of bastard feudalism. Unlawful maintenance involved the corruption of the legal system and the connected problem of champerty (supporting an unjust claim to land for a share of the profits).[12] Illegal livery was concerned with the artificial expansion of affinities for violent purposes. While the laws concerning both livery and maintenance were connected to problems associated with bastard feudalism, no one was indicted simultaneously for both offences.

The main concern about widespread retaining that the legal records indicate was their potential to help facilitate instances of local disorder and unrest across the kingdom. The most extreme cases involved feuding by powerful noble families. Historians now tend to emphasise the importance of the feud in pre-modern societies as a legitimate means of creating stability and addressing grievances without recourse to the state. Excessive or continual recourse to the state to sort out local disputes was problematic because the functioning of the

---

[6] Stubbs, *Constitutional History* , iii, 579.
[7] *PROME*, vi, 50.
[8] *PROME*, viii, 38.
[9] *PROME*, vi, 50; vii, 124; vii, 239–40; viii, 11–12, 38; viii, 400; ix, 354–5, 402–3; xiii, 65; xv, 131–2, 371.
[10] Saul, 'Abolition of Badges', 313.
[11] See in particular: Rose, *Maintenance in Medieval England*.
[12] Hicks, *Bastard Feudalism*, 119–24, 223, 227.

state was predicated on the cooperation of nobles.[13] Yet that should not disguise the fact that when they did erupt, noble feuds posed a distinct threat to the lives of those who became entangled in them. The English state was more extensive than any of its medieval contemporaries in Europe and, in general, adopted a stronger stance against feuding than many other places, with feuding being unacceptable within England's legal frameworks. The ability for even peasants in Germany to legally wage their own feuds, provided it was conducted with adherence to strict legal processes, would be unthinkable for even the richest of English dukes.[14] It is perhaps instructive of the unacceptability of feuding in late medieval England, in theory if not in practice, that a collection of essays on feuding in medieval and early modern Europe included no essay on late medieval England.[15] This is unfortunate, given the fact that the violent noble feuds of the 1450s were one of the main causes of the Wars of the Roses.[16] Endemic violence was not the norm anywhere in medieval Europe, including England, but nevertheless there were plenty of occasions when the squabbles of local elites led to instances of maiming, disfiguring and the loss of life. Local lawlessness and feuding was particularly problematic in England, as such problems could easily become entangled with personal rivalries near the centre of government, which created a clear connection between lawlessness and rebellion.

It is within the context of this comparative lack of tolerance of feuding that many prosecutions for illegal liveries and retaining occurred. This concern is evident in the preamble of many of the acts which highlight problems of lawlessness and violent local feuding. A petition presented to the parliament of 1459 complained about the numerous robberies, extortions, rapes and other violent crimes across the kingdom committed by men who had 'been so favoured and assisted with persones of grete myght, havyng towardes theym of their lyverey, expressely ayenst youre lawes' and included the names of twenty-one offenders.[17] These complaints were not part of a conscious policy of the crown

[13] There is a large body of literature on this topic. The key studies that have helped shape this discussion are: R.R. Davies, 'The Survival of the Bloodfeud in Medieval Wales', *History*, liv (1969), 338–57; Howard Kaminsky, 'The Noble Feud in the Later Middle Ages', *P&P*, clxxvii (2002), 55–83; Jenny Wormald, 'Bloodfeud, Kindred and Government in Early Modern Scotland', *P&P*, lxxxvii (1980), 54–97. For a more recent study that adopts an explicitly comparative perspective, including a valuable discussion of late medieval England, see: Grant, 'Murder Will Out', 193–226.
[14] Christine Reinle, 'Peasants' Feuds in Medieval Bavaria (Fourteenth–Fifteenth Century)' in *Feud in Medieval and Early Modern Europe*, eds. Jeppe Büchert Netterstrøm and Bjørn Poulsen (Aarhus, 2007), 161–74.
[15] *Feud in Medieval and Early Modern Europe*, eds. Netterstrøm and Poulsen.
[16] Although rather old, the classic account of this remains: Storey, *The End of the House of Lancaster.*
[17] *PROME*, xii, 499500.

to reduce the military might of the nobility because, as previously stated, the initial impetus for legislation came from the Commons in parliament as opposed to the crown. The initial petitions highlighted the abuses of noble retainers wearing liveries that emboldened them to disrupt the legal system.[18] Yet, in many instances the problems were localised. A petition from Henry Popham, esquire, in c.1404–5 illustrates the problem caused by liveries in relation to the execution of justice. Popham complained about an attack upon him by Lord Lovell and, because some of the JPs in Wiltshire received Lovell's fees and robes, they were partial in his favour.[19] Such concerns were not confined to the late fourteenth and early fifteenth centuries when the impetus for discussions about liveries came from the Commons. Robert Hawtmount, a tenant of Edward, prince of Wales in the manor of Watlington, presented a petition to the prince and his council in 1481 complaining about John Abrey of South Weston who wore the prince's livery and used it to commit 'robberyes escapes of felons wronges and grete extorcions'.[20] Henry VII also recognised retaining as a means of causing local disorder and did not always view the practice as a threat to his sovereignty. In 1494 he claimed in a letter to the steward of the honour of Pickering that he had been informed about poaching in his woods and blamed unlawful retaining as a method employed by offenders to gather men for such purposes.[21]

Not every case can be explained by either the escalation of private feuds or central government's arbitrary enforcement of the law as a means of attacking political opponents. Retaining men by grants of livery or fees contrary to the statutes was a crime and therefore it should be expected that those offending would be indicted. Yet these interrelated problems of lawlessness and rebellion can help to shed light on the reasons why many lords and gentry retained men illegally, especially as the extant sources help to contextualise certain cases. However, this approach is at the mercy of the surviving sources providing additional scraps of information, sometimes incidentally, that shed additional light on the context of specific cases. In many instances, no such information exists. One case of illegal livery, not found in the records of the King's Bench, illustrates this problem. In 1483, John Howick, physician, was presented to a jury in Nottingham for being retained by Richard, duke of Gloucester and illegally using his livery.[22] No additional information can be found about this case and it has not been possible to establish the exact context in which Richard, duke of Gloucester encountered this physician.[23] This rather enigmatic case involving

---

[18] See Chapter 3 for a full discussion of this point.
[19] SC8/135/6710.
[20] SC8/344/E1306.
[21] DL37/62 rot. 21.
[22] *Records of the Borough of Nottingham*, ii, 330–1.
[23] For instance, the most detailed study of Richard III's servants, Horrox, *Richard III: A*

the man who, a few months later, would become king in the most dramatic of fashions is illustrative of a key problem with many cases of illegal livery: the difficulty in establishing the broader context of many cases.

Despite these concerns, there is sufficient evidence, primarily from indictments, from which to draw some broad conclusions about illegal livery and acts of lawlessness. Indictments provide important information regarding the dates and locations of offences and such evidence can be compared with indictments for other crimes committed by the same, or similar, groups of people. When examining the indictments it is necessary to heed Rees Davies' warning to historians not to turn chaos into order at the stroke of a pen by arranging isolated and unrelated episodes into 'neat causal patterns', a danger to which those who study war and revolt are particularly susceptible.[24] This warning is applicable to violent feuding and petty lawlessness which, along with civil war and revolt, were possible reasons why men would distribute and receive liveries contrary to the statutes. There is similarly a danger of assigning every instance of illegal retaining a sinister motive in which a lord was preparing either to strong-arm or to overawe a local quarter session, engage in private feuding or, in extreme cases, rebel against the sovereign. Such generalisations distort our understanding of specific cases and the contexts in which they arose. Yet it is also clear that liveries were distributed at times to wage feuds. The uneven nature of the surviving evidence relating to retaining as a mechanism for waging feuds means that it is not possible to draw any meaningful conclusions from a quantitative analysis of all of the cases. Instead, the best way to approach this is through a series of case studies that indicate the various reasons why illegal retaining occurred. The following two chapters examine the context of specific cases. This chapter analyses specific cases, and groups of cases, to highlight the various reasons for illegal retaining, while the next chapter examines similar instances in the broader urban context.

The key point for many cases is that those indicted for illegal livery comprised only part of a larger following indicted for various breaches of public order. This is evident in the indictment of Sir William Courtenay of Powderham, whose father, also William Courtenay, had played a key role in local administration under Edward IV and Richard III, dying in 1485.[25] In 1491 William Courtenay was indicted for giving livery illegally to ninety-three men.[26] At the same there

---

Study in Service, includes no references to Howick.

[24] R.R. Davies, *The Revolt of Owain Glyn Dŵr* (Oxford, 1995), 263.

[25] For an overview of the career of William Courtenay, the father, see: J.A.F. Thomson, 'The Courtenay Family in the Yorkist Period', *BIHR*, xlv (1972), 231, 236–7. William Courtney who was indicted for illegal livery was given livery of his lands on 20 September 1485: *CPR, 1485–1494*, 9.

[26] KB29/121 rott. 15–16.

were various indictments for riot and mayhem in Devon. Courtenay was indicted for rioting together with forty of the men indicted for illegally receiving his livery, meaning 43 per cent of those in receipt of his livery illegal were involved in the same riot. Most of those indicted for rioting were yeomen or craftsmen, although one gentleman, Robert Prous, was indicted for taking illegal livery and rioting.[27] The indictment with relevant information about the date and place of the offence does not survive and therefore precise details are unknown. However, the writs of *venire facias* indicated that those illegally in receipt of Courtenay's livery only comprised one element of a larger force. The one exception to this trend comes from two cases in Leicestershire during Henry VIII's reign. In 1516, Lord Hastings was indicted for illegally retaining 184 men and the marquess of Dorset was indicted for illegally retaining 158 men at Loughborough on 20 April. This was part of a long-running feud between the two men and they were ordered to appear before the justices of the King's Bench for various 'transgressions, riots and assemblies' as well as illegal livery.[28] This was the only large-scale case in which it is demonstrable that a large group of men were *all* indicted for receiving illegal livery in conjunction with another crime.

Staffordshire – 1414

The indictments show that there was a basis for the concern that retaining was a method of recruitment for feuding. The origins of the twenty-one cases in Staffordshire in 1414 stretched back to the second half of Henry IV's reign when the dominance of the Lancastrian affinity in the county caused resentment among other local gentry. In particular the Erdswick family, led by Hugh Erdswick and his brothers, were the main opponents of the Lancastrians in the county and were involved in a string of disturbances from at least 1408 onwards.[29] A petition was presented to parliament in 1410 listing their deeds, which Henry IV had converted into an indictment in King's Bench for which Hugh Erdeswick obtained a pardon.[30] The feud re-erupted early in Henry V's reign; this led to a commission of *oyer et terminer* visiting the county which produced the twenty-one cases of illegal livery. It is clear that the distribution of livery was used by both sides in this dispute to enhance their military strength for other crimes. Robert Erdeswyke

---

[27] KB29/121 rot. 14.
[28] KB29/148 rot. 16; KB27/1021 rott. 22–3 rex. For a discussion of this feud see: Robertson, 'Court Careers and County Quarrels', 153–70.
[29] For a discussion of these events see: Helen Castor, *The King, the Crown and the Duchy of Lancaster: Public Authority and Private Power, 1399–1461* (Oxford, 2000), 213–24; Given-Wilson, *Henry IV*, 479–80; Powell, *Kingship, Law and Society*, 208–16.
[30] *PROME*, viii, 471–6; KB27/597 rex rot 11; *CPR, 1408–1413*, 269, 275–7.

was indicted for illegally distributing livery to six yeomen,[31] two of whom were also indicted, along with four others, for breaking into Chartley Park, held by his rival in the county Edmund Ferrers, and murdering one of Ferrers' servants, Ralph Page, on 1 April 1414 (Palm Sunday). The indictment makes clear that Robert Erdeswyke had raised men for this purpose, stating he had 'procured and abetted them'.[32] In 1414 Hugh Erdeswyke assembled a group of around 1,000 men 'with a view of killing Edmund de Ferrers, the lord of Chartley'. The figure of 1,000 men is almost certainly an exaggeration meant to convey the scale of the gathering. Only twelve of the supposed 1,000 men are actually named in the indictment together with Erdeswyke[33] and only three of those twelve were also indicted for illegally receiving livery from him.[34] The nine others given livery illegally by Erdeswyke may have been part of the 1,000 men Erdeswyke is alleged to have assembled, although this can only be speculated.

The Percy–Neville Feud

Another prominent feud, which effectively turned into a full-scale private war, in which liveries were distributed to gain supporters was between the Percy and Neville families in Yorkshire during the 1450s.[35] This was a more serious feud than in Staffordshire a generation earlier and the families in question were members of the peerage, with the two families holding the earldoms of Northumbria (Percy) and Salisbury (Neville) respectively. These titles gave both families large sways of lands, offices and, above all, influence in the region. The families were also key for the defence of the Scottish border and became prominent figures in national politics. The feud was one of many that contributed to the breakdown of Lancastrian government during the 1450s and helped to contribute to the alignments made at the First Battle of St Albans where the Neville family sided with Richard, duke of York while the Percy family sided with the Lancastrian forces and where the earl of Northumberland and his son, Thomas Percy, were killed.[36] Although the feud became embroiled in the crises of national politics, the cases of illegal livery related to disputes on a local and regional, as opposed to national, level.

---

[31] KB9/113 m. 2.
[32] KB9/113 mm. 1, 24, 32, 39, 47; 'Extracts from the Plea Rolls of the Reigns of Henry V and Henry VI', 5.
[33] KB9/113 m. 14; 'Extracts from the Plea Rolls of the Reigns of Henry V and Henry VI', 7.
[34] KB9/113 mm. 2, 40.
[35] For a discussion of the Percy–Neville feud see: Griffiths, 'Local Rivalries and National Politics', 589–632; Storey, *End of the House of Lancaster*, 124–32.
[36] On the alignments at the First Battle of St Albans see: Michael Hicks, *Wars of the Roses* (London, 2010), 109–13.

Cases of illegal livery shed additional light on the feud and the nature of the military strength of the feuding factions, particularly the Percy family who were indicted. The key event was on 23 August 1453 when two of the earl of Northumberland's sons, Thomas Percy, Lord Egremont and Richard Percy led 710 other named men in an attack against members of the Neville family, including the earl of Salisbury, while they were returning home from the wedding of Sir Thomas Neville and Maud Stanhope. This was an attempt to assassinate Salisbury and other prominent members of the Neville family. A commission of *oyer et terminer* a year later indicted the Percies and their affinity for numerous crimes around this time, including illegal livery. Yet the indictments indicate that most of the violence involved legal retainers as the Percy brothers along with 710 other men were alleged to have attacked the Nevilles, but were only indicted for giving illegal livery to twenty-eight men between them.[37] The number of men indicted for illegal livery in both cases was clearly only a small percentage of the men involved in wider instances of lawlessness.

Although comparatively few accomplices were indicted for illegal livery, these indictments are important for understanding the nature of the feud. The dates on which liveries were distributed suggests that the Percies were temporarily enlarging their affinity in order to wage a local feud. Egremont was indicted for four offences against the statutes of livery, of which the date of two offences is given in the indictment: on 12 May 1453 at Healaugh[38] and on 4 February 1454 at York.[39] The offence committed at Healaugh occurred while he was missing the second session of the 1453 parliament and ignoring an order to go to Guienne for military campaigning.[40] The third case involving Egremont is only known by the surviving writ instructing the justices to determine the place and date of the offence.[41] His brother, Richard Percy, was indicted for giving illegal livery to four men, but this is also known only from a writ sent to the justices to inquire into when the offence was committed. The writ does, however, state that Richard Percy had given illegal livery to the men at three separate places in the East Riding of Yorkshire: Foston, Brandesburton and Brigham.[42] This suggests that Richard Percy travelled around the East Riding distributing liveries over an unknown period of time. This could have been an ongoing activity of his, but when considered in conjunction with the fact that his brother was also distributing

---

[37] KB9/148/2 mm. 31, 38, 54, 55; KB9/149/1 mm. 20–1, 49, 53; Griffiths, 'Local Rivalries and National Politics', 597–8.

[38] KB9/149/1 m. 49.

[39] KB9/149/1 m. 53.

[40] *PROME*, xii, 210, 212, 222–3, 324.

[41] KB9/149/1 m. 21. Egremont's indictment for illegally retaining a man in the city of York is only known by writs of *venire facias* which do not record the date or place of an offence: KB9/148/2 mm. 31, 38, 54–5.

[42] KB9/149/1 m. 20.

livery in 1453 it is likely that this was a short-term event, particularly in the context of later events which suggest that the Percies were illegally, and probably legally, giving livery to a large number of men in Yorkshire in the build-up to an attack on the Neville family.

This chronology also has implications for the dating of the origins of the feud. R.L. Storey and Ralph Griffiths argued that the territorial and political ambitions of the two families made violence inevitable and that the origins of conflict can be dated from at least the late 1440s.[43] In contrast A.J. Pollard and Michael Hicks have argued that violence between the two families was not inevitable. Pollard noted that during the 1440s and early 1450s the two families were able to coexist and cooperate in the running of local government in the north-east, including the shire election of 12 January 1453. The outbreak of violence in the county was a result of Neville aggrandisement in the Percy-dominated East Riding of Yorkshire, which was evident with the announcement of the marriage of Sir Thomas Neville and Maud Stanhope. Thereafter, relations between the two families deteriorated quickly into open violence.[44] For Hicks there was nothing inevitable about the feud and it 'seems to have arisen abruptly in the summer of 1453'.[45] The fact that livery was being distributed during the spring of 1453 at the very latest indicates that the hostilities emerged before the summer of 1453.

Others argue that the origins of the feud were located outside Yorkshire. Considering the feud from the context of their influence in the north-west, Peter Booth has shown that there were instances of violence in Cumbria in 1450 caused by the introduction to the county of the sons of Salisbury and Northumberland during the late 1440s.[46] The three-year difference between the violence in Cumbria and Yorkshire suggests that feuding between the two affinities was contained and managed in Cumbria and that these events were precursors to the more widespread feud in Yorkshire later in the decade. Moreover, no one from Cumbria was given illegal livery by the Percies, although thirty-eight men were indicted from the county, probably legal retainers considering the amount of land owned by the Percy family in the county.[47] Kay Lacey and M.W. Warner argued that a surviving document relating to a precedence dispute indicates personal animosity between Richard Neville, earl of Sailsbury and Henry Percy, earl of Northumberland as early as 1442.[48] Although there may have been animosity

---

[43] Griffiths, 'Local Rivalries and National Politics', 592–3; Storey, *End of the House of Lancaster*, 124–6.

[44] Pollard, *North-Eastern England*, 245–8, 255–6.

[45] Michael Hicks, *Warwick the Kingmaker* (Oxford, 1998), 86.

[46] Peter Booth, 'Men Behaving Badly? The West March Towards Scotland and the Percy–Neville Feud' in *The Fifteenth Century III: Authority and Subversion*, ed. Linda Clark (Woodbridge, 2003), 101–3.

[47] Ibid., 115–16.

[48] M.W. Warner and Kay Lacey, 'Neville vs. Percy: A Precedence Dispute, *circa* 1442',

between the two earls a decade before the disturbances in Yorkshire, there was nothing to suggest that those problems could escalate into full-scale private war. The distribution of illegal livery from at least 12 May 1453 indicates that the latest possible start to the feud was spring 1453, though tensions had existed for several years by that point.

Derbyshire – 1434 and 1468

There were two serious outbreaks of gentry violence in Derbyshire during the fifteenth century that resulted in indictments for illegal livery. The first, in 1434, centred on several interconnected rivalries in Derbyshire relating to property disputes and competition for local influence. These disputes resulted numerous murders, rapes, thefts and assaults across the county, particularly between the Pierpoint and Foljambe families.[49] Royal government took the disturbances seriously and two high-ranking nobles, John, duke of Bedford and William, earl of Suffolk were included on a commission of *oyer et terminer*.[50] The event that prompted the commission was probably the murder of Henry Longford and William Bradshaw at Chesterfield parish church on 1 January 1434, an incident in which Sir Henry Pierpoint was also maimed. The commissioners empanelled two juries from all six of Derbyshire's hundreds and the borough of Derby, with the maimed Henry Pierpoint sitting on one of those juries. Susan Wright noted that the relatively high status of the jurors may have helped them withstand pressure from those engaged in such activities.[51]

The commission identified twelve instances of illegal livery involving several leading gentry such as Ralph, Lord Cromwell, Henry, Lord Grey of Codnor, Sir Richard Vernon (indicted twice), Sir John Cockayne, Joan Beauchamp and Thomas Foljambe, gentleman.[52] One apparent link between many of those indicted for distributing illegal livery was Richard Broun of Repton who received livery illegally from Richard Vernon, Ralph Cromwell and Joan Beauchamp, and who was also accused of embracery to get Thomas Foljambe acquitted.[53] The indictments indicate a degree of factionalism in the county but there is little evidence that liveries were distributed to raise support for planned acts of violence, which is evident in the indictments against Thomas Foljambe. In addition to illegal

---

Historical Research, lxix (1996), 211–17.

[49] For a discussion of these events see: Castor, *The King, the Crown and the Duchy of Lancaster*, 239–50; Wright, *Derbyshire Gentry*, 128–31.

[50] *CPR, 1429–36*, 353.

[51] Wright, *Derbyshire Gentry*, 129.

[52] For the relevant illegal livery indictments see: KB9/11 mm.s. 15, 17.

[53] KB9/11 m. 14.

livery, Foljambe was indicted by the jury that did not include Pierpoint of aiding and abetting the murders of Longford and Bradshaw.[54] Foljambe was one of the lead instigators of the disorders at Chesterfield. He was accused of distributing liveries in Easter 1433, which makes it unlikely that men were retained in preparation for the attack at Chesterfield the following January. This fits with a more general pattern of the illegal livery cases from this commission, which are difficult to interpret because the offences were committed around a major religious festival when liveries were normally distributed to servants as a means of asserting a lord's standing.[55] Ten out of the twelve cases of illegal livery prosecuted by the commission were committed on or around *Clausum Pasche* (the Sunday after Easter) between 1426 and 1433, while one was committed at Christmas 1429 and one on 1 December 1431. Derbyshire in the late 1420s and early 1430s was a county in which there was a significant amount of unrest, particularly between feuding gentry families, yet the indictments for illegal livery do not suggest that liveries were distributed by local gentry with any specific actions in mind because many instances occurred around significant religious feasts when it was expected such liveries would be distributed. The fact that some of those in receipt should not have been given such liveries suggests an attempt to maintain a larger following and local influence than the statutes permitted, not to commit any specific act, but to maintain a sufficient support within the county.

The commission also indicted Henry, Lord Grey of Codnor, for attempting to impede the free election of knights of the shire by appearing at the electoral meeting, reportedly with 200 men on 24 June 1433.[56] Grey himself was indicted for giving illegal livery to eleven men on 20 April 1433.[57] At first sight it may appear that Grey was building up his affinity for the purposes of electoral interference. Such instances were not unheard of in the fifteenth century. Roger Virgoe argued that electoral malpractices and the manipulation of returns by leading magnates were well known in the fifteenth century, although the extent of such practices is uncertain.[58] Simon Payling has argued that 'it seems that the politics of intimidation, even in the fifteenth century, were insufficiently subtle to carry an election'.[59] The indictments in Derbyshire are the only instances of a prosecution for illegal livery coinciding with an attempt to overawe a parliamentary election. The only comparable case was a private suit

---

[54] KB9/11 m. 14.
[55] Davies, *Lords and Lordship*, 65.
[56] KB9/11 m. 17.
[57] KB9/11 m. 15.
[58] Roger Virgoe, 'Three Suffolk Parliamentary Elections of the Mid-Fifteenth Century', *BIHR*, xxxix (1966), 185–96; Roger Virgoe, 'The Cambridgeshire Election of 1439', *BIHR*, 46 (1973), 95–101; Roger Virgoe, 'An Election Dispute of 1483', *Historical Research*, lx (1987), 24–44.
[59] Payling, *Political Society*, 162–4.

in Nottinghamshire, in 1451, when Sir John Talbot (later earl of Shrewsbury) accused Sir John Stanhope of illegally distributing livery to twenty-four men at Rampton on 20 January 1450, presumably so that Stanhope could mobilise his supporters and ensure his election.[60]

The chronology of events in Derbyshire suggests that liveries, on this occasion, were not distributed solely for the purposes of impeding a free election. The writ for parliamentary summons was sent on 24 May 1433, five weeks after Grey had distributed illegal livery, and the opening of parliament scheduled for 8 July, suggesting that it was assembled in haste.[61] A possible shire election could not have been the reason why Grey distributed livery in April 1433, though it did help him bolster his support in the county. Moreover, Grey was also not alone in attempting to interfere with the free election. His main rivals at the election, Sir Richard Vernon and Sir John Cokayne, likewise appeared at the election with reportedly 300 men.[62] Both men were also indicted for illegal livery. Vernon was indicted for offences committed on Christmas 1429, 1 December 1431 and 24 April 1430 while John Cokayne was indicted for an offence on 7 April 1426. They were also accused of receiving illegal livery along with three gentlemen from Ralph Cromwell on 9 April 1431.[63] The events are complicated by the fact that Vernon and Cokayne were indicted for illegally receiving livery from Grey in 1433. Susan Wright suggested that if Grey had given livery to Vernon and Cokayne to influence the election it was ineffectual, but the summons to parliament was not sent out until after the livery offence was committed.[64] Grey seems to have had a disagreement with Vernon and Cokayne in the weeks between the distribution of livery and the shire election. None of the livery offences by men involved in electoral interference were committed between the issuing of a parliamentary summons and the holding of the shire election, although it is likely that the men who were given illegal livery were involved in attempts to impede free elections.

There were several other outbreaks of disorder in Derbyshire during the fifteenth century, but the only other outbreak that produced cases of illegal livery was in 1468.[65] The disorder was caused by issues in local politics, notably the exclusion of the Vernon family, particularly Henry Vernon, from political life in the county. Around 11pm on the evening of 3 December 1467 Henry's uncle, Roger Vernon, was murdered by Bartholomew Davenport, gentleman, who was a

---

[60] CP40/763 rot. 483; CP40/769 rot. 138.

[61] *PROME*, xi. 66.

[62] Discussed in: Simon Payling, 'County Parliamentary Elections in Fifteenth-Century England', *Parliamentary History*, xviii (1999), 246; Wright, *Derbyshire Gentry*, 114.

[63] KB9/11 m. 15.

[64] Wright, *Derbyshire Gentry*, 132.

[65] For a full discussion of the disorders in Derbyshire during the fifteenth century see: Wright, *Derbyshire Gentry*, 119–42, particularly 138–42 for the events around 1468 in this paragraph and the following paragraph.

member of Henry, Lord Grey of Codnor's household, and John Lord, yeoman.[66] Despite the fact that Codnor was later indicted for illegal livery,[67] neither of these murderers was indicted for illegal livery as they were presumably retained legally. Such a case may have highlighted the need for the law to be extended beyond liveried servants to other forms of retaining. There was more to these disturbances than one murder. Roger Vernon's murder was the most serious incident in a string of murders and assaults that were heard by the commission. The commission sat during a period of increased tension in national politics, particularly between Edward IV and his brother George, duke of Clarence. In addition to Codnor, John Talbot, third earl of Shrewsbury, was also indicted for giving illegal livery.[68] According to the pseudo-Worcester chronicler, those around Edward IV favoured Codnor while those around Clarence favoured the earl of Shrewsbury who was an ally of Richard Vernon, and eventually aligned with Clarence and Warwick.[69] However, it would be a mistake to assume any political partisanship in these indictments, especially as several leading nobles including Richard, earl of Gloucester, William, Lord Hastings, the earl of Warwick and earl Rivers were all named on the commission.[70]

Many of the indictments were for offences that had happened several years earlier and were presumably remembered by local informants or jurors. Two of the offences dated back to 1461: one involving Sir John Gresley illegally giving livery to one esquire and three gentlemen;[71] and one involving Walter Blount, Lord Mountjoy giving illegal livery to ten men.[72] A further two indictments were for offences committed in 1464, those against Lord Grey of Codnor[73] and John Cokeyn, esquire.[74] The only livery offence committed in the months immediately preceding the commission was by Talbot, who illegally distributed livery to twenty-two men on 23 February 1468.[75] This was ten days after Edward issued the commission, though it is uncertain whether Talbot knew this and simply distributed liveries to gain support in the region before the commission arrived.[76] What is clear is that he was giving livery to known criminals. Five

---

66 KB9/13 mm. 24, 39, 51.
67 KB9/13 m. 20. Note: he was the son of the Henry, Lord Grey of Codnor who was indicted in 1434.
68 KB9/13 m. 23.
69 'Annales', 789. For the local politics see: Hicks, '1468 Livery Act', 19–20; Wright, *Derbyshire Gentry*, 139.
70 *CPR, 1467–1477*, 69–70.
71 KB9/13 m. 19.
72 KB9/13 m. 22.
73 KB9/13 m. 20.
74 KB9/13 m. 21.
75 KB9/13 m. 23.
76 *CPR, 1467-1477*, 69–70.

yeomen who received illegal livery from Talbot had been involved in the murder of Nicholas Colyer two years earlier, although it is uncertain whether they were actively seeking the earl's support to avoid any indictments or whether the earl was wanting to recruit violent men to help in local disputes.[77] The key point is that liveries were still being given out after the murder of Richard Vernon, probably on the assumption that the disruptions could have escalated. Liveries were distributed at regular intervals by the Derbyshire gentry in the 1460s as a means of building networks of support, although the extent to which those wearing liveries were used in nefarious activities is uncertain. Yet Edward IV was clearly concerned with the extent of lawlessness in the county, which led to a wide-ranging commission with indictments for offences that were several years old. The commission was zealous in its prosecution of offences and the indictments for illegal livery were both a punishment to the gentry of Derbyshire for years of lawlessness and a warning about their future conduct.

The Dukes of Norfolk and Suffolk and the Siege of Caister Castle

Property disputes relating to the will of Sir John Fastolf were behind the conflict between the Paston family and the two dukes, along with several other members of the East Anglian gentry at this time.[78] Sir John Paston claimed that Fastolf made a nuncupative will two days before he died in November 1459 which made Paston along with Fastolf's chaplain Thomas Howes responsible for administering his estates, excluding the ten other executors named in a will written in June of that year. Paston then obtained all of Fastolf's lands in fee simple for a fee of 4,000 marks. Several of these properties were claimed or seized by others during that decade, including the duke of Norfolk who seized Caister Castle in 1461 and the duke of Suffolk who claimed the manors of Hellesdon and Drayton. The dispute continued after John I's death in 1466 with his son Sir John Paston II continuing to try to maintain the estates. In October 1468 some of the trustees named in Fastolf's initial will of June 1459 sold Caister to the duke of Norfolk. The dispute was cause by the probable opportunism of the Paston family who claimed the Fastolf estates which was enabled by the complexities of medieval land law.

On 14 June 1469 a commission of *oyer et terminer* heard the indictment against John Howard, duke of Norfolk, for giving illegal livery to a total of 134 men at

[77] Hicks, '1468 Statute of Livery', 18.
[78] These events are the basis of: Colin Richmond, *The Pastons in the Fifteenth Century: Fastolf's Will* (Cambridge, 1996). For this paragraph see also: Helen Castor, 'John Paston (1421–1466)', *ODNB*, xlii, 987–8; Helen Castor, 'John Paston (1422–1479)', *ODNB*, xlii, 988–9.

Framlington on 29 May and 1 June that year and John de la Pole, duke of Suffolk for giving illegal livery to twenty-five men at Wingfield on 1 June.[79] Both dukes were able to tap into existing local connections in order to raise men at this time. For instance, Gilbert Debenham, esquire, served on five out of nine commissions of the peace in Suffolk between 20 November 1467 and 11 September 1473 with the duke of Norfolk, from whom Debenham had illegally received livery.[80] Similarly, Sir Robert Wyngfeld was appointed to three commissions of the peace along with the duke of Norfolk between 4 July 1471 and 11 September 1473, despite having previously received Norfolk's livery illegally.[81] This was part of a general pattern of appointments because Wyngfeld was named on the eleven commissions of the peace in Norfolk with the duke between 20 February 1466 and 10 November 1475. This trend is evident for several other men indicted in 1470 for illegally receiving livery from the dukes of Norfolk and Suffolk such as Sir John Heveningham, Sir William Calthorp and John Knyvet, esquire.[82]

These cases highlight the use of livery as a means of waging local feuds and raise questions about the efficiency of the legal system. The cases were heard before a commission of *oyer et terminer* given to many members of Edward IV's family and inner circle for the whole realm of England.[83] The case was heard by the king's father-in-law, Earl Rivers, and his chamberlain, William, Lord Hastings, and others, which gave the commission the necessary clout to indict East Anglia's principal resident magnates. The time lag of only two weeks between the offences being committed and their prosecution was remarkably quick by fifteenth-century standards, indicating the seriousness with which Edward IV regarded the situation. A few months earlier, in January 1469, the king wrote to John Paston ordering him to stop assembling people in his dispute with the duke of Norfolk over Caister Castle.[84] There were several disturbances at this point. The duke of Suffolk led a group of men to tear down the Paston lodge at Hellesdon, an act in which Edward IV refused to intervene but would 'let the lawe proced' as the Pastons might have brought bills against the duke when his *oyer et terminer* commission was in Norwich.[85] The seriousness with which the authorities took instances of illegal livery is indicated by the fact that forty-five men who wore the livery of either of the two dukes were outlawed.

Yet the indictments did not deter the dukes because two months later the duke of Norfolk laid siege to the Paston-owned Caister Castle between 21 August and

---

[79]   KB27/839 rex rott. 31–2.
[80]   KB29/99 rot. 32.
[81]   *CPR, 1467–1477*, 630–1.
[82]   *CPR, 1461–1467*, 568; *CPR, 1467–1477*, 622–3.
[83]   *CPR, 1467–77*, 170.
[84]   *PL*, ii, 393–4.
[85]   *PL*, i, 544–5.

27 September 1469, eventually forcing the Pastons to surrender. During the siege Walter Writtle drafted a letter to four of the duke of Norfolk's men, asking them to speak with John Paston in order to 'avoide the sheedying of Cristyn blode'.[86] The four men to whom the letter was addressed (Sir John Heveningham, Thomas Wyngfeld,[87] Gilbert Debenham and William Brandon) were all indicted for illegal livery at the same time as the duke of Norfolk.[88] Nine men from a list of thirty-five present at the siege of Caister Castle compiled by William Worcestre were indicted for receiving illegal livery.[89] There was little direct correlation between those indicted for illegal livery and those participating in the siege of Caister Castle. The most plausible reason for this is that most of those present at the siege were legal retainers of the duke of Norfolk. While Master Philip Wentworth, knight and Master Simon Fitzsymonde of Essex, esquire, were at Caister Castle but not indicted for illegal livery, there were members of their families who were indicted for illegal livery but not at Caister Castle – Robert Fitzsymond, esquire, Thomas Wentworth, esquire, and Henry Wentworth, esquire – which suggests that the families were linked to the duke of Norfolk. It should be emphasised that Worcester's list principally named those of gentry rank and above. Therefore, there is no evidence that the yeomen who were indicted for receiving livery in 1469 were present at the siege. Similarly, many of the gentry that were present at Caister Castle were not indicted for receiving illegal livery a few months earlier.

In many ways these indictments conform to the general pattern in which illegal retainers formed only part of a larger force raised by a feuding party in a property dispute. This case differs from others because the indictments did not end the feud: the duke of Norfolk laid siege to Caister Castle *after* he had been indicted for distributing illegal liveries. Soon after this commission sat, Warwick the Kingmaker launched his first brief coup against Edward IV, issuing a manifesto at Calais along with his brother, archbishop Neville, and George, duke of Clarence, the king's brother. The Battle of Edgecote on 26 July and the king's brief imprisonment left a vacuum of royal authority which enabled the duke of Norfolk to lay siege to Caister Castle. Later the duke of Norfolk became one of Edward IV's key allies when he retook the throne in 1471, but at this point

---

[86] *PL*, ii, 577–8.
[87] Around the same time Writtle also drafted a separate letter intended only for Wyngfeld – *PL*, i, 578–9.
[88] KB29/99 rott. 31–2.
[89] William Worcestre, *Itineraries*, ed. John H. Harvey (Oxford, 1969), 189. In addition to the four previously cited there was: John, duke of Norfolk; his brother, John Lord Loveday, referred to as 'Loveday his brother' by Worcestre; Sir William Calthorp; Reynold Broke, described by Worcestre as 'Master Broke, son of Lord Cobham esquire'; and Robert Timperley, esquire, described by Worcestre as 'Master Timperley, esquire'.

actions were based on local issues.[90] Edward evidently trusted him enough in 1474 when an indenture was made between the king and Norfolk in preparation for the king's French campaign which obliged the duke to provide 300 archers 'well and sufficiently armed' for his planned invasion of France.[91] The duke's actions in 1469, however, were shaped by the context of that year as opposed to any future cordial relations between the king and the duke. As Colin Richmond noted: 'it is unlikely that he had a subtle enough mind to embark on the siege of Caister as a way to embarrass Warwick and Clarence' in order to make the realm ungovernable and restore Edward.[92] Indeed, both dukes must have implicitly acknowledged the legitimacy of the Readeption government as they purchased pardons for their livery offences in late 1470.[93] The effectiveness of indictments to deter further acts of violence and lawlessness, particularly those involving prominent regional magnates, depended on the ability of royal government to enforce further sanctions if necessary.

Henry Bruyn, Esquire – 1452

The instances discussed thus far have concentrated on illegal livery cases connected to large magnate disputes and events of national significance. Yet illegal livery was also prosecuted in connection with more localised instance of more petty lawlessness. The example which best illustrates this is against the Hampshire esquire Henry Bruyn, whose career as law-enforcer and law-breaker had a distinctly maritime dimension. Bruyn had been given a commission of the peace on 16 February 1446[94] and was sheriff of Hampshire when a commission was given to him and several others on 1 August 1448 to arrest certain known pirates in Portsmouth.[95] The maritime aspect of his career was prominent in both his legal and illegal activities. His father, Maurice Bruyn, had granted him land in Rowner on the Hampshire coast[96] which was his main place of residence at this time. Bruyn's landholdings affected the nature of some commissions he was given. He was regarded as a man capable of maintaining order on the Isle of Wight and had the military capability to help organise the defences of the island against 'the gretyst juperdye and danger' that the island was facing. The islanders therefore asked for him to be made lieutenant of the Isle of Wight

---

[90]   For an account of these events see: Hicks, *Wars of the Roses*, 190–8; Ross, *Edward IV*, 126–45.
[91]   E101/71/5 m. 961.
[92]   Richmond, *Fastolf's Will*, 197.
[93]   KB27/839 rex rott. 31–2.
[94]   *CPR, 1452–1461*, 478.
[95]   *CPR, 1446–1452*, 140.
[96]   *Cal. Inquisitions Misc., 1422–1485*, no. 353.

since the previous lieutenant, John Newport, had been discharged for various 'mysgovernances'.[97]

Despite Bruyn's role in upholding public order around the Hampshire coast, on 16 October 1451 a writ was sent to the justices in Hampshire to enquire into his activities, including the giving of illegal liveries.[98] In addition to livery, Bruyn was charged for attacking a Portuguese ship at Southampton on 3 November 1447,[99] and coming into possession of stolen goods and chattels from another Portuguese ship that had been attacked on 10 August 1450.[100] It was at this time that he was indicted for illegally distributing livery at Rowner on 20 January 1451.[101] Royal government was also taking measures to curb the problem of piracy during the period. On 12 December 1450 a commission of *oyer et terminer* was given to the keeper of the privy seal and several gentry to investigate acts of piracy against Burgundian ships by vessels owned by Henry, duke of Exeter, Henry Bruyn, esquire, and 'a vessel called *le Carvell* of Portsmouth'.[102] A subsequent commission of enquiry on 19 August 1451 concerned an attack on 'a hulk called *le George* of Lescluse' which was contrary to a naval truce between Henry VI and Philip the Good.[103] Bruyn was also involved in an attack upon a Genoese ship in September 1450, wounding the merchants, taking them captive and seizing their cargo.[104] The surviving indictments from the first commission suggest, at the most, minimal involvement of Bruyn or his affinity. Robert Jorde of Titchfield was the only man who received livery from Bruyn and was indicted by this commission.[105] Moreover, despite being the MP for Portsmouth in 1450, Bruyn was unable to prevent himself from being named by the commission as one of those involved in piracy against Burgundian vessels. His political affiliations at this time are difficult to determine. Despite having links with the duke of York, he was also a continual royal servant at this time and seems to have avoided becoming embroiled in the feud between the dukes of York and Somerset.[106] Henry Bruyn's case is a clear example of a 'fur-collar crime' or, to be more specific, 'fur-collar piracy', in which a member of the gentry distributed liveries to followers who were, in effect, a criminal gang.[107]

---

[97] SC8/28/1352; SC8/28/1353.
[98] KB9/265 m 84.
[99] KB9/265 m. 85.
[100] KB9/265 m. 86.
[101] KB9/265 m. 88.
[102] *CPR, 1446–1452*, 434–5.
[103] *CPR, 1446–1452*, 480.
[104] KB9/109 m. 11.
[105] KB9/109 m. 6.
[106] Linda Clark, unpublished article for History of Parliament Trust, London, on Henry Bruyn.
[107] For the concept of 'fur-collar crime' see: Barbara A. Hanawalt, 'Fur-Collar Crime: The

Conclusion

The cases of illegal livery discussed here were concentrated on local disputes. Feuds such as the Percy–Neville feud and the siege of Caister Castle took on greater national significance, but illegal liveries were distributed on these occasions for waging local disputes. This does not mean that illegal liveries were not given in instance of rebellion. The earl of Northumberland's confession at the 1404 parliament indicates that the Percies distributed liveries to supporters in the build-up to the Battle of Shrewsbury.[108] Similarly, the fact that the rebel army at Empingham in 1470 wore the duke of Clarence's livery suggests that illegal liveries were distributed as a means of recruitment for that rebellion.[109] Yet the indictments reveal little of the use of illegal liveries as a means of recruiting men as a direct threat to the reigning king. The indictments against Lord Bergavenny in 1507 were exceptional because his retaining practices were viewed as a direct challenge to Henry VII, while the indictments against the Stanley family were part of a concerted effort to dismantle their hegemony in the north-west. Such overtly political indictments were rare, particularly in the aftermath of rebellions when such practices may have been common. At the end of a rebellion or civil war, reconciliation with many on the defeated side was just as important for political stability as punishing the leaders of such risings. Political expediency trumped dogmatic enforcement of the law because the need to reconcile with rebellious factions meant the full force of the law could not realistically be used to prosecute individuals for comparatively minor offences. The commissions of *oyer et terminer* dealing with local feuding, in contrast, had a greater emphasis on punishment of offenders as a means of restoring law and order. This was evident in Staffordshire in 1414 when Henry V intervened to restore order in the county. Many feuds originated in disputes about landholding because the complexities of the English legal system allowed more room for manipulation of legal processes and satisfactory resolutions were almost impossible to achieve.[110] Feuding was also linked to competition for local hegemony and the increase in the number of local offices and commissions only exacerbated such competition. Liveries were distributed by feuding parties in order to obtain support in local disputes, but those men given illegal livery only formed one component of a larger force.

Pattern of Crime among the Fourteenth-Century English Nobility', *Journal of Social History*, viii (1975), 1–17.
[108] *PROME*, viii, 231–2.
[109] *Chronicle of the Rebellion in Lincolnshire*, 10–11.
[110] Harriss, *Shaping the Nation*, 197–202.

9

The Urban Experience

As Chapter 5 demonstrated, townsmen were a component of many bastard feudal affinities and many townsmen were indicted for illegal livery. The problems associated with townsmen wearing the liveries of feuding lords are illustrated by a mandate given to the mayor and aldermen of Kingston-upon-Hull on 27 June 1443 which ordered them to inquire into all transgressions against the statutes of livery. Certain burgesses had accepted the livery of magnates, which meant that 'a grievous quarrel has arisen among the burgesses of the town'.[1] Concerns about townsmen wearing noble liveries are evident in the initial debates about liveries during the late fourteenth century. A Commons petition in 1393 complained about the lack of enforcement of the 1390 act and stated that among those engaged in these disruptive practices were people with various urban occupations such as tailors, drapers, cobblers, fishmongers and butchers.[2] The Livery Act of 1429 exempted mayors during their period in office,[3] while the 1468 act gave to the relevant civic officials 'within eny such cite, burgh, towne port' the power to hear cases.[4] This clause essentially formalised certain existing practices. Earlier royal charters had given the right to hear and determine livery cases to Norwich in 1452,[5] Canterbury in 1453,[6] Derby in 1459,[7] and Rochester[8] and Colchester in 1462.[9] The statutes acknowledged that urban communities were part of a wider system of retaining and livery granting and many townsmen were indicted, but there has been no attempt to consider this phenomenon more broadly.

In a seminal article on medieval government Gerald Harriss noted the importance of the nobility and leading churchmen in the governing of England, in particular when the king was unable to govern because he was too young, too infirm or out of the kingdom.[10] However, one aspect of government not

---

[1]   *CPR, 1436–41*, 180–1.
[2]   *PROME*, vii, 239–40.
[3]   Ibid., viii, 547.
[4]   Ibid., xiii, 384–5.
[5]   *Calendar of Charter Rolls*, iv, 115.
[6]   Ibid., 124.
[7]   Ibid., 132.
[8]   Ibid., 151.
[9]   Ibid., 179.
[10] Gerald Harriss, 'Political Society and the Growth of Government in Late Medieval England', *P&P*, cxxxviii (1993), 28–57.

considered by Harriss was towns.[11] Although towns were not involved in the running of the kingdom when the king was unable to fulfil his duties, they were key partners in the operation of government. English towns enjoyed various rights and liberties which successive kings granted them, and towns operated within the wider political system of late medieval England that had patronage at its heart. Yet Christian Liddy has warned against reducing analyses of town–crown relations to 'a story of favours bought and gifts given', as kingship required the king to uphold the common good for everyone, not simply his own servants.[12] Urban governments had a degree of autonomy and power but the amount that English towns enjoyed was significantly less than many of their continental counterparts. Mayors, aldermen and other civic authorities were members of the partnership between royal government and local power structures. As Chris Given-Wilson has noted, 'royal government … was not something Englishmen could ignore, wherever they lived and however great they were'.[13] Civic governments held their power and authority directly from the king and therefore had to uphold his laws. Failure to uphold royal law jeopardised those urban liberties which towns cherished and fiercely guarded.

Town, Crown and the Upholding of the Statutes

One way in which urban governments helped to uphold the king's laws was by ensuring that those laws were known and disseminated widely. As towns were centres of commerce where goods and produce were traded, many people visited towns regularly or, at the very least, knew someone who did. Towns were therefore ideal places for communicating the royal will in the form of proclamations that reminded people of their duty to enforce the statutes. Proclamations were made outside towns but their comparatively dense populations made towns ideal locations to disseminate such orders to localities where problems were presumably believed to exist.[14] On various occasions late medieval kings ordered specific civic authorities to proclaim that the statutes of livery were to be upheld, with several proclamations being made during politically sensitive times. The earliest example of this was in April 1400 when Henry IV ordered the mayor and sheriff of London to proclaim the livery act passed during his first parliament

---

[11] Liddy, *War Politics and Finance*, 14 also notes this omission.
[12] Ibid., 3.
[13] Given-Wilson, *Henry IV*, 5.
[14] On the value of proclamations see: James A. Doig, 'Political Propaganda and Royal Proclamation in Late Medieval England', *Historical Research*, lxxi (1998), 254–5; Steven Gunn, *Early Tudor Government, 1485–1558* (Basingstoke, 1995), 188.

in 1399.[15] On 5 November 1413 Henry V ordered the sheriffs of London to proclaim that the 1401 statute was to be observed as part of his broader campaign against lawlessness at the start of his reign.[16] Beyond London, in April 1457 proclamations were made in Dover ordering that no one was to take the livery of any lord or gentleman.[17] In 1469, a proclamation was made in the city of Nottingham ordering that the previous year's act was to be upheld.[18] Only a few such orders from the Lancastrian and Yorkist kings survive, mainly from local and urban records as opposed to those from central government. While this may indicate a limited use of proclamations, beyond the dissemination of new acts of parliament, it is illustrative of the various strategies open to kings to ensure their laws were upheld.

Tudor monarchs used proclamations with increasing regularity, developing a system begun by their late medieval predecessors.[19] The surviving records indicate that Henry VII, like his predecessors, used urban governments as the vehicle for reminding his subjects to uphold the livery laws. R.W. Heinze was surprised that the only surviving royal proclamation from Henry VII's reign relating to retaining was issued in 1502 and only sought to ensure that the existing laws were upheld.[20] Heinze missed an earlier proclamation from 1488 which indicates Henry's concern that his tenants would be illegally retained, reflecting the concerns expressed in the 1487 act.[21] Henry VII ordered the mayor and bailiffs of the town of Lancaster to make a proclamation that no one in the town was to retain or be retained by any means 'but as may and shal accord with oure lawes' or to come to any assemblies unless responding to a commission or commandment.[22] The fact that this order was given to Lancaster suggests that this proclamation was part of a broader strategy to improve the management of his duchy of Lancaster estates and prevent royal tenants from being retained by potentially rebellious lords. The proclamation in Lancaster was a means of implementing a broader policy evident in the 1487 act and in several writs sent to various duchy of Lancaster officials.[23] The problem of liveries and/or retaining was included in several preambles to proclamations along with various other crimes because it had become a standard problem that kings claimed to be combating. Henry VIII ordered the sheriffs of London and Middlesex to make

[15] *CCR, 1399–1402*, 182.
[16] *Calendar of Letter-Books of the City of London*, i, 119.
[17] HMC, *5th Report* (London, 1876), 492, 521.
[18] *Records of the Borough of Nottingham*, ii, 425.
[19] Gunn, *Early Tudor Government*, 189.
[20] R.W. Heinze, *The Proclamations of the Tudor Kings* (Cambridge, 1976), 79; *Tudor Royal Proclamations*, i, no. 50.
[21] *PROME*, xv, 375–6.
[22] DL37/62 rot. 4.
[23] DL37/62 rott. 5, 6d, 14, 17d, 19, 21, 30d, 41, 42d.

a proclamation 'that by reason of murders, riots, routs, unlawful assemblies, maintenance and embraceries due to neglect of the statutes against liveries and retainers, these statutes will henceforth be strictly enforced'.[24] A similar proclamation was made in Leicester in 1520.[25] Determining the effect, if any, that these proclamations had on either the enforcement of the statutes or the practice of illegal retaining is not possible from the surviving records. The key point here is that such proclamations reveal a conscious decision on the part of successive kings to remind their subjects in specific areas to adhere to the statutes.

Beyond communicating the royal will, urban governments were responsible for ensuring that livery and retaining laws were upheld.[26] The emphasis on the fact the laws were the king's law is evidence in a decree made by Edward IV on 4 October 1471 in the Star Chamber which referred to 'grete riottis, excesses and mysgouernances' in Nottingham. It went on to state that Edward had asked Henry, Lord Grey of Codnor, if those accused were his servants, which Grey denied. Despite Grey's denial Edward responded by saying that neither Grey nor his servants were to do anything to the mayor, aldermen or 'cominalte' of Nottingham contrary to his laws and peace and that Grey himself was not to retain anyone in the town against the form of the statutes.[27] Failure to uphold the king's laws was potentially disastrous for certain towns since urban liberties were threatened if mayors and aldermen failed in their responsibility to maintain law and order. In March 1457 Henry VI named York as a major centre of riots and unlawful assemblies which has led to 'gret slaughters, murder of oure people, and other mischeves'. He therefore ordered the mayor to proclaim that the riots that had recently occurred in the city were unlawful and that that the city would forfeit its liberties if such riots and the displays of weapons and noble liveries continued.[28] Henry VII's letter to York about retaining a few months after a minor Yorkshire uprising in 1486 included a thinly veiled threat to the mayor, aldermen, sheriffs and common counsel of the city, saying that 'if ye shew your self remise or negligent in thexecucion of this our commaundement, we shall soo correct and ley the default theror to your discharge, that it shalbe to heavy for you to bere the same, ye may be assured'.[29] In 1495 Henry VII threatened to replace the mayor of York and the city's magistrates if they failed to keep king's peace.[30]

---

[24] *L&P Hen. VIII*, i, no. 3353.
[25] *Records of the Borough of Leicester*, iii, 12.
[26] See also: Attreed, *The King's Towns*, 281.
[27] *Records of the Borough of Nottingham*, ii, 384–7. The decree was enrolled in the town's records on 13 November 1471.
[28] Attreed, *The King's Towns*, 294.
[29] *The York House Books, 1461–1490*, 2 vols., ed. Lorraine Attreed (Stroud, 1991) ii, 521.
[30] *York Civic Records*, ed. A Raine, 8 vols., York Archaeological Society, Records Series (Wakefield and York, 1939–53), ii, 115–16. See also: Christian Liddy, 'Urban

Threatening to take away urban liberties was the most extreme of a multitude of options open to kings who wished to address illegal retaining and other threats to public order in towns. Successive kings, for various reasons, either ordered specific towns to enforce the statutes or made an ordinance prohibiting retaining or distributing livery in that town or city. Rosemary Horrox has argued that such letters were probably issued at the request of the recipient town.[31] Yet the contexts in which these letters were sent indicate that they were issued on the king's initiative because of genuine concerns about large groups of men being assembled in a relatively short space of time.

In total, there are nineteen known royal letters to civic governments about urban retaining between 1449 and 1522, seventeen of which are from 1470 onwards.[32] It is impossible to estimate how representative the surviving sample of letters is of what was originally sent. Eight out of the nineteen known letters are from Richard III's short two-year reign because of the unique survival of his signet book, which was evidently not archived with the rest of the signet office's records which were destroyed in the Banqueting House fire of 1619.[33] Although the number of lost letters is impossible to quantify, it is clear that there must have been other letters that are now lost. Richard III's signet book indicates that no standard letter was sent to every town in the kingdom but that letters were targeted to specific towns. Rosemary Horrox argued that this collection of documents is unlikely to represent any form of 'administrative innovation'.[34] The letters about retaining similarly do not necessarily reveal a new royal policy towards urban retaining but a continuation of earlier practices.

Three letters that Edward IV sent, all from 1470 onwards, suggest that Edward began to take a more stringent view of urban retaining. The earliest known letter about retaining that was connected to a political crisis at national level was sent by Edward IV. On 9 January 1470 he wrote to the bailiff, burgesses and inhabitants of Scarborough prohibiting everyone in the town from taking the livery of 'eny lord or estate whatsouer'. The letter's preamble suggests that Edward was concerned that liveries would be distributed in order to raise troops against him: 'yet neither arise ne stirre towar ony Journay at the request or desire of eny persone whatsoever he been onlesse thon ye have a special commaundement from vs in that bihalue'.[35] When Edward wrote to Scarborough he was

---

Enclosure Riots: The Risings of the Commons in English Towns, 1480–1525', *P&P*, ccxxvi, (2015), 74–5.

[31] Rosemary Horrox, 'Urban Patronage and Patrons in the Fifteenth Century' in *Patronage, the Crown and the Provinces in Later Medieval England*, ed. Ralph A. Griffiths (Gloucester, 1981), 165 n. 78.

[32] See Appendix 3.

[33] *Harleian 433*, i, p. xvi.

[34] Ibid.

[35] North Yorkshire Country Record Office, DC/SCB, White Velum Book of Scarborough,

attempting to reconcile with his brother George, duke of Clarence, and Richard Neville, earl of Warwick, after their coup which led to Edward's temporary imprisonment. The coup began in the guise of a popular uprising led by Robin of Redesdale centred in Warwick's estates in Richmondshire leading to a Yorkist defeat the Battle of Edgecot.[36] '[O]ny Journay' must have meant accompanying a magnate who was in open rebellion against the king. Scarborough's close proximity to the centre of the rebellion is likely to have left the town, and indeed most of the region, under suspicion. A possible connection between men from Scarborough and the earl of Warwick was evident after the second phase of the Wars of the Roses in which Edward IV was deposed for six months.[37] As part of Edward's attempts to reassert his authority and punish traitors, several men from Scarborough were named in various commissions given by Edward in summer 1471 to arrest numerous men, seize their goods and bring them before the king's council.[38] When Edward wrote to Scarborough in January 1470 he did not know there would be another attempted coup, but the letter does indicate that he was concerned about the potential for retaining as a mechanism for raising troops for an armed rebellion.

Edward IV's other letter to a town about retaining was sent to Coventry in February 1472 in which he ordered that the statutes be upheld because of various crimes and seditions that had recently occurred. The privy seal writ was also proclaimed in the open market. The preamble noted Henry VI's readeption: 'Callyng to our Remembraunce and consideracion the gret tempests, diusions & troubles that in late daies haue be in this our Reaume'. Edward then stated that his order was 'for the pacificacion, defence, and suretee of the same our land and subgittes, both inwards & outwards'.[39] The letter was sent ten months after Edward regained his throne and was sent to a town with connections to the earl of Warwick. In 1471 prominent townsmen, including the mayor, loaned Warwick the Kingmaker £66 13s. 4d. and contributed soldiers to the Lancastrian army at the Battle of Barnet.[40] Soon after Edward IV began his second reign, an oath of alliance to him was recorded in the town's Leet book[41] and the town paid £200 to have its liberties restored.[42] Edward IV's letter formed part of an

---

f. 53. I would like to thank Professor Michael Hicks for supplying me with his transcription of this document.

[36] Hicks, *Warwick*, 270–8; A.J. Pollard, *Warwick the Kingmaker: Politics, Power and Fame* (London, 2007), 67.

[37] Warwick was killed in the aftermath of the Battle of Barnet. For a more detailed discussion of these events see: Ross, *Edward IV*, 166–73.

[38] *CPR, 1467–1477*, 286–7.

[39] *Coventry Leet Book*, i, 374.

[40] Ibid., 364–6.

[41] Ibid., 367.

[42] Ibid., 370.

attempt to address Coventry's potential as a recruiting ground for supporters and funds by rebellious nobles.

Richard III's signet book provides further examples of kings writing to towns and cities. The first two letters sent by Richard III – to Northampton on 3 August 1483[43] and to Southampton on 12 September 1483[44] – occurred between his usurpation and the duke of Buckingham's rebellion. Both letters mention that liveries had 'caused oftentimes gret divisione & geoperdie' as well as 'gret divisions troubles descencions and debates'. The 'gret divisione' refers to the previous thirty years of intermittent conflict that resulted in three usurpations between 1461 and 1471. Curbing retaining in towns, as well as the countryside, was a means of stabilising Richard's rule. Yet his concern about a potential rebellion was only one reason why the inhabitants of Northampton and Southampton were not to be retained contrary to the statutes. The phrase 'good reuelle to be had & continued within oure said Towne' in the letter to Northampton also relates to internal urban conflicts that were exacerbated by retaining, which is apparent in letters issued after the repression of Buckingham's Rebellion. Richard's letter to Canterbury on 4 January 1484 ordered that the statutes were to be upheld in the town for good rule and 'theschewing of divysion discordes & variaunces that mighte growe amonges the subgiettes of this oure Royaulme'.[45] Similar sentiments are found in all the remaining letters to urban governments that he sent. Richard III's letters about retaining addressed two interconnected concerns that were fundamental to kingship and good government: campaigning against threats to public order and pre-empting any rebellions.

Although royal letters to urban governments about retaining are most concentrated in Richard III's reign, the practice of writing to towns about retaining was another method of ruling developed by the Yorkists which Henry VII adapted to suit his needs. Shortly after his usurpation he wrote to the mayor and JPs of Coventry on 31 January 1486 ordering them not to permit illegal retaining in the town.[46] In November 1486 he wrote to the mayor, aldermen, sheriffs and common council of York, a few months after a minor rising in the county.[47] Writing to towns about retaining shortly after a local rebellion replicated Edward IV's practices. Henry VII's main adaptation was to place stronger emphasis on the special obligations owed to him in the duchy of Lancaster since he was also duke of Lancaster. As early as 1449 Margaret of Anjou had written to the town of Leicester about the distribution of illegal liveries in light of various disturbances in the town and surrounding area. The letter was not an example of a conscious

---

[43] *Harleian 433*, ii, 10.
[44] Ibid., 19.
[45] Ibid., i, 69.
[46] HMC, *The Manuscripts of Shrewsbury and Coventry Corporations*, 120.
[47] *York House Books*, ii, 521.

policy of royal government about retaining. It was not addressed to any specific person but rather 'to all men to whom tis present writyng endented shall come' and was written by Margaret in a private capacity because the town was part of her dower when she became queen.[48] Edward IV was the first king to issue a specific ordinance about retaining to a town in the duchy when he ordained that no one in Halton was to be retained 'contrarie to the statutes'.[49] The ordinance also emphasised the special obligations that duchy inhabitants had towards the king, stating that they were 'to attende upon noo man but oonly upon the kinges highnesse' or Lord Stanley in the king's absence. The first occasion in which Henry VII wrote directly to towns in the duchy of Lancaster about retaining was the order to the town of Lancaster to proclaim that the statutes were to be upheld.[50] Henry placed a stronger emphasis on the loyalty owed to him by towns in the duchy of Lancaster in his letter to Leicester in 1498 which noted that Leicester was 'parcell of our duchie of Lancastre' and stated that 'for the tranqullite and peax to be had thrugh this oure said royaume' no one was to be retained by 'cloth, cognisaunce, othe or otherwise, contrarie to our said lawes & statutz'.[51]

Henry's practice of writing to towns and cities about retaining and tailoring the order to address the specific context of the recipient town or city is evident in his letter to the mayor and brethren of Carlisle in February 1498. Here, the order was tailored to address the needs of a militarised city on the Scottish border that was on the frontline against any invasion threats. The letter is the clearest articulation of royal fears that retaining in the city would be the method of recruitment for a rebellion and in this instance could coincide with a Scottish invasion.[52] Carlisle's importance in terms of national security was stated in the preamble when Henry stated that the city was 'oon of the chief keyes and fortessies to the defense of this our Realm'. Consequently, no one living in the city was to 'hensfurthe [be] reteyned with any man be he spiritual or temporall lord or other by lyveree baggnen clothing cognoissance or any other wise'. Furthermore, nobody was to ride out of the city to become involved in local disorder, but instead was 'to be abiding and attending at all seasons bothe of warre and of peax in the same oure citie for the defens and suretie therof'. The city's government was to swear oaths of fealty to the bishop of Carlisle and tender sureties to him; this is the only letter of its kind to stipulate this. The letter suggests Henry was concerned about the political elite in Carlisle and the surrounding area, hence the need to extract oaths of fealty and remind the city's government of their obligations to

---

[48] *Records of the Borough of Leicester*, ii, 256–7. See also Chapter 4.
[49] DL5/1 fol. 136. Printed in Myers, *Crown, Household and Parliament*, 327.
[50] DL37/62 rot. 4.
[51] *Records of the Borough of Leicester*, ii, 354.
[52] Cumbria Record Office, Carlisle, Ca2/150. For a more detailed discussion of this document see: McKelvie, 'Henry VII's Letter to Carlisle in 1498', 149–66.

uphold the retaining laws. Thomas, Lord Dacre, warden on the west march, was the dominant figure in Carlisle and its hinterland and had served Richard III in the north. Despite making peace with Henry VII early in the new reign, Dacre was never fully trusted by the new king.[53] Such concerns were coupled with problematic foreign relations. A Scottish invasion the previous year had, in all likelihood, alerted Henry to the problems that could be caused by illegal retaining in the city, either as a means of recruiting for a fifth column to coincide with a Scottish invasion or hindering the defences of a key stronghold on the Scottish border if such an invasion did manifest itself. It is unlikely that Henry had received news that the Scottish king James IV had ratified a truce five days before Henry wrote to Carlisle[54] and even if he did, there is nothing to suggest that Henry trusted James to stick to the truce. Henry's letter to Carlisle therefore demonstrates concerns about retaining in relation to law and order, possible rebellions and the defence of the realm.

The militarised nature of Carlisle means that it is not a typical example of the towns to which kings wrote about retaining. The most useful comparison with Carlisle is Calais, which received no known letter about retaining, despite the fact that Calais was a source of much military strength during the Wars of the Roses because of the professionalism of the garrison.[55] Here the concern about retaining was not addressed by the king but by the captain of the garrison as part of a broader strategy to maintain discipline. The relevant example dates from Edward IV's reign when, in order to maintain discipline in the garrison, Richard Neville, earl of Warwick, passed several ordinances on 26 July 1467 including one stating that those in the garrison were only permitted to give livery to 'the persones being within his retinu upon peyn of forfeiture of Cs'.[56] In many ways this ordinance built on older military ordinances that pre-date any laws restricting the distribution of noble liveries. Clause 23 of the ordinances for Richard II's campaign in Scotland in 1385 stated that no captain was to retain the services of someone already contracted for the campaign. The clause was part of an attempt to develop a sense of unity in the army, which was probably heterogeneous in its composition, and to prevent any quarrelling between rival captains.[57] The context of Warwick's ordinances suggests that his order about

[53] On Dacre see in particular: Steven G. Ellis, 'A Border Baron and the Tudor State: The Rise and Fall of Thomas, Lord Dacre of the North', *Historical Journal*, xxxv (1992), 253–77; Summerson, *Medieval Carlisle*, ii, 466–76.
[54] *CDS*, iv, no. 1644.
[55] See in particular: David Grummitt, *The Calais Garrison: War and Military Service in England, 1436–1558* (Woodbridge, 2008); G.L. Harriss, 'The Struggle for Calais: An Aspect of the Rivalry between Lancaster and York', *EHR*, lxxv (1960), 30–53.
[56] For all of Warwick's Calais ordinances discussed in this paragraph see: C47/149 rot. 14.
[57] Anne Curry, 'Disciplinary Ordinances for English and Franco-Scottish Armies in

liveries was also intended to maintain discipline and prevent quarrelling. In total Warwick issued nine ordinances 'for the assured governaunce and prosperite of the seid towne' with the first ordinances stating that they were to be diligent in their duties. Other ordinances related to treason or military discipline and one suggestive ordinance was against adultery. The latter in particular indicates a desire to maintain cohesion within the garrison. A set of disciplinary ordinances in Lancastrian Normandy in 1421 prohibited soldiers from keeping concubines, or other women in adulterous relationships, because such women 'plunder, steal, take away, demand and extort the goods of our lieges and subjects' in order to 'sustain their sensual and hedonistic lifestyle'. Although the ordinance refers to such acts 'provoking the wrath of the divine majesty', one cannot help but think that the ordinance was more concerned with the very real worldly problem of quarrels between competing lovers.[58] This desire to maintain cohesion within a group of trained fighters who were part an English outpost that existed with the lingering threat of a French attack was also evident in Warwick's ordinances from Calais in 1467. Similarly, Carlisle was a clear target for a Scottish attack if hostilities commenced in 1498. Ordinances about retaining in such military outposts formed one element of wider attempts to maintain cohesion by deterring captains from retaining each other's men.

The inclusion of liveries in the military ordinances of Calais is representative of the broader point that urban governments were concerned about a proliferation of noble liveries within their walls. Moreover, towns and cities were capable of addressing such concerns without needing a royal command. Indeed, to view urban authorities simply as the passive conduits of the royal will would be mistaken, as the maintenance of law and order was a concern shared by urban and royal governments. For instance, in 1504 the town of Gloucester passed an act against retaining because of the 'dyvers myscheffs and greate ennormytyes that in this towne before this time hath bene usyd'.[59] Eleven such ordinances survive in various urban archives between 1460 and 1516, including Warwick's ordinance in Calais in 1467.[60] In total, six of these ordinances were passed during the 1460s while a further four were passed during Henry VII's reign. The earliest known urban ordinance regarding the distribution of livery was in Northampton in 1460 when an ordinance given on 25 May forbade anyone in the town from

---

1385: An International Code?', *Journal of Medieval History*, xxxvii (2011), 269–94, particularly 291 (no. 23) for the relevant ordinance. See also: Maurice Keen, 'Richard II's Ordinances of War in 1385' in *Rulers and Ruled in Late Medieval England*, eds. Rowena Archer and Simon Walker (London, 1995), 33–48.

[58] The ordinances are edited in: Anne Curry, 'Disciplinary Ordinances for English Garrisons in Normandy in the Reign of Henry V' in *The Fifteenth Century XIV: Essays Presented to Michael Hicks*, ed. Linda Clark (Woodbridge, 2015), 10–12.

[59] HMC, *Twelfth Report, Appendix, Part IX* (London, 1891), 436.

[60] See Appendix 4.

taking 'eny maner [of] Clotyng or Synges of eny lorde squyer or any other person unfraunchesed excepte the kyng' on pain of imprisonment. Furthermore, no one was to enter into any unlawful oath, promise or assurance with anyone without the king's permissions.[61] As the ordinance was passed during the first phase of the Wars of the Roses, it is likely that Northampton did not want to become entangled in the conflict by having its inhabitants recruited into the rebel Yorkist army. Such ordinances were local remedies to deal with specific local issues that were reinforced by the existing parliamentary statutes.[62] The ordinances do not replicate each other or the parliament acts, as all had slight variations to adapt to local circumstances. In some towns there was an absolute ban on retaining and livery distribution, such as in Nottingham in 1463 when an ordinance stated that any burgess taking livery, presumably of a noble, was to be 'disfranchised and inpresoned and fyned att ye discretion of the Maior and Councell'.[63] This was an extreme measure when compared to similar ordinances, as a complete ban on liveries and retaining was rare. On most occasions the focus was on reminding urban communities of the existing laws. In 1503 the city of York ordained 'that no fruanchesed person were no connisaunce or leverey of any lord or gentilman contray unto the statutez thereappon provided'.[64] The clause stating that retaining was not to happen against the existing statutes was also included in most of the royal letters. Edward IV's letter to Coventry in 1472 stated that retaining was not to happen in the town 'contrarie to our laws & statutes ordeigned & prouided in suche behalfe'.[65] Variations of these phrases are found in the majority of royal letters and urban ordinances and, presumably, those entitled to wear a lord's livery could continue to do so. Kings and towns were not concerned about the practice of retaining within towns provided it was within the terms of the statutes. Their key concern was that widespread retaining and the giving of liveries would lead to the creation of large unwieldy noble affinities that could be used to conduct private feuds or mount rebellions.

Urban Feuding

During the later middle ages several large towns were awarded county status in their own right and returned cases to King's Bench separate from the surrounding countryside. Three cases of illegal livery were returned to the King's Bench

---

[61] *Records of the Borough of Northampton*, ed. C.A. Markham, 2 vols. (London, 1898), i, 297–8.
[62] Cavill, *The English Parliaments of Henry VII*, 182.
[63] *Records of the Borough of Nottingham*, ii, 425.
[64] *YCR*, ii, 181.
[65] *Coventry Leet Book*, i, 374.

operating in towns rather than the county at large: London in 1439;[66] Coventry in 1480 when Thomas Shirwood, gentleman, was indicted;[67] and Nottingham in 1501 when a glover was indicted.[68] Unfortunately, these cases seem to be isolated instances with no further contextual information available about them. It is therefore difficult to extrapolate any broader significance from them. However, there are cases involving townsmen in returns made by local JPs and commissions of *oyer et terminer* for which there is further contextual information. These cases illuminate the role of towns and urban communities in examples of noble feuds and retaining.

The involvement of prominent members of the urban community in outbreaks of violence was evident in Chester. Jane Laughton described fifteenth-century Chester as a place where 'feuding country gentlemen and their rival affinities strutted the city streets and caused serious disturbances'.[69] These disturbances are evident in cases of illegal livery that originated in the city. In 1428 the city's mayor, John Hope, was charged with illegally giving livery to a baker and a yeoman from Chester on 4 November 1426 at Chester.[70] Hope was a member of a small group of families who formed the civic elite that had dominated the city during the fourteenth and fifteenth centuries.[71] He was a former sheriff of Chester (1412–15) and was elected mayor of Chester seven times between 1419 and 1428.[72] On 19 October 1419, only a few days after he had been elected mayor, a group of armed men attempted to murder Hope, his brother Robert, Robert's son and three other townsmen. It was alleged that, since his election as mayor, Hope, himself of Welsh descent, had routinely gone through Chester accompanied by a band of English and Welsh supporters wearing coats of mail and carrying swords and poleaxes.[73] The Welsh element in this, however, should not be exaggerated. Despite feelings of mutual antagonism between Wales and Cheshire, particularly in the aftermath of the Glyndŵr Rebellion, Philip Morgan has argued that 'ethnicity may well have been used as a weapon whose use was enabled in response to the [Glyndŵr] Revolt, but it was not the cause of disorder'.[74] Hope

---

[66]   KB29/72 rot. 30.

[67]   KB29/110 rot. 17.

[68]   KB29/140 rot. 31; KB29/143 rot. 41.

[69]   Jane Laughton, 'The Control of Discord in Fifteenth-Century Chester' in *Survival and Discord in Medieval Society*, eds. Richard Goddard, John Langdon and Miriam Müller (Turnhout, 2010), 213.

[70]   CHES25/12 mm. 16.

[71]   *A History of the County of Chester: Volume V Part 1, The City of Chester, General History and Topography*, eds. C.P. Lewis and A.T. Thacker (London, 2003), 60.

[72]   *A History of the County of Chester: Volume V Part 2*, 309–10; Laughton, *Life in a Late Medieval City*, 119.

[73]   CHES25/11 mm. 17–18. Discussed in Laughton, *Chester, 1275–1520*, 34.

[74]   Philip Morgan, 'Cheshire and Wales' in *Power and Identity in the Middle Ages*, eds.

and his retainers were involved in violent and intimidating acts, which was why they were indicted for illegal livery. Their Welsh decent only exacerbated tensions that previous actions had caused. At the same time, another former mayor of Chester, John Whitmore, was also indicted for giving illegal livery to five men in November 1423.[75] Whitmore was also a member of the city's ruling elite and was mayor during the period in which Hope was sheriff.[76] In Cheshire the ruling oligarchy was involved in instances of lawlessness over a sustained period and the indictments against two former mayors of the city for illegal livery were connected to their other activities in both the city and the surrounding countryside.

The cases from Chester are unusual because there is a clear connection between the distribution of livery and factional violence within the urban community. More often, townsmen were retained illegally by nobles as part of a broader recruitment campaign in the waging of feuds with other nobles. One such case occurred in 1505 when the Hampshire knight William Sandys was indicted for illegally retaining seven men, five of whom were townsmen. Sandys illegally retained one vintner from Winchester along with a fishmonger, a mercer, a draper and one of the town clerks of Andover.[77] Out of these seven men John Hacker, fishmonger of Andover, was the only man fined for his involvement with Sandys in outbreaks of violence in Chute Forest against members of the Lisle family.[78] Yet the fines for this brawl indicate that Sandys drew upon an urban support base in his feud with the Lisle family. Both William Sandys and his son Richard were noted as being resident in Andover. In addition, two gentlemen, three mercers, three innholders, a smith, a constable, a caster, a tanner, a husbandman and sixteen yeomen from Andover, along with John Paulet, gentleman of Basingstoke, were amongst those fined with Sandys for their involvement in the brawl at Chute Forest.[79] It is clear that Sandys was drawing on his urban support base, or 'affinity', in conducting his own private feud.

These feuds were relatively minor compared to the large-scale feuds of the mid-fifteenth century that were, in effect, private wars. Evidence from indictments relating to the feuding of the 1450s demonstrates clearly that feuding nobles were perfectly able and willing to recruit townsmen into their affinities. The most notable instance of nobles employing townsmen in their disputes was in Yorkshire during the Percy–Neville dispute in which 15.3 per cent of the 710 men indicted for ambushing the earl of Salisbury and other prominent members of the

---

Huw Price and John Watts (Oxford, 2007), 195–210, quotation on 209.
[75] CHES25/12 mm. 16.
[76] *Victoria County History Cheshire*, v 60 (1), 309 (2).
[77] KB9/436 m. 13. This was in addition to a yeoman from Anport and a husbandman from Clatford.
[78] KB27/969, fines.
[79] KB27/969, fines; Luckett, 'Crown Office and Licensed Retinues', 232.

Neville family were from York.[80] However, only three men from York, a waller, a yeoman and a fletcher, were indicted for illegally receiving livery from Thomas Percy. Indeed, only twenty-seven men were indicted for receiving livery illegally from either Thomas or Richard Percy in the months leading up to the attack on the Nevilles.[81] The scale of the Percy–Neville feud means it is unsurprising that some townsmen did become involved making a sizeable minority of the Percy following in the summer of 1453, although very few are known to have received illegal livery from the Percies.

Hereford in the 1450s

A more extreme example of urban communities being drawn into wider conflicts was in Herefordshire in the 1450s, where the city of Hereford became a space for the public display of factionalism. These cases are atypical in scale and context but they highlight the connection between urban communities and feuding nobles. Although there are no known royal letters or civic ordinances relating to livery in Hereford, these cases show that many of the ordinances and letters common in the second half of the fifteenth century were grounded in concerns about very plausible scenarios. All the offences in Herefordshire during the 1450s occurred in either the city of Hereford or Leominster, the county's second largest town, and many men from both places were indicted for receiving illegal livery from local lords and gentry. Unfortunately the records do not state the precise location in Hereford or Leominster where the livery was distributed, for instance in a public place such as the market or a tavern, or at a private residence. Nevertheless, when the context in which many of the livery offences occurred is considered, it is clear that towns and cities were being used as both recruiting centres and stages on which to make a show of strength.

One of the main disruptors of the peace in Hereford during this decade was Sir Walter Devereux, a close associate of Richard, duke of York. Devereux used the county's two main towns as his rallying points where he could distribute liveries to a large number of men, and was indicted on three occasions.[82] The cases of illegal livery involving him, and his close associates, were a product of both local feuding in the county and broader national events connected to the increasing alienation of the duke of York from the Lancastrian court. There is sufficient evidence to demonstrate a close connection between Devereux and the duke of York including appearing on the duke's retinue rolls, receiving an annuity

---

[80] Griffiths, 'Local Rivalries and National Politics', 597–8.

[81] KB9/149/1 mm. 20–1, 49, 53.

[82] KB9/34/1 m. 5; KB9/34/2 m. 142; KB9/35 mm. 6, 69.

from him and acting as a witness to a charter he inspected.[83] Devereux was also connected to the events in September 1450 when Richard, duke of York returned unannounced from Ireland to set himself up as the leader of the faction opposed to a circle of men around Henry VI, led by Edmund Beaufort, duke of Somerset. In the first of two bills that York presented to Henry VI in 1450 Devereux was named, along with Edmund Mulso, as someone whom it was rumoured was to be imprisoned because of malicious stories that were being circulated by the royal favourites about York's role in the loss of Normandy.[84]

The indictments against Devereux for illegal livery in Herefordshire in both 1452 and 1457 were part of a series of indictments against him on both occasions, and show that he was granting liveries in major urban centres. In 1452 Devereux was indicted for giving illegal livery to thirty-one men from Hereford on 4 January 1452.[85] This was one month before Richard, duke of York wrote to the town of Shrewsbury requesting support against Henry VI's favourites[86] and two months before members of the Yorkist faction in Herefordshire made a pact of mutual assistance and then demonstrated in favour of the duke of York on 3 March, the day after the Dartford incident.[87] Devereux also was indicted for staging a demonstration in Hereford in 1452 in favour of the duke.[88] R.L. Storey argued that Walter Devereux 'undoubtedly instigated the [1452] rising in Herefordshire' since he was 'York's leading adherent' in the county.[89] The political context of Devereux's retaining activities in 1452 indicates that the town of Hereford was used by Devereux as a place to gain supporters as part of an attempt to broaden the support for Richard, duke of York.

Five years later, in 1457, another commission of *oyer et terminer* was more wide-ranging in its attack on the Yorkist faction in Herefordshire. It was triggered by an act of large-scale lawlessness by Devereux and his son-in-law, Sir Walter Herbert. In August 1456 they were alleged to have gathered a force of around 2,000 men from Hereford, Webley and other parts of Herefordshire and the Welsh Marches and laid siege to Carmarthen Castle to retake it for the duke. After the siege, Edmund Tudor, earl of Richmond was imprisoned, dying, possibly of plague, shortly after his release. Both Devereux and Herbert were later imprisoned by the government for their role in these events.[90] Although Devereux was indicted, the leader of the Yorkist faction by this point seems to have been his

---

[83]   E101/53/33; *CPR, 1446–1452*, 231; Johnson, *Duke Richard of York*, 230–1.
[84]   Griffiths, 'York's Intentions', 204.
[85]   KB9/34/1 m. 5; KB9/34/2 m. 142.
[86]   *EHD*, iv, 269–70.
[87]   Storey, *End of the House of Lancaster*, 230.
[88]   KB9/34/1 m. 48.
[89]   Storey, *End of the House of Lancaster*, 230.
[90]   KB9/35 m. 24. The context is discussed in greater depth in Storey, *End of the House of Lancaster*, 179–80.

son-in-law William Herbert. William Worcestre referred to the commission in a letter to John Paston in May 1457, but only mentioned the part played by Herbert in these events, stating that he would appear before the king and lords at Leicester 'so he make amendys to theym he hath offended', later referring to the 'Herbert partye' and 'ell Herbery and hys affinité'.[91] The indictments indicate that Herbert was a key instigator of unrest in Herefordshire and the Welsh Marches around this time as he was indicted for distributing illegal livery to three men on 12 March 1456[92] and was indicted for eight other crimes by the commission.[93] On 22 May he was granted back seven tuns of Gascon wine that he forfeited at Bristol after judgements against him at the session at Hereford.[94] In June he was pardoned and restored to his possessions, which may have been part of an attempt to detach him from other Yorkist rebels in the region.[95]

Although Herbert had become the most active agitator in the region by 1457, it is clear that the Devereux family maintained a prominent place in inciting disturbances in the region. Sir Walter Devereux was indicted for giving illegal livery to one tailor from Hereford on 10 May 1455[96] and fifty-seven men from across Herefordshire on 1 April 1456 in Leominster.[97] He was indicted for seven other violent offences in 1457 that indicate that he distributed illegal livery in preparation for large demonstrations of strength in the county.[98] Devereux was indicted for crimes that were allegedly committed before the 1452 commission sat, when he was indicted for seizing and imprisoning a man called Richard Lulwalle in May 1451.[99] Another alleged crime of Devereux's was committed around the time that the 1452 commission was sitting when he was indicted for disturbing the king's peace with forty unknown men by attacking and then dispossessing Humphrey Blount, esquire, of his half manor of Ayssherton.[100] Devereux's son, the future Lord Ferrers of Chartley, Walter Devereux, esquire, illegally gave livery to four men on 12 July 1456 and was also involved in the capturing of Carmarthen Castle.[101] Beyond his family, his key support in the county seems

---

[91] *PL*, ii, no. 572.

[92] KB9/35 m. 69.

[93] KB9/35 mm. 44, 52, 60, 70, 72, 102, 115, 117.

[94] *CPR, 1452–1461*, 353. The order to the chancellor to make this the grant was given under the privy seal on 13 May – PSO1/20 no. 1008.

[95] *CPR, 1452–1461*, 360; Ralph Griffiths, 'William Herbert, First Earl of Pembroke (c.1423–1469)', *ODNB*, xxvi, 729–31.

[96] KB9/35 m. 69.

[97] KB9/35 m. 6.

[98] KB9/35 mm. 24, 40–1, 48, 70–2.

[99] KB9/35 m. 41.

[100] KB9/35 m. 48.

[101] KB9/35 m. 67; Ralph Griffiths, 'Walter Devereux, First Baron Chartley (c.1432–1485)', *ODNB*, xv, 969–71.

to have been the gentleman Hugh Shirely who, soon after the end of York's Second Protectorate, on 2 March 1456, distributed illegal livery to sixteen men at Leominster[102] but was pardoned soon after the commission of *oyer et terminer*.[103] Shirley probably received liveries from Devereux on 1 April too, although his name was later crossed out on the indictment.[104]

These indictments also demonstrate the intertwining of urban, county and national political rivalries in which members of the gentry distributed liveries in an urban setting, in this case Hereford, to recruit men for violent activities. As stated, Herbert was distributing liveries on 12 March 1456.[105] Significantly, one of Herbert's kinsmen, Walter Vaughan, was murdered the following day and on 15 March 1456 Herbert and Devereux's son, along with a large group of men, interrupted a session of the peace to ensure the execution of those believed to be responsible for the murder, subsequently taking control of the city of Hereford for thirty-six hours.[106] The murder of one of Herbert's kinsmen the day after he had been distributing livery is suggestive of wider political manoeuvrings and the motivation of the Yorkists faction in the county. The indictment against Herbert only states the men to whom *illegal* livery was given, and does not state anyone who was given *legal* livery. As one of Herbert's kinsmen it is conceivable that Vaughan was given livery legally with many other permanent household servants. If this deduction is correct then the clear conclusion is that Vaughan's murder, Herbert's distribution of livery and the Yorkist takeover of the city of Hereford within three days of each other were all inextricably inter-linked. Vaughan's murder occurred at a time when Herbert was gathering his retainers to disturb the peace in the city of Hereford. The chronology of events means that it can be reasonably speculated that this visible display of faction by Herbert was the catalyst for a murder as a pre-emptive strike against the Herbert affinity in the city. If large numbers of men were being given livery by the known Yorkists, that may have exacerbated any Lancastrian fears which, in turn, precipitated Vaughan's murder.

Tensions between the Yorkist faction in the county and the city's elite continued. On 7 April 1456, six days after giving illegal livery to more than sixty men in Leominster,[107] Devereux, along with two other men, allegedly seized and imprisoned Richard Green, the former mayor of Hereford.[108] Green was mayor in

---

[102] KB9/35 m. 6; Herbert, 'Herefordshire, 1416–61', 121 n. 73.
[103] *CPR, 1452–1461*, 353.
[104] KB9/35 m. 6.
[105] KB9/35 m. 69.
[106] KB9/35 mm. 44, 61–2, 65–6, 72; KB9/282 m. 31; Herbert, 'Herefordshire, 1416–61',111; Storey, *End of the House of Lancaster*, 180.
[107] KB9/35 m. 6. At least four of the men originally named on the indictment had their names subsequently scored out.
[108] There are two indictments relating to this arrest: KB9/35 mm. 40, 65.

1447–8 and had a reputation for corruption and lawlessness.[109] The two men who accompanied Devereux, John Burton, gentleman, and John ap Harry, esquire, were not indicted for receiving illegal livery from him. It is possible that they were with Devereux at Leominster on 7 April but were entitled to receive his livery and therefore do not appear in the indictments for illegal livery. The time difference between the two offences was too short to believe that the distribution of liveries was anything other than a calculated display of power by Devereux. Moreover, three of the men in receipt of his livery were former or future MPs for Leominister, which indicates that they held some local prominence.[110] Although the exact motives for this imprisonment are uncertain, the chronology of events suggests that Devereux was involved in Hereford's internal politics and used the county's second largest urban settlement as a recruiting ground before making this show of strength.

The internal urban politics of Hereford gave the Yorkist gentry in the county supporters when they engaged with national political events. Around thirteen of the fifty-three people named along with Herbert and the Devereuxs in the indictment for taking 2,000 men to take Carmarthen Castle are known to have received illegal livery in the spring of 1456.[111] Many of those named on the indictment may have also received liveries in the spring of 1456 but were not indicted as they were legally entitled to receive them. The indictments against the Devereuxs and Herbert indicate that they became embroiled in urban politics during the 1450s and that such towns were in themselves an ideal recruiting ground to gain supporters for wider acts of lawlessness and rebellion.

When looking below the level of the factional leaders in such feuding, it seems that townsmen in Herefordshire aligned themselves with Devereux and Herbert as a means of gaining powerful local support for their own legal problems, since many were indicted for a variety of other crimes. Ailsa Herbert calculated that 285 out of the 397 (72 per cent) men indicted by this commission 'were associates of Devereux, Herbert or members of their affinities'.[112] Richard Sherman, ironmonger of Hereford, was indicted, along with unknown others, for assaulting and leaving for dead John Forte at Leominster on 3 June 1452.[113] Philip Moseley, shoemaker, was indicted for receiving illegal livery from Walter Devereux in 1452 and from his son Walter Devereux, esquire, in 1457. Surviving indictments from the 1452 commission attest to his involvement in several other instances of violence, although none of these seem to have been directly connected with either

---

[109] Herbert, 'Herefordshire, 1413–61', 110.
[110] The three men were: William Hood, John Hood and Thomas Bradford. Wedgwood, *Biographies*, 100, 467.
[111] KB9/35 m. 24.
[112] Herbert, 'Herefordshire, 1413–61', 115.
[113] KB9/34/1 m. 45.

Devereux or Herbert.[114] Likewise, Thomas, Richard and Henry Monyngton, who received illegal livery from Walter Devereux,[115] were indicted for a multitude of offences unrelated to the activities of Devereux and Herbert.[116] There was also John Weobley, described as both a yeoman and a tailor, who was indicted for receiving Devereux's livery in 1452 and had previously been involved in much of the violence that had become commonplace at Hereford's mayoral elections. His earliest known crime was from 1446, when he is reported to have incited a man to commit murder. It has been suggested that Weobley was one of many criminals who sought out Devereux's support.[117] Many of the men indicted for receiving illegal livery in Herefordshire in 1452 and 1457 were part of a complex network and were involved in committing various crimes both with the men who gave them illegal livery and with each other.

However, not all of those indicted by the 1457 commission in Herefordshire were Yorkists, as three known Lancastrians, James Tuchet, Lord Audley, Thomas FitzHarry and Henry Oldcastle were indicted. For all three, distributing illegal livery was the only crime for which they were indicted and they do not appear to have been involved in any of the nefarious activities of many of the other men indicted for distributing illegal livery. All three were trusted Lancastrians, which indicates that the commission was not simply intent on imposing 'exemplary retribution on York's retainers in his heartland'.[118] James, Lord Audley, also a retainer of the duke of Buckingham, was indicted for giving livery to a vintner and a draper on 28 May 1455.[119] Four years later Audley was killed leading the Lancastrian army at Blore Heath.[120] Thomas FitzHarry, esquire, was indicted for giving livery illegally to Walter ap Gynon at Hereford in April 1456.[121] FitzHarry was also a retainer of the duke of Buckingham, held numerous local offices during the 1450s, and was escheator in Hereford at the time of Sir Walter Devereux's inquisition *post mortem* in 1459.[122] He was eventually attainted for his Lancastrian activities by the parliament of 1461.[123] Henry Oldcastle, esquire, was indicted for giving livery to two butchers and a baker on 6 August 1455.[124] Oldcastle's career is more opaque although his appearance in several commissions towards the

---

[114] KB9/34/2 mm. 18, 86, 95, 113, 165.
[115] KB9/35 m. 6
[116] KB9/34/2 mm. 149, 128, 90, 77; KB9/35 mm. 13, 17, 39, 42, 46, 50, 59.
[117] Storey, *End of the House of Lancaster*, 228–30.
[118] Hicks, *Warwick*, 131.
[119] KB9/35 m. 69; Rawcliffe, *The Staffords*, 223.
[120] *An English Chronicle*, 79.
[121] KB9/35 m. 68.
[122] C139/176 no. 22; *CPR, 1452–1461*, 48, 153, 347, 403, 408, 444, 459, 559, 562, 565 612, 632, 666, 671; Rawcliffe, *The Staffords*, 223; Wedgwood, *Biographies*, 331–2.
[123] *PROME*, xiii, 51.
[124] KB9/35 m. 69.

end of the 1450s in Herefordshire indicates that he was seen as reliable by the Lancastrian government.[125] There is a distinct possibility that the indictments were a token gesture designed to give the impression that the commission was not simply a one-sided attack upon the duke of York's men. Two of them, Audley and FitzHarry, were retainers of the duke of Buckingham who sat on the commission.[126] This may be evidence that the commission was not just a one-sided affair only interested in the punishment of known Yorkists. Blatantly ignoring the crimes of Lancastrians while indicting Yorkists for every crime possible, however, would leave the commission open to criticism. All three were indicted for giving livery illegally to a small number of men, and Oldcastle and Audley seem to have been able to obtain a pardon with relative ease.[127] The service that a retainer had to perform for a lord could encompass a wide range of duties. It is possible that part of the service required of Audley and FitzHarry was to be complicit in their indictment. This is not to argue that the charges were made up, or that no instances of illegal retaining occurred. Rather, offences were committed and therefore indicted, but the cases were not subsequently pursued by the justices. In order that justice was seen to be done it was a wise move politically to indict several leading Lancastrians for the minor offence of illegal livery, a crime they could easily ignore or for which they could obtain a pardon. The fact that two of the men were retainers of the duke of Buckingham, who sat on the commission, gives further credence to the suggestion that the commission was made to be shown that it was not overtly partisan.

Conclusion

The cases from Herefordshire in the 1450s were the most extreme example of liveries being distributed in towns in order to build support bases for rebellious purposes, and it is therefore important not to generalise from a set of very untypical cases. Nevertheless, the range of surviving evidence relating to urban retaining examined here – indictments, royal letters and urban ordinances – enables broad conclusions about the role of townspeople in the turmoil of the fifteenth century to be drawn. Many letters to towns were, in part, intended to prevent such towns becoming recruiting grounds for rebellion. The fact that towns were the most densely populated parts of the kingdom meant that they had the potential to provide any faction engaged in civil war or rebellion with a comparatively large number of supporters quickly. Distributing livery to, or retaining, a large number

---

[125] *CPR, 1452–61*, 559, 667.
[126] Rawcliffe, *The Staffords*, 223; *CPR, 1452–61*, 348–9.
[127] For Oldcastle: KB27/784 rex rot. 34. For Audley: KB27/785 rex rot. 2.

of men in a public place during periods of political unrest was a potential show of strength for a particular faction. This could encourage onlookers to join and thus garner support for them. Connected to rebellion was the problem of disorder, which was rhetorically linked with rebellion in many royal letters regarding retaining. Indeed, livery was used in some cases to exacerbate internal civic problems but was also used by particular factions to bolster their numbers in violent feuds. However, towns were not purely passive and simply implementing the royal will, as evidenced by the fact that numerous towns had by-laws that tried to prevent noble retaining. Urban governments, like many kings, did not want the troubles brought by unregulated retaining in towns and sought sufficient remedies. Towns and townsmen were not detached from the wider political events of late medieval England, and they did not seek to shut themselves off. Granted, towns were keen to uphold and guard their liberties and many sought to prevent undue aristocratic influence. However, the evidence about retaining and livery distribution in late medieval English towns clearly shows that townsmen entered into bastard feudal relationships and, if it suited them, would become embroiled in larger aristocratic disputes.

Conclusion

At the 1628 parliament all of the statutes about retaining and the distribution of livery were repealed, apparently without being debated.[1] Presumably retaining by fees and livery was no longer deemed the problem it had been during the late medieval period. Retaining was an integral part of sixteenth-century England and there is no evidence that the statutes of livery or Henry VII's increased enforcement of the statutes stopped legal retaining.[2] Retaining remained one of several methods by which Henry VIII's armies were raised.[3] Simon Adams argued that the earl of Leicester's expedition to the Netherlands (1585–6) was the last major military campaign to utilise bastard feudal methods in military recruitment.[4] The continuation of retaining and the distribution of liveries throughout the sixteenth century meant that illegal retaining was something that Tudor government kept a firm eye on. From around 1541 the patent rolls begin to record licences for nobles and gentry to retain a specified number of men, a practice also evident in the reigns of Edward VI, Mary I and Elizabeth I.[5] The retinue list for Sir Thomas Lovell from 1508[6] proves such licences were granted before 1541 and that the developments from 1541 might simply be a new method of recording such licences which has created a better survival rate, or may genuinely reflect greater crown oversight of the matter. The reasons for this change of practice has yet to be investigated. According to Simon Adams, 'Elizabeth's hostility to retaining was open and consistent, but she sought to regulate it by proclamation rather than by fresh legislation'.[7] One particular proclamation in 1572 against illegal retaining and vagrancy was part of a response to disorder and sedition in the aftermath of the 1569 rebellion against Elizabeth I.[8] Such a tactic was used

---

[1] *Stat. Realm*, v, 27–30.
[2] J.P. Cooper, 'Retainers in Tudor England' in *Land, Men and Beliefs: Studies in Early-Modern History*, eds. G.E. Aylmer and J.S. Morrill (London, 1983), 78–96.
[3] Steven Gunn, *The English People at War in the Age of Henry VIII* (Oxford, 2018), 55–61.
[4] Simon Adams, 'A Puritan Crusade? The Composition of the Earl of Leicester's Expedition to the Netherlands, 1585–86' in *The Dutch in Crisis, 1585–1588: People and Politics in Leicester's Time*, ed. Paul Hofthijzer (Leiden, 1988), 7–34.
[5] Cooper, 'Retainers in Tudor England', 87.
[6] HMC, *Manuscripts of His Grace the Duke of Rutland*, iv, 559–66.
[7] Adams, 'Baronial Contexts?', 168.
[8] Roberts, 'Elizabethan Players and Minstrels and the Legislation of 1572 against Retainers and Vagabonds', 29–31.

on numerous occasions by Edward IV and Henry VII and was a continuation of older monarchical responses to excessive retaining. During the reigns of Elizabeth I and James I illegal retaining and the distribution of liveries remained a concern and was regularly included in commissions necessary for the upkeep of justice.[9] As such illegal retaining remained an issue throughout the Tudor period of English history.

Although bastard feudalism 'was very much alive in Tudor and Early Stuart England', the terminal date for this study has been 1520 for several reasons, the first of which relates to the historiography and available source material.[10] Cases in the King's Bench appear to wane around this time as the only known cases from the 1520s were in Norfolk in 1522.[11] Throughout the fifteenth century the law was enforced sporadically, and therefore the absence of cases between 1522 and 1530 may suggest a further lull in enforcement, representing a wider trend. In this respect the problem is perhaps the types of question that historians of the sixteenth century tend to address compared to those who focus on the fifteenth century.[12] J.P. Cooper noted the continuation of retaining into the sixteenth century and attempts to address illegal retaining throughout the century but did not highlight any indictments.[13] Instances of illegal livery were recorded in the *York Civic Records* in 1547 and 1577–8 but there is no indication how representative these cases are of enforcement.[14] Since then there has been no work on illegal retaining from the mid-sixteenth century onwards and, if the statutes did not continue to be enforced, the range of material available would warrant a full-scale study on its own right.

There is scope for future work on bastard feudalism and illegal retaining from the mid-sixteenth century onwards. This book has examined illegal livery and illegal retaining during the fifteenth century, which was the high point of bastard feudalism. Michael Hicks argued that an examination of the 'statutes of livery can be used to cast light on bastard feudalism, its evolution and regulation', and that his article on the 1468 act could act as a 'fixed point for more wide ranging interpretation'.[15] Although the statutes *were* enforced sporadically, few cases were resolved and fines were rare. The lack of the enforcement of the statutes highlights the interaction of the law and politics in late medieval England. Furthermore, such enforcement provides an additional source base, the records

[9] *Select Statutes and other Constitutional Documents Illustrative of the Reigns of Elizabeth and James I*, 144, 362, 377, 382, 386.
[10] For quotation see: Hicks, *Bastard Feudalism*, 4.
[11] KB29/154 rot. 32.
[12] Steven Gunn, 'Henry VII in Context: Problems and Possibilities', *History*, xcii (2007), 302.
[13] Cooper, 'Retainers in Tudor England', 78–96.
[14] *YCR*, ii, 14; iii, 1; iv, 157. Discussed in D.M. Palliser, *Tudor York* (Oxford, 1979), 15.
[15] Hicks, '1468 Statute of Livery', 15.

of the King's Bench, for understanding the nature of lord–retainer relationships in late medieval England, albeit ones that were deemed unacceptable and therefore legislated against. The statutes illuminate two interconnected and overarching themes: the nature of the enforcement of the statutes and what the cases reveal about the nature of bastard feudalism.

After the passing of the initial acts at the end of the fourteenth century, there was no immediate enforcement despite repeated petitions complaining about the inability of the statutes to address the problems of liveried retainers. Richard II's use of his own personal affinity was one of the main grievances that led to him lacking sufficient supporters to face down Henry Bolingbroke's rebellion.[16] Once Henry IV was king, liveries remained a sensitive issue at the early Lancastrian parliaments but, except for one private suit in 1410, enforcement was lacking.[17] It was only after the accession of Henry V that the first wave of enforcement occurred, as part of the new king's law-and-order drive in the midlands. Henry V had no conscious policy to enforce the statutes but identified such cases because the gentry who were distributing illegal liveries were involved in much of the feuding in Staffordshire and Shropshire from the latter years of Henry IV's reign. Enforcement was sporadic but increased during the fifteenth century, reaching its apex during Henry VII's reign.

Cases became more regular during the 1450s, not because of any deliberate policy from Henry VI to stamp out illegal livery but because it was a mechanism used for waging the serious feuds during that decade. Large clusters had previously occurred in Staffordshire in 1414 and Derbyshire in 1434 but these were not connected to significant events in national politics in the manner that cases relating to the Percy–Neville feud or in Herefordshire in 1452 and 1457 related to national affairs. The feuds and civil unrest of the 1450s were the catalyst for a change in impetus for new legislation relating to liveries from 1461. After 1468, the statutes developed to deal with other forms of retaining, not just the giving of liveries. The earlier acts from the late fourteenth century originated from Commons petitions, whereas the acts of Edward IV and Henry VII were crown-driven affairs. In one sense, this can be viewed in the traditional manner of Yorkist and Tudor kings being examples of the 'new monarchies' that sprang up across Europe from the late fifteenth century, who increased the central power of the monarchy at the expense of the old aristocracy, limiting the importance of parliament as a forum for dissent and the crafting of legislation.[18] Yet this view

---

[16] On the Lancastrian usurpation see in particular: Given-Wilson, *Henry IV*, 138–54; Saul, *Richard II*, 405–34.

[17] KB27/596 plea rot. 76. Printed in *Select Cases in the Court of King's Bench Under Richard II, Henry IV and Henry V*, 192–4.

[18] On the new monarchies see in particular: Cavill, *English Parliaments of Henry VII*, 199–44; Anthony Goodman, *The New Monarchy: England, 1471–1534* (Oxford,

is too deterministic and does not really explain why the statutes became a more 'crown-driven' affair. It was the Wars of the Roses, and in particular the First War (1459–61), that made Yorkist and Tudor kings more concerned about illegal livery and retaining than their Lancastrian predecessors. The feuds of the 1450s which contributed to the outbreak of the First War were, in part, exacerbated by excessive retaining by the nobility. However, civil war rarely led to indictments of illegal livery. It is perfectively conceivable that some who fought in the Wars of the Roses turned up to battles wearing the liveries of lords that they were not permitted by law to wear, but the need for reconciliation in the aftermath of civil war meant the statutes were rarely enforced in connection with these events, as such prosecutions were impracticable and petty compared to the more serious offences of treason and homicide.

Crucial to this study has been the role of Henry VII in the development and enforcement of the statutes. Henry VII has been seen as helping to dismantle the private power of the old aristocracy, particularly their ability to build up large private followings. In part this was a view developed by older historiographical traditions that viewed the Battle of Bosworth and the end of the Wars of the Roses as marking a new era in English history. Radical change in fundamental socio-political structures could not happen instantly and the reign of Henry VII was viewed as a bridge between the medieval and early modern. Steven Gunn has argued that historians have not developed a greater understanding of the reign of Henry VII because of his 'liminal' position in history, between the end of the late medieval period and the start of the early modern period.[19] James Ross has taken a slightly different line on Henry VII, stating that he was both the last medieval and first early modern king, noting that he still required the cooperation of the nobility as much as his predecessors did.[20] In terms of illegal livery and retaining, Henry VII developed many of the practices that Edward IV initiated, such as writing to towns about retaining and ensuring that new acts were passed that further defined the law. The key changes in Henry VII's reign were the scale of the enforcement and its geographical spread, particularly after the 1504 act. There were more cases during Henry VII's reign than any other, but peers were not necessarily the target. Indeed, peers were just as likely to be indicted during the reign of Edward IV or during the first decade of Henry VIII's reign as they were during Henry VII's reign. Henry VII had more cases and used more flexible systems for law enforcement and the collection of fines, but this should not be read as a conscious attack on the older nobility. The indictments against

1988); Steven Gunn, 'Politic History, New Monarchy and State Formation: Henry VII in European Perspective', *Historical Research*, lxxxii (2009), 380–92.
[19] Gunn, 'Henry VII in Context', 301–17. For similar arguments about Henry VII's parliaments: Cavill, *The English Parliaments of Henry VII*, 1–18.
[20] Ross, *John de Vere*, 227.

Bergavenny and James Stanley during Henry VII's reign were the largest and were clearly connected to political uncertainty, but these were targeted prosecutions. Francis Bacon's story from the seventeenth century about Henry VII fining the earl of Oxford was likely caused by a misunderstanding of cases against men indicted for wearing the earl's livery without his consent. Nevertheless, the story is representative of a persistent misconception about Henry VII: that he targeted the retaining practices of the entire noble class and used retaining laws to achieve this objective. The target of most of the prosecutions during Henry VII's reign was the gentry, not because the king objected to them retaining or being retained, but because Henry VII's regime adopted a firmer stance on the enforcement of the statutes. Henry VII's views on nobles and gentry retaining were consistent with those of earlier kings, who recognised it was necessary for the operation of medieval government and society. The main difference in Henry VII's reign was that the laws were more aggressively enforced.

The relatively large number of gentry indicted for both distributing and receiving illegal liveries and retaining helps to address another overarching point: the nature of bastard feudalism as evident in the legal records. The range of people who were indicted for illegal livery and the number of opportunities there were for illegal retaining illustrate the extent to which retaining was an integral part of late medieval society. This has implications for understanding bastard feudalism as thought of in the 'narrow' sense that Andrew Spencer identified as a set of socio-political bonds.[21] In particular, Colin Richmond's confident declaration that 'Bastard Feudalism is dead: I do not think I ever believed it was alive' is problematic.[22] Richmond's conclusion was based on the assumption that bastard feudalism was about a particular magnate dominating the local politics of a county, which the work of Simon Walker on John of Gaunt's affinity and Simon Payling on Lancastrian Nottinghamshire disproved.[23] Bastard feudalism was about obtaining service, not necessarily perverting the legal system or dominating county politics, which were simply possible ways of using such retained service, not necessarily the reason for retaining.[24]

Bastard feudalism was not confined to members of the peerage retaining members of the gentry, which was the most documented form of retaining. Although accepting the validity of the term 'bastard feudalism', Nigel Saul argued that there were members of the gentry in fourteenth-century Sussex who operated 'outside the embrace' of bastard feudalism because they had no formal

---

[21] Spencer, *Nobility and Kingship*, 100–9.
[22] Richmond, 'An English Mafia?', 240.
[23] Payling, *Political Society in Lancastrian England*, 87–108; Walker, *Lancastrian Affinity*, 235–61.
[24] On the importance of service, see in particular: Horrox, *Richard III: A Study in Service*, 1–27.

known connections to specific peers.[25] Christine Carpenter has noted that any claim that there were any independent gentry can only be sustainable from negative evidence. Once such evidence is found they can no longer be classed as 'independent gentry'. Indeed, connections with peers have been subsequently identified for two of the examples of 'independent gentry' cited by Saul.[26] The medieval gentry, as Colin Richmond argued elsewhere, were not simply 'Pavlovian dogs, jumping at the chance of a fee, a rent charge, a stewardship here, a parkership there',[27] but that is because they were lords in their own right to those of a lower social status as well as the retainers of magnates.[28] The cases discussed here show that it was the gentry who were indicted for illegally retaining, not because it illegal for them to retain, but because it was illegal for them to retain *in certain circumstances*. The records of the King's Bench indicate that the gentry normally retained men from the county in which they were resident, but rarely from the same place where they resided. It was acceptable, and even necessary for the operation of government, for the gentry to be permitted to retain men, provided it was within reasonable means. The provisos and exemptions in the statutes articulated the occasions on which it was permitted to retain and the key ceremonial events in which liveries were necessary for display.

A further reason for this confusion has been the interchangeable use of the terms 'retinue' and 'affinity'. Jan Burgers and Mario Damen have noted that affinities is now the preferred term that English historians use, as opposed to retinues.[29] A distinction needs to be made between a 'retinue', which was a lord's military power, and who in times of peace offered him protection, and an 'affinity', which consisted of all a lord's servants, including his military retinue.[30] The indenture of retainer was primarily used to retain men for military purposes, which in part explains why there are more indentures of retainer for John of Gaunt, a noble whose life 'was dominated by war and the rumours of peace' to a greater extent than most other medieval aristocrats.[31] The indenture of retainer and the letter patent were not, as K.B. McFarlane argued, bastard feudalism's 'peculiar instruments', but represented only one type of bastard feudal relation, which was not necessarily the most common one.[32] Indeed, these indentures

---

[25] Saul, *Knights and Esquires*, 260–1.
[26] Christine Carpenter, 'Law, Justice and Landowners', *Law and History Review*, i (1983), 206 n. 7.
[27] Colin Richmond, 'After McFarlane', *History*, lxviii (1983), 57.
[28] Hicks, *English Political Culture in the Fifteenth Century*, 141–2, 154–6.
[29] Jan W.J. Burgers and Mario Damen, 'Feudal Obligation or Paid Service? The Recruitment of Princely Armies in the Late Medieval Low Countries', *EHR*, cxxxiii (2018), 780.
[30] Hicks, *Bastard Feudalism*, 43–68, 185–93.
[31] Walker, *Lancastrian Affinity*, 39.
[32] McFarlane, 'Bastard Feudalism', 164.

were 'more the exception than the rule' in forming such relationships.[33] Bastard feudalism was about the construction of affinities to meet the needs of various lords, with servants rewarded with cash payments as opposed to the creation of tenurial relations. The military dimension of the bastard feudal affinity was one part of a lord's broader affinity. Widows and clerics did not need to construct large military retinues but they did need affinities of household servants, estate officials and legal counsel. It was for this reason that various acts made explicit that women and clerics were bound by the same terms of the statutes that peers and gentry were.

The statutes conformed to the social, governmental, political and cultural realities of late medieval England and therefore only restricted certain forms of retaining, because bastard feudalism and the wearing of livery for ceremonial purposes were too pervasive to prohibit. The statutes themselves restricted retaining to certain categories of servants in a bid to limit widespread lawlessness. Enforcement was sporadic and normally linked to periods and localities where there was widespread local disorder, although those indicted for distributing and receiving illegal livery and retaining were not always those indicted for other crimes. The Wars of the Roses meant that retaining and the widespread distribution of liveries became associated with the recruitment of men for rebellion, but such instances rarely led to prosecutions because the practicalities of reconciliation after such wars could make indictments seem petty. Ultimately, the statutes of livery worked within acceptable frameworks on both practical and ideological levels in order to limit the excesses of bastard feudalism.

[33] Carpenter, 'Bastard Feudalism in the Fourteenth Century', 61.

Appendix 1

Number of Cases by Reign

Reign	Number of Cases
Richard II	1
Henry IV	0[1]
Henry V	31
Henry VI	72
Edward IV	46
Edward V	0
Richard III	0
Henry VII	150
Henry VIII (to 1522)	36

[1] This figure, as discussed in Chapter 1, excludes cases from private suits such as in Derbyshire in 1410: KB27/596 plea rot. 76. Printed in *Select Cases in the Court of King's Bench Under Richard II, Henry IV and Henry V*, 192–4.

Appendix 2

Number of Cases in each County[1]

County	Number of Cases
Bedfordshire	2
Berkshire	3
Buckinghamshire	0
Cambridgeshire	13
Cheshire	39
Cornwall	1
Coventry	1
Cumbria	0
Derbyshire	22
Devon	4
Dorset	1
Durham, bishopric of	0
Essex	2
Gloucestershire	6
Hampshire	7
Herefordshire	20
Hertfordshire	14
Huntingdonshire	1
Kent	21
Lancashire	0
Leicestershire	3
Lincolnshire	3
London	1
Middlesex	0
Norfolk	3
Northamptonshire	4

[1]   The only towns with county status that are included in this table are the ones for which cases of illegal livery have been identified.

Number of Cases in each County

Northumberland	0
Nottingham, town of	1
Nottinghamshire	1
Oxfordshire	2
Rutland	1
Shropshire	10
Somerset	2
Staffordshire	25
Suffolk	13
Surrey	14
Sussex	10
Warwickshire	19
Westmorland	0
Wiltshire	1
Worcestershire	28
York, city of	1
Yorkshire	36

Appendix 3

List of Letters to Towns and Lordships

Margaret of Anjou to Leicester – 20 May 1449[1]

Henry VI to York – March 1457[2]

Edward IV to the bailiff, burgesses and inhabitants of Scarborough – 9 January 1470[3]

Edward IV to the mayor and sheriffs of Coventry – 11 February 1472[4]

Edward IV to Halton – 27 August 1476[5]

Richard III to the mayor and bailiffs of Northampton – 3 August 1483[6]

Richard III to the mayor and sheriffs of Southampton – 12 September 1483[7]

Richard III to the mayor, sheriff, aldermen and burgess of Canterbury – 4 January 1484[8]

Richard III to Nicholas Steward of the monastery of Burton and bailiff of the town of Burton – 4 January 1484[9]

Richard III to the inhabitants of Tonbridge and lordships of Penshurst, Brasted, Hadlow and *Ealding* – 22 January 1484[10]

Richard III to the mayor, sheriff and bailiffs of Southampton – 5 July 1484[11]

Richard III to the mayor and bailiffs of Bedford – 26 September 1484[12]

Richard III to the bailiff and inhabitants of Tamworth – 12 October 1484[13]

Henry VII to mayor and JPs of Coventry – 31 January 1486[14]

[1]   *Records of the Borough of Leicester*, ii, 256–7.
[2]   Attreed, *The King's Towns*, 294, n. 44.
[3]   North Yorkshire Country Record Office, DC/SCB, White Vellum Book of Scarborough, f. 53.
[4]   *Coventry Leet Book*, i, 373–5.
[5]   DL5/1 fol. 136; printed in Myers, *Crown, Household and Parliament*, 327.
[6]   Ibid., 10.
[7]   Ibid., 19.
[8]   Ibid., 69.
[9]   Ibid., 69–70.
[10] Ibid., 81.
[11] HMC, *11th Report, Appendix, Part 3: The Manuscripts of the Corporations of Southampton and King's Lynn* (London, 1887), 16.
[12] *Letters and Papers Illustrative of the Reigns of Richard III and Henry VII*, ed. James Gardiner, 2 vols. (1861–3), ii, 288; *Harleian 433*, ii, 162–3.
[13] *Harleian 433*, ii, 166–7.
[14] HMC, *The Manuscripts of Shrewsbury and Coventry Corporations*, 120.

Henry VII to the mayor, aldermen, sheriffs and common counsel of York – 19 November 1486[15]

Henry VII to Wells – between 22 August and 30 September 1497[16]

Henry VII to the mayor and brethren of Carlisle – 15 February 1498[17]

Henry VII to the mayor and brethren of Leicester and the recorder of the duchy of Lancaster – 20 March 1498[18]

Henry VIII to the mayor and brethren of Leicester and the recorder of the duchy of Lancaster– 20 March 1522[19]

---

[15] *York House Books*, ii, 521.

[16] HMC, *1st Report, Appendix* (London, 1874), 107. The report does not provide the date for the letter. The date here has been deduced by the fact that the following entry relates to a visit by Bishop Oliver King on 30 September 13 Henry VII. The letter is likely to have been received prior to this date during this regnal year.

[17] Cumbria Record Office, Carlisle, CRO, Ca2/150. Printed in: McKelvie, 'Henry VII's Letter to Carlisle', 165–6.

[18] *Records of the Borough of Leicester*, ii, 354; DL 37 rot. 30d.

[19] *Records of the Borough of Leicester, Volume 3: 1509–1603*, ed. M. Bateson (Cambridge, 1905), 20–1.

Appendix 4

List of Local Ordinances[1]

Northampton – 1460[2]
Nottingham – 1463[3]
Worcester – 1466[4]
Calais – 1467[5]
London – 1467[6]
Leicester – 1467[7]
High Wycombe – 1490[8]
Worcester – 1496[9]
York – 1503[10]
Gloucester – 1504[11]
Newcastle on Tyne – 1516[12]

---

[1] An earlier list, of which this appendix is an expansion, is given in: Winifred I. Haward, 'Gilbert Debenham: A Medieval Rascal in Real Life', *History*, xiii (1929), 308 n. 2.

[2] *Records of the Borough of Northampton*, i, 297–8.

[3] *Records of the Borough of Nottingham*, ii, 425.

[4] *English Gilds: The Original Ordinances of More than One Hundred Early English Gilds, Together with Þe Olde Usage of Þe Cite of Wynchester; the Ordinances of Worcester; the Office of the Mayor of Bristol; the Costomary of the Manor of Tettenhall*, ed. Toulmin Smith (London, 1870), 388.

[5] C47/149 rot. 14.

[6] *Calendar of Letter-Books of the City of London, L*, 73, and 73 n. 1.

[7] *Records of the Borough of Leicester*, ii, 293.

[8] *The First Ledger Book of High Wycombe*, ed. R.W. Greaves, Bucks Record Society, xi (1947), 50–1.

[9] *The Ordinances of Worcester*, 388–9.

[10] *YCR*, ii, 181.

[11] HMC, *Twelfth Report*, 436.

[12] John Drake, *The History and Antiquities of the Town and County of the Town of Newcastle upon Tyne*, 2 vols. (London, 1789) ii, 179.

Appendix 5

Letters from Henry VII to Duchy of Lancaster Officials

To Richard Gardiner, mayor of Lancaster and Thomas Eskryg and Giles Drynkall, bailiffs of the said town to make proclamation about retaining – 13 March 1488.[1]

To Brian Sandford, esquire of the body, constable of Pickering, steward of the honour and lordship – 5 July 1489.[2]

To Viscount Well, the stewards of his lordship of Sutton in Holland Lincolnshire – 16 February 1489.[3]

To Henry Wentworth, steward of the honour of Pontefract – 18 June 1492.[4]

To John Villers, steward of the lordship of Chesterfeld and Skardsdale – 8 November 1493.[5]

To Brain Sandford, steward of the honour of Pickering and Pykerynglith, parcel of the duchy of Lancaster in Yorkshire and Richard Cholmeley, gentleman – 20 February 1494.[6]

To the lord Hastings, steward of all our honour of Leicester, part of the duchy of Lancaster – 12 July 1494.[7]

To the mayor and brethren and recorder of the town of Leicester – 20 March 1498.[8]

To Bryan Palmer, deputy steward of the honour of Pontefract – 28 November 1500.[9]

---

[1] DL37/62 rot. 4.
[2] DL37/62 rot. 5.
[3] DL37/62 rot. 6d. Note: name added later, large gap after 'To'.
[4] DL37/62 rot. 14.
[5] DL37/62 rot. 17.
[6] DL37/62 rot. 19.
[7] DL37/62 rot. 21.
[8] DL37/62 rot. 30. Also printed in: *Records of the Borough of Leicester*, ii, 354.
[9] DL37/62 rot. 41.

To George Talbot fourth earl of Shrewsbury and the inhabitants of the honour of Tickhill – 21 May 1501[10]

To Sir Thomas Worsley, knight of the body, Henry, duke of York's deputy in the honours of Pontefract and Knarseborough – 26 May 1501.[11]

---

[10] DL37/61 rot. 42.
[11] DL37/61 rot. 43.

Bibliography

Archives

The National Archives, London

C1 – Early Chancery Proceedings.
C47 – Chancery Miscellanea.
C49 – Parliament and Council Proceedings.
C139 – Inquisitions *Post Mortem*, Henry VI.
C255 – Tower and Rolls Chapel Series, Miscellaneous Files and Writs.
CHES25 – Indictment Rolls, Cheshire.
CP40 – Court of Common Pleas, Plea Rolls.
DL5 – Duchy of Lancaster: Court of Duchy Chamber: Entry Books of Decrees and Ordinances.
DL37 – Duchy of Lancaster and Palatinate of Lancaster: Chanceries: Enrolments.
DURH13 – Durham, Plea Rolls.
E36 – Miscellaneous Books.
E101 – King's Remembrancer.
E154 – King's Remembrancer and Treasury of Receipt: Inventories of Goods and Chattels.
E163 – Exchequer Miscellanea.
E159 – King's Remembrancer: Memoranda Rolls and Enrolment Books.
E210 – King's Remembrancer, Ancient Deeds, Series D.
KB 8 – *Baga de Secretis.*
KB 9 – Ancient Indictments.
KB 27 – *Coram Rege* Rolls.
KB 29 – Controlment Rolls.
KB145 – King's Bench, Recorda.
PL15 – Plea Rolls, Lancashire.
PSO1 – Warrants of the Privy Seal.
SC8 – Ancient Petitions.
STAC2 – Court of Star Chamber: Proceedings of Henry VIII

British Library, London

Additional Charters.
Additional Manuscripts.
Lansdowne.

Cumbria Record Office, Carlisle

Ca. – City of Carlisle Records.

Hampshire Record Office, Winchester
5M53 – Wriothesley Papers.

Magdalen College, Oxford
GD – McFarlane Papers.
Fastolf Papers.

North Yorkshire Country Record Office
DC/SCB – White Vellum Book of Scarborough

Published Primary Sources: Records

The Anglica Historia of Polydore Vergil, AD 1486–1537, ed. and trans. Denys Hay, Camden Society, lxxiv (London, 1950).
Bacon, Francis, *The History of the Reign of King Henry VII and Selected Works*, ed. Brian Vickers (Cambridge, 1998).
The Book of Chivalry of Geoffroi de Charney: Text, Context and Translation, eds. Richard W. Kaeuper and Elspeth Kennedy (Philadelphia, 1996).
British Library, Harleian Manuscript 433, eds. Rosemary Horrox and P.W. Hammond, 4 vols. (Gloucester, 1979).
Calendar of Charter Rolls Preserved in the Public Record Office, Volume VI, 1427–1516 (London, 1927).
Calendar of Close Rolls Preserved in the Public Record Office, 42 vols. (London, 1900–47).
Calendar of Documents Relating to Scotland, Volume 4: 1357–1509, ed. Joseph Bain (Edinburgh, 1888).
Calendar of Inquisitions Miscellaneous, 1399–1422 (London, 1968).
Calendar of Inquisitions Miscellaneous, 1422–1485 (London, 2003).
Calendar of Inquisitions Post-Mortem and other Analogous Documents Preserved in the Public Record Office, 26 vols. (London, 1905–54; Woodbridge, 2002–10).
Calendar of Inquisitions Post-Mortem and other Analogous Documents Preserved in the Public Record Office. Henry VII, 3 vols. (London, 1898–1955).
Calendar of Patent Rolls Preserved in the Public Record Office, 49 vols. (London, 1893–1916).
Calendar of Letter-Books of the City of London, I: 1400–1422, ed. Reginald R. Sharpe (London, 1909).
Calendar of Letter-Books of the City of London, L: Edward IV to Henry VII, ed. Reginald R. Sharpe (London, 1932).
Calendar of Wills Proved and Enrolled in the Court of Husting, London: Part 2, 1358–1688, ed. Reginald R. Sharpe (London, 1890).

The Chronica Maiora of Thomas Walsingham (1379–1422), ed. David Preest (Woodbridge, 2005).

The Chronicle of Adam Usk, 1377–1421, ed. and trans. Christopher Given-Wilson (Oxford, 1997).

Chronicle of the Rebellion in Lincolnshire, 1470, ed. John G. Nicholas, Camden Society (London, 1847).

Chronicles of the Revolution, 1397–1400: The Reign of Richard II, ed. and trans. Christopher Given-Wilson (Manchester, 1993).

Court Rolls of Elmley Castle, 1347–1564, ed. Robert K. Field, Worcestershire Historical Society, xx (2004).

The Crowland Chronicle Continuations: 1459–1486, eds. Nicholas Pronay and John Cox (London, 1986).

Death and Dissent: The Dethe of the Kynge of Scotis and Warkworth's Chronicle, ed. Lister M. Matheson (Woodbridge, 1999).

Drake, John, *The History and Antiquities of the Town and County of the Town of Newcastle upon Tyne*, 2 vols. (London, 1789).

Elizabeth de Burgh, Lady of Clare (1295–1360): Household and Other Records, ed. Jennifer Ward (Woodbridge, 2014).

An English Chronicle 1377–1461, ed. William Marx (Woodbridge, 2003).

English Gilds: The Original Ordinances of More than One Hundred Early English Gilds, Together with Þe Olde Usage of Þe Cite of Wynchester; the Ordinances of Worcester; the Office of the Mayor of Bristol; the Costomary of the Manor of Tettenhall, ed. Toulmin Smith (London, 1870).

English Historical Documents IV, 1327–1485, ed. A.R. Myers (London, 1968).

English Historical Documents V, 1485–1558, ed. C.H. Williams (London, 1967).

'Extracts from the Plea Rolls, 16 to 33 Edward III', ed. G. Wrottesley, *Collections for the History of Staffordshire*, xvii (1896), 1–173.

Fortescue, J., *Governance of England*, ed. C. Plummer (Oxford, 1885).

Hall's Chronicle; Containing the History of England during the Reign of Henry the Fourth and Succeeding Monarchs to the End of the Reign of Henry the Eighth, ed. H. Ellis (London, 1809).

The Historical Collections of a Citizen of London in the Fifteenth Century, ed. J. Gairner, Camden Society, new series, vii (1876).

HMC, *1st Report, Appendix* (London, 1874).

———— *5th Report* (London, 1876).

———— *6th Report* (London, 1877).

———— *11th Report, Appendix, Part 3: The Manuscripts of the Corporations of Southampton and King's Lynn* (London, 1887).

———— *12th Report, Appendix, Part IX: The Manuscripts of the Duke of Beaufort, KG, the Earl of Donoughmore, and Others* (London, 1891).

———— *Report 24: Manuscripts of His Grace the Duke of Rutland*, iv (1908).

———— *Report of the Records of the City of Exeter* (London, 1916).

Historie of the Arrivall of Edward IV in England and the Final Recouerye of his Kingdomes from Henry VI. A.D. M.CCC. LXXI., ed. John Bruce, Camden Society (London, 1838). Reprinted in *Three Chronicles of the Reign of Edward IV*, ed. Keith Dockray (Gloucester, 1988), 131–198.

Household Accounts and Disbursement Books of Robert Dudley, Earl of Leicester, ed. Simon Adams, Camden fifth series, vi (Cambridge, 1995).

Letters and Papers, Foreign and Domestic, of the Reign of Henry VIII, 1509–1547, eds. J.S. Brewer et al., 21 vols. (London, 1862–1932).

Letters and Papers Illustrative of the Reigns of Richard III and Henry VII, ed. J. Gardiner, 2 vols. (London, 1861–3).

The Life of Edward the Second, trans. and ed. Noël Denholm-Young (London, 1957).

The Maire of Bristowe Is Kalendar, ed. Peter Fleming, Bristol Record Society, lxvii (Bristol, 2015).

Parliamentary Rolls of Medieval England, eds. Christopher Given-Wilson et al., 16 vols. (Woodbridge, 2005).

Paston Letters and Papers of the Fifteenth Century, vols. 1 and 2 ed. Norman Davis (Oxford, 1971-6), vol. 3 eds. Richard Beadle and Colin Richmond (Early English Text Society, special series xxii, 2005).

'Private Indentures for Life Service in Peace and War', eds. Michael Jones and Simon Walker, *Camden Miscellany*, xiii (London, 1994), 35–66.

Proceedings Before the Justices of the Peace in the Fourteenth and Fifteenth Centuries, Edward III to Richard III, ed. Bertha Putnam (London, 1938).

Proceedings and Ordinances of the Privy Council, Volume 1L: 10 Richard II to 11 Henry IV, ed. Harris Nicholas (London, 1834).

Proceedings in the Parliaments of Elizabeth I: Volume 1, 1558–1581, ed. T.E. Hartley (Leicester, 1981).

Records of the Borough of Leicester, Volume 2: 1327–1509, ed. M. Bateson (London, 1901).

Records of the Borough of Leicester, Volume 3: 1509–1603, ed. M. Bateson (Cambridge, 1905).

Records of the Borough of Northampton, ed. C.A Markham, 2 vols. (London, 1898).

Records of the Borough of Nottingham, Vol 2: 1399–1485, ed. W.H Stevenson (Nottingham, 1883).

Records of the Gild of St George in Norwich, 1389–1547, ed. Mary Grace, Norfolk Record Society, ix (1937).

Records of Some Sessions of the Peace in Lincolnshire, 1381–1396, Volume I: The Parts of Kesteven and The Parts of Holland, ed. Elisabeth G. Kimball (Hereford, 1955).

Records of Visitations Held by William Alnwick, Bishop of Lincoln, 1436–1449, Part I, ed. A. Hamilton Thompson (London, 1919).

Register of Edward, The Black Prince, IV, 1351–1365 (London, 1933).

Royal and Historical Letters During the Reign of Henry the Fourth, Volume 1, 1399–1404, ed. F.C. Hingeston (London, 1860).

Select Cases in the Court of King's Bench Under Richard II, Henry IV and Henry V, ed. G.O. Sayles, Selden Society, lxxxviii (London, 1971).

Select Statutes and other Constitutional Documents Illustrative of the Reigns of Elizabeth and James I, ed. G.W. Prothero, 4th edition (Oxford, 1919).

Shropshire Peace Roll, 1400–1414, ed. E.G. Kimball (Shrewsbury, 1959).

Statutes of the Realm, 11 vols. (London, 1810–28).

The Coventry Leet Book or Mayor's Register, 1420–1555, ed. M.D. Harris, Early English Text Society (London, 1907–13).

The Estate and Household Accounts of William Worsley Dean of St Paul's Cathedral, 1479–1497, eds. Hannes Kleineke and Stephanie R. Hovland, London Record Society, xl (2004).

The First General Entry Book of the City of Salisbury, 1387–1452, ed. David R. Carr, Wiltshire Record Society, liv (2001).

The First Ledger Book of High Wycombe, ed. R.W. Greaves, Bucks Record Society, xi (1947).

The Scrope and Grosvenor Controversy, ed. N.H. Nicholas, 2 vols. (London, 1832).

The York House Books, 1461–1490, 2 vols., ed. Lorraine Attreed (Stroud: Alan Sutton, 1991).

Tudor Royal Proclamations, eds. Paul L. Hughes and James F. Larkin (New Haven, 1961).

Worcestershire Taxes in the 1520s: The Military Survey and Forced Loans of 1522–3 and the Lay Subsidy of 1542–7, ed. Michael A. Faraday, Worcestershire Historical Society, xix (2003).

York Civic Records, ed. A. Raine, 8 vols., York Archaeological Society, Records Series (1939–53).

Books and Articles

Adams, Simon, 'Baronial Contexts? Continuity and Change in the Noble Affinity, 1400–1600', in John L. Watts (ed.), *The End of the Middle Ages? England in the Fifteenth and Sixteenth Centuries* (Stroud, 1998), 155–98.

———— 'A Puritan Crusade? The Composition of the Earl of Leicester's Expedition to the Netherlands, 1585–86' in *Leicester and the Court: Essays on Elizabethan Politics* (Manchester, 2002), 176–95.

Acheson, Eric, *A Gentry Community: Leicestershire in the Fifteenth Century, c.1422–c.1485* (Cambridge, 1992).

Allmand, Christopher, *Henry V* (London, 1992).

Archer, Rowena E., 'Rich Old Ladies: The Problem of Late Medieval Dowagers' in A.J. Pollard (ed.), *Property and Politics: Essays in Later Medieval English History* (Gloucester, 1984), 15–35.

Bean, J.M.W., *The Estates of the Percy Family, 1416–1537* (Oxford, 1958).

———— *From Lord to Patron: Lordship in Late Medieval England* (Manchester, 1989).

Bellamy, J.G., 'Justice under the Yorkist Kings', *American Journal of Legal History*, ix (1965), 135–55.

———— *Crime and Public Order in England in the Later Middle Ages* (London, 1973)

———— *Bastard Feudalism and the Law* (London, 1989).

Bennett, Michael J., *Community, Class and Careerism: Cheshire and Lancashire Society in the Age of Sir Gawain and the Green Knight* (Cambridge, 1983).

Bernard, G.W., 'The Tudor Nobility in Perspective' in G.W. Bernard (ed.), *The Tudor Nobility* (Manchester, 1992), 1–48.

Blatcher, Marjorie, *The Court of King's Bench, 1450–1550: A Study in Self-Help* (London, 1978).

Bindoff, S.T., *Tudor England* (Harmondsworth, 1950).

Booth, Peter, 'Men Behaving Badly? The West March Towards Scotland and the Percy–Neville Feud' in Linda Clark (ed.), *The Fifteenth Century III: Authority and Subversion* (Woodbridge, 2003), 95–116.

Britnell, Richard, 'Town Life' in Rosemary Horrox and W. Mark Ormrod (eds.), *A Social History of England, 1200–1500* (Cambridge, 2006), 134–78.

Brown, R.A., 'Bastard Feudalism and the Bishopric of Winchester, c.1280–1530' (unpublished PhD thesis, University of Winchester (Southampton), 2003).

Burgers, Jan W.J., and Damen, Mario, 'Feudal Obligation or Paid Service? The Recruitment of Princely Armies in the Late Medieval Low Countries', *EHR*, cxxxiii (2018), 777–805.

Burt, Caroline, 'A "Bastard Feudal" Affinity in the Making? The Followings of William and Guy Beauchamp, Earls of Warwick, 1268–1315', *Midland History*, xxxiv (2009), 156–80.

Cameron, Alan, 'The Giving of Livery and Retaining in Henry VII's Reign', *Renaissance & Modern Studies*, xviii (1974), 17–35.

Carpenter, Christine, 'The Beauchamp Affinity: A Study of Bastard Feudalism at Work', *English Historical Review*, xcv (1980), 514–532.

———— 'Sir Thomas Malory and Fifteenth-Century Local Politics', *Bulletin of the Institute of Historical Research*, liii (1980), 31–43.

———— 'Law, Justice and Landowners', *Law and History Review*, i (1983), 205–37.

———— *Locality and Polity: A Study of Warwickshire Landed Society, 1401–1499* (Cambridge, 1992).

―――― 'Gentry and Community in Medieval England', *Journal of British Studies*, xxxiii (1994), 340–80.

―――― 'Political and Constitutional History: Before and After McFarlane' in R.H Britnell and A.J. Pollard (eds.), *The McFarlane Legacy: Studies in Late Medieval Politics and Society* (Stroud, 1995), 175–206.

―――― 'William Beauchamp V', *ODNB*, iv, 607–9.

―――― 'Bastard Feudalism in Fourteenth-Century England' in Steve Boardman and Julian Goodacre (eds.), *Kings, Lords and Men in Scotland and Britain, 1300–1625*, (Edinburgh, 2014), 59–92.

Carpenter, David, 'The Second Century of English Feudalism', *P&P*, clxviii (2000), 30–71.

Castor, Helen, *The King, the Crown and the Duchy of Lancaster: Public Authority and Private Power, 1399–1461* (Oxford, 2000).

―――― 'John Paston (1421–1466)', *ODNB*, xlii, 987–8.

―――― 'John Paston (1422–1479)', *ODNB*, xlii, 988–9.

Cavill, Paul R., 'The Problem of Labour and the Parliament of 1495' in Linda Clark (ed.), *The Fifteenth Century V: 'Of Mice and Men': Image, Belief and Regulation in Late Medieval England*, (Woodbridge, 2005), 143–55.

―――― *The English Parliaments of Henry VII* (Oxford, 2009).

―――― 'The Enforcement of the Penal Statutes in the 1490s: Some New Evidence', *Historical Research*, lxxxii (2009), 482–92.

―――― 'Heresy, Law and the State: Forfeiture in Late Medieval and Early Modern England', *EHR*, cxxix (2014), 270–95.

Chapman, Adam, '"Dug fi at y Dug o Iorc" [He took me to the Duke of York]: Henry Griffith, a "Man of War"' in B.J. Lewis and D.F. Evans (eds.), *'Gwalch Cywyddau Gwŷr': Essays on Guto'r Glyn and Fifteenth Century Wales* (Aberystwyth, 2013), 103–34.

Cherry, M., 'The Courtenay Earls of Devon: The Formation and Disintegration of a Late Medieval Aristocratic Affinity', *Southern History*, i (1979), 71–97.

―――― 'The Struggle for Power in Mid-Fifteenth Century Devonshire' in Ralph A. Griffiths (ed.), *Patronage, the Crown and the Provinces in Later Medieval England* (Gloucester, 1981), 123–44.

Chrimes, Stanley, *English Constitutional Ideas in the Fifteenth Century* (Cambridge, 1936).

Clark, Linda, 'Magnates and their Affinity in the Parliaments of 1386–1421' in Richard Hugh Britnell and Anthony James Pollard (eds.), *The McFarlane Legacy: Studies in Late Medieval Politics and Society* (Stroud, 1995), 217–53.

―――― unpublished article for History of Parliament Trust, London, on Henry Bruyn, Portsmouth, for 1422–60 section.

Clayton, Dorothy J., 'Peace Bonds and the Maintenance of Law and Order in Late Medieval England: The Example of Cheshire', *BIHR*, lviii (1985), 133–48.

―――― *The Administration of the County Palatine of Cheshire, 1442–85* (Manchester, 1990).

Cohn, Samuel K., *Popular Protest in Late Medieval English Towns* (Cambridge, 2013).

Colson, Justin, and Rally, Robert, 'Medical Practice, Urban Politics and Patronage: The London "Commonalty" of Physicians and Surgeons of the 1420s', *EHR*, cxxx (2015), 1102–31.

Conway, Agnes, *Henry VII's Relations with Scotland and Ireland, 1485–1498* (Cambridge, 1932).

Cooper, C.H., *The Lady Margaret: A Memoir of Margaret, Countess of Richmond and Derby*, ed. J.E.B. Mayor (Cambridge, 1874).

Cooper, J.P., *Land, Men and Beliefs: Studies in Early Modern History*, eds. G.E. Aylmer and J.S. Morrill (London, 1983).

Coss, P.R., 'Bastard Feudalism Revised', *Past & Present*, no. 125 (1989), 27–64.

Coward, Barry *The Stanleys, Lord Stanley and the Earls of Derby: The Origins, Wealth and Power of a Landowning Family*, Chetham Society, 3rd series, xxx (Manchester, 1983).

Crouch, David B., Carpenter, David, and Coss, P. R., 'Bastard Feudalism Revised', *Past & Present*, 131 (1991), 165–203.

Crouch, David, *William Marshall: Court, Career and Chivalry in the Angevin Empire* (London, 1990).

―――― *Tournament: A Chivalric Way of Life* (London, 2005).

Cunningham, Sean, 'The Establishment of the Tudor Regime: Henry VII, Rebellion and the Financial Control of the Aristocracy' (unpublished PhD thesis, Lancaster University, 1995).

―――― 'Henry VII and Rebellion in North-Eastern England, 1485–1492: Bonds of Allegiance and the Establishment of Tudor Authority', *Northern History*, xxxii (1996), 42–74.

―――― 'Henry VII, Sir Thomas Butler and the Stanley Family: Regional Politics and the Assertion of Royal Influence in North Western England' in Tim Thornton (ed.), *Social Attitudes and Political Structures in the Fifteenth Century* (Stroud, 2002), 220–41.

―――― *Henry VII* (London, 2007).

―――― 'St Oswald's Priory, Nostell v Stanley: The Common Pleas of Lancaster, the Crown, and the Politics of the North-West in 1506' in Paul Brand (ed.), *Foundations of Medieval Scholarship* (York, 2008), 141–61.

―――― *Prince Arthur: The Tudor King Who Never Was* (Stroud, 2016).

Davies, R.R., 'The Survival of the Bloodfeud in Medieval Wales', *History*, liv (1969), 338–57.

―――― *The Revolt of Owain Glyn Dŵr* (Oxford, 1995).

―――― *Lords and Lordship in the British Isles in the Middle Ages*, ed. Brendan Smith (Oxford, 2009).

Denholm-Young, Noël, *Seignorial Administration in England* (London, 1937).

Devine, Melanie, 'The Lordship of Richmond in the Later Middle Ages' in Michael Prestwich (ed.), *Liberties and Identities in the Medieval British Isles* (Woodbridge, 2008), 98–110.

Dodd, Gwilym, *Justice and Grace: Private Petitioning and the English Parliament in the Late Middle Ages* (Oxford, 2007).

———— 'Thomas Paunfield, the 'heye Coirt of rightwisenesse' and the Language of Petitioning in the Fifteenth Century' in W. Mark Ormrod, Gwilym Dodd and Anthony Musson (eds.), *Medieval Petitions: Grace and Grievance* (Woodbridge, 2009), 12–46.

Doig, James A., 'Political Propaganda and Royal Proclamation in Late Medieval England', *Historical Research*, lxii (1998), 253–80.

Dunham, William H., *Lord Hastings' Indentured Retainers, 1461–83: The Lawfulness of Livery and Retaining under the Yorkists and Tudors*, Transactions of the Connecticut Academy of Arts & Sciences xxxix (New Haven, 1955).

Dyer, Christopher, 'England's Economy in the Fifteenth Century' in Linda Clark (ed.), *The Fifteenth Century XIII: Exploring the Evidence: Commemoration, Administration and the Economy* (Woodbridge, 2014), 201–25.

Ellis, Steven G., 'A Border Baron and the Tudor State: The Rise and Fall of Thomas, Lord Dacre of the North', *Historical Journal*, xxxv (1992), 253–77.

Fleming, P.W., 'Household Servants of the Yorkist and Early Tudor Gentry' in Daniel Williams (ed.), *Early Tudor England: Proceedings of the 1987 Harlaxton Symposium* (Woodbridge, 1989), 19–36.

Forrest, Ian, *The Detection of Heresy in Late Medieval England*, (Oxford, 2005).

Fritze, Ronald H., 'William Sandys, First Baron Sandys (c.1470–1540)' *ODNB*, xlviii, 935–6.

Given-Wilson, Chris, *The Royal Household and the King's Affinity: Service, Politics and Finance in England, 1360–1413* (London, 1986).

———— 'The King and the Gentry in Fourteenth-Century England', *Transactions of the Royal Historical Society*, 5th series, xxxvii (1986), 87–102.

———— *The English Nobility in the Late Middle Ages* (London, 1987).

———— 'Service, Serfdom and English Labour Legislation, 1350–1500' in Anne Curry and Elizabeth Matthew (eds.), *The Fifteenth Century I: Concepts and Patterns of Service in the Later Middle Ages* (Woodbridge, 2000), 21–37.

———— 'The Rolls of Parliament, 1399–1421' in Linda Clark (ed.), *Parchment and People in the Middle Ages* (Edinburgh, 2004), 57–72.

———— 'The Exequies of Edward III and the Royal Funeral Ceremony in Late Medieval England', *EHR*, cxxiv (2009), 257–82.

———— 'Rank and Status among the English Nobility, c.1300–1500' in Thorsten Huthwelker, Jörg Peltzer and Maximilian Wemhöner (eds.), *Princely Rank in Late Medieval Europe: Trodden Paths and Promising Avenues* (Ostifildern, 2011), 97–118.

—— *Chronicles: The Writing of History in Medieval England* (London, 2004).

—— *Henry IV* (London, 2016).

Goldberg, P.J.P., 'What Was a Servant?' in Anne Curry and Elizabeth Matthew (eds.), *The Fifteenth Century I: Concepts and Patterns of Service in the Later Middle Ages* (Woodbridge, 2000), 1–20.

Goodman, Anthony, *The New Monarchy: England, 1471–1534* (Oxford, 1988).

Grant, Alexander, 'Murder Will Out: Kingship, Kinship and Killing in Medieval Scotland' in Steve Boardman and Julian Goodacre (eds.), *Kings, Lords and Men in Scotland and Britain, 1300–1625*, (Edinburgh, 2014), 193–226.

Green, David, 'The Later Retinue of Edward the Black Prince', *Nottingham Medieval Studies*, xliv (2000), 141–51.

Gribit, Nicholas A., *Henry of Lancaster's Expedition to Aquitaine, 1345–46: Military Service and Professionalism in the Hundred Years War* (Woodbridge, 2016).

Griffiths, Ralph A., 'Gruffydd ap Nicholas and the Rise of the House of Dinefw', *National Library of Wales Journal*, xiii (1964), 256–68.

—— 'Local Rivalries and National Politics: The Percies, the Nevilles, and the Duke of Exeter, 1452–55', *Speculum*, xliii (1968), 589–632.

—— 'Duke Richard of York's Intentions in 1450 and the Origins of the Wars of the Roses', *Journal of Medieval History*, i (1975), 187–209.

—— 'Richard of York and the Royal Household in Wales, 1449–1450', *Welsh History Review*, viii (1976), 14–25.

—— 'Gruffydd ap Nicholas and the Fall of the House of Lancaster', *Welsh History Review*, viii (1976), 213–31.

—— 'The Winchester Session of the 1449 Parliament: A Further Comment', *Huntingdon Library Quarterly*, xlii (1979), 181–91.

—— *The Reign of Henry VI: The Exercise of Royal Authority, 1422–1461* (London, 1981).

—— *King and Country: England and Wales in the Fifteenth Century* (London, 1991).

—— 'Richard, Duke of York, and the Crisis of Henry VI's Household in 1450–1: Some Further Evidence', *Journal of Medieval History*, xxxviii (2012), 244–56.

—— 'Walter Devereux, First Baron Chartley (c.1432–1485)', *ODNB*, xv, 969–71.

—— 'William Herbert, First Earl of Pembroke (c.1423–1469)', *ODNB*. xxvi, 729–31.

Griffiths, Ralph A., and Thomas, Roger S., *The Making of the Tudor Dynasty*, revised edition (Stroud, 2005).

Grummitt, David, *The Calais Garrison: War and Military Service in England, 1436–1558* (Woodbridge, 2008).

Gundy, Alison, 'The Earl of Warwick and the Royal Affinity in the Politics of the

West Midlands, 1389–99', in Michael Hicks (ed.), *The Fifteenth Century II: Revolution and Consumption in Late Medieval England* (Woodbridge, 2001), 57–70.

Gunn, Steven, 'The Regime of Charles, Duke of Suffolk, in North Wales and the Reform of Welsh Government, 1509–25', *Welsh History Review*, xii (1985), 461–94.

———— 'Chivalry and the Politics of the Early Tudor Court' in Sydney Anglo (ed.), *Chivalry in the Renaissance* (Woodbridge, 1990), 107–28.

———— 'The Accession of Henry VIII', *Historical Research*, lxiv (1991), 278–88.

———— *Early Tudor Government, 1485–1558* (Basingstoke, 1995).

———— 'Sir Thomas Lovell (c.1449–1524): A New Man for a New Monarchy?' in John L. Watts (ed.), *The End of the Middle Ages? England in the Fifteenth and Sixteenth Centuries* (Stroud, 1998), 117–53.

———— 'Henry VII in Context: Problems and Possibilities', *History*, xcii (2007), 301–17.

———— 'Politic History, New Monarchy and State Formation: Henry VII in European Perspective', *Historical Research*, lxxxii (2009), 380–92.

———— *Henry VII's New Men and the Making of Tudor England* (Oxford, 2016).

————*The English People at War in the Age of Henry VIII* (Oxford, 2018).

Gunn Steven, Grummitt, David, and Cool, Hans, *War, State and Society in England and the Netherlands, 1477–1559* (Oxford, 2007).

Guy, John A., 'Wolsey and the Tudor Polity' in Steven J. Gunn and Philip G. Lindley (eds.), *Cardinal Wolsey: Church, State and Art* (Cambridge, 1991), 54–75.

Gwyn, Peter, *The King's Cardinal: The Rise and Fall of Thomas Wolsey* (London, 1991).

Hanawalt, Barbara A., 'Fur Collar Crime: The Pattern of Crime among the Fourteenth-Century English Nobility', *Journal of Social History*, viii (1975), 1–17.

Harrison, C.J., 'The Petition of Edmund Dudley', *EHR*, lxxxii (1972), 82–99.

Harriss, Gerald L., 'The Struggle for Calais: An Aspect of the Rivalry between Lancaster and York', *EHR*, lxxv (1960), 30–53.

———— *King, Parliament and Public Finance in England to 1369* (Oxford, 1975)

———— 'Political Society and the Growth of Government in Late Medieval England', *P&P*, cxxxviii (1993), 28–57.

———— *Shaping the Nation: England, 1360–1461* (Oxford, 2005).

———— 'Stourton Family (*per*, c.1380-1485)', *ODNB*, lii, 975.

Harvey, I.M.W., *Jack Cade's Rebellion of 1450* (Oxford, 1991).

Haward, Winifred I., 'Gilbert Debenham: A Medieval Rascal in Real Life', *History*, xiii (1929), 300–14.

Hawkyard, Alasdair, 'George Neville, Third Baron Bergavenny (c.1469–1535)', *ODNB*, xl, 495–7.

Heinze, R.W., *The Proclamations of the Tudor Kings* (Cambridge, 1976).

Herbert, Alisa, 'Herefordshire, 1413–61: Some Aspects of Public Disorder' in Ralph A. Griffiths (ed.), *Patronage, the Crown and the Provinces in Later Medieval England* (Gloucester, 1981), 103–22.

Hicks, Michael, 'Attainder, Resumption and Coercion, 1461–1529', *Parliamentary History*, iii, (1984), 15–31.

——— 'The Yorkshire Rebellion of 1489 Reconsidered', *Northern History*, xxii (1986), 39–62.

——— *Richard III and His Rivals: Magnates and their Motives in the Wars of the Roses* (London, 1991).

——— *False, Fleeting, Perjur'd Clarence: George, Duke of Clarence 1449–78*, revised edition (Gloucester, 1992).

——— 'The 1468 Statute of Livery', *Historical Research*, lxiv (1991), 15–28.

——— *Bastard Feudalism* (London, 1995).

——— *Warwick the Kingmaker* (Oxford, 1998).

——— 'Bastard Feudalism, Overmighty Subjects and the Idols of Multitude during the Wars of the Roses', *History*, lxxxv (2000), 386–403.

——— *English Political Culture in the Fifteenth Century* (London, 2002).

——— 'King in Lords and Commons: Three Insights into Late Fifteenth-Century Parliaments, 1431–85' in Keith Dockray and Peter Fleming (eds.), *People, Places and Perspectives* (Stroud, 2005), 131–53.

——— 'Crowland's World: A Westminster View of the Yorkist Ages', *History*, xc (2005), 172–90.

——— *The Wars of the Roses* (London 2010).

——— 'Retainers, Monks and Wine: Three Insights into Everyday Life' in Michael Hicks (ed.), *The Later Medieval Inquisitions Post Mortem: Mapping the Medieval Countryside and Rural Society* (Woodbridge, 2016), 174–93.

Hillaby, Joe, and Hillaby, Caroline, *Leominster Minster, Priory and Borough, c.660–1539* (Woonton Almeley, 2006).

Hilton, Rodney, 'Reasons for Inequality among Medieval Peasants', *Journal of Peasant Studies*, v (1978), 271–83.

Holford, Matthew, '"Thrifty Men of the County"? The Jurors and Their Role' in Michael Hicks (ed.), *The Fifteenth Century Inquisitions Post Mortem: A Companion* (Woodbridge, 2012), 201–22.

Holford, M.L., and Stringer, K.J., *Border Liberties and Loyalties: North-East England, c.1200–c.1400* (Edinburgh, 2010).

Holmes, G.A., *The Estates of the Higher Nobility in Fourteenth-Century England* (Cambridge, 1957).

Horrox, Rosemary, 'Urban Patronage and Patrons in the Fifteenth Century' in Ralph A. Griffiths (ed.), *Patronage, the Crown and the Provinces in Later Medieval England* (Gloucester, 1981), 145–66.

———— 'The Urban Gentry in the Fifteenth Century' in John A.F. Thomson (ed.), *Towns and Townspeople in the Fifteenth Century* (Gloucester, 1988), 22–44.

———— *Richard III: A Study of Service* (Cambridge, 1989).

Hoyle, R.W., 'The Earl, the Archbishop and the Council: The Affray at Fulford, May 1504' in Rowena E. Archer and Simon Walker (eds.), *Rulers and Ruled in Late Medieval England* (London, 1995), 239–56.

Ives, Eric W., 'Crime, Sanctuary and Royal Authority under Henry VIII: Exemplary Sufferings of the Savage Family' in Morris S. Arnold, Thomas Andrew Green, S.A Scully and S.D. White (eds.), *On the Laws and Customs of England* (Chapel Hill, 1981).

James, Mervyn, *Society, Politics and Culture: Studies in Early Modern England* (Cambridge, 1986).

Johnson, P.A., *Duke Richard of York, 1411–1460* (Oxford, 1988).

Jones, Michael K., and Underwood, Malcolm G., *The King's Mother: Lady Margaret Beaufort, Countess of Richmond and Derby* (Cambridge, 1992).

Kaminsky, Howard, 'The Noble Feud in the Later Middle Ages', *P&P*, clxxvii (2002), 55–83.

Keen, Maurice, *Chivalry* (London, 1984).

———— 'Richard II's Ordinances of War in 1385' in Rowena E. Archer and Simon Walker (eds.), *Rulers and Ruled in Late Medieval England* (London, 1995), 33–48.

Kesselring, K.J., *Mercy and Authority in the Tudor State* (Cambridge, 2003).

King, Andy, 'Sir William Clifford: Rebellion and Reward in Henry IV's Affinity' in Linda Clark (ed.), *The Fifteenth Century IX: English and Continental Perspectives* (Woodbridge, 2010), 139–54.

Kleineke, Hannes, 'Why the West was Wild: Law and Disorder in Fifteenth-Century Cornwall and Devon' in Linda Clark (ed.), *The Fifteenth Century III: Authority and Subversion* (Woodbridge, 2003), 75–94.

———— 'Þe Kynes Cite: Exeter in the Wars of the Roses' in *The Fifteenth Century VII: Conflicts, Consequences and the Crown in the Late Middle Ages*, ed. Linda Clark (Woodbridge, 2007), 137–56.

———— 'Poachers and Gamekeepers: Four Fifteenth Century West Country Criminals' in John C. Appleby and Paul Dalton (eds.), *Outlaws in Medieval and Early Modern England: Crime, Government and Society, c.1066–c.1600* (Farnham, 2009), 129–48.

———— 'Robert Bale's Chronicle and the Second Battle of St Albans', *Historical Research*, lxxxvii (2014), 744–50.

Lacey, Helen, *The Royal Pardon: Access to Mercy in Fourteenth-Century England* (Woodbridge, 2009).

Lachaud, Frédérique, 'Liveries of Robes in England, c.1200–c.1330', *English Historical Review*, cxi (1996), 279–298.

Lambert, Craig L., *Shipping in the Medieval Military: English Maritime Logistics in the Fourteenth Century* (Woodbridge, 2011).

Lander, J.R., 'Bonds, Coercion and Fear: Henry VII and the Peerage' in J.G Rowe and W.H. Stockdale (eds.), *Florilegium Historiale* (Toronto, 1971), 327–67.

―――― *English Justices of the Peace, 1461–1509* (Gloucester, 1989).

Laughton, Jane, *Life in a Late Medieval City: Chester, 1275–1520* (Oxford, 2008).

Lavell, Ryan, *Alfred's Wars: Sources and Interpretations of Anglo-Saxon Warfare in the Viking Ages* (Woodbridge, 2010).

Laynesmith, Joanne L., *The Late Medieval Queens: English Queenship, 1445–1503* (Oxford, 2004).

Lewis, P.S., *Essays in Later Medieval French History*, (London, 1985).

Liddy, Christian, *War, Politics and Finance in Late Medieval English Towns: Bristol, York and the Crown, 1350–1400* (Woodbridge, 2005).

―――― *The Bishopric of Durham in the Late Middle Ages: Lordship, Community and the Cult of St Cuthbert* (Woodbridge, 2008).

―――― 'Urban Enclosure Riots: The Risings of the Commons in English Towns, 1480–1525', *P&P*, ccxxvi (2015), 41–77.

Luckett, Dominic, 'Crown Office and Licensed Retinues in the Reign of Henry VII' in Rowena E. Archer and Simon Walker (eds.), *Rulers and Ruled in Late Medieval England* (London, 1995), 223–38.

MacDonald, Alastair J., *Border Bloodshed: Scotland, England and France at War, 1369–1403* (Edinburgh, 2000).

MacDougall, Norman, *James III*, 2nd edition (Edinburgh, 2009).

Mackman, Jonathan S., 'The Lincolnshire Gentry and the Wars of the Roses' (unpublished D.Phil thesis, University of York, 1999).

Maddern, Philippa C. *Violence and Social Order: East Anglia, 1422–1442* (Oxford, 1992).

―――― '"Best Trusted Friends": Concepts and Practices of Friendship among Fifteenth-Century Norfolk Gentry' in Nicholas Rogers (ed.), *England in the Fifteenth Century* (Stamford, 1992), 100–17.

Madden, F., 'Political Poems of the Reigns of Henry VI and Edward IV', *Archaeolgia*, xxix (1842), 318–47.

Maddicott, J.R, *Thomas of Lancaster, 1307–1322: A Study in the Reign of Edward II* (Oxford, 1970).

―――― 'Law and Lordship: Royal Justices as Retainers in Thirteenth and Fourteenth Century England', *P&P*, supplement iv (1978).

―――― *Simon de Montfort* (Cambridge, 1994).

McFarlane, K.B., 'Parliament and Bastard Feudalism', *TRHS*, 4th series, xxvi (1944), 53–79.

―――― 'Bastard Feudalism', *Bulletin of the Institute of Historical Research*, xx (1945), 161–80.

——— 'The Wars of the Roses', *Proceedings of the British Academy*, i (1964), 87–119.

The Nobility of Late Medieval England: The Ford Lectures of 1953 and Related Studies (Oxford, 1973).

McHardy, A.K., 'Haxey's Case, 1397: The Petition and its Presenter' in James L. Gillespie (ed.), *The Ages of Richard II* (Stroud, 1997), 93–114.

——— '*De Heretico Comburendo*' in Margaret Aston and Colin Richmond (eds.), *Lollardy and the Gentry in the Later Middle Ages* (Stroud, 1997), 112–23.

McKelvie, Gordon, 'The Legality of Bastard Feudalism: The Statutes of Livery, 1390 to c.1520' (unpublished PhD thesis, University of Winchester, 2013).

——— 'The Livery Act of 1429' in Linda Clark (ed.), *The Fifteenth Century XIV: Essays in Honour of Michael Hicks* (Woodbridge, 2015), 55–65.

——— 'Henry VII's Letter to Carlisle in 1498: His Concerns about Retaining in a Border Fortress', *Northern History*, liv (2017), 149–66.

——— 'Kingship and Good Lordship in Practice: Henry VII, the Earl of Oxford and the Case of John Hale (1487)', *Journal of Medieval History*, xlv (2019), 504–22.

McNiven, Peter, *Hersey and Politics in the Reign of Henry IV: The Burning of John Badby* (Woodbridge, 1987)

McRee, Benjamin R., 'Unity or Division? The Social Meaning of Guild Ceremony in Urban Communities' in Barbara A. Hanawalt and Kathryn L. Reyerson (eds.), *City and Spectacle in Medieval Europe* (Liverpool, 1994), 189–207.

Mercer, Malcolm, *The Medieval Gentry: Power, Leadership and Choice during the Wars of the Roses* (London, 2010).

Mertes, Kate, *The English Noble Household 1250–1600: Good Governance and Politic Rule* (Oxford, 1988).

Miller, Helen, *Henry VIII and the English Nobility* (Oxford, 1986).

Moore, R.I., *The First European Revolution, c.970–1215* (Oxford, 2000).

Morgan, Philip J., *War and Society in Medieval Cheshire, 1277–1403*, Chetham Society, 3rd series, xxiv (Manchester, 1987).

——— 'Cheshire and Wales' in Huw Price and John Watts (eds.), *Power and Identity in the Middle Ages* (Oxford, 2007), 195–210.

Murphy, Neil, 'Receiving Royals in Later Medieval York: Civic Ceremony and the Municipal Elite, 1478–1503', *Northern History*, xliii (2006), 241–55.

——— 'Henry VIII's First Invasion of France: The Gascon Expedition of 1512', *EHR*, cxxx (2015), 25–56.

Myers, A.R., 'Parliamentary Petitions in the Fifteenth Century', *EHR*, lii (1937), 385–404, 590–613.

——— 'A Parliamentary Debate of the Mid-Fifteenth Century', *Bulletin of the John Rylands Library*, xxii (1938), 388–404.

———— 'A Parliamentary Debate of 1449', *BIHR*, li (1978), 78–83.

———— *Crown, Household and Parliament in Fifteenth Century England* (London, 1985).

Ormrod, W. Mark., 'Agenda for Legislation, 1322–c.1340', *EHR*, cv (1990), 1–33.

———— 'On – and Off – the Record: The Rolls of Parliament, 1337–1377' in Linda Clark (ed.), *Parchment and People in the Middle Ages* (Edinburgh, 2004), 39–56.

———— 'The Rebellion of Archbishop Scrope and the Tradition of Opposition to Royal Taxation' in Gwilym Dodd and Douglas Biggs (eds.), *The Reign of Henry IV: Rebellion and Survival, 1403–13* (Woodbridge, 2008), 162–79.

———— 'Introduction: Medieval Petitions in Context' in W. Mark Ormrod, Gwilym Dodd and Anthony Musson (eds.), *Medieval Petitions: Grace and Grievance* (Woodbridge, 2009), 1–11.

———— 'Voicing Complaint and Remedy to the English Crown, c.1300–c.1460' in W. Mark Ormrod, Gwilym Dodd and Anthony Musson (eds.), *Medieval Petitions: Grace and Grievance* (Woodbridge, 2009), 135–55.

———— 'The New Political History: Recent Trends in the Historiography of Later Medieval England' in Troels Dahlreup and Per Ingesman (eds.), *New Approaches to the History of Late Medieval and Early Modern Europe* (Copenhagen, 2009), 37–59.

———— *Edward III* (London, 2011).

Palliser, D.M., *Tudor York* (Oxford, 1979).

Payling, Simon J., 'The Widening Franchise: Parliamentary Elections in Lancastrian Nottinghamshire' in Daniel Williams (ed.), *England in the Fifteenth Century* (Woodbridge, 1987), 167–85.

———— *Political Society in Lancastrian England: The Greater Gentry of Nottingham* (Oxford, 1991).

———— 'County Parliamentary Elections in Fifteenth-Century England', *Parliamentary History*, xviii (1999), 237–57.

———— 'The Rise of Lawyers in the Lower House, 1395–1536' in Linda Clark (ed.), *Parchment and People in the Middle Ages* (Edinburgh, 2004), 103–20.

Penn, Thomas, *Winter King: Henry VII and the Dawn of Tudor England* (London, 2011).

Phillips, Gervase, 'Edward Stanley, First Baron Monteagle (c.1460–1523)', *ODNB*, lii, 174.

Pollard, A.J., 'The Family of Talbot, Lord Talbot and the Earls of Shrewsbury in the Fifteenth Century' (unpublished PhD thesis, University of Bristol, 1969).

———— 'The Northern Retainers of Richard Nevill, Earl of Salisbury', *Northern History*, xi (1976 for 1975), 52–69.

———— 'Richard Clervaux of Croft: A North Riding Squire in the Fifteenth Century', *Yorkshire Archaeological Journal*, vi (1978), 151–69.

——— *North-Eastern England during the Wars of the Roses: Lay Society, War and Politics, 1450–1500* (Oxford, 1990).

——— 'Edward Stanley, First Baron Monteagle (c.1460–1523)', *ODNB*, lii, 174.

Powell, Edward, 'Arbitration and the Law in England in the Late Middle Ages', *Transactions of the Royal Historical Society*, 5th series, xxxiii (1983), 49–67.

——— 'Proceedings before the Justices of the Peace at Shrewsbury in 1414: A Supplement to the Shropshire Peace Roll', *EHR*, xcix (1984), 535–50.

——— *Kingship, Law and Society: Criminal Justice in the Reign of Henry V* (Oxford, 1989).

——— 'After "After McFarlane": The Poverty of Patronage and the Case for Constitutional History' in Dorothy J. Clayton, Richard G. Davies and Peter McNiven (eds.), *Trade, Devotion and Governance: Papers in Later Medieval History* (Stroud, 1994), 1–16.

Prestwich, J.O., 'War and Finance in the Anglo-Norman State', *TRHS*, 5th series, iv (1955), 19–34.

——— 'Military Household of the Anglo-Norman Kings', *EHR*, xcvi (1981), 1–35.

Prestwich, Michael, *War, Politics and Finance Under Edward I* (London, 1972).

Purser, Toby Scott, 'The County Community of Hampshire, c.1300–c.1530, with Special Reference to the Knights and Esquires' (unpublished PhD thesis, University of Winchester (Southampton), 2001).

Pugh, T.B., 'The Magnates, Knights and Gentry' in S.B. Chrimes, C.D. Ross and R.A. Griffiths (eds.), *Fifteenth Century England* (Manchester, 1972), 86–128.

——— 'Richard, Duke of York and the Rebellion of Henry Holland, Duke of Exeter, in May 1454', *Historical Research*, lxiii (1990), 248–62.

——— 'Henry VII and the English Nobility' in G.W. Bernard (ed.), *The Tudor Nobility* (Manchester, 1992), 49–110.

——— 'Edward Neville, First Baron Bergavenny', *ODNB*, xl, 488–9.

Putnam, Bertha, *The Enforcement of the Statutes of Labourers During the First Decade after the Black Death, 1349–1359* (New York, 1908).

Rawcliff, Carole, *The Staffords: Earls of Stafford and Dukes of Buckingham* (Cambridge, 1978).

——— 'Richard, Duke of York, the King's "Obesiant Liegeman": A New Source for the Protectorates of 1454 and 1455', *Historical Research*, lx (1987), 232–9.

Reeves, A.C., 'Ralph Cromwell', *ODNB*, xiv, 353–5.

Reid, Rachel R., *The King's Council in the North* (London, 1921).

Reinle, Christine, 'Peasants' Feuds in Medieval Bavaria (Fourteenth and Fifteenth Century)' in Jeppe Büchert Netterstrøm and Bjørn Poulsen (eds.), *Feud in Medieval and Early Modern Europe* (Aarhus, 2007), 161–74.

Richmond, Colin, 'The Nobility and the Wars of the Roses', *Nottingham Medieval Studies*, xxi (1977), 71–86.

——— *John Hopton: A Fifteenth Century Suffolk Gentleman* (Cambridge, 1981).

——— 'After McFarlane', *History*, lxviii (1983), 46–60.

——— *The Paston Family in the Fifteenth Century: The First Phase* (Cambridge, 1990).

——— 'An English Mafia?', *Nottingham Medieval Studies*, xxxvi (1992), 235–43.

——— *The Pastons in the Fifteenth Century: Fastolf's Will* (Cambridge, 1996).

Roberts, Peter, 'Elizabethan Players and Minstrels and the Legislation of 1572 against Retainers and Vagabonds' in Anthony Fletcher and Peter Roberts (eds.), *Religion, Culture and Society in Early Modern Britain* (Cambridge, 1994), 29–55.

Rose, Jonathan, *Maintenance in Medieval England* (Cambridge, 2017).

Ross, Charles, *Edward IV* (London, 1974).

——— *Richard III* (London, 1981).

——— 'Rumour, Propaganda and Popular Opinion during the Wars of the Roses' in Ralph A. Griffiths (ed.), *Patronage, the Crown and the Provinces in Later Medieval England* (Gloucester, 1981), 15–32.

Ross, James, 'Seditious Activities: The Conspiracy of Maud de Vere, Countess of Oxford, 1403–4' in Linda Clark (ed.), *The Fifteenth Century III: Authority and Subversion* (Woodbridge, 2003), 25–42.

——— *John de Vere, Thirteenth Earl of Oxford (1442–1513): 'The Foremost Man of the Kingdom'* (Woodbridge, 2011).

——— '"Mischieviously Slewen": John, Lord Scrope, the Dukes of Norfolk and Suffolk, and the Murder of Henry Howard in 1446' in Hannes Kleineke (ed.), *The Fifteenth Century X: Parliament, Personalities and Power: Papers Presented to Linda Clark* (Woodbridge, 2011), 75–96.

——— 'A Governing Elite? The Higher Nobility in the Yorkist and Early Tudor Period' in Hannes Kleineke and Christian Steer (eds.), *The Yorkist Age: Proceedings of the 2011 Harlaxton Symposium* (Donnington, 2013), 95–115.

——— '"Contrary to the Ryght and to the Order of the Lawe": New Evidence of Edmund Dudley's Activities on Behalf of Henry VII in 1504', *EHR*, cxxvii (2012), 24–45.

——— 'The English Aristocracy and Mesne Feudalism in the Late Middle Ages', *EHR*, cxxxiii (2018), 1027–59.

Saul, Nigel, *Knights and Esquires: The Gloucestershire Gentry in the Fourteenth Century* (Oxford, 1981).

——— *Scenes From Provincial Life: Knightly Families in Sussex, 1280–1400* (Oxford, 1986).

——— 'The Commons and the Abolition of Badges', *Parliamentary History*, ix (1990), 302–15.

——— 'Richard II and the Vocabulary of Kingship', *EHR*, cx (1995), 854–77.

——— *Richard II* (London, 1997).

Simon, Monika, 'Of Lands and Ladies: The Marriage Strategies of the Lords Lovell (c.1200–1487)', *Southern History*, xxxiii (2011), 1–29.

Sinclair, Alexandra, 'The Great Berkeley Law Dispute Revisited, 1417–39', *Southern History*, ix (1987), 34–50.

Spencer, Andrew, 'The Comital Military Retinue in the Reign of Edward I', *Historical Research*, lxxxiii (2010), 46–59.

——— *Nobility and Kingship in Medieval England: The Earls and Edward I* (Cambridge, 2014).

Storey, R.L., 'The Wardens of the Marches of England towards Scotland, 1377–1489', *EHR*, lxxii (1957), 593–615.

——— *The End of the House of Lancaster*, 2nd edition (Gloucester, 1986).

——— 'Liveries and Commissions of the Peace, 1388–90' in F.R.H. Du Boulay and C.M. Barron (eds.), *The Reign of Richard II* (London, 1971), 131–52.

Strickland, Matthew, '"All Brought to Nought and Thy State Undone": Treason, Disinvesture and the Disgracing of Arms under Edward II' in Peter R. Coss and Christopher Tyerman (eds.), *Soldiers, Nobles and Gentlemen: Essays in Honour of Maurice Keen* (Woodbridge, 2009), 279–304.

Strohm, Paul, *England's Empty Throne: Usurpation and the Language of Legitimation, 1399–1422* (New Haven and London, 1998).

Stubbs, William, *Constitutional History of England in the Middle Ages*, 3 vols. (Oxford, 1880).

Summerson, Henry, *Medieval Carlisle: The City and the Borders from the Late Eleventh to the Mid-Sixteenth Century*, 2 vols. (Kendal, 1993).

Thomson, J.A.F., 'The Courtenay Family in the Yorkist Period', *BIHR*, xlv (1972), 230–46.

——— 'Scots in England in the Fifteenth Century', *Scottish Historical Review*, lxxix (2000), 1–16.

Thornton, Tim, *Cheshire and the Tudor State, 1480–1560* (Woodbridge, 2000).

——— 'Savage Family', *ODNB*, xlix, 63–6.

Tout, T.F., *Chapters in Administrative History of Medieval England*, 6 vols. (Manchester, 1920–33).

Vale, Malcolm, *War and Chivalry* (London, 1981).

——— *The Princely Court: Medieval Courts and Culture in North-West Europe, 1270–1380* (Oxford, 2004).

Vaughan, Richard, *Philip the Good: The Apogee of Burgundy*, new edition (Woodbridge, 2002).

Virgoe, Roger, 'Three Suffolk Parliamentary Elections of the Mid-Fifteenth Century', *BIHR*, xxxix (1966), 185–96.

——— 'The Cambridgeshire Election of 1439', *BIHR*, xlvi (1973), 95–101.

——— 'An Election Dispute of 1483', *Historical Research*, lx (1987), 24–44.

Walker, Simon, *The Lancastrian Affinity, 1361–1399* (Oxford, 1990).

—————— *Political Culture in Later Medieval England*, ed. Michael J. Braddick, intro. by G.L. Harriss (Manchester, 2006).

Ward, Jennifer C., *English Noblewomen in the Later Middle Ages* (London and New York, 1992).

Ward, Matthew, *The Livery Collar in Late Medieval England and Wales: Politics, Identity and Affinity* (Woodbridge, 2016).

Warner, M.W., and Lacey, Kay, 'Neville vs. Percy: A Precedence Dispute, *circa* 1442', *Historical Research*, lxix (1996), 211–17.

Watts, John, *Henry VI and the Politics of Kingship* (Cambridge, 1996).

Waugh, Scott L., 'Tenure to Contract: Lordship and Clientage in Thirteenth-Century England', *EHR*, ci (1986), 811–39.

Woolgar, C.M., *The Great Household in Late Medieval England* (London, 1999).

Wormald, Jenny, 'Bloodfeud, Kindred and Government in Early Modern Scotland', *P&P*, lxxxvii (1980), 54–97.

Wright, Susan M., *The Derbyshire Gentry in the Fifteenth Century*, Derbyshire Record Society, viii (Chesterfield, 1983).

Youngs, Deborah, *Humphrey Newton (1466–1536): An Early Tudor Gentleman* (Woodbridge, 2008).

Reference Works

The Complete Peerage of England, Scotland, Ireland, Great Britain and the United Kingdom, ed. Vicary Gibbs, new edition, 6 vols. (London, 1910).

A History of the County of Chester: Volume V Part 1, The City of Chester, General History and Topography, eds. C.P. Lewis and A.T. Thacker (London, 2003).

A History of the County of Chester: Volume V Part 2, The City of Chester, Culture, Buildings, Institutions, eds. C.P. Lewis and A.T. Thacker (London, 2005).

A History of the County of Lancaster: Volume 8, eds. William Farrer and J. Brownbill (London, 1914).

Oxford Dictionary of National Biography, eds. Brian Howard Harrison and H.C.C. Mathews, 60 vols. (Oxford, 2000).

The History of Parliament: The House of Commons, 1386–1421, ed. J.S. Roskell, 4 vols. (Stroud, 1992).

Wedgwood, Josiah C., *History of Parliament: Biographies of the Members of the Commons House, 1439–1509* (London, 1936).

Index

Forte, John, 198
Fortescu, Sir John, from Hertfordshire,
    indicted in 1491, 125
Fortescue, Sir John, chief justice the king's
    bench, 62–3
forty-shilling freeholders, 114
Foston (Yorkshire), 169
Fox, Richard, bishop of Winchester, 93, 138
Framlington (Suffolk), 176
France, 17, 43
    campaigns of Henry V in, 49, 89
    campaign of Edward IV (1475), 178
    expedition in 1513, 96
    nobility of, 27
    potential invasion by (1491), 115
    potential invasion by (1511), 78
    potential invasion by (1513), 115
    view of English as king killers, 162
    war with England (1512), 23
Fulford (Yorkshire), 83, 117, 134

gaol delivery, 67
Gardiner, Richard, mayor of Lancaster, 215
Gascoigne, William, chief justice of the
    king's bench, 49
Gascony,
    campaign in 1294, 89
    loss of, 59
    wine from, 196
Gaunt, John of, duke of Lancaster, x, 8,
    19–20, 25, 36, 38, 40, 106, 159, 206
Genoa, ships of, 179
Germany, peasant feuds in, 164
Glorious Revolution, 3
Gloucester, Humphrey, duke of, 55
Gloucester, town of, 190
    ordinance about retaining (1504), 190, 214
Gloucestershire, 79, 122, 136, 142, 210
Glyn Dŵr, Owain, 45
good lordship, 1, 13, 112, 119, 150
Govely, Raulyn, esquire, 42
Gregory's Chronicle, 64
Grenefield, Thomas, gentleman, 141, 148
Greenham, Nicholas, husbandman, 144
Greenham, Robert, husbandman, 144
Gresley, Sir John, 174
Grey, Edward, Viscount Lisle, 82, 86, 109
Grey, Henry, sixth lord Codnor, 66, 109 fn.
    28, 111, 127, 171–3
Grey, Henry, seventh lord Codnor, 108, 110
    fn. 33, 173–5, 184
Grey, John, of Exeter, 129

Grey, John, lord Wilton, 82, 86, 109, 143–4,
    153, 156
Grey, Thomas, marquis of Dorset, 79, 83,
    110–11, 113, 141, 167
Greystoke, John, baron, 152–3
Greystock, Sir Ralph, 9, 126, 152
Griffith, Sir Walter, 116
Griffith, Sir William, 84
Griffiths, Henry ap, esquire, 61–2
Gyon, Walter ap, 199

Hadlow, lordship of, 212
Haklut, Sir Ralph, 98
Halton (Cheshire), 69, 188, 212
Hampshire, 58, 59, 70, 77, 79, 83, 85, 95,
    115–17, 132, 141, 148, 153, 155, 178–9,
    193, 210
Hankford, William, chief justice of the king's
    bench, 49
Harrington, John, junior, 156
Harrington, John, senior, 156
Hastings, Edward, lord, 215
Hastings, Sir Edmund of Roxby, steward of
    Pickering, rebel, 72
Hastings, George lord, (created earl of
    Huntingdon in 1529), 79, 83, 110–11, 113,
    141, 156, 167
Hastings, Sir Ralph, 9,
Hastings, William lord, 21, 67–8, 106, 159,
    174, 176
Hawtmount, Robert, tenant of Edward prince
    of Wales, 165
Haxey, Thomas, x, 41–2
Haydon, Henry, of London, 126
Haye, Richard, 90 fn. 69
Healaugh (Yorkshire), 169
Hellesdon, (Norfolk), 25, 68, 175–6
Henry II, 54
Henry IV, 22–3, 26, 42–9, 54, 56, 72, 97,
    121, 134, 156, 162, 167, 182, 204, 209
    as Henry Bolingbroke, 42, 204
    becomes king (1399), 26, 42, 45, 162, 204
Henry V, 48–50, 54–6, 70, 209
    as prince of Wales, 45–6
    campaigns against lawlessness, 49, 56, 95,
        139, 147, 167, 180, 183
    French wars, 49, 89
Henry VI, 30, 49–51, 61–3, 65, 70, 93, 103,
    110–11, 184, 195, 209, 212
    deposed (1461), 22, 64, 162
    depose (1471), 162
    mental breakdown, 59